FROM WOUNDED KNEE
TO THE GALLOWS

FROM WOUNDED KNEE TO THE GALLOWS

THE LIFE AND TRIALS OF LAKOTA CHIEF
TWO STICKS

PHILIP S. HALL
MARY SOLON LEWIS

UNIVERSITY OF OKLAHOMA PRESS : NORMAN

Publication of this book is made possible through the generosity of Edith Kinney Gaylord.

Library of Congress Cataloging-in-Publication Data

Names: Hall, Philip S., 1943– author. | Lewis, Mary Solon, 1936– author.
Title: From Wounded Knee to the gallows : the life and trials of Lakota chief Two Sticks / Philip S. Hall and Mary Solon Lewis.
Description: Norman : University of Oklahoma Press, [2020] | Includes bibliographical references and index. | Summary: "The story of the Lakota chief Can Nopa Uhah, Two Sticks, who was wrongfully accused of murdering four white cowboys and hung in 1894. Uses government records, newspaper accounts, and unpublished manuscripts to give a clear and candid account of the Oglala's struggles in the events leading up to and in the wake of Wounded Knee"—Provided by publisher.
Identifiers: LCCN 2019058088 | ISBN 978-0-8061-6491-5 (paperback)
Subjects: LCSH: Two Sticks, 1832?–1894. | Lakota Indians—Biography. | Oglala Indians—Social conditions—19th century. | LCGFT: Biographies.
Classification: LCC E99.T34 H35 2020 | DDC 978.004/9752440092 [B]—dc23
LC record available at https://lccn.loc.gov/2019058088

The paper in this book meets the guidelines for permanence and durability of the Committee on Production Guidelines for Book Longevity of the Council on Library Resources, Inc. ∞

Copyright © 2020 by the University of Oklahoma Press, Norman, Publishing Division of the University. Manufactured in the U.S.A.

All rights reserved. No part of this publication may be reproduced, stored in a retrieval system, or transmitted, in any form or by any means, electronic, mechanical, photocopying, recording, or otherwise—except as permitted under Section 107 or 108 of the United States Copyright Act—without the prior written permission of the University of Oklahoma Press. To request permission to reproduce selections from this book, write to Permissions, University of Oklahoma Press, 2800 Venture Drive, Norman, OK 73069, or email rights.oupress@ou.edu.

CONTENTS

List of Illustrations vii
Acknowledgments ix

Prologue 1
1. Staring at the Hangman's Noose 4
2. The Political Road to Wounded Knee 6
3. The Indian Unrest That Brought Can Nopa Uhah to the Gallows 17
4. The Killing of Ike Miller 39
5. The Peacemaker 46
6. A Good Indian Is Murdered 52
7. The Indian Who Killed Lieutenant Casey 59
8. Plenty Horses's Second Trial 70
9. Frontier Justice 83
10. For What, Simply Killing an Indian? 96
11. Pine Ridge, 1891: A Time of Gloom 106

12. Pine Ridge, 1892: A Year of Resistance.   121
13. No Water and His Camp of Malcontents   131
14. The Brown–Eastman Dispute   137
15. Looking at the Brown–Eastman Dispute through
    Others' Eyes.   149
16. Can Nopa Uhah's Crime   163
17. Catching the Culprits   175
18. The Frontier Peers into the Twentieth Century   185
19. The Wheels of Justice Turn Slowly.   196
20. Two Sticks's Trial.   211
21. The Hanging   224

Notes.   231
Bibliography   265
Index.   271

ILLUSTRATIONS

Richard F. Pettigrew	7
Daniel Royer	13
Area of operation of Sixth Cavalry, December 1890	33
Little, instigator of the 1890 Indian revolt	37
Young Man Afraid of His Horses	47
Tasunka Ota (Plenty Horses)	61
Participants in Plenty Horses's second trial	81
Map of Sioux Indian lands, showing the diminished reservations and ceded lands	85
Sioux delegation of 1891	116
No Water's village	132
Dr. Charles A. Eastman	147
Elaine Goodale Eastman	147
Father Florentine Digmann	153
Two Sticks, Joe Bush, Cyrus Fry, and Chris Matthiessen	182

Indians held in the Lawrence County Jail in October 1894 209
Drawing of White Clay Creek area 214
Drawing of the halfway camp dugout 215

ACKNOWLEDGMENTS

Many people aided us in this project, and we thank them profusely. In particular, at Black Hills State University, Sarah Freng, research librarian, always greeted our requests to order microfilm and to search out other possible mother lodes of information with a smile; Scott Ahola, assistant director, was never too busy to help; and the late Bobbi Sago, director of the Case Archives and Special Collections, directed us to out-of-print rare books containing nuggets. Lori Terrill, the newly installed director of the Case Archives and Special Collections, guided us to several useful pictures from the Collins Collection. Hannah Marshall, archivist at Deadwood History, most graciously assisted us in our search for information about Two Sticks's attorney, William McLaughlin. She also brought our attention to historic photos in the Deadwood History collection. Then there is Mark Thiel, archivist and curator of special collections at Marquette University, who, not incidentally, once lived on the Pine Ridge Reservation and was the archivist at Oglala Lakota College in Kyle, South Dakota.

At the South Dakota State Historical Society, Ken Stewart, research room administrator, Matthew Reitzel, manuscript archivist, and Virginia Hanson, government records archivist, always welcomed us to their domain, seemingly unconcerned about reels of microfilm that would need refiling when we departed.

Carol Hauck, librarian at Deadwood Public Library, was of considerable assistance, as was Lori Cox-Paul, director of archival operations at the National

Archives in Kansas City, who promptly responded with federal court records of Plenty Horses's trials. Paige Litz assisted with photos and final preparation.

We are especially indebted to our three editors from the University of Oklahoma Press. We were just plain lucky that Alessandra Tamulevich, the acquisitions editor, was willing to venture into our hand-dug coal mine, scrutinize it closely, and decide that in capable hands it could produce enough nuggets of historical gold to justify bringing the manuscript into the light of day. Alessandra skillfully and tenaciously shepherded the manuscript up the decision-making ladder from committee to committee until the publishing light flashed green. She then placed the weighty manuscript in the capable hands of Emily Schuster, manuscript editor, and Peg Goldstein, copy editor. They corroborated in a well-choreographed literary dance that magically made these two hayseeds appear smart and scholarly.

Wasta, South Dakota
August 7, 2019

PROLOGUE

On August 17, 1854, Second Lieutenant John Lawrence Grattan, a recent graduate of West Point, marched into a Lakota encampment of six hundred, with twenty-nine soldiers and an interpreter, to demand that Chief Conquering Bear surrender High Forehead because he had killed a Mormon's cow and must be punished. When the situation became tense, a nervous soldier shot an Indian brave. Gunfire erupted. The Indians killed Grattan and all his men.[1]

Thus began the Sioux Indian Wars. The clashes that ensued over the course of the next thirty-six years include the Blue Water Creek Massacre (1855), Fetterman Massacre (1866), Wagon Box Fight (1867), Battle of Honsinger Bluff (1873), Battle of the Rosebud (June 17, 1876), Battle of the Little Bighorn (June 25, 1876), Slim Buttes Battle (September 9, 1876), and Battle of Wolf Mountain (1877). Those epic battles evoke mesa-like images that today punctuate the historical landscape of the American West and color its sunsets crimson.

During these years of war, some Lakota gradually came to believe that trying to stop the white men's intrusions into their land was futile. Instead of fighting soldiers and seeing their women and children killed, they concluded that the best strategy was to acquiesce when the whites demanded land and, in exchange, to settle for peace, rations, annuities, and provisions that would gradually, but not too quickly, prepare the Lakota to walk the white man's road. Accordingly, Indian chiefs and headmen signed the Fort Laramie Treaty of 1868. Article 2 of the treaty established the Great Sioux Reservation for the "absolute and undisturbed use and occupation of the Indians." Almost equally as important, Article 10 promised each Indian one pound of beef and one pound of flour per day for the next four years.[2] Although not generous, at least the rations were sufficient. It was the last equitable treaty between the Sioux and the U.S. government. Subsequent treaties with the Sioux were land grabs.

The first land grab treaty occurred in September 1876 when a handful of Lakota chiefs and headmen reluctantly put their signatures, or "marks," to the Agreement of 1877—"the sell or starve treaty." The agreement demanded the Lakota cede the gold-rich Black Hills in exchange for the continuation of their rations and annuities until the Indians could support themselves.[3] Six years later, in 1883, Congress sent commissioners to Sioux agencies to try to convince them to further break up the Great Sioux Reservation. They failed, as did the Pratt Commission of 1888. However, in 1889 a third commission convinced the Sioux to sell nine million acres of the Great Sioux Reservation. Whereas the Sioux Bill of 1889 did not address the issue of rations, the commissioners promised the Lakota that signing the bill would not result in a reduction of rations.[4] It was a promise Congress did not let the commissioners keep. Beginning in July 1890, the start of a new fiscal year, the Oglala's beef ration was reduced 20 percent.[5] Their flour ration was cut from four ounces daily to two.[6] (Two ounces of flour is comparable to a thinly cut slice of bread.)

The meager rations were insufficient and typically of poor quality at best and, at worst, literally rotten. The Oglala became malnourished. With malnourishment came its handmaiden—infectious diseases. Measles, influenza, and whooping cough ran rampant. The more deadly infectious diseases were scrofula, erysipelas, and consumption, all names for tuberculosis. Afflicted Indians suffered slow, painful deaths. The incident rate of tuberculosis on Pine Ridge was twenty-five per thousand, twelve times the national average.[7] In 1890 the death rate among the Oglala from all causes, but primarily infectious diseases, shot up to forty-five per month,[8] meaning 10 percent of the Oglala died that year.

The despair spawned hopelessness. Hopelessness created unrest, and unrest ignited the last pitched battle between the Sioux and the U.S. Army. On December 29, 1890, beside a creek called Wounded Knee, soldiers gunned down more than two hundred Lakota men, women, and children. The massacre was followed by several weeks of running skirmishes as the troops formed a ring around the hostiles' holdout and gradually tightened it. Surrounded and running low on grass for their horses, and wood for warming fires and food, more than four thousand Lakota paraded into Pine Ridge on the morning of January 15, 1891, and surrendered. Kicking Bear symbolically laid his rifle at the feet of General Nelson A. Miles, commander of the Division of the Missouri.[9] The Lakota's long-running armed conflict with the U.S. government was over. However, their struggle for survival was beginning.

That story—the Oglala's struggle to survive—is not uplifting. It tells of human suffering and of unconscionable injustice inflicted on the defenseless and voiceless Oglala by the actions, deeds, and intentional neglect of the politically powerful. As unpleasant as the story is, it must be told. It is what happened.

All the Oglala suffered during those years. One of them was Can Nopa Uhah. He was born in 1832 or thereabouts, a Brulé Sioux and a member of Two Strike's band. For most of his life, his name was Red Elk (Heraka Luta). In 1890 or possibly a year or two prior, Red Elk fell from a horse, resulting in a compound fracture of the femur of his right leg. While the leg was healing, he got around by using two crutch-like sticks. As is customary in Lakota culture, he was given a fitting moniker: Can Nopa Uhah was known as such on Indian census rolls, "can" being the Lakota word for wood or sticks; "nopa" meaning two; and "uhah" indicating broken. A direct translation of Can Nopa Uhah is "Sticks—Two—Broken." Newspaper reporters of the time and most whites referred to him as Two Sticks, although the U.S. federal court documented his case as "United States vs. Cha Nopa Uhah alias Two Sticks." Few Lakota endured more pain or paid a higher price.

⋆ 1 ⋆

STARING AT THE HANGMAN'S NOOSE

Wincing in pain, Can Nopa Uhah climbed the gallows slowly on the morning of December 28, 1894. The rope binding his arms behind his back cut into his wrists and pulled at the scar tissue from a bullet wound to his chest, inflicted when he resisted arrest for the murder of four white men. Despite all, he closely inspected the carpenter's work. Finding the work satisfactory, he said, "Was-te" (Good).[1] At the top of the gallows, the hangman's noose was dangling in the air. Death was waiting for Can Nopa Uhah.

Only hours before, Two Sticks had eaten his last meal, a hearty breakfast of steak broiled over live coals, several slices of bread, and two cups of strong coffee. Shortly after breakfast, Father Florentine Digmann, a Jesuit priest from the Holy Rosary Mission on the Pine Ridge Reservation, went into Two Sticks's jail cell to comfort the sixty-two-year-old Indian and administer the last rites. A half hour later William L. McLaughlin arrived. The attorney had a telegram. When Digmann had offered to pay the cost of a telegram, McLaughlin had agreed to make an eleventh-hour plea to Grover Cleveland, president of the United States. At Digmann's behest, McLaughlin had asked the president to commute Two Sticks's sentence from death to life in prison. The telegram in McLaughlin's hand was from Henry Thurber, the president's private secretary. McLaughlin dispassionately read President Cleveland's reply. Digmann translated the one-sentence missive: "The President has refused to interfere with the execution of the sentence of Two Sticks."[2]

At 9:30 A.M. U.S. Marshal Otto Peemiller and Deputy U.S. Marshals Andrew Bray and Frank Beiglemeir entered the jail cell. They were accompanied by Frank Young, the interpreter for the Pine Ridge Agency; Sheriff Arthur Bartlett of Dawes County, Nebraska, representing the county of residence of two of the murdered men; and Sheriff Ed W. Blakely of Fall River County, South Dakota, representing the county of residence of the other two murdered men. Several newspaper reporters were also present.

Two Sticks rose from his chair and shook their hands. Wasting no time, Marshal Peemiller read the death warrant. Frank Young interpreted the marshal's words to Two Sticks. When Peemiller finished reading the death warrant, he asked Two Sticks if there was any reason the death sentence should not be carried out.

Turning toward Peemiller, the condemned prisoner spoke in Lakota. Frank Young translated. In a clear, resonant voice, Two Sticks said,

My heart is not bad. I did not kill the cowboys. The Indian boys [First Eagle, Fights With, White Face Horse and Two Two] killed them. I never killed a white man. I never pulled a gun on a white man. The Great Father and the men under him should talk to me and I would show them I am innocent. The white men are going to kill me for something I haven't done. I am a great chief myself. I have always been a friend of the white man. The white men will find out in time that I am innocent, and then they will be sorry they killed me. The Great Father will be sorry, too, and he will be ashamed. My people will be ashamed, too. My heart is straight and I like everybody. God made all hearts the same. My heart is the same as a white man's. If I had not been innocent, I would not have come up here so good when they wanted me. They know I am innocent or they would not let me go around here. [During his long incarceration, Two Sticks was often allowed out of his cell to roam about within the jail.] My heart knows I am not guilty, and I am happy. I am not afraid to die. I was taught that if I raised my hands to God and told a lie, God would kill me that day. I never told a lie in my life."[3]

Was Two Sticks innocent? Was the federal government's justice system about to hang an innocent man? And if Two Sticks was innocent, how did it happen that he was about to be hanged for murder?

❋ 2 ❋

THE POLITICAL ROAD TO WOUNDED KNEE

Can Nopa Uhah's date with the hangman on December 28, 1894, was an inextricable consequence of the Indian unrest of 1890 that culminated in the Wounded Knee Massacre. If there had been no Indian unrest, the crime for which Two Sticks was executed would not have occurred. While there were multiple causes for the Indian unrest, the principal one unfolded in 1889 at a most unlikely place—a smoke-filled room in the small, frontier town of Pierre, Dakota Territory.[1]

Anticipating statehood for South Dakota, newly elected legislators met in Pierre on the morning of October 15, 1889, to select two men to represent South Dakota in the United States Senate.[2] They elected Gideon Moody, a resident of the Black Hills and an associate justice of the territorial supreme court, and Richard F. Pettigrew.[3]

Pettigrew was six feet tall, ramrod straight, well proportioned, and endowed with a keen mind that looked out at the world through steely gray penetrating eyes. While he had the appearance of a statesman, any further resemblance to a principled man ended there. Hidden behind Pettigrew's outward facade was a double-dealing, unscrupulous, self-serving politician who covered his own crooked trail with trumped-up accusations against anyone who opposed him.[4]

Upon being elected to the U.S. Senate, Pettigrew informed a loyal constituent, "I intend to close out all of the Indian Reservations [in South Dakota] just

Richard F. Pettigrew, U.S. senator, 1889–1901. (South Dakota State Historical Society.)

as soon as possible. We have either got to pursue that course or else the course implemented by the other western states—that of getting rid of the Indians in one way or another. (Otherwise) we cannot develop and build up a State with such vast areas of unoccupied and untaxable property."[5]

Senator Pettigrew's other goal was to use the well-oiled spoils system to strengthen his political base. To that end, the newly elected senator secured the appointment of loyal South Dakota Republicans to be bank examiners, postmasters, town site commissioners, artesian well examiners, census enumerators, and law clerks. He selected a United States attorney and the veterinary surgeon at the newly founded state agricultural college in Brookings.[6] Pettigrew also nominated Cyrus J. Fry to be the U.S. marshal for the District of South Dakota.

Fry, whose life was destined to intersect with Can Nopa Uhah's, moved to Vermillion, Dakota Territory, with his wife, Christiana, and their family in 1882 to engage in farming. In 1884 Fry was elected county commissioner, an office he held for three years, until elected county treasurer.[7] He was sworn in as U.S. marshal on January 2, 1890, by Judge Alonzo Edgerton in Pettigrew's law office.[8] At the time, Fry had two secrets. In November 1883 he had returned to his former home in Great Bend, Kansas, to appear in court on a civil charge. Shortly after the hearing, Fry heard a rumor that several parties in Great Bend were going to bring suits against him and hold him in jail until the cases could be tried. He slipped out of town and returned to Vermillion, putting himself beyond the reach of Kansas law enforcement.[9] Fry's wife undoubtedly was aware of that concealment. However, it was possible that Mrs. Fry did not know about her husband's other personal problem until she received a telegram from Deadwood in 1893.

Pettigrew's most egregious abuse of the spoils system was on the seven Indian reservations with headquarters in South Dakota: Cheyenne River, Pine Ridge, Rosebud, Yankton, Crow Creek, and Lower Brulé, the latter two administered by the same agent; and the Sisseton-Wahpeton Reservation, which was partially located in North Dakota but had its agency headquarters was in Sisseton. Another small reservation was based at Flandreau, but it was administered by the agent in charge of the Santee Reservation in Nebraska and therefore was not under Pettigrew's purview.

As soon as Senator Pettigrew ensconced himself in Washington, he set out to get on the Senate Indian Affairs Committee, which had oversight of the Bureau of Indian Affairs. Once he was on the committee, all six South Dakota–based Indian agents were at Richard Pettigrew's mercy. He set out to replace agents who were Democrats with South Dakota Republicans and then pressured them to rid their reservations of employees who were Democrats and to replace them with additional loyal South Dakota Republicans.

One party loyalist who wanted to be an Indian agent was Perain P. Palmer. Palmer and his wife, Mary, were relative newcomers to South Dakota, having arrived in Estelline in 1883 from Baraboo, Wisconsin, where he was a plasterer. In Estelline, Palmer had served as township assessor, and that position kindled within him a yen for politics. He was on the ballot in November 1888 for a seat in the Dakota Territory legislature.[10] His campaign touted his military service as a sergeant in the Wisconsin First Heavy Artillery Regiment during the Civil War. His competitor did not have a comparable distinction. That difference was likely the reason Palmer won. When Palmer joined the territorial legislature of 1889, he found himself on the same side of the aisle as fellow Republican Richard Pettigrew.[11]

In the spring of 1890, Palmer solicited Pettigrew's support to become the Indian agent for the Cheyenne River Reservation, and Pettigrew decided Palmer was worthy of a political plum. On April 12, 1890, he wrote to Palmer, "I saw the Secretary of the Interior and the President today. The Secretary tells me that he will try to secure your appointment next Tuesday as agent at Cheyenne. If this is done, I shall want to change all employees at the agency as soon as possible. It is very important that the employees shall all be Dakota Republicans."[12]

To Pettigrew's surprise and chagrin, President Benjamin Harrison refused to immediately install Palmer as the new agent. He believed the current agent, Dr. Charles E. McChesney, had done an exceptional job. Among other accomplishments, many of McChesney's employees were Indians and they supported him. As was apparent in McChesney's final report to the commissioner of Indian affairs, he valued them: "I wish to express my sincere thanks to the employees for their hearty and intelligent assistance. They have always responded promptly and cheerfully to the many calls made upon them for the discharge of important duties and by their active cooperation have done much to render possible whatever success has attended my administration of the affairs of this agency since 1886."[13] Harrison saw no reason to insult an honorable and capable man by terminating him a few months before his term expired.

Pettigrew was infuriated that Harrison had the audacity to thwart his control over patronage on the reservations in South Dakota. He responded by trumping up corruption charges against McChesney and putting the charges on the desk of Thomas J. Morgan, the commissioner of Indian affairs. Morgan was not intimidated by the upstart senator. He informed Pettigrew that even if the corruption charges were filed, he would not immediately remove McChesney. Instead, he would appoint a special agent to investigate the matter; McChesney would remain at his post until the investigation was completed, which would take at least until mid-August. By then McChesney's voluntary resignation would be effective. Morgan went further than that. With Harrison's backing, he put Pettigrew on notice that competent agency employees were not going to be dismissed simply because they were Democrats.[14] Morgan's admonition did not deter Pettigrew. Instead, it increased his resolve and made him more devious.

Pettigrew did not wait for Palmer to take up his duties at Cheyenne River before sending him the names of South Dakota Republicans desiring political plums. On July 3, 1890, Pettigrew wrote to Palmer:

Carl Sherwood of Clark County wants to have C. A. Fountain appointed one of the clerks at *your* [emphasis added] agency. I think either as your issue clerk or a storekeeper. He also wishes to have another gentleman appointed as farmer. I have told him that I thought you could also give the gentleman a place as a blacksmith, or a wheelwright, or a carpenter. As soon as you get possession [of the agency] I think it is best to change all the employees and put in a lot of Dakota Republicans. I am not at all afraid. The service will be all right if we change the whole crowd. I see there are at least two additional farmers at $600 per year. I should like to have Theo. Berndt of Tyndall, South Dakota, appointed to one of these places.[15]

When Palmer finally became the agent, Pettigrew sent him a congratulatory letter, complete with expectations. "I am glad to know," Pettigrew wrote, "you are in charge of that agency. I want to change the farmers as soon as possible. The first appointment I want is Theodore Berndt of Tyndall. I am very particular to have this appointment made as I think it will affect the success of the legislative ticket in Bon Homme County. I also want young McCormack of Hyde County taken care of beyond any question because I told his father he would have one [a job]."[16]

Pettigrew's other tactic to replace agency employees with Dakota Republicans was deceit. When he wanted the superintendent of the boys' school at the Cheyenne River Agency to be dismissed and replaced by J. M. Corbin, a Republican from Templeton, South Dakota, Pettigrew wrote a letter to the commissioner of Indian affairs. In it he claimed to have received a letter from Palmer conveying the new Indian agent's desire to change the superintendent: "He says the present teacher is unable to control the boys and the police are constantly being kept busy bringing them back to the school. Mr. Palmer is a very capable man. I have confidence in his statement and believe his recommendation should be carried out."[17] Pettigrew then wrote to Palmer, telling him to terminate the current superintendent and hire J. M. Corbin.[18]

Like many of Pettigrew's political appointments, Palmer was incompetent and unethical. He had been in control of the Cheyenne River Reservation for a little more than a year when evidence revealed that he and his clerk, George B. Shoenfeldt, who was Palmer's son-in-law, and a mixed-blood interpreter, William Benoist (known to the press as Billy Benway), had pocketed thousands of dollars by falsifying records about money paid to individual Indians for the sale of their cattle. The ill-gotten gain from that scam alone was between fifteen and twenty thousand dollars.[19] Other charges included purchasing hay from individual Indians for two to five dollars a ton and charging the Bureau of Indian Affairs ten dollars a ton.[20] It was also alleged that Palmer allowed his son-in-law, Shoenfeldt, to get a 10 percent kickback on supplies purchased from area merchants. Under the threat of being charged with defrauding the government, Perain Palmer and Shoenfeldt simultaneously submitted their resignations in January 1892.[21]

George Wright was the Indian agent for the Rosebud Reservation. He entered the Indian Service in July 1883, serving as a farmer under his father, James Wright, who was at the time the Indian agent. When James Wright retired in 1886, Agent Lebbeus "Foster" Spencer replaced him. Spencer was dismissed in 1889, allegedly for corruption but more likely at the insistence of the Sioux Bill commissioners because Spencer had actively discouraged the Brulé from signing the Sioux Bill of 1889.[22] Upon General George Crook's recommendation, George Wright was named the Indian agent.

Pettigrew did not attempt to remove Wright because the newly installed Indian agent had the good fortune of being both a South Dakotan and a Republican. Pettigrew assumed Wright would be another conduit for patronage. As Pettigrew told one of his constituents, "I have written the agent [Wright] asking him to weed out the Democrats and fill their places with Dakota Republicans."[23] He immediately inundated Wright with the names of Dakota Republicans who needed jobs: "Mr. Rouse would like a place as a teacher at your agency. I have sent a gentleman from McCook County to you. I think you will find he will make a good man."[24] In yet another letter to Wright, Pettigrew wrote, "I hope you will be able to take care of Mr. Haspshuld of Clifton, South Dakota."[25] More requests followed. One letter to Wright said, "[T]he farmers that I should like to have appointed are Fred Barth and Theodore Berndt."[26]

Pettigrew's choice for the Indian agent at the Crow Creek and Lower Brulé Reservations was James Stephens, a staunch Republican from Springfield, South Dakota, who had worked to convince legislators from the southeast corner of the state to vote for Pettigrew in the contest for U.S. Senate. However, O. S. Gifford was South Dakota's newly elected legislator to the United States House of Representatives and a member of the House Committee on Indian Affairs. Gifford insisted on having at least some of the political spoils that came with victory. He wanted Andrew Dixon to become the agent at Crow Creek. Dixon had the politically correct credentials. First and foremost, he was a Republican.

He was also the ex-sheriff of Lincoln County. Moreover, both Dixon and O. S. Gifford were from the little town of Canton, South Dakota. They were friends.

Pettigrew did not oppose Gifford's pick for Indian agent at Crow Creek and Lower Brulé because he believed "Dixon will recommend the removal of every one of the employees at the agency, and we will send him first class, active Republicans."[27] When Dixon was installed as the Indian agent, Pettigrew did not have any compunction about usurping Gifford's patronage privileges; he instructed Dixon as to the South Dakota Republicans who should be awarded jobs. "I have written Burkholder," Pettigrew wrote Dixon, "to come and see you as I desire to have him appointed chief clerk. There will be another chief clerk in charge of the Indians at Lower Brulé, and we will correspond about that in the future. I shall also want to correspond with you about other employees at the agency. I want Fred Barth of Wittenberg to be one of the farmers at that agency."[28] In another letter to Dixon, Pettigrew wrote, "I think we will persuade him [the commissioner of Indian affairs] to change pretty near all of the employees. You will have to recommend removals, giving your reasons why and send them to the Commissioner. Notify me, and I will go down and look after it."[29] Pettigrew sometimes handed out jobs to loyal South Dakota Republicans without input from the appropriate Indian agent or without even extending the courtesy of informing the agent. A case in point is a letter he wrote to Emery Potter of Salem, South Dakota: "I can have you appointed at once as a sub-teacher at Rosebud. The position pays 50 dollars per month for yourself and 25 dollars for your wife."[30] Pettigrew's letters to Indian agents about South Dakota Republicans who should be given jobs on their reservations were not suggestions or even requests. They were directives from a U.S. senator, who made it clear to the agents that they served at his pleasure.

Of all Pettigrew's nominees to be Indian agents, the most incompetent was Daniel F. Royer. In 1883, the thirty-two-year-old Royer and his family moved from Pennsylvania to Alpena, Dakota Territory. There, Royer set about becoming a big man in a small town. He was postmaster, doctor, city treasurer, chairman of the board of education, member of the territorial board of pharmacy, coroner for Jerauld County, proprietor of the drugstore, and owner of the lumberyard and the livery stable. He also had financial interests in the bank and the newspaper.[31] Upon establishing himself in Alpena, Royer formed a close friendship with Richard Pettigrew. When a daughter was born in 1886 to Royer and his wife, RosAnnah, they named her Maude Pettigrew Royer and chose Pettigrew to be her godfather. Royer was elected to the Dakota territorial

Daniel Royer, Pine Ridge agent, 1890. (South Dakota State Historical Society.)

legislature in November 1886 and reelected in November 1888. There, he forged a political alliance with Pettigrew.

Pettigrew rewarded Royer for his friendship and political loyalty by nominating him to be the Indian agent at Pine Ridge. On March 17, 1890, he notified Royer: "I have filed a letter endorsing you for Pine Ridge. If you secure the appointment, I shall want to clean out the whole force of farmers, teachers and clerks as far as possible and put in Dakota men. You cannot make any appointment until you consult [Senator] Moody and I about it."[32]

When Royer's appointment did not happen as soon as expected, Pettigrew wrote him a reassuring letter: "You will be appointed the agent at Pine Ridge. I have this promise from the Secretary of the Interior. The President refuses to remove the present agent, and his term does not expire until September."[33] In mid-August Pettigrew sent Royer the news the aspirant had been hoping for: "You were confirmed yesterday, no objections having been filed against you and the President notified."[34]

Royer took charge of Pine Ridge Reservation on October 9, 1890, replacing Colonel Hugh Gallagher, a man of impeccable honesty and highly regarded by both his employees and the Oglala.[35] Royer was not of the same ilk. For his issue clerk, Royer selected Bishop J. Gleason, a Republican from Potter County who in 1889 was a delegate to the Republican Convention in Huron.[36] Royer and Gleason did not come to Pine Ridge to help the Oglala; they came to steal from them. Reflecting on the transition from Gallagher's administration to Royer's, Robert Pugh, a longtime agency employee, related: "[W]hen Gallagher left there were three hundred cords of wood, 150 tons of hay, 600,000 lbs. of corn and oats on hand. [When Royer came] the wood, hay and grain were stolen remorselessly—stolen clean. The wood went with such dispatch that the boarding school had to burn tree tops and other inferior fuel. Vouchers were signed for supplies that never made it to the agency. Cattle were bought at inflated prices." Pugh related one such fraudulent transaction: "A drover came in with a large herd of trail-gaunt cattle. Under Gallagher's administration, the cattle would have been bought as 950-pound steers and put on the reservation grass to fatten. But Royer's clerk, B. J. Gleason, purchased the steers at 1,200 pounds." Pugh calculated that the government paid for eighty thousand pounds of beef that did not exist. The fraudulently obtained $41,250 was split among the drover, Gleason, and Royer.[37]

Royer's arrival at Pine Ridge, coupled with Pettigrew's patronage practices, unleashed a sudden, unexpected assault on the Oglala's culture, values, and tradition. Previously, the wrongdoings, deceptions, and manipulations hoisted upon the Oglala were done by white men who came into their land, held councils seldom lasting more than a few days, got the land they wanted, and left. Few Lakota could even remember their names and as quickly as possible forgot their faces. The white men were out of sight and out of mind and, most importantly, out of Indian Country. With the exception of an Indian agent and his small staff composed of a combination of whites and Indians, the Oglala were then left to govern themselves in their traditional ways and to decide among themselves the course of their lives. Freedom of choice, something endemic to the viability of all groups and cultures, was still theirs. The Oglala instantly lost that when Pettigrew's patronage practices flooded the reservation with white people. As American Horse remarked, "The white men are [now] so numerous [at the agency] that they fairly trample on the Indians."[38]

Some white people came to Pine Ridge with the noble mission of "civilizing" the Indians. Their easiest, most convenient target was Indian children. Thisba Hutson was one of the civilizers. She arrived just prior to the start of school in 1890 to teach at the government boarding school, replacing Clarence Three Stars, an Oglala Sioux. Like all the new teachers, Hutson believed that Indian children only needed a little motivation to adopt the ways of civilized people, and she saw it as her job to be the prod. However, she was surprised to discover that the majority of the Indian children were reluctant students. When instruction commenced that fall,

> many of the children had to be arrested and brought to school by force. Immediately upon arriving each child was stripped naked and placed in a bathtub filled with water as hot as could possibly be used. In it was a generous amount of kerosene. Plenty of yellow soap was then applied by the vigorous use of scrubbing brushes. The child's head was pushed under the kerosene-laced water several times to kill the myriad of supposed insects and vermin the children had unwittingly brought with them. If their camp clothes were good enough to salvage, the garments were given to the parents to take home. Generally, the garments were burned. After the bath, a girl's hair was dried and put into one long braid. The boys had their long hair cropped, making them feel humiliated, immodest and naked. The boys were then dressed in school uniforms and their feet stuffed into army-issue brogans furnished by the government.[39]

(The brogans were not shaped for a right or left foot; all the shoes were the same shape. Until the brogans gradually softened by wear to take the shape of the foot, the boys hobbled around on blistered feet.) The children were given English first names, by which they were to be known at school. All classes were taught in English. The boarding school children were forbidden to speak Lakota, even in the evening, and punished if they did. Many children ran away from the schools. When they ran away, the agent sent the Indian police after them. If parents refused to send their children back to school, the family's rations were terminated until the children returned to school.[40]

Runaway children invariably showed up back home, tearfully reported the harsh, humiliating treatment they received at the hands of white teachers, and begged their parents not to return them to school. But what were parents to do when an Indian police officer arrived to tell them that if their children were not returned to school, their rations would be terminated?

Many of the white people who came to Pine Ridge did not have as principled a purpose as Thisba Hutson. They came because the work demands were few and the idle time gave them opportunity to exploit the Indians. As Elaine Goodale observed, "[T]he assistant farmer . . . was usually a political henchman or the needy favorite of some man higher up. Such posts were poorly paid and regarded as desirable mainly because of opportunities for private pickings. As was commonly quipped by those even on the lowest rung, assistant farmers, 'We're none of us here for our health.'"[41] Most of the newly appointed farmers did not have any qualifications to be farmers, and they did not pretend to have an interest in the welfare of the helpless Natives. They kept their jobs by feeding the bureaucrats in the Bureau of Indian Affairs glowing but falsified reports of their success at advancing the Indians' agricultural progress.[42]

It is little wonder that after Royer had been in charge for only one month and three days, the Oglala's animosity toward their white overseers was so widespread and so intense that all it would take to set off an Indian uprising was a single spark.

❖ 3 ❖

THE INDIAN UNREST THAT BROUGHT CAN NOPA UHAH TO THE GALLOWS

The Sioux Indian Wars began in 1854 when an Indian killed a Mormon's cow. Ironically, the armed conflict that ended the Sioux Indian Wars was also precipitated by an Indian killing a critter. The Indian who killed the beef was known as Little, possibly because of his small stature. The animal did not belong to a white man or to the U.S. government. It belonged to Little's brother, and he was not concerned about the butchered beef. Government officials were. Hearing that hungry Indians were killing breeding stock for food, the Bureau of Indian Affairs had issued a regulation mandating that an Indian obtain permission from the government herder before killing any livestock. Royer coupled the mandate with an order that the animal had to be slaughtered at the agency.[1]

When word reached the agency that Little had killed a steer without permission, Royer ordered the Indian police to arrest him. Early Wednesday morning, November 12, 1890, while most Indian families were headed for the agency to collect their rations, Lieutenant Thunder Bear and a contingent of Indian police arrived at Big Road's camp on Wounded Knee Creek to arrest Little. As per Lakota tradition, Thunder Bear informed the headman of the camp, in this case Big Road, that the Indian police had come to arrest Little. Big Road likely scoffed at them. Why herd an animal fifteen miles to the agency, kill it, and then haul the carcass home in the back of a wagon? Big Road sent the Indian police away.

Later that same day, thousands of Oglala were at the agency for their rations. At noon they milled around in the street, waiting for the issue building to reopen at one o'clock. Little was among them, and the Indian police spotted him. Thunder Bear, Standing Bear, and several other police slipped into the crowd. Separating and visiting as they went, the policemen edged toward Little. When Standing Bear reached Little, he grabbed him. Whereas Little was a small man, he was cat quick and sinewy strong. He wrestled Standing Bear to the ground. As Little released Standing Bear, he drew his knife, to let Standing Bear know that if he wanted to, he could kill the policeman. But Little released Standing Bear and backed away.[2]

The attempted arrest infuriated the Oglala waiting in the street for the issue building to reopen. They swarmed around the Indian policemen. They were angry because in the attempt to arrest Little, the police, their own kinsmen, were enforcing the edict of a dishonest white man who was stealing their rations and plundering the reservation to line his pockets. Some began shouting that the time had come to burn the agency to the ground and kill all the whites. The commotion could be heard in the council room. American Horse, a principal chief, rose from the council and went into the street. He pushed his way to the entrapped police. "My brothers," he called to the crowd, "what are you going to do? Are you going to kill these men of our own race? . . . Thousands of white soldiers will be here in three days. . . . What will become of your families?"[3]

At that instant, the one o'clock bell rang. Unsuspecting clerks opened the doors of the issue building. Returning from his lunch, Robert Pugh walked into the confusion. He saw that the door to the back room was slightly ajar. Royer was peering out. The terrified Indian agent beckoned Pugh to the back room. Barely able to speak, Royer whimpered, "We have almost been massacred." Pugh, a longtime resident of Pine Ridge, with an Oglala wife and mixed-blood children, who knew the Oglala as well as any white man could, told Royer that the seemingly volatile scene between the Indians and the Indian police was only a war of words; no further trouble would ensue. Despite the assurance, Royer declared he was going to take his family and leave. Pugh advised him not to do that, as it would bring his career as an Indian agent to an end.[4]

Pugh went out of the issue building and walked among the Indians, most of whom he personally knew. He latched onto the collar of one of the men and led him into the issue building while trying to talk some sense into him. Pugh loaded the man up with eatables, filled his own arms with boxes of crackers and other provisions, and walked into the crowd. Handing out the crackers, he called out, "Take these and go home. You are making it unpleasant at the agency." They dispersed. Quiet again reigned.[5]

By then Royer had his team ready and his family in a buggy. As he was leaving, Royer told Pugh that he was the acting Indian agent because he had successfully quelled the disturbance. Pugh advised Royer against demanding troops, as there was no need. With an impatient nod, Royer cracked his buggy whip and fled with his family to Rushville.[6]

Three days later Royer, still badly frightened despite his refuge at Rushville, telegraphed Thomas Morgan, the commissioner of Indian affairs: "Indians are dancing in the snow and are wild and crazy. I have fully informed you that employees and government property at this Agency have no protection and are at the mercy of these dancers. Why delay by further investigation? We need protection and we need it now. The leaders should be arrested and confined in some military post until the matter is quieted and this should be done at once."[7]

In reporting that "Indians are dancing in the snow," Royer was referring to the Ghost Dance. The Ghost Dance constituted a new religion, brought to the Lakota reservations in the spring of 1890 by seven delegates who had ridden the Union Pacific train to Pyramid Lake, Nevada, to learn about it from a Paiute medicine man named Wovoka. The Ghost Dance was a ritualistic ceremony in which the Indians danced clockwise in a circle, emulating the motion of the sun across the sky, until each fell unconscious on the ground. Later, when revived, they told about seeing and talking with their recently deceased relatives. The believers were told that their dancing would usher forth the biblically promised Second Coming of the Messiah, meaning Jesus Christ. This time he was coming to save the Indians, his chosen people, and upon his arrival, he would cause all whites to die by sinking into the earth.[8] To hungry, exploited, and subjugated people, it was an appealing belief. However, there was an ominous component of the Ghost Dance as practiced on the Lakota reservations. Short Bull and Kicking Bear, the two ardent proselytizers, told the Lakota that bullets could not pierce their ghost shirts,[9] meaning soldiers could not kill them. When Robert Belt, the acting commissioner of Indian affairs, learned of the Messiah craze, he instructed Indian agents at the five Lakota reservations to put a stop to the Ghost Dance. This they were unable to do.[10]

When Royer did not get the solicited support from Morgan, on November 16 he sent an urgent telegram to Brigadier General John R. Brooke, commanding officer of the Department of the Platte:

In attempt to arrest an Indian Tuesday [actually Wednesday] for violating regulations, he drew a butcher knife on the police and in less than two minutes over two hundred armed Indians, ready to fight, ran to his assistance. This occurred close to my office. They threatened the agent and were only prevented from burning all the government buildings and supplies by older and wiser heads. The situation here is serious. We have no protection. Our police are overpowered and can do nothing. I received a communication from the offender Tuesday that if I did not discourage [Royer probably scrawled "discharge," but the telegraph operator misread it] the police who attempted to arrest him by next issue day I might expect trouble. We need protection and we need it now. The Indians are buying all the ammunition they can get and are well armed. Delay is dangerous.[11]

Brooke forwarded the telegram to the assistant adjutant general at the Division of the Missouri in Chicago who showed it to General Nelson Miles, commander of the division. Miles forwarded a copy of Royer's telegram to the secretary of war.

Several days later, Pugh was in his office when he heard the clear notes of a bugle. Walking out to the street, he saw a column of three troops of cavalry approaching with the redoubtable Agent Royer driving safely in the center. A detachment from the Fifth Cavalry stationed at Fort Robinson was giving Royer the assurance he needed to return to Pine Ridge.[12]

By then Royer's panic-fueled telegrams had gotten the attention of John Noble, secretary of the interior; Redfield Proctor, secretary of war; and President Harrison. On November 13 Harrison directed the secretary of war to "assume responsibility for the suppression of any threatened outbreak."[13] Accordingly, in the predawn hours of November 20, 230 soldiers under the command of Lieutenant Colonel A. T. Smith took up positions on the outskirts of the Rosebud Agency. When the morning sun announced their presence, Short Bull, a medicine man, feared the worst. He led several thousand panic-stricken Brulé northwest to Chief Lip's camp at the confluence of Pass Creek and White River. They commenced ghost dancing frenetically.[14] That same day, Chief Two Strike and Crow Dog led upward of one thousand followers northwest toward the badlands.[15] Among them were Can Nopa Uhah; his wife, Sits in Lodge (Timahel Yanka); and their sons First Eagle (Wanbli Tokaha), age twenty-seven; Fights With (Wasaglefis, also known as Mark Red Elk), age seventeen; Hiyuiciya (Dismounts, also known as Thomas), age nine; and Slohan Ku (Comes Crawling), age six.

That same morning, November 20, the Oglala at the Pine Ridge Agency awoke and looked up at the hills above their camp to see Gatling guns and Hotchkiss cannons trained on them. Terrified, many Oglala fled fifteen miles down White Clay Creek to Chief No Water's camp.[16]

Upon learning that thousands of Brulé and Oglala had left their agencies and congregated in the remote areas of the Pine Ridge Reservation, many white settlers living adjacent to the Lakota reservations convinced themselves that an Indian uprising was about to commence. Settlers as far north as Mandan, North Dakota, as far south as Valentine, Nebraska, and at all points in between flocked to the nearest towns for safety. General stores as far from Pine Ridge as Lincoln and Omaha, Nebraska, sold out entire supplies of guns and ammunition.[17] Some settlers were reluctant to abandon their homes. They thought it best to fortify themselves and prepare for an Indian attack. A group of settlers living just south of the Pine Ridge Reservation converted a root cellar into a log bunker, measuring twenty-four by twenty-four feet, and covered the roof with timber, on top of which they put dirt. They dubbed the impregnable structure Fort Nendle after the homesteader on whose land it was built.[18]

James "Scotty" Philip and Charley Waldron, West River ranchers, were among those concerned by the Lakota's reaction to the presence of troops on their reservations. On the evening of November 22, they knocked on the door of Governor Arthur Mellette's residence in Pierre. The governor greeted them warmly. His welcome was not unexpected, as some of the seventeen hundred cattle Philip ran on his ranch belonged to the governor. But the cowboys did not seek out the governor to talk about cows. They came to inform Mellette that the sudden, unexpected appearance of troops on Rosebud and Pine Ridge had pushed the Indians to the verge of an uprising. The ranchers told the governor that Short Bull, the medicine man for Chief Lip's village near the mouth of Pass Creek, had brought the Ghost Dance to his band in late September. When Robert Whitfield, the boss farmer assigned to the band, learned of the ghost dancing, he convinced Chief Lip to tell Short Bull that he and his new Ghost Dance religion were not welcome in the village and that Short Bull should leave. A week later Indians broke into Whitfield's house and absconded with his entire supply of winter food and his horses. Philip and Waldron also told Mellette that a few days earlier Indians had wantonly killed twenty of Philip's cattle and seven of Waldron's. Philip related that the previous day he had talked to Yellow Thigh, a subchief who was taking his small band to join Short Bull at the ghost dancers' camp on Pass Creek. Yellow Thigh told Philip that if soldiers tried to stop the ghost dancing, they would be killed by a hailstorm.[19]

Mellette sent a telegram to General Miles, telling him of the ranchers' ominous concerns.[20] Mellette also asked Philip, John Holland, and Crow Eagle, a Sioux chief whose band lived peaceably in a small village thirty miles up from the mouth of Bad River, if they would undertake the hazardous mission of reconnoitering Short Bull's camp of ghost dancers. They agreed to do it. Upon reaching the ghost dancers' camp on Pass Creek, the three scouts were stunned to find it abandoned. Signs indicated that the Indians had gone west along the south bank of White River.[21] When the scouting report was shared with Mellette, he was alarmed to learn that the hostiles were headed in the direction of isolated whites squatting on land along the north bank of the White River, land the Indians had recently and reluctantly ceded. For all Mellette knew, Short Bull's ghost dancers were even then killing the isolated whites.

Desperate for more information, Mellette wired Valentine T. McGillycuddy, president of the Lakota Bank in Rapid City but formerly an Indian agent at Pine Ridge, requesting him to go to Pine Ridge and assess the situation. Only hours after the governor's telegram reached McGillycuddy, he caught the train for Rushville and thence went by team and buggy to the agency. He expected that a telegram from Commissioner Morgan would be waiting for him at Rushville, appointing him to replace Daniel Royer, the agent whose incompetence had made it necessary to move troops onto the reservation. McGillycuddy expected the appointment because he knew Morgan wanted Royer removed and because Herbert Welsh, secretary of the influential Indian Rights Association, also wanted McGillycuddy in the job.[22] Welsh went so far as to prompt several newspaper editors to write opinion pieces designed to pressure Secretary Noble and President Harrison to reinstate McGillycuddy.[23] Pettigrew used his position on the Senate's Indian Affairs Committee to oppose the removal of Royer and the reinstatement of McGillycuddy. "If McGillycuddy shows up on the reservation," Pettigrew instructed Royer, "put him off the agency. I consider him a scoundrel. Furthermore, he would like to be your successor."[24]

In the end, Harrison succumbed to political considerations because thousands of soldiers were being rushed to Sioux reservations at taxpayer expense and panic-inciting but baseless newspaper articles had the public believing an Indian uprising had erupted. If Harrison were to suddenly announce that the crisis could be handled by one individual—even V. T. McGillycuddy—the political ramifications could be severe. There was no telegram waiting for McGillycuddy at Rushville reinstating him as Indian agent. However, he had Governor Mellette's telegram in his pocket and used it as his admission ticket to the agency. Shortly after arriving on the scene, McGillycuddy asked General John R. Brooke, commander of the troops at the agency, for permission to go to the hostile camp on White Clay Creek and try to persuade the Indians to come into the agency. Brooke denied the request.[25] He opted for a military solution.

With more troops arriving almost daily at the agency and others taking up positions around the border of Pine Ridge, the Indians became increasing frightened. On November 30 panicked Brulé and Oglala met at the confluence of Grass Creek and White River. Joining forces, they forded the river and headed west toward a badland table the Sioux called Oonagazhee, the sheltering place. Now known as Stronghold Table, it was a natural fortress deep in the recesses of the rugged badlands. There, they ghost danced with renewed frenzy while five hundred Indian women dug a defensive trench five feet deep across the narrow neck of land connecting Stronghold to a much larger table to the south, now called Cuny Table.[26]

The settlers quickly learned that the Indians had taken up a defensive position on Stronghold Table and were alarmed. On December 1, John Brennan, proprietor of the Harney Hotel in Rapid City, received a wire from W. F. Steele at Pine Ridge: "Scouts just came in. Report about eight hundred Indians near Badlands—still dancing. There may be trouble here."[27]

Believing an Indian outbreak was imminent, the small towns adjacent to Pine Ridge prepared for it. Buffalo Gap, only seventeen miles from the reservation, was the first town to organize. Forty men convened at W. J. Wood's general store to form a home guard, with N. L. Pope in command. Pickets were put three miles to the east of town and also to the south. The *Buffalo Gap Republican* boasted, "If the government cannot control the redskins, the Buffalo Gap Destroyers offer their services to settle the whole matter."[28] Well, they would settle the whole matter if they had guns. They sent a telegram to Governor Mellette: "Please send immediately one hundred guns with one hundred rounds of ammunition for each."[29] Oelrichs, Hot Springs, Hermosa, Custer, Rapid City, and number of other towns also formed home guards.

The formation of home guards and the appeals for guns put Mellette on the sharp horns of a dilemma. Mellette knew that nearly every West River man owned a rifle and knew how to use it. They did not need more guns. But if he did not arm the citizens and an Indian killed even one South Dakotan, he would be blamed. In a move that could be described as better safe than sorry, Mellette dispatched Brigadier General George W. Carpenter, chief of supply for the South Dakota Militia, to organize citizens along the eastern edge of the Missouri River in the vicinity of the Crow Creek and Lower Brulé Reservations.[30] He requested General Miles to put troops at Chamberlain and he wired the secretary of war, asking for a thousand guns and ammunition.[31]

Redfield Proctor, secretary of war, authorized the release of rifles and ammunition from the army arsenal in Rock Island, Illinois. The guns shipped to the governor were Springfield .45- and .50-caliber breach-loading rifles. The bullets had copper casings that expanded when fired, often preventing the cartridge from ejecting. When that happened, the rifle's only use was as a club. In 1890 those rifles were antiquated. Nearly every settler on the frontier owned a Model 1873 Winchester, the famous lever-action repeating rifle that won the West. Arming the settlers with Springfield rifles was simply a symbolic gesture of support. But settlers living adjacent to the Pine Ridge Reservation interpreted the rifles as more than symbolic. To them, the governor's distribution of guns was official authorization to go Indian hunting. Before the month was out, settlers would kill a considerable number of Indians. With one exception, their deaths were never recorded and their graves, like their names, are unknown.

Mellette could not have foreseen those tragic outcomes when he shipped rifles and ammunition to the following places on December 4, 1890: Aberdeen and Chamberlain each received one hundred rifles and five thousand cartridges; Redfield, sixty rifles and three thousand cartridges; Gann Valley and Woonsocket, forty rifles and two thousand cartridges each; Highmore, Mound City, and Ree Heights, twenty rifles each along with one thousand cartridges. Two days later one hundred rifles and five thousand cartridges were consigned to Merritt H. Day at Rapid City.[32]

That same day, December 6, Mellette sent a telegram to Day, a Rapid City attorney. It read: "You are hereby appointed my aide-de-camp to dispose of all ordnance and manage the Hills campaign. Present to Mayor Wood."[33] Day's appointment was interesting because he was an ardent Democrat. His military service dated back twenty-five years to when he was a captain in the Eleventh Wisconsin Volunteer Infantry during the Civil War.

Day likely solicited Mellette for the appointment and Mellette likely granted it because of their long-standing friendship. In 1878 Day was a young, aspiring attorney in Springfield, Dakota Territory, and Mellette worked just down the block as the head of the public land office. Their friendship continued over the intervening years and was strengthened that summer when Mellette's son Charley was a dinner guest in the Day home during his visit to the Black Hills. There were also the ever-present political reasons. Day had strengthened the Republicans' hand in 1885 when he joined the diversionist movement, fracturing the Democratic Party.[34]

Mellette probably believed Day would do little more with the appointment than make a few fiery speeches, convince the old-timers in Rapid City to have a military parade that he could lead, and adorn the wall of his law office with the meaningless telegram. If that was what the governor expected, he was wrong.

The next day, December 7, Day and Charley Allen loaded the rifles and rounds of ammunition into a wagon and set out to arm the ranchers along the west bank of the Cheyenne River. Upon reaching the river, "Lieutenant Colonel" Day armed area ranchers and young cowboys and had them sign a document enlisting them into the "Dakota Militia." He placed George Cosgrove in charge of fifty men and stationed them at Frank Stanton's ranch on Spring Creek. They were to patrol from Rapid Creek south to Battle Creek. Day put Gene Akin in command of forty-six cowboys and stationed them at Joe McCloud's ranch on Battle Creek, instructing them to patrol south from Battle Creek to Beaver Creek.[35] Day then returned to Rapid City and promptly sent a letter to Mellette, informing the governor of the actions taken and assuring him that "the men are good ones . . . if the Indians attack God help them."[36]

As Day was arming the ranchers along the Cheyenne River, the Indians on Stronghold Table were fervently ghost dancing. Up on Stronghold, young men envisioned themselves as warriors, protectors of women and children, and providers. Can Nopa Uhah's two oldest sons, First Eagle, age twenty-seven, and Fights With, age seventeen, were among the believers. With hopes of earning the right to wear an eagle feather, the young Lakota men were anxious to mount their war ponies and go looking for glory. Traditionally, glory was obtained by stealing horses from the Pawnees or the Crows. But in 1890 the only enemy horses to steal belonged to white ranchers. Fortuitously, the enemy and their horses were not far away.

The first clash between the Dakota Militia and the hostiles occurred on December 9 at the Daly-Torkelson Ranch, located four miles downriver from the mouth of French Creek. Early that morning a half dozen armed Indians burst into Jack Daly and Nels Torkelson's ranch house just as the two were preparing breakfast. Holding the ranchers at gunpoint, the Indians relieved Daly of $150 and gathered up the ranchers' hats and coats. The raiding party then retreated back across the river, taking with them all the horses in the corral. Daly and Torkelson suffered a cowboy's worst humiliation by having to walk to the Warren Ranch on Battle Creek and confess that they had been set afoot by Indians.

The next morning, December 10, Joe McCloud rode with Daly and Torkelson back to their ranch. From the river bluff they saw that Indians had taken it over. Two Indians were in the corral working a herd of stolen horses. The cowboys also saw smoke coming out of the cabin's chimney, but they had no way of knowing how many Indians, if any, were inside. In time, one man came out. When the cowboys realized that only three Indians were holding the ranch, they rode down on the cabin, firing their guns and yelling as if they were leading a cavalry charge. The ruse worked. The Indians jumped on their horses and fled across the river.

The cowboys rode back to the Warren Ranch and boasted of their accomplishment. Gene Akin, the newly appointed "captain" for the Dakota Militia, brought them up short. The ranch, he pointed out, was again abandoned and might already be back in Indian hands. He ordered Sam Bell, Gus Haaser, Ike Miller, Lew Peck, T. M. Warren, Alex Webb, and Shorty West to ride back to the ranch and hold it.

The seven cowboys arrived at the Daly-Torkelson Ranch shortly after midday. They put their horses in the corral and went into the cabin to make coffee. Just as the water came to a boil, they heard the hooves of galloping horses. The men rushed out the cabin door to get a fleeting glimpse of three Indians herding the cowboys' horses across the river. Shame-faced, they too walked back to the Warren Ranch and related that Indians had stolen their horses and left them afoot.

Captain Akin decided to set a trap for the horse-stealing Indians. Late that night, Akin, George Tarbox, Will Brisbin, Jim Ferguson, Charley Edgerton, Farley Sprague, Mel McGregor, and H. J. Sprague rode back to the Daly-Torkelson Ranch. They hid their horses in the barn and slipped into the cabin. Not wanting chimney smoke to reveal their presence, they endured a cold night.

Early the next morning, December 11, George Cosgrove and five of his men, attached to the northern branch of the Dakota Militia, patrolled upriver. When they reached the Daly-Torkelson Ranch, Cosgrove posted Neal Dennis on a high knoll to stand guard while everyone else went into the cabin to fix lunch. They swung the door open on a cabin full of grinning cowboys, who ribbed them about ruining their ambush. The cabin walls were still echoing with laughter when Joe McCloud, Jack Daly, and Nels Torkelson rode in with food for the eight men presumed to be hiding in the cabin.

Coffee, bacon, and biscuits were being served when Neal Dennis rushed in to report that a bunch of horsemen were riding fast toward the cabin. Cosgrove grabbed his binoculars. "They're Indians," he exclaimed. "There's seventeen of 'em. Everyone hide behind something and don't shoot until I holler."[37]

As we consider seventeen young Lakota riding toward the Daly-Torkelson Ranch, intent on gaining glory by stealing horses, it is timely to examine the context of what was about to unfold. In 1890 the Lakota were aware of a larger world and their diminutive place in it. By then many of the significant Lakota chiefs had boarded trains to travel a thousand miles through countless towns and cities to visit Washington, D.C., where they craned their heads to peer up at multistory buildings. A fair number of Oglala had traveled with Buffalo Bill's Wild West Show when it had toured eastern North America and even Europe. Every one of the seventeen braves had listened intently to the stories told by their worldly elders, and they too had seen some of that larger world during occasional trips to Rushville, Chadron, and even Rapid City, perhaps even participating in Fourth of July parades. As for George Cosgrove, he knew that by stepping into the open and firing a shot harmlessly into the air, the young braves would turn tail and retreat back to Stronghold. But he didn't. At that brief moment and in that unique place, both the young warriors and the white cowboys wanted to believe it was once again 1876 on the Dakota frontier.

So Cosgrove ordered every one of the men to hide behind something and not shoot until he hollered.[37] Charley Edgerton hid behind a big downed cottonwood tree north of the cabin. Riley Miller, a noted crack shot, found a good position. Francis Rousch ducked behind the door frame and continued chewing his biscuit. As the Indians pulled up their horses at the corral gate, one of them, almost certainly a young Brulé named White Horse, reached down from his horse to slide back the gate pole. As he did, White Horse saw that they had ridden into an ambush. He raised his gun in the air and fired a warning shot. Not waiting for Cosgrove to holler, Edgerton shot White Horse. The young Indian fell from his saddle; his lifeless body lay draped across the wooden gate poles. Two warriors rode up, leaned down from their saddles, and picked him up. Under a withering barrage of rifle fire, the Indians retreated. Judging from the riderless horses that splashed back across the river, the Dakota Militia concluded that they had killed or seriously wounded at least three Indians. Some of the cowboys recognized one of the Indian warriors as a young man who had recently returned from the Carlisle Indian School.[38] That man was Plenty Horses. White Horse was his cousin.

Upon hearing about the shootout, Day telegraphed the governor: "There was a skirmish yesterday noon at French Creek. Three Indians killed, none of my men. Will write you the details, but situation is becoming serious for the settlers who are unarmed. Can you supply fifty good rifles and ammunition so the settlers can defend themselves?"[39]

A telegram was not a private communication; every telegraph operator along the railroad line east across Nebraska, north to Sioux Falls, and then west to Pierre was privy to it. News of the skirmish spread quickly. Upon meeting someone on the street, the first words exchanged were, "Did you hear about the Indian outbreak at French Creek?" Mellette wrote back to Day: "I was pleased to get your message stating that in a skirmish three Indians were killed by 'our men' without a loss to the whites. . . . Be discreet in killing Indians."[40]

Pine Ridge and Rosebud were not the only Lakota reservations in the throes of Indian unrest. Up north on the Standing Rock Reservation, a rumor reached Agent McLaughlin that Sitting Bull and his band of fervent ghost dancers intended to join the hostiles on Stronghold. On orders from McLaughlin, the Indian police entered Sitting Bull's village in the early morning of December 15 to arrest the aged medicine man. When Sergeant Red Tomahawk and Private Bull Head stepped out of Sitting Bull's cabin with him in tow, a melee broke out and Sitting Bull was shot and killed.[41] He did not die because the Indian police botched their attempt to arrest him. He died because the arrest order had no moral authority and everyone at Sitting Bull's village that fateful morning, including the Indian police, knew it. After all, what crime had Sitting Bull committed?

Before the sun set that day, Mellette learned that Sitting Bull had been shot and killed. He immediately issued more guns and ammunition. Day received the lion's share—two hundred rifles and seven thousand cartridges shipped to Rapid City. Sixty rifles and three thousand cartridges went to Aberdeen; Bangor, Mound City, and Custer each received forty rifles and two thousand cartridges; twenty rifles and one thousand cartridges each were allotted to Hot Springs, Minnikahta, and Cedar Post Office.[42]

That same morning but 160 miles south, another Indian was killed. On the evening of December 14, as M. D. Cole was finishing his evening chores at his ranch on Spring Creek, he spotted an Indian up on the hillside, reconnoitering the place from behind a clump of sagebrush. Cole figured he knew what the

Indian intended. After dark he slipped back to the barn and hid in the hay loft. In the predawn morning of December 15, the barn door creaked open and an intruder slipped in. Cole pulled the trigger on his 10-gauge shotgun and blasted the would-be horse thief into the barnyard.[43]

Joseph Gossage, proprietor and editor of the *Rapid City Journal*, announced somewhat proudly, "The ball which made him a good Indian struck him in the left temple."[44] The *Battle River Pilot*, Hermosa's weekly newspaper, lauded Cole for "letting the settlers know what a good Indian looks like."[45]

Word that Cole had shot and killed an Indian quickly spread up and down the Cheyenne River valley, prompting some Dakota Militia men to lay plans that evening for a daring raid. What they planned was in defiance of Mile's orders that no offensive action should be taken against Indians when they were on their own reservation, and the Dakota Militia men knew it. Yet in the predawn hours of December 16, George Cosgrove led more than a dozen heavily armed men across the Cheyenne River and onto the Pine Ridge Reservation. Their destination was a place along Little Corral Draw where it briefly narrowed into a steep-sided canyon. There, Cosgrove, Roy Coates, Joe Erdman, Frank Lockhart, Charley Allen, Bill Lindsey, Riley Miller, John Hart, and others turned their horses onto an animal trail that wound its way up the side of the canyon and then across twenty yards of bare badland crowning the top. They tied their horses in a hidden basin and walked back down the trail far enough to hide among the big rocks and cedars. Pete Lemley, Frank Hart, Paul McClelland, and Francis Rousch continued to the head of Little Corral Draw. There, at the base of the northwest corner of Stronghold, stood one hundred tepees set up by Indians who had moved off the top of the windswept table. Their large herd of horses grazed nearby. Stealthily working their way through the horse herd, the cowboys were undetected. Upon reaching the southwest edge of the herd, they fired their guns and yelled at the top of their lungs, sending the horses stampeding toward the Cheyenne River. As anticipated, a group of young Indian braves were soon in hot pursuit. The cowboys guided the horses down Little Corral Draw and past where their comrades lay in ambush. The ambushers opened fire on the pursuing Indians and killed a good number of them.[46]

Two days later, December 17, Valentine McGillycuddy, accompanied by John Brennan and Will McFarland, arrived at the Cheyenne River to assess the situation. Their first stop was Cole's ranch. En route to the ranch, they were joined by John Farnham and his full-blooded Oglala wife, Ellen. The couple lived across from the confluence of Rapid Creek and the Cheyenne River on land that only months earlier had been part of the Great Sioux Reservation. When the group reached Cole's place, they discovered that the ghost-shirted Indian Cole had shot and killed was still lying in the corral. Ellen Farnham recognized him. In a hushed voice, she said his name was Dead Arm, a Hunkpapa from Sitting Bull's band, only nineteen years old. Kicking Bear was his uncle and the slain youth was her cousin. The party dug a grave. As dirt was being shoveled onto Dead Arm's body, Farnham, a white man with little schooling, recited from memory a lengthy and appropriate passage from the Bible.[47]

While the burial party was conducting its brief services, members of Gene Akin's platoon of Dakota Militia were on the reservation attempting to set up yet another ambush. Farley Sprague had noticed that the Indian warriors always waited until midday to ford the river and go looking for horses and cattle to steal. He observed that they left a signaler back on the top of the west-facing river brakes. The warrior would scan the country with field glasses and use a mirror to alert his comrades if a Dakota Militia patrol was in the area. Farley decided to use the same tactic to foil the Indians. He sneaked onto the reservation early that morning, picketed his horse among a cluster of cedar trees, and hid. About noon he spotted three Indians making their way to the Cheyenne River. He flashed a mirror, signaling Gene Akin, Joe McCloud, and George Tarbox to join him.[48]

By coincidence, Frank Hart and Pete Lemley had crossed onto the reservation that morning in search of a critter to drive back, butcher, and provide meat for Cosgrove's platoon of men. They were herding a suitable animal back to Stanton's ranch when they came under fire from three Indians surveying the countryside in preparation for their raid.[49] When Akin's men heard the gunfire, they immediately surmised some cowboys were in trouble and galloped their horses toward the source of the gunshots. The Indians' own rifle fire muffled the sound of the cowboys' horses, allowing Akin's men to come in from behind undetected. The cowboys killed all three—the last Indians killed by the Dakota Militia.[50]

The Dakota Militia was unsure how many Indians they killed during those two weeks in December. A conservative count would be at least a dozen, but a reasonable estimate would be as many as eighteen. The slain Indians were the kinsmen, brothers, or sons of the Lakota seeking refuge on Stronghold. The inflicted emotional wounds festered, creating a pain that could be mitigated only by retribution, if not immediately then eventually.

The next day, December 18, McGillycuddy set out on a personal peace mission to Stronghold. He was accompanied by Brennan and McFarland. Their guide across the rugged badlands was Americus Thompson, an affable old bachelor living halfway down Rapid Creek. In past years Thompson had often joined the Oglala on their hunting trips, and he could speak Lakota well enough to make himself understood. Most importantly, he knew the rugged, almost impassable badlands like the back of his hand.

The party approached within three miles of Stronghold and was close enough to make out the tepees at the northern base of the table when an uncomfortably close voice said, "Hau! Putin Cigala" (Hello, Little Beard—the Oglala's name for McGillycuddy). Following the sound, the men saw a solitary figure sitting motionless not twenty-five yards away. The old man, a friend of McGillycuddy's, told them the Indians would continue fighting until the soldiers were taken away and that the little band of whites (the Dakota Militia) was in a dangerous position and should get out of there. He said the people on Stronghold knew Sitting Bull had been killed and their hearts were bad. They vowed to kill the next white man who came to them talking peace. The old Indian advised McGillycuddy and his party to go back.

McGillycuddy did not doubt the Indian's sincerity, question his assessment, or ignore his advice. Realizing the situation had deteriorated to the point where he was helpless to alter the course of events, he and his party retreated. As they backtracked, a roving band of Indian braves fired at them from a distance, not so much to kill anyone but to underscore the extent of the Indians' anger and defiance.[51]

As the calendar slid into the last two weeks of 1890, the weather in southwestern South Dakota continued to be unseasonably mild, with Indian summer days, which happen when warm weather returns following a hard frost. The warm weather brought out hibernators such as prairie dogs, badgers, and skunks and put them, as well as people, on the move.

One of the people on the move was Deputy U.S. Marshal George Bartlett. He arrived in Deadwood on December 23 with Little, the man whose harmless killing of a beef had brought the army onto the reservation and ignited the Indian unrest. Little was incarcerated in the Lawrence County Jail and held there pending the spring term of federal court.[52]

That same day, December 23, a delegation of friendlies headed by Little Wound, Big Road, and Fast Thunder arrived at Stronghold with several wagonloads of rations. It was the third attempt to convince Short Bull, Two Strike, and the other holdouts to give up their refuge on Stronghold. The warm reception suggested that the ghost dancers might soon come into the agency.[53]

The situation was not as auspicious on the Cheyenne River Reservation. Late that same afternoon, Big Foot and his band of approximately 335 ardent ghost dancers abandoned their log cabins on Deep Creek, loaded their wagons, and struck out to the south. They fled because of fear (correctly founded) that the army intended to arrest Big Foot and possibly, as had been done to Sitting Bull, kill him. At seven o'clock that evening, Colonel Edwin Sumner, commander of the Eighth Cavalry, stationed near the forks of the Cheyenne River to monitor activities in Big Foot's village, learned that the chief and his band had hastily fled south. Sumner surmised that the Miniconjous were headed for Pine Ridge to join the hostiles on Stronghold. He immediately alerted his superiors and other officers of the ominous development. Adhering to the advice of local men who knew the country well, the army assumed Big Foot would intercept the Fort Pierre–Fort Laramie Trail and follow it through the only known pass in the north badland wall where it was possible to descend with wagons.

About two o'clock on the afternoon on December 24, Big Foot and his band reached the north badland wall at a place, known only to the Indians, where it was possible to lead a saddle horse down a narrow spine of badland to the floor two hundred feet below. Using axes and spades, Big Foot's band carved a passageway down the wall and descended.[54] In the evening dusk, they peaceably passed two miles west of Charley Gallagher's isolated cabin,[55] crossed White River, and camped for the night, Christmas Eve, on the Pine Ridge Reservation.[56]

Later that day Lieutenant Joseph Byron asked Captain Almond Wells for permission to take a dozen soldiers from Troop L (Cheyenne Indians recruited from the Pine Ridge Reservation) and make a recognizance of badlands adjacent to Stronghold. He wanted to determine whether it was possible to get cannons up the west end of Cuny Table and within range of the Indian encampment on Stronghold. Three local cowboys, one of whom was Gus Haaser, were Byron's guides. On the way back from their surveillance, Byron's patrol spotted a band of six Indian warriors leaving the east bank of the Cheyenne River and heading back to Stronghold.

Byron and his Cheyenne scouts hid along the Indian warriors' apparent route and when they were within rifle range killed every one of them. They dumped the dead Indians in the bottom of a flash-flood gully and pried off the overhanging edge of the cut bank to cover their bodies. The warriors' guns

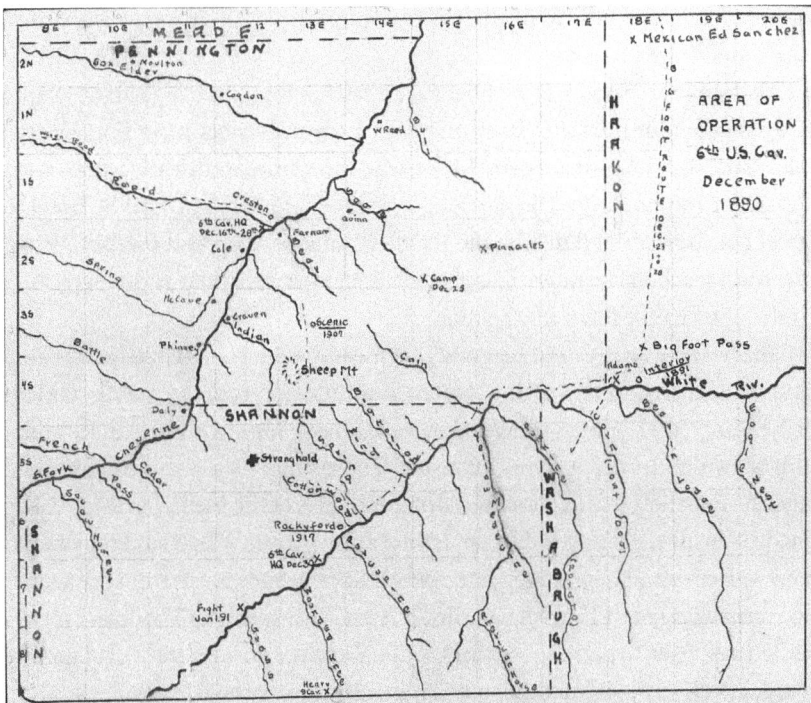

Area of operation of Sixth Cavalry, December 1890. (South Dakota State Historical Society)

and other weapons were similarly buried a short distance away. As soon as Byron got his patrol on the west bank of the Cheyenne River, he lined them up and sternly instructed them that no one was to say a word about the killings to anyone, warning that if word that they had killed the Sioux warriors on their own reservation got out, all of them would be jailed, court-martialed, and possibly hanged.[57]

In the nearly treeless badlands, a rifle shot can be heard for miles, especially when fired through winter-thick air. Byron's killing of the Lakota warriors on their own land did not go unnoticed by the Indians on Stronghold. Late that afternoon, warriors from Stronghold splashed their horses across the shallow Cheyenne River seeking revenge. Their leader was Kicking Bear. Whether Plenty Horses or Can Nopa Uhah's sons First Eagle and Fights With were along is unknown, but possibly they were. At dusk Kicking Bear's war party fired into the camp of Byron and his Cheyenne scouts. For several hours bullets flew in both directions, but no casualties were inflicted to either side.[58] The killing of the Lakota warriors on their own reservation went unavenged that day.

That same afternoon, December 24, an eastbound train chugged into Rapid City. Lieutenant Edward Casey and his Cheyenne scouts from Fort Keogh, Montana, were aboard. General Miles, who was commanding the troops from a suite of rooms in the Harney Hotel, walked a block north of the hotel to greet his young friend during the train's temporary stop at the depot. When the train reached Hermosa, Casey and his platoon debarked and set up camp at the outskirts of town for the night.[59]

The next day was Christmas, and that morning Big Foot's band broke camp and made their way to a spring located four miles up from the mouth of Medicine Root Creek. Having traveled more than one hundred miles in less than thirty-two hours, they were exhausted. The spring, its surrounding timber, and the impenetrable badland walls on both sides of the Medicine Root Valley made it an ideal place to hide from roving army patrols.[60] That same day Major Guy V. Henry and four troops of the Ninth Cavalry rode north from the agency to Harney Springs. (The Oglala called it Ash Grove Springs.) The detachment's assignment was to patrol north and south along the Fort Pierre–Fort Laramie Trail, effectively blocking the only approach to Stronghold.[61]

Casey and his Cheyenne scouts were also on the move. The same morning they broke camp at Hermosa, rode down Battle Creek, passed through Lieutenant Colonel Robert H. Offley's encampment with the Seventeenth Infantry, and proceeded to the Cheyenne River. After a ride of twenty-five miles, they camped for the night.[62]

The next morning, December 26, Casey and his detachment proceeded eight miles upriver to where Lieutenants Byron and L. H. Struthers were camped with Troop L. They reached the encampment that afternoon, but Struthers and Byron were not there. They were on the reservation making another reconnaissance of the hostiles on Stronghold Table. It was well after dark when Byron and Struthers and a number of their Cheyenne scouts rode in with startling news. They had ridden to the southeast end of a badland table (now known as Blind Man Table), which put them at nearly the same elevation as Stronghold. From that vantage point, they glassed the encampment of the ardent ghost dancers and what they saw surprised them. The hostiles were striking their tepees and loading them into wagons.[63] It appeared that the Indians intended to start early the next morning for Pine Ridge, presumably to surrender to General Brooke. If handled properly, it was possible the Sioux Indian uprising might be drawn to an end with no more bloodshed.

Casey immediately sent a courier upriver on a fast horse to deliver the news to Offley, encamped with the Seventeenth Infantry on Battle Creek. From there, the auspicious information was carried eighteen miles into the little town of Hermosa and telegraphed to General Miles. Late that night the courier came back with Miles's instructions. Casey and his scouts were to set out at first light for Stronghold Table. If the hostiles had departed, they were to follow them at a prudent distance, but under no circumstances was Casey to allow his Cheyenne scouts to initiate hostile actions against the retreating Sioux.

At sunup on the morning of December 27, Casey, his platoon of scouts, and their guide, Americus Thompson, mounted up. Never one to miss an adventure, Frederic Remington, the famous artist and author, swung his three-hundred-pound carcass into a saddle and rode with them, hoping to get more fodder for his fluid pen.[64] The raconteur did not have any trepidation about riding toward the encampment of hostile Indians because he had supreme confidence in Casey. "Lt. Casey could," Remington boasted to Richard Hughes, a reporter for the *Rapid City Journal*, "make a Sioux Indian herd sheep."[65]

Casey and his platoon rode downriver to a point across from the mouth of a creek now known as Quinn Draw. There they encountered members of the Dakota Militia wanting to accompany Casey to Stronghold, their justification being to retrieve some of their stolen livestock.[66] Casey heartily welcomed the cowboys because of their knowledge of the rugged, difficult-to-traverse badlands.

Americus Thompson and the cowboys guided the cavalry platoon to the northwest corner of Stronghold Table, where a precipitously steep path wound to the top. The path was ice covered in places, making it treacherous. The men dismounted and led their reluctant horses up the trail. They often had to stand to the side so the horses could jump over icy patches.[67] When the men reached the top of Stronghold, they did not find any cattle or horses contentedly grazing. Instead, they saw hundreds of cattle carcasses. "It looks like a slaughter house," one of the cowboys commented, "for which we provided the cattle."[68]

Riding at a fast trot, the Cheyenne Indian scouts and the cowboys crossed the five-mile-wide Cuny Table. At the rim of the mesa they could see clear to the White River, eighteen miles away. Just below them a cloud of tan-colored dust caught their eye. It was the hostiles heading toward the agency.[69] Can Nopa Uhah, his warrior sons First Eagle and Fights With, and the rest of the family were undoubtedly with them.

Descending the east side of Cuny Table, Casey's platoon fell in behind the retreating Indians and followed them at a comfortable distance. Upon reaching the ford, the Indians crossed the White River. They went a short distance up Grass Creek and camped for the night.[70]

When Casey and his detachment reached the ford, they stopped. They were soon joined by Captain Almond Wells, in command of Troops A and B of the Eighth Cavalry out of Fort Meade and a troop from the Fifth Cavalry. Together with Casey's detachment, Wells's troops camped. Because the Fifth Cavalry soldiers were from Leavenworth, Kansas, the encampment was called Camp Leavenworth. Wells ordered the erection of a defensive position along the west bank of the river so the soldiers could, if necessary, prevent the hostiles from slipping back into the protective terrain of the badlands.[71]

Meanwhile and elsewhere on the reservation, at noon on December 27, Big Foot and his band of 350 Miniconjou struck out for the Pine Ridge Agency, where they expected to join the hostiles from Stronghold and peaceably parade into the agency.[72]

The next morning, December 28, the hostiles from Stronghold went four miles upriver to the mouth of White Clay Creek, which they followed five more miles to No Water's village. Short Bull and his band of Brulé stopped there. Others continued another five miles to Young Man Afraid of His Horses's camp. Finding that Young Man Afraid of His Horses's band was in Wyoming on a hunting trip, some hostiles took shelter in the band's temporarily abandoned cabins. Others continued on to the Drexel Mission. There, only five miles from the agency, they too went into camp.[73]

At sunup on the morning of December 29, the hostiles encamped outside the gates of the mission hitched up their teams and prepared to go to the agency. They expected to meet Chief Big Foot and his band of Miniconjou at the outskirts of the agency. The combined force of Brulé, Oglala, and Miniconjou would parade into Pine Ridge with much ceremony and pride, peaceably bringing the Sioux uprising to an end.

As the hostiles broke camp that morning, they heard the sound of Hotchkiss cannons reverberating across the frozen prairie and surmised that soldiers were attacking Big Foot's band. Several thousand peaceful Indians camped at the agency also heard the cannon fire. Panic-stricken, more than four thousand Indians fled down White Clay Creek. Caught between General Brooke's forces to the southeast and Captain Wells's entrenched soldiers at the river ford, the hostiles stopped at No Water's village and waited for events to unfold.[74]

Little, instigator of the Indian revolt at Pine Ridge, 1890. Photo by John Grabill, circa 1891, at Deadwood. (South Dakota State Historical Society.)

That same morning, December 29, Americus Thompson and a Swedish teamster at Camp Leavenworth set out in a wagon for Pine Ridge, twenty-five miles to the southeast, to procure provisions and get messages. Frederic Remington and two Cheyenne Indian scouts mounted their horses and rode along. A little later, Sam Bell, T. M. Warren, Willis McDermond, and Isaac Miller also rode out from Camp Leavenworth and headed on horseback for the Pine Ridge Agency, where they expected to witness the hostiles from Stronghold Table surrender to General Brooke.

The cowboys had ridden only nine miles when they met a team of heavily lathered horses pulling a government wagon and three outriders racing down the White Clay Creek road. As the galloping team with its wagon and occupants approached, Thompson shouted, "Go back! Go back!" At that moment shots fired by pursuing hostiles whistled past the cowboys' ears and kicked up dust. With the well-mounted cowboys providing a rear guard, everyone raced for the protection of Wells's bivouacked troops.[75]

By noon on December 29, General Miles knew about the battle on Wounded Knee Creek. He immediately wired the secretary of war, asking for all available troops in the United States. Before sunup the next morning, December 30, he vacated his command center at the Harney Hotel and boarded a special train for Pine Ridge.[76] Upon reaching Pine Ridge, he took charge, strengthened perimeter defenses, moved the Seventh Cavalry inside the earthwork from its camp a mile northwest, and bolstered the troops at Pine Ridge to three thousand.[77]

After a few weeks, a semblance of calm was restored at Pine Ridge. Many of the Brulé who had taken refuge in No Water's village returned to the Rosebud Reservation, but not Can Nopa Uhah, chief of a small group of Brulé Sioux known as the Broken Arrow band. He and his band stayed in No Water's village.

As for Little, whose arrest resulted in thousands of troops being rushed to the Dakotas and precipitated the bloody massacre wherein several hundred Miniconjou were killed, on March 10, 1891, a grand jury met in Deadwood to examine the evidence against him. The jurors found that the evidence was insufficient to indict Little of felonious assault. The next day the government paid for the ticket that allowed him to return to the reservation aboard the Elkhorn train.[78]

⋈ 4 ⋈

THE KILLING OF IKE MILLER

The details of the battle at Wounded Knee Creek spread coast to coast within days.¹ Many saw the battle as the precursor of a full-scale Indian uprising. The Rushville home guard was given notice to make every possible preparation for defending the town and seeing that adjacent settlers were notified.² The panic spawned rumors such as the baseless but widely believed report that a band of Indians had abducted the wife and daughter of a rancher named Miller and burned his ranch.³

In South Dakota, the caption of a leading newspaper read, "The 6,000 Indians at Pine Ridge on the Point of Open Rebellion."⁴ Another newspaper reported, "Panic Reigns Supreme."⁵ Indeed it did. Ranchers and homesteaders living west of the reservation poured into towns along the Fremont, Elkhorn and Missouri Valley Railroad. At Buffalo Gap, citizens held a town meeting and decided to leave in place the pickets that had been continuously posted all through December. Plans were drawn up for a twenty-by-fifty-foot blockhouse. Just in case the Indians might try to burn them out, a sixteen-by-fifteen-foot excavation was dug in the middle to a depth of four feet.⁶ In Hermosa, the citizens excavated a thirty-by-thirty-foot hole, four feet deep, built up the four sides with several feet of logs, and laid sod against the logs. They roofed "Fort Buckingham" with heavy timbers, over which dirt was liberally spread.⁷ The citizens of Hill City, twenty crow-fly miles west of Hermosa and in the heart of the Black Hills, formed a home guard.⁸ "Colonel" Merritt Day organized twenty-eight men living along upper Spring Creek (west of Hermosa) into a third company of Dakota Militia. William McClelland was installed as captain.[9] Governor Mellette sent the Buffalo Gap home guard another shipment of one hundred rifles and more ammunition.[10] He also received numerous letters seeking his attention. One letter dated January 6, 1891, came from Thomas Littleton, a resident of Vermillion, a town that was about as far as one could get from Pine Ridge and still be in South Dakota. The letter read: "I offer my services in organizing volunteers to help suppress the Indian uprising. . . . I can enroll fifty or more good men here and mount them and procure arms for part of them (Winchester rifles). Send me authority and instructions at once."[11] That kind of hysterical overreaction concerned Mellette, but what worried him were letters from people living adjacent to the reservation who had firsthand knowledge of developments. One such letter came from Scotty Philip. In a letter dated January 12, 1891, Philip wrote, "Indians have now run off over eight hundred head of cattle [some of which likely belonged to the governor] and seventy-five head of horses in the last twelve days. Now that ruins me as it does a good many others in my neighborhood, and it is a good deal hard to bear as it is all through negligence on the part of the government as we done all in our power to get protection. I am going up to my ranch in about a week and I would like to know what you want done with your cattle, if there is any left."[12]

In response to those letters and other information, Mellette sent additional rifles to Sturgis, Hat Creek, Fort Pierre, Whitewood, Pierre, Oelrichs, Smithwick, Fairburn, Hermosa, Rapid City, Minnesela, Rousseau, Cheyenne City, and White River,[13] and he applied to the secretary of war for an additional one thousand rifles and two hundred thousand rounds of ammunition.[14] Even Sturgis, only two miles west of Fort Meade, formed a home guard—just in case the hundreds of soldiers at the fort should be overrun by Indians. Mellette sent Miles M. Cooper a telegram appointing him "colonel" of the Sturgis home guard. On the eastern edge of the recently ceded Great Sioux Reservation, eighty fear-stricken settlers flooded into Fort Pierre.[15]

Amos Barber, the newly elected governor of Wyoming, received telegrams from settlers residing in and near Lusk and Douglas asking for arms with which to protect themselves. Governor Barber sent a Major Stilzer of the Wyoming State Militia to investigate and determine whether the residents were in danger. Stilzer reported back to the governor: "Situation serious. Request the state militia be sent there at once."[16]

A headline in the *St. Paul Globe* said it all: "Chadron's Danger! The Little Nebraska Town Is Now Full of Terrified Women and Children With Fighting All Around. In Consequence, the Sheriff Demands of Gov. Thayer Militia, Arms and Ammunition to Protect the Frightened Settlers."[17]

James Dahlman, the colorful sheriff of Chadron, who was not immune to the influence of groundless rumors and even capable of perpetuating them, wired the governor of Nebraska, John Thayer: "Indians have been fighting here for two days. The city is full of women and children, and no arms. Can't you order out militia and send guns?"[18]

In response Thayer wired orders to state militia commanders stationed at the towns of Fremont, Central City, Ord, and Tekamah to leave on the first train with their troops for the state's northern border with the Pine Ridge Reservation. General Leonard Colby of the state militia ordered eighteen companies to patrol the towns just south of the Rosebud and Pine Ridge Reservations, an area stretching 150 miles from Valentine through Cody, Gordon, Rushville, Hay Springs, Chadron, and Crawford to Harrison. Panicked homesteaders poured into these little towns by the hundreds.[19]

Even Iowa responded. Although its western border was 275 miles from Pine Ridge, the Sixth Regiment of the Iowa National Guard was ordered to hold itself in readiness to march to Pine Ridge for service against the Indians.[20]

As if the official information about troop movements, actual skirmishes with Indians, and preparations for war by state governments were not sufficiently alarming, the stories printed in newspapers from coast to coast were downright frightening. It was reported that along the White River, hostile Indians had burned scores of houses to the ground.[21] Another newspaper said that three cattlemen living near the mouth of Hay Creek (just south of the Black Hills) were missing and feared killed.[22] It was reported that two teamsters from Rushville were found dead ten miles from the agency and that a foraging party of Indians had attacked the ranch of Douglass Points, killed him, and driven away his six hundred head of cattle.[23] Those stories were patently false, but reporting them sold newspapers, which in turn fueled panic.

When 1891 was but one day old, Captain Almond Wells's troops and Dakota Militia cowboys were still bivouacked on the west bank of the White River at Camp Leavenworth. No one arrived to give them reliable information about what was unfolding at No Water's village or at the agency. The soldiers and cowboys were starving for information and curious. Furthermore, just sitting around a campfire trying to keep warm was not a cowboy's nature. One of the cowboys was Ike Miller. He had been more or less quarantined on the west bank of White River since the afternoon of December 28 and was bored.

The sun rose on the first day of the New Year to announce that a snowstorm of the previous evening had passed quickly and was gone, replaced by a dome of high pressure and moderating temperatures that prompted energetic men to become restless. Miller was not immune to the affliction. Unable to take the suspense any longer, Miller announced he was going to ride the twenty-seven miles to the agency and see for himself what was going on. His friends tried to talk him out of his foolhardy idea, but Miller was not to be dissuaded. He told them that he had worked for three years as a government herder on the reservation and reminded them "that at one time or another, every buck on the reservation had stopped to eat at my fire; and I didn't have an enemy among them." With that, Miller tied his bedroll behind his saddle and started in the direction of the agency.[24] His intended route would take him up the White Clay Creek road and right past No Water's village, the refuge of the ardent ghost dancers from Stronghold, who remained outraged at the ranchers and settlers along the Cheyenne River who had killed so many of their kinsmen.

Isaac Miller was not your typical cowboy—far from it. He stood only five feet, five inches tall in his stocking feet, and on those feet there were no toes. His feet were also clubbed, forcing him to drag each foot along the ground for a few inches before lifting it. Walking was not much to Miller's liking. He also had stiffness in his hands, preventing him from being a good roper, a much-demanded skill for a cowboy. His face was reddish, his auburn hair was thin to the point of balding, and he had sandy-colored whiskers.[25] His physical characteristics suggest that he was born with Adams-Oliver syndrome, a rare genetic disorder, usually accompanied by learning problems, making it likely that Miller could neither read nor write.

He had come into the West River country in 1879, from where no one rightly knew. It was rumored that he had drifted down from Canada. Others believed he came up from Missouri, a belief supported by census data. No one on the Dakota frontier was all that sure about his age. Some thought he was as young as thirty-six;[26] others guessed him to be at least forty-one.[27] Actually, Miller was forty-four.[28]

After arriving in the West River country, Miller lived in the evening shadow of the Black Hills. He was a drifter, taking ranch-hand jobs where he could find them. When the work at one ranch was finished, Miller and his horse wandered off in search of the next place where there was work to do in exchange for a full stomach and place to sleep. One of his longest employments was from January 1887 to June 1890, when he worked for John Darr, the man in charge of the government cattle on Pine Ridge.[29] While working for Darr, Miller never gained the status of cowboy. He was the cook.

Such were the looks and the nature of the man who ignored his friends' advice and struck out from Camp Leavenworth on the morning of January 1, 1891 for the agency. After riding nine miles, Miller came to Philip Wells's log cabin and stopped. Wells was not home, but his wife, Mary, was. Mary Wells was acquainted with Miller and invited him in. When he told her that he was on his way to the agency, she informed him that a mile farther up the creek there was a large gathering of Indians at No Water's village, frenetically ghost dancing and in an ugly mood. She advised him against going any farther. But Miller stuck to his line that he was sure none of the Indians had a quarrel with him and that he intended to go on to the agency.

As Ike was preparing to leave, Mary Wells requested a favor. She asked Miller if he would carry a heavy chest out from the back room. When he stepped into the dimly lit room, Wells shut the door and locked him in. She triumphantly informed Miller that he would stay there until he came to his senses.

Miller eventually promised Wells that if she let him out, he wouldn't continue on his intended trip to the agency. She unlocked the door. Miller promptly mounted his horse and rode away, but he didn't head back down the road toward the encampment of soldiers. Instead, he rode up the creek in the direction of No Water's village.[30]

Several days passed without Miller returning to Almond Wells's encampment of soldiers. Miller's friends feared he had been killed, but they had no way of knowing.

Miller's fate was not known until January 7, when a team and wagon was spotted coming up White Clay Creek road toward the agency. The driver was Red Eagle, and in the back of his wagon was Ike Miller's frozen corpse.[31]

No one knew how Ike Miller had met his death other than that he had been shot. To fill the void, rumors took the place of facts. One story had it that he was shot through the hip as he rode peaceably into No Water's village, fell off his horse, and lay there for two days, begging the Indians for help before he succumbed to his wound and the cold.[32]

Another version of the killing was told by Frank M. Stewart, an alias that earlier had allowed Valentine McGillycuddy's brother to hold the position of issue clerk at Pine Ridge. Stewart announced that Miller had ridden up the

White Clay Creek road until it divided. Seeing an Indian coming down one road, Miller had taken the other. Just as Miller reached the point where the two trails merged and while riding at a gallop, Stewart said, he encountered a small band of hostile Indians and was shot from his horse. According to Stewart, Miller was only slightly wounded. Upon rising to his feet, Miller recognized the leader of the warriors as Eagle Hawk, one of No Water's sons. Knowing Eagle Hawk well and having shown him favors, Miller threw down his gun and told Eagle Hawk that he was merely going into the agency on business. In answer, Eagle Hawk rode up to Miller and shot him in the head, killing him instantly.[33]

Like the first story, Stewart's version of Ike Miller's death was not true. All that was known for sure was that Miller nearly made it to No Water's camp before he was killed. His body lay along the White Clay Creek road for a week. The hostile Indians had no regard for it, and no white person could get close enough to the hostiles' encampment to retrieve the body.

When Red Eagle finally brought Ike Miller's body into the agency, no one knew of any next of kin who might come claim the body and take it home for burial, so he was buried the next day in Pine Ridge. There were no friends at the graveside to say a few kind words about Ike Miller, recount his finer qualities, or even posthumously thank him for his friendship or a meal eaten at his campfire. A couple of soldiers, men who never knew Miller, were detailed to put his cold, stiff body in the bottom of a six-foot-deep hole and cover the corpse with dirt. It was not so much a funeral as a planting.

On February 16, an Indian presumed to have killed Ike Miller was arrested and taken to the agency.[34] The man was not Eagle Hawk. He was Leaves His Woman, also known as Young Skunk, another of Chief No Water's sons.[35] Two days later Leaves His Woman was transported to Fort Meade and locked in the guardhouse.[36] He was held there until a grand jury convened at Deadwood during the second week of March. After hearing the evidence, the grand jury indicted Leaves His Woman for the murder of Ike Miller. He was returned to Fort Meade and confined there while awaiting trial. However, authorities eventually learned that Young Skunk was not the murderer. Upon being informed that the incarcerated Indian was innocent, Secretary of War Redfield Proctor wired Lieutenant Colonel Edwin Sumner, the post commander at Fort Meade, ordering him to release Young Skunk. He was put aboard the train at Sturgis and escorted by Private John Stevenson back to Pine Ridge, where he was released.[37]

Who was Ike Miller's killer? McGillycuddy, former Indian agent at Pine Ridge, tapped into his contacts, trying to determine the guilty party.

McGillycuddy received a letter dated April 18 from his friend Fast Horse, who had once served in McGillycuddy's Indian police force.[38] Fast Horse informed McGillycuddy that Miller had been killed by Shoots the Enemy, a young Brulé from Rosebud. After Shoots the Enemy killed Miller, he took Miller's gun belt and pistol. There were two other Brulé with Shoots the Enemy when he killed Miller. One of them, known as Tracks, took Miller's horse; the other man was Walks Outside.[39]

No attempt was made to arrest Shoots the Enemy. Perhaps that was because the frontier was not concerned about justice for a diminutive man who drifted from one ranch to another in search of a warm place to sleep and a hot meal. Moreover, attention had already been drawn to the killings of other men, better known and more important.

5

THE PEACEMAKER

With his defenses of Pine Ridge in place, General Miles set out to convince the hostiles at No Water's village that they should peaceably come into the agency. To do that, he needed an intermediary, someone to whom the hostiles would listen. In January 1891 there was only one man on the Dakota frontier who could accomplish that—Young Man Afraid of His Horses.

Young Man Afraid of His Horses, whose name should be correctly translated as "His Enemies Are Even Afraid of His Horse," was born in 1836 to a distinguished Lakota family. His boyhood friends included Hunts the Enemy (later known as Man Who Carries the Sword, also known as George Sword), Little Wound, He Dog, and Crazy Horse. As young men, they fought valiantly in the Fetterman fight and the Wagon Box conflict, decisive battles that forced the government to close the Bozeman Trail and remove forts strategically located along the upper North Platte River. During this tumultuous time, the Oglala selected four outstanding warriors to be shirt wearers and granted them full authority to protect the people.[1] One of them was Young Man Afraid of His Horses.

That responsibility fell particularly heavy on Young Man Afraid of His Horses's shoulders when the Oglala split into two factions. The whites dubbed one faction the nontreaty Oglala and the other faction the progressives. The two Oglala factions were alternately known as the northern Oglala and the agency Oglala. Young Man Afraid of His Horses's first test as to

Young Man Afraid of His Horses in front of his tepee. (National Archives photo no. 111-SC-82521.)

whether he could mediate conflicts between the two factions arose in 1873 when the government wanted to take a census of the Indians. Fearing that a correct count of the Oglala would result in decreased rations, the nontreaty Oglala refused to allow a census to be taken. The Indian agent retaliated by threatening to cut off their rations and summon troops if they refused to be counted. Young Man Afraid of His Horses and Man Who Carries the Sword called a council of Oglala chiefs and headmen and convinced them to acquiesce to the census.

Young Man Afraid of His Horses also stepped forward in 1875 when the Allison Commission came to the Red Cloud Agency intent on convincing the Lakota to sell the Black Hills. The commissioners brought along 120 cavalrymen for their protection. As negotiations became heated, the commissioners and cavalry suddenly found themselves encircled by three hundred armed warriors, whose leader, the northern chief Little Big Man, announced that if any agreement was made to sell the Black Hills, they would kill the commissioners and the first chief who stepped forward to sign it. At that tense moment, Young Man Afraid of His Horses's warriors formed a protective shield around the vastly outnumbered cavalrymen and commissioners.[2]

In 1877 Young Man Afraid of His Horses assisted in convincing Crazy Horse to abandon his struggle against the soldiers and come into the Red

Cloud Agency. When the Indian agent promised them a buffalo hunt, Young Man Afraid of His Horses, ever the diplomat, suggested that Crazy Horse be given the honor of hosting the anticipated buffalo feast.[3]

When Valentine McGillycuddy arrived on March 10, 1879, to become the Indian agent of the newly formed Pine Ridge Agency, Young Man Afraid of His Horses demonstrated his ability to modify his thinking to the changing realities on the frontier. He supported the new agent in alliances he saw as beneficial to the Oglala. Among other areas of cooperation, he assisted McGillycuddy in establishing an Indian police force. He recommended that Man Who Carries the Sword (George Sword), a fellow shirt wearer, be appointed captain of the Indian police. Young Man Afraid of His Horses also organized a board of councilmen to regulate Indian conduct and punish offenders. The councilmen selected him to be president. In turn, McGillycuddy often consulted Young Man Afraid of His Horses and usually took his advice.[4]

However, Young Man Afraid of His Horses did not blindly support the government. A case in point was in 1889 when General George Crook brought a three-man commission to Pine Ridge, seeking to convince the Oglala to cede nearly nine million acres and break the Great Sioux Reservation into six small reservations. Young Man Afraid of His Horses opposed giving up any more land. Due in large part to his opposition, the requisite three-fourths of the adult Oglala males did not sign the agreement.[5]

This was why, in January 1891, Young Man Afraid of His Horses was the only person who could convince the hostiles in No Water's village to come peaceably into the agency and surrender.

Unfortunately, as the New Year began, Young Man Afraid of His Horses was not at Pine Ridge. When the army arrived at Pine Ridge on November 20, 1890, he saw that bloodshed was likely and asked for permission to take his Cih Hu Ha Tum band on a hunting trip to Wyoming. A pass was granted.[6]

On the evening of November 24, 1890, the peacemaker and his band were ten miles from Minnesela, a little settlement near the mouth of the Red Water River. By then, most whites in the Black Hills had read or at least heard the editor of the *Black Hills Daily Times*'s warning about the dangers of the Messiah craze:

> Eighteen hundred years ago the Jews of Israel received a Messiah. The Messiah came announcing that the kingdom of God was at hand . . . the Jewish people became aroused to such a pitch they would have sacrificed their lives if their Messiah had commanded it.

Today another people, the Indians, have received a Messiah.... Under this Messiah's teaching, these warring tribes have ceased their dissensions against each other and are all united. He has promised them that they shall, under his guidance come in possession of their hunting grounds and the enemy, the white man, shall be no more.

What does all of this signify to us with 30,000 Indians about us aroused to a pitch of frenzy by a religious craze? It means this. That this savage and ferocious people will, unless checked by the strong hand of the government, commence this spring in their work of destroying the white man.[7]

That article and other such fearmongering engaged in by every newspaper on the frontier convinced many whites living in the Black Hills they had reason to fear an Indian outbreak. The very week Young Man Afraid of His Horses's band was traveling along the northern edge of the Black Hills, the *Black Hills Daily Times* opined as to the best way for towns and settlers to protect themselves against the impending Indian outbreak: "It is firmly resolved that no halfway measures should be adopted. The Indians must be killed as fast as they make an appearance and before they can do any damage. It is better to kill an innocent Indian occasionally than to take chances on goodness. To exterminate them it will be necessary to employ first-class killers regardless of expense."[8]

It is little wonder that when someone in Minnesela spotted Young Man Afraid of His Horses's band on the journey to Wyoming, an urgent telegram was sent to Fort Meade, asking for soldiers to come protect the defenseless white settlers. Troop D was dispatched and the army patrol cautiously rode into Man Afraid of His Horses's temporary camp. Upon determining that the Indians had a pass to be off the reservation, the officer allowed the Oglala chief and his band to continue their trip.[9]

Young Man Afraid of His Horses kept his band in the Powder River country all of December. In the later part of the month, he went farther west to visit his friends, the Northern Cheyenne and then the Crow.[10] Soon after the first of the year, they started for home. On January 6 they were approaching the newly established town of Newcastle, Wyoming, when an army officer hailed them. He told Young Man Afraid of His Horses that General Miles urgently needed him. The army officer secured passage for himself, Young Man Afraid of His Horses, and three of the chief's headmen on the Chicago, Burlington and Quincy Railroad, which just that year had built tracks into a newly discovered coal seam in eastern Wyoming. When the train reached Crawford, Nebraska, Captain John O'Connell of the First Infantry and a detachment of his soldiers boarded the train. They accompanied Man Afraid of His Horses and his headmen to Rushville. From there, the Indians were taken by wagon to the agency, where General Miles anxiously awaited their arrival.[11]

The very day, January 7, the army escort was hurrying Young Man Afraid of His Horses to Pine Ridge, Lieutenant Edward W. Casey of the Twenty-second Infantry mounted his big, black thoroughbred and set out early in the morning with White Moon and Rock Road, two of his Cheyenne scouts, to make a reconnaissance of the hostile encampment ten miles to the southeast. Baptiste Garnier, a mixed-blood from Pine Ridge who was serving as an army scout during the uprising, arrived just in time to warn Casey not to get too close to the hostiles' encampment.[12] Garnier knew the Indians were bent on getting revenge for their kinsmen killed by Cheyenne River ranchers and were especially angry at the army patrol that had ambushed Lakota braves on their own reservation.

Whether the hostiles were aware that Casey took no part in any of the killings is unknown but irrelevant. They knew Casey and Joseph Byron camped together, and they had seen with their own eyes that it was Casey, Byron, and the murderous cowboys who had scaled Stronghold and cut off their option of a retreat. Beyond a doubt, a good many young warriors in the hostile encampment longed for a chance to kill him. When White Moon returned to Camp Leavenworth later that morning to report that an Indian had shot and killed the lieutenant within a quarter mile of the hostile encampment,[13] Garnier would not have been surprised.

A detachment of soldiers was immediately dispatched to retrieve the body,[14] and word of Casey's killing soon reached the agency. It was a hard blow to General Miles. Casey had been under Miles's command when both were stationed at Fort Keogh, Montana. There, Casey had recruited fifty Northern Cheyenne men and transformed them into army scouts, complete with uniforms and military discipline. Miles was enthusiastically supportive of Casey's efforts and the two became good friends.[15] Upon learning of Casey's death, Miles retained his focus on the big picture—bringing the Messiah craze to an end without further bloodshed. To achieve that, he needed Young Man Afraid of His Horses.

When the chief arrived at Pine Ridge on January 8, he was immediately taken to Miles's headquarters.[16] The next morning, Young Man Afraid of His Horses went to No Water's village and counseled with the hostiles' leaders. He returned late that afternoon to assure Miles that many of the hostiles would come into the agency the next day or the day following.[17] Once more the peacemaker fulfilled his responsibilities as a shirt wearer.

On January 12, the entire body of nearly four thousand hostiles moved within sight of the agency. Their head chiefs sent messengers to the agency to tell Miles they desired peace. On January 15 the Indians paraded into the agency and surrendered. Their surrender brought the Indian uprising to an end with a climax befitting a Shakespearian tragedy. Three thousand army troops who only six weeks earlier had been brought onto the reservation from as far away as Texas and New Mexico vanished almost overnight. Another two thousand soldiers positioned in strategic locations around the borders of the Lakota reservation similarly disappeared.[18]

Many whites living on the Dakota frontier were dissatisfied with the outcome. They protested that the Sioux had not been completely stripped of their guns and set afoot, and they had not been handed yokes of oxen and plows and told to cultivate the land or starve. Worse yet, from the perspective of the whites in western South Dakota, not an acre of land had been taken from them.

Citizens of Hermosa passed a resolution roundly condemning General Miles for the way the conflict was resolved. They produced a medal for Miles that bore the following inscription:

> Veni Vidi Vici [I came, I saw, I conquered]
> Brutum Fulmen [an empty threat]
> In Commemoration of the Mastery
> Inactivity of the Commander
> General in the Field during the
> Indian War of 1890–91
> The Beautiful Leather Medal is
> Dedicated to General Miles
> By the disgusted residents of
> The Black Hills.[19]

Although it was not the outcome the greedy white settlers wanted, many on the frontier were convinced that the Indian uprising was over and Casey was the last fatality. They were wrong.

⚔ 6 ⚔

A GOOD INDIAN IS MURDERED

Following the hostiles' surrender to General Miles, most Brulé went back to the Rosebud Reservation and the various bands of Oglala returned to the widely scattered little villages where they had lived prior to the appearance of soldiers. The Pine Ridge Reservation quickly took on the appearance of normalcy. However, an ominously large number of former hostiles, including Plenty Horses, Can Nopa Uhah, his wife, and four sons, chose to stay in No Water's village. Some whites living next to the boundaries of the reservation believed these hostiles, now dubbed "malcontents," would soon reignite the Indian war.[1]

The doomsayers did not have to wait long before an incident threatened to unravel the fragile peace. On the morning of January 11, a skirmish occurred between white ranchers living in Meade County and some Indians. The widely read *Rapid City Journal* informed its readers of the incident:

> On Saturday evening [January 10] two bucks and two squaws with two teams and wagons camped at the mouth of Alkali Creek. Settlers and stockmen who have been on the lookout for Indians learned that late Saturday night they were joined by a band of about twenty bucks, who were mounted. The band had with them about forty horses, among which were several belonging to the Culbertsons and some with the cross X brand. A party of six men, in which were Pete and Andy Culbertson,

Squire Jones, and Alva Marvin, approached the camp about sunrise Sunday morning and proceeded to cut out the horses when they were fired upon by the Indians. The fire was briskly returned and continued for some time. The sound brought other settlers and stockmen to the scene when most of the Indians who had secured their horses broke for the rough ground in the brakes adjacent. Two bucks, a squaw and two horses were killed on the ground. A buck and a squaw started north with one of the teams and wagons and five wounded Indians followed.[2]

In a subsequent article, the *Rapid City Journal* informed West River folk that "several parties were in town yesterday from Alkali and Elk Creek valleys. They state that the report of Sunday morning's fight . . . as published by the *Journal*, was substantially correct."[3]

The *Sturgis Weekly Record* did not get news of the skirmish to its readers until January 16: "There was a report on Sunday that a big fight had occurred on Lower Alkali and several Indians were killed. The *Record* has tried to get 'the straight of it' from several parties who came down this way:"

> It seems to be . . . that a hunting party of Crows had come down from the north and when on the divide between Alkali and Elk Creek two ponies played out. There were ten to a dozen bucks in the party with wagons, etc. They shot the two ponies and then their horsethieving [sic] proclivities came to the surface. They started to round up some ranch horses and were caught in the act. Ranchers interfered and several shots were fired by white men, just as there would have been if a party of white men tried to run off stock. The Record's informant didn't know whether anybody had been killed, but didn't think none had.[4]

A distorted rumor of the incident eventually reached the white employees at Pine Ridge. Gossip had it that a roving band of "savages" was raiding ranches near Colonel Edwin Sumner's command when they were discovered by cowboys. The Indians, who numbered fifty, fired at the cowboys without effect. Four troopers of the Eighth Cavalry joined the cowboys in a running fight with the Indians and killed two of them. They also recovered forty horses and a wagon the Indians had stolen. The Indians fled southwest toward their sanctuary on Pine Ridge Reservation.[5]

None of the initially told stories about the skirmish at the mouth of Alkali Creek were true. The sad, horrific, but factual story was that when Young Man

Afraid of Horses's band finished a successful hunt in Wyoming, they continued west to visit the Northern Cheyenne and then the Crow. The antelope meat the band obtained through hunting was loaded into two wagons. In one wagon were Few Tails and his wife, Clown. One Feather; his wife, Red Owl; their thirteen-year-old daughter, Otter Robe; and an infant daughter were in the other wagon. Each wagon was pulled by a team of horses, with two horses tied behind. Even by alternating the horses, the wagons were so heavily loaded that their progress was slow. As the two Indian families proceeded toward Pine Ridge, they did not know that thousands of troops had arrived to squelch the Messiah craze. They also were unaware that nearly every West River town had formed an armed-to-the-teeth home guard. For Few Tails and One Feather, Wounded Knee was nothing more than a spring-fed creek that flowed north in search of the White River.

On the evening of January 10, 1890, the two families camped at the confluence of Alkali Creek and the Belle Fourche River. Sergeant Frank Smith, who was in charge of the courier station at Peter Quinn's ranch, seven miles from the mouth of Alkali Creek, rode into their camp. Few Tails showed Smith his pass to be off the reservation and the officer rode away.

The next morning the two families broke camp to resume their journey. Few Tails's wagon was in the lead. He went only three hundred yards when a hail of gunfire erupted from a brush-covered knoll. Two bullets struck Few Tails, killing him instantly. Clown was also shot. One bullet struck her in the leg; another hit her in the breast. She fell backward into the wagon.

One Feather turned his wagon and fled. The white men mounted their horses and pursued him. Handing the reins to his wife, One Feather used his breech-loading .45-caliber rifle to keep his pursuers at a distance.

One of the pursuers, Andrew Culbertson, turned aside. He rode to Quinn's ranch to inform the four soldiers stationed there that he and his brothers had been attacked by Indians trying to steal their horses. Culbertson asked the soldiers to help. Two soldiers jumped on their horses and raced with Culbertson toward the sound of the gunfire.[6] Hearing gunshots, area ranchers V. P. Shoun and Abe Jones also joined the chase.[7]

After being pursued for ten miles, One Feather and Red Owl reached Elk Creek at a place where it could not be crossed by a wagon. Using the protection of the timber along Elk Creek, One Feather made a stand. When a rifle ball grazed the palm of Pete Culbertson's hand, the pursuing white men took cover. Red Owl unhitched the team. She put Otter Robe on one horse and placed the infant in her arms. She and One Feather mounted the other horse. The Indian family headed toward the Cheyenne River, twenty miles to the east. Upon reaching the river, they crossed it and their pursuers abandoned the chase.[8]

Two of the Culbertson brothers rode fifteen miles downriver to Camp Cheyenne, located at the fork of the Belle Fourche and Cheyenne Rivers. The two hundred soldiers bivouacked there since April of 1890 had passed eight months monitoring the ghost dancing at Big Foot's village ten miles to the east and a few miles up from the mouth of Deep Creek. After Big Foot and his band fled from their village on December 23, there was little for the soldiers to do. Boredom hung heavily over their heads, relieved only by the six boxes of "ammunition" smuggled in on January 7 by Henry Wyttenbach, co-owner of a Sturgis liquor store. Each box held a gallon of whiskey.[9]

When the Culbertsons reached Camp Cheyenne, they invented a story about having had a skirmish that morning with a party of Indians attempting to steal their horses. The next day, Lieutenant Colonel Henry Merriam dispatched Lieutenant Francis Marshall to the scene of the skirmish with orders to conduct a thorough investigation. George W. Ladd, the county surveyor, and Meade County sheriff Valentine Beaver accompanied Marshall. They found Few Tails's body still in the wagon box. A meticulous examination of the immediate area uncovered empty bullet casings in a clump of bushes about twenty yards away from Few Tails's wagon. Some of the cartridges were from a .45-caliber rifle, about twenty cartridges came from Winchester rifles, and a few were from a .42-caliber rifle. The investigators concluded that the cartridges marked the spot where the white men hid to ambush the Indians. They also examined the wagon tracks and the horses' hoofprints.[10] Everything about the scene convinced Marshall and his investigative team that Few Tails had been murdered. Marshall relayed his findings and conclusion to General Miles,[11] who sent a copy of Marshall's report on to Governor Mellette. Mellette, in turn, sent the report to Meade County state's attorney Alex McCall with instructions to investigate and institute criminal proceedings against all concerned if warranted.[12]

After crossing the Cheyenne River, the One Feather family struggled to get home. Their infant daughter died of starvation and exposure as they passed through Chief Lip's abandoned village near the confluence of Pass Creek and the Cheyenne River. The family did not reach the safety of the Rosebud Agency until January 24.[13]

As for Clown, when the ranchers left the scene of the ambush to pursue One Feather and his family, she crawled under the canvas tarp covering the wagonload of meat and throughout the day lay there hidden. Late that afternoon Peter Quinn, a local rancher, directed one of his young sons to go to the nearby scene of the attack and bring home the wagon. Upon reaching the site, the boy reached his arm under the canvas covering of the wagon. He was startled to feel the warm leg of a human being and he hurriedly left the scene.[14] It was now dusk. Clown crawled out from under the canvas tarp, mounted a horse bareback, and escaped. Upon reaching the house of a white family, possibly the home of Frank Cottle at the mouth of Elk Creek, Clown slid off her horse and limped to the house. She knocked and a white man came to the door. Seeing the caller was an Indian, he ordered her to leave. She did, but her untethered horse had walked off into the darkness.

Clown had no option but to walk southward along the west bank of the Cheyenne River. She hobbled on her wounded leg all through the night. When the sun rose, she hid until dusk and then resumed walking. After walking thirty-one miles, she reached the post office/general store that constituted the settlement of Creston near the mouth of Rapid Creek. Although Clown had traded at the store, she was afraid to stop.

The old Chamberlain–Rapid City freighting route ran right past the Creston store. Clown followed the freighting trail across the frozen-over Cheyenne River, up Spring Creek and into the badlands. Hearing a wagon coming, she hid in the darkness and let it go by. After twelve miles, Clown struck the grass-filled ruts of the Fort Pierre–Fort Laramie Trail. Turning south, she followed the trail eighteen miles to the White River. From there the trail and the White River veered southwest. Clown followed the trail until she came to Captain Wells's Camp Leavenworth at the ford near the mouth of Grass Creek. It was dark. She had walked sixty-six miles in seven days in the dead of winter. Exhausted, wounded, and unable to take another step, Clown collapsed.

The next morning, January 18, Gus Craven, a civilian guide and husband of a part-Indian woman, found Clown lying behind his tent. She was taken to the field hospital at the agency and nursed back to health.[15]

When Clown sufficiently recovered, she told of the killing of Few Tails and her ordeal. The story swept through the Oglala community like a tornado, uprooting the semblance of calm Young Man Afraid of His Horses had achieved. Upon hearing the tragic story, half a dozen warriors in No Water's village galloped their horses to the top of a high hill, firing their rifles as they rode.[16]

When the turmoil at No Water's village was reported to General Miles, he immediately sent for Young Man Afraid of His Horses to again solicit his support in quieting the renegade Indians. By then Young Man Afraid of His Horses had heard of Clown's ordeal and knew that white men had killed Few Tails, a close friend and relative. The chief was in no mood to help pacify the hostiles. It took all of Miles's diplomacy to calm Young Man Afraid of His Horses and persuade him to once again pacify the hostiles.[17]

On January 20 Miles and Young Man Afraid of His Horses induced an assemblage of Oglala chiefs and headmen to come into the agency. Miles assured them that the army was not responsible for Few Tails's death. He told the Indians it was his conclusion that Few Tails had been murdered, and he promised them justice would be done.[18] The next day acting Indian agent Captain Francis Pierce ordered the distribution of twenty days of additional rations[19] and an extra-large issue of beef. However, empathy, promises, extra rations, and beef were not enough to mollify the Indians. They wanted Few Tails's killers punished.

When C. C. Moody, proprietor of the *Sturgis Weekly Record*, learned that General Miles was convinced that Few Tails had been killed without provocation, the paper changed its tune: "It appears that the Indians who were fired into and one killed were on a friendly visit to the Crows. It seems very strange that some people could not see that Indians with wagons and women were not on the warpath." As for justice being done, Moody was not optimistic: "It will be difficult, if not impossible, to convict the killers of Few Tails."[20] Porter Warner, editor of the *Daily Deadwood Pioneer-Times*, agreed: "Few Tails' killers will never be punished and probably never even brought to justice.[21]

East River residents viewed the killing of Few Tails through a different lens. An article in the *Mitchell Capital* on January 23 read: "When the treacherous whites in Bear Butte County [meaning Meade County, where Bear Butte is located] wantonly murdered old Few Tails and wounded his squaw, they committed an outrage."[22] The *Argus-Leader*, a Sioux Falls newspaper, opined that Few Tails was one of the most reliable and progressive Indians on the [Pine Ridge] agency and that "his killing was one of the most cold-blooded and unjustifiable murders ever committed on the frontier."[23] The *Pierre Weekly Free Press*, a newspaper aligned with its West River constituents, countered: "The slobbering sentiment displayed by both the Sioux Falls dailies . . . would indicate that they might become the mouthpiece of Dr. Bland."[24] (Thomas Bland was head of the National Indian Defense Association.)

News about Few Tails's killing spread far beyond South Dakota. The rest of America was dismayed that white men had killed an innocent Indian and appalled that the white men responsible for the killing had not been indicted for murder.[25]

As January came to a close, the white men who had killed Few Tails had not been charged. But Miles overlooked that injustice and instead pressed Young Man Afraid of His Horses for assistance in facilitating the arrest of the Indians who had allegedly killed Lieutenant Casey. Young Man Afraid of His Horses became incensed. "No," he said angrily, "I will not surrender them; but if you will bring the white men who killed Few Tails, I will bring the Indians who killed the white soldier . . . and right out here in front of your tepee I will have my young men shoot the Indians, and you have your soldiers shoot the white men; and then we will be done with the whole business. They were all bad men."[26]

⚜ 7 ⚜

THE INDIAN WHO KILLED LIEUTENANT CASEY

When Lieutenant Edward Casey was shot and killed on January 7, there were five Indians, three of them Sioux, within ten feet of him. There was no doubt as to who killed Casey. He was a young Brulé whose Lakota name was Sunkewakan Ota ("Sunkewakan" meaning horse, and "Ota" meaning many).[1] To a white man's ear, the phonetic spelling was Tasunka-Ota, and he was known to whites as Plenty Horses. The Lakota name was given to him by his grandfather Moon That Ever Shines. Shortly after Tasunka-Ota's birth, Moon That Ever Shines returned from a raid in Nebraska, likely on the Pawnee, with one hundred horses. He gave ten of the horses to his infant grandson, and with them came the name Plenty Horses.[2]

At the age of fourteen, Plenty Horses and thirteen other Lakota children (nine boys and four girls) were more or less rounded up, put on a train, and sent thirteen hundred miles east to the Carlisle Indian Industrial School in Pennsylvania. He arrived on November 14, 1883, not knowing more than a few words of English. A considerable portion of his education at Carlisle was in the "outing program," where he was an unpaid laborer for white farmers. Plenty Horses worked for B. F. Schofield from September 1886 to August 1887, John Vance from September 1887 to May 1888, and Fred Vanartsdalen from September 1888 to April 1889. Plenty Horses, Arrow Running Horse, Frank Janis, and Hope Blue Teeth all departed Carlisle on July 8, 1889, and returned home.[3] Plenty Horses had then lived away from his people and off the reservation for five and one-half years. He arrived back on the reservation with only fourth-grade academic skills.

In the days following Casey's killing, that was what the authorities learned about Plenty Horses, but knowing his name and background was one thing; apprehending the alleged murderer was another. Plenty Horses evaded arrest for more than a month, and in that he had assistance. The residents of No Water's village refused to surrender Plenty Horses until the white men who had killed Few Tails were arrested.[4] When General Miles promised that Few Tails's killers would be brought to justice, the Indians' willingness to shield Plenty Horses dissipated.

A tip was received as to Plenty Horses's location, and twenty-three-year-old Sydney A. Coleman, a recent graduate of the U.S. Military Academy,[5] was assigned to make the arrest. He and fifty Indian police rode into a small Indian camp on a tributary of White Clay Creek (likely Trail Creek) on February 16 and reined up their horses at the opening to a lodge belonging to Corn Man, Plenty Horses's grandfather. Plenty Horses and two other young warriors were inside. They were ordered to come out, but they refused and Coleman wisely withdrew. The next morning he and the Indian police again went to the Indian camp. As expected, almost everyone had gone to the agency for their rations, leaving only six men behind. One of them was Plenty Horses. Another was Leaves His Woman, the Indian who allegedly had murdered Ike Miller. Coleman captured both suspects and took them to the agency.[6]

Ironically, it was Lieutenant Joseph Byron and a detachment of Cheyenne scouts who arrived at Pine Ridge on February 18 to take custody of Plenty Horses and Leaves His Woman. Byron transported the alleged murderers to Fort Meade, where they were locked in the guard house. To ensure that Plenty Horses did not escape, a blacksmith welded shackles around his ankles and a guard checked on him hourly.[7]

A grand jury met in Deadwood from March 6 to March 11 to review whether the evidence against a long list of suspects warranted indicting any of them. Plenty Horses, the accused murderer of Casey, was on that list. Judge Alonzo Edgerton presided and Valentine T. McGillycuddy, the former Indian agent at Pine Ridge, was the jury foreman. During the proceedings, Plenty Horses was called upon to testify on his own behalf. "I am an Indian," he told the grand jury. "For five years I attended Carlisle and was educated in the ways of the white man. I was lonely. I shot the lieutenant so I might make a place for myself among my people. Now I am one of them. I shall belong, and the

Tasunka Ota (Plenty Horses), the slayer of Lieutenant Edward Casey, near Pine Ridge. (Library of Congress, Prints and Photographs Division, John C. H. Grabill Collection, LC-DIG-ppmsc-02523.)

Indians will bury me as a warrior. They will be proud of me. I am satisfied." Based on the suspect's admission, the grand jury indicted Plenty Horses for the murder of Edward Casey.[8]

John Burns, a Deadwood attorney, notified Herbert Welsh, secretary of the Indian Rights Association (IRA), that he had been approached by Plenty Horses and his father, Living Bear, to serve as the defense attorney. Burns decided that Plenty Horses's best defense was that he had shot Casey in the context of an ongoing war. Burns was willing to take on the case but wanted at least five hundred dollars as compensation. On behalf of the Indian Rights Association, Herbert Welsh offered two hundred. Burns held out for five, which the Indian Rights Association refused to pay.[9]

The thought of hosting Plenty Horses's highly visible trial put smiles on the faces of Deadwood's businessmen. In 1891 the country, especially drought-stricken South Dakota, was experiencing hard times. Deadwood's business-men looked forward to the bevy of reporters from far-flung newspapers who would come to town, dine at their eateries, and lodge in their hotels. At federal government expense, the jurors would stay in Deadwood day after day. In the businessmen's collective mind's eye, they also saw the Lawrence County courtroom packed with curious spectators who would need lodging and food during the long trial. The mere thought of all those new dollars coming to town had Deadwood's businessmen drooling. But they were soon disappointed.

Judge Alonzo Edgerton was an East River man. He did not believe Plenty Horses could get a fair trial in Deadwood given the reputation of West River denizens for prejudice against Indians. Edgerton ordered that Plenty Horses be tried in Sioux Falls at the spring session of federal court. His ruling did not sit well with the Deadwood business community. The *Black Hills Daily Times* opined that "Judge Edgerton changed the venue because he doesn't like the Hills people."[10] The editor's jab at Edgerton had less to do with a perceived insult and more to do with thin wallets.

At that point the Plenty Horses case and the Few Tails case became inter-twined. U.S. district attorney for South Dakota William Sterling had turned Few Tails's case over to Meade County state's attorney Alex McCall. But McCall did not summon a grand jury to determine whether anyone should be indicted for Few Tails's murder, causing many Black Hills citizens to conclude that the state's attorney intended to dismiss the case because it would be impossible to find a jury of Meade County residents who would convict Few Tails's killers.[11]

Fearing that Few Tails's killers might never see the inside of a courtroom, General Miles concluded that he needed to act, and act he did. When U.S. deputy marshal Chris Matthiessen arrived at Fort Meade on March 12 to take custody of Plenty Horses and transport him to Sioux Falls, post commander Edwin Sumner told Matthiessen that he had orders from General Miles not to hand over the prisoner.[12] It was a power play. Miles was not going to allow

Plenty Horses to be put in the hands of the civilian authorities until the Meade County state's attorney secured indictments against the men who had killed Few Tails.

The shrewd move worked. U.S. Attorney William B. Sterling promised the secretary of war that charges would be brought against the white men who had killed Few Tails if the army handed Plenty Horses over to civilian authorities. With that promise made, Secretary of War Redfield Proctor wired Sumner on March 18, instructing him to release Plenty Horses to civilian authorities.[13]

Deputy Matthiessen received a telegram on March 27 from his boss, U.S. Marshal Cyrus Fry, instructing him to proceed to Fort Meade and take custody of Plenty Horses. The deputy arrived at Fort Meade the next day and transported his prisoner two miles to the Meade County jail and locked him up for the night.[14] The next day the deputy and his prisoner, whose legs were still shackled, boarded the train for Sioux Falls. There, Plenty Horses was taken to a blacksmith, who filed off the leg irons. Plenty Horses was secured in the Minnehaha County Jail to await the spring session of federal court.[15]

While Plenty Horses bided his time in jail, his father, Living Bear, went around the Pine Ridge Reservation trying to sell two old ponies and in other ways raise money for his son's legal defense.[16] Little money was raised, and Plenty Horses had no legal counsel. In those days there were no public defenders. However, in highly visible cases such as Plenty Horses's trial, the court could appoint legal counsel. Accordingly, David E. Powers and George Nock were appointed to defend Plenty Horses. They were to be paid three hundred dollars plus whatever Plenty Horses's father could scrape together, about two hundred dollars. Both men had recently moved from Rome, New York, to Sioux Falls and were regarded as brilliant young attorneys of great promise.[17] Despite the paucity of funds, the attorneys threw themselves into the case and immediately went to work. Monday, April 13, Nock filed seven demurrers petitioning the court to squash the indictment against Plenty Horses. All the demurrers were based on technicalities. One demurrer called for dismissal on the grounds that the name of the presiding judge was not specifically stated when the indictment was made. Another demurrer was that the indictment did not state by whose order the grand jury in Deadwood was adjourned. The next day Judge Edgerton reviewed the seven demurrers for dismissal and denied all of them.[18] Having exhausted all legal avenues for avoiding a trial, Nock entered Plenty Horses's plea: not guilty.[19]

Just days before the trial was scheduled, Living Bear traveled all the way from Pine Ridge to visit his son in jail. Upon entering Plenty Horses's jail cell, Living Bear grasped his son's hand and cried. Amid his sobs he said, "Tasunkta Ota, you have had a bad heart. You killed Casey. You are a man, and you must suffer." On leaving the jail cell, Living Bear handed his son a large bright yellow handkerchief.[20]

When court convened on April 24, Judge Oliver P. Shiras of the Federal Court for the North District of Iowa and Judge Edgerton of the South Dakota Federal Court presided. The prosecuting attorneys were U.S. District Attorney W. B. Sterling, Assistant U.S. District Attorney Charles Howard of Redfield, and Captain John G. Ballance of the Army Judge Advocate Corps, whose knowledge of the army and Indian matters was particularly useful to the prosecution.[21]

The first task was selecting twelve jurors from the venire of twenty-five. Half of the venire declared upon examination that they had prejudice against Indians and were therefore summarily dismissed. An additional venire of thirteen men was examined in the afternoon.[22] After the defense exercised its twenty preemptory challenges, twelve jurors were impaneled late in the afternoon.[23] The jurors were Henry Ramsdell, McCook County; Howard Hall, Kingsbury County; A. H. Wright, Parkston; W. L. Miner, Eden; Thomas Hennegar, Charles Mix County; Daniel Birdsell, McCook County; F. L. Stevens, Bon Homme County; N. J. House, Canton; Wallace L. Dow, Sioux Falls; Fred. L. Speyr, Sioux Falls; G. W. Lowry, Sioux Falls; and Cyrus H. Ormiston, Sioux Falls.[24] When the jury was seated, U.S. Attorney Sterling gave a graphic account of Casey's killing. Court was then adjourned for the day.[25]

When court convened Saturday morning at nine-thirty, the spectators included a number of fashionably dressed women, including Marie Blaine, wife of James Blaine Jr. and daughter-in-law of the U.S. secretary of state. She was escorted to the first row. Also attending were William Larrabee, the ex-governor of Iowa, and Dr. Daniel Dorchester, superintendent of the Indian schools of the United States.[26] So many people wanted to attend the trial that the two U.S. deputy marshals stationed at the entrance had to turn away spectators for lack of standing room.

Defense attorneys Nock and Powers were all smiles when court convened. They had just received a telegram from Herbert Welsh, secretary of the Indian Rights Association, assuring them that the IRA would furnish all necessary funds to defend Plenty Horses.[27]

The prosecutors' first witness was Dr. B. L. Ten Eyck, the army surgeon who had examined Casey's body ten hours after the shooting. He confirmed that Casey had died instantly from a single bullet entering the back of his head and exiting just below his right eye.

White Moon, one of the Cheyenne scouts who had accompanied Casey that fateful morning, was the next witness.[28] Unfortunately, there is no record, official or otherwise, of his testimony. The prosecution then called Rock Road, the other Cheyenne scout who had accompanied Casey that day, to the stand. Rock Road testified that he, White Moon, and Casey rode from the soldiers' encampment on the west bank of the White River to where they encountered a group of about forty Indians butchering some cattle. He related that two of the Indians rode up to them. One was Broken Arm; the other was Plenty Horses. As the five of them talked, a rider (Bear That Lays Down) came down the road from the direction of the hostile camp and joined them. He was requested to take a message to the chiefs in the hostile camp, telling them that Casey wished to talk with them. As the men waited for Bear That Lays Down to come back, Casey told Rock Road to return to the soldiers' encampment in their defensive position at the ford on White River.[29]

Bear That Lays Down, the messenger, then testified. He said he was married to a sister of Plenty Horses's mother, making him Plenty Horses's uncle. Bear That Lays Down confirmed the testimony of the two previous witnesses regarding meeting with Casey on a hill near where a band of Indians were butchering several beeves. He also testified that Rock Road asked him to take a message to Red Cloud's camp, telling the chiefs that Casey would like to meet with them. Upon returning with Red Cloud's reply, Bear That Lays Down related, he was accompanied by Peter Richard. While Casey and Richard talked, White Moon, Broken Arm, Plenty Horses, and he held their horses close together and listened. Bear That Lays Down said that his horse was directly in front of Casey. He watched Plenty Horses back up his mount, raise his rifle, and shoot Casey. As Casey fell from his horse, Plenty Horses galloped his horse toward the hostile camp.

Sterling jumped on that piece of testimony to ask the critical question, "Who murdered Casey?" Bear That Lays Down replied, "Tasunka-Ota [Plenty Horses]." At that, court was adjourned for the day.[30]

On Monday, April 27, Bear That Lays Down was cross-examined. The next witness was Peter Richard, a mixed-blood and son-in-law of Red Cloud, who told the court that Red Cloud sent back a message advising the lieutenant to return at once to the soldiers' encampment. Richard said that he and Casey then discussed how to get the hostile and friendly Indians to merge together and cease their warfare. At the time, he did not think Casey was in any danger, so he was surprised when Plenty Horses raised his gun and fired.[31]

Henry C. Thompson, an interpreter, testified. He was followed on the witness stand by Captain George W. Llewellyn, a field deputy U.S. marshal for the Northern District, Eighth Circuit of Iowa.[32] The prosecution's final witness was Broken Arm;[33] his testimony provided no new information.[34] With that, the prosecution rested its case.

The defense team then had its turn. George Nock informed the court that the defense would not dispute that Plenty Horses had killed Casey. However, they would present evidence showing that the killing was justified because a state of war existed at the time between the hostile Indians and the army.

Their first witness was Philip Wells, chief of the U.S. scouts for General Brooke during the Messiah craze. As Wells strode to the witness stand, a palpable tension arose in the courtroom. Everyone expected the defense attorneys to ask Wells questions designed to elicit answers that would support their contention that a state of war existed at the time. If a picture can be worth a thousand words, then the thin white scar across Wells's nose that resulted from an Indian attempting to stab Wells to death during the Wounded Knee battle said it all. The scar was testament to the defense's contention that a state of war existed at the time.

While Wells sat in the witness seat and listened, a hot debate erupted between prosecuting attorney William Sterling and defense attorney George Nock. Judge Shiras brought the rancorous argument to an end by saying that he would consider the legal merits of the "state of war" defense that evening and give his ruling in the morning. "Court," he then thundered, "is adjourned until tomorrow morning."[35]

When court resumed Tuesday morning, April 28, Shiras rendered his decision. He ruled that the defense could argue that Plenty Horses was not guilty because a state of war existed when he killed Casey.[36] Wells was recalled to continue his testimony. He described the fight of December 30 that he participated in just outside the gates of the Drexel Mission, giving in detail the location of the troops and the hostiles. When Powers asked Wells to describe the Ghost Dance, the audience hung on the scout's every descriptive word. They listened intently as he related that Indians caught up in the Ghost Dance expected whites to be destroyed for the wrongs they had committed against the

Indians and that they also believed that the white men's bullets could not pierce their ghost shirts. Powers then asked Wells questions designed to convince the jurors that the Indians, including Plenty Horses, were, at the time, in a peculiar, unrealistic state of mind.[37]

The defense's next witness was Living Bear, Plenty Horses's anguished father. Although the attorneys dressed Living Bear dapperly in a white shirt and plain suit and made sure his long hair was neatly brushed, he walked up to the witness stand with obvious trepidation. Yet when Living Bear spoke, his voice was firm and resolute. He gave his age as fifty and said he was a Brulé Sioux, a cousin of Two Strike's and a member of his band. Living Bear related that he was not present at the Drexel Mission fight, being too old for combat: "The younger men of the tribe went to the fight. We older ones decided it would be of no use for us to go. The creek was deep and well-sheltered, and we intended to make our stand there.... We dug rifle pits and put logs in front of them. We were surrounded by different camps of soldiers and we expected they would come after us."[38]

Prosecuting attorney Sterling mounted a severe cross-examination of Living Bear, trying to show that peace reigned at the time of Casey's death and that the Indians were at the point of peacefully coming into Pine Ridge, all to no avail. He could not shake Living Bear's testimony.[39]

The next witness was fifty-one-year-old He Dog. He Dog was Red Cloud's nephew and a brother of Short Bull, the leading medicine man for the hostile Indians. It was widely known among army officers and others on the frontier that He Dog was a noted Lakota warrior, having fought soldiers on Rosebud Creek, the Little Bighorn, Slim Buttes, and Wolf Mountain, and that he was with Crazy Horse when the war chief came into Fort Robinson in 1877 to surrender.[40]

He Dog was of medium height and despite his age had the look of an athlete. His long hair hung straight down without being pushed back or braided. His face was round, full, and surly. On the stand, he was an eloquent and passionate speaker. In answer to Powers's questions, He Dog related that the Oglala were mortified when they learned that Big Foot and most of his band, including woman and children, had been shot down in cold blood. He described the fortifications the hostile Indians had erected at No Water's village and the rifle pits they dug to defend themselves from an anticipated attack by the army. His testimony was underscored by his demeanor of sincerity but was related with the aura of a man who was reluctant to tell all he knew. Upon cross-exam, the best Sterling could do was to chip away at He Dog's credibility by pointing out some inconsistencies regarding his recollection of dates.[41]

Bear That Lays Down was again called to the stand. Earlier in the trial, while testifying for the prosecution, he emphatically stated that Plenty Horses had killed Casey. The defense now called upon him to tell the court about the fortifications surrounding the hostile encampment. In response to the defense attorney's questions, Bear That Lays Down informed the court that the Indians had built the fortifications because they expected to be attacked by the army. He also told about the hardships suffered by the people in the hostile camp, relating that everyone in No Water's village, including women and starving children, went fourteen days without any rations. Having rushed to No Water's village in haste, they did not have the clothing and bedding needed to cope with the intense winter cold, and they suffered greatly.[42]

A. B. Melville was the defense team's next witness.[43] What he related was not of sufficient importance to warrant any attention from the newspaper reporters in the galley.

John McDonough, a reporter for the *New York World*, then took the stand. McDonough testified about the in-depth jail cell interview he had with Plenty Horses prior to the trial. According to McDonough, Plenty Horses was certain he would be hanged for killing Casey, and he did not hold back on relating the incident. In response to the defense attorney's questions, McDonough underscored his veracity by often referencing notes he had taken during the interview. The effect was to give the jurors a vivid picture of Plenty Horses's state of mind, both when he shot Casey and in the days before the shooting. McDonough said Plenty Horses had great animosity toward the army soldiers and officers for their senseless killing of women and children at Wounded Knee. The reporter said that Plenty Horses was a participant in the Drexel Mission fight and that he joined the fight to get revenge against the whites. McDonough concluded his testimony by telling the jury that, in his opinion, Plenty Horses had no sense of guilt or remorse about killing Casey.[44]

The defense called its last witness to the stand—Plenty Horses. As he rose, Plenty Horses pulled his blanket to his shoulders and strode to the stand, accompanied by Philip Wells, the defense's interpreter. Sterling objected to having Wells interpret for Plenty Horses. "This man has an education and can get along without the aid of an interpreter," Sterling argued. Nock interposed, insisting that Plenty Horses's command of the English language was limited, making it likely he would misinterpret some questions and not adequately answer them. Judge Edgerton directed some questions at Plenty Horses. When Plenty Horses gave satisfactory answers, Edgerton ruled that no interpreter was needed. Nock again appealed, "And if that [the request for an interpreter] be refused, you will force us to close our case without a word from the defendant in his behalf."

"It is not necessary to make a threat," Judge Shiras angrily retorted.

"Then we refuse to permit Plenty Horses to testify, and we also close our case."

Plenty Horses's eyes turned toward the open window. Not the slightest expression could be seen on his face.[45]

When court convened Wednesday morning, April 29, Charles T. Howard, gave the prosecution's summation. Powers and Nock gave the summation for the defense.[46] Judge Shiras assured the jurors that the court had jurisdiction over the case because Indians living on reservations were at all times subject to the authority of the United States government. He then gave the jurors their instructions. In these instructions, Shiras informed the jurors of the legal distinction between manslaughter and murder, stating that the jurors could, if the evidence supported it, find Plenty Tails guilty of either charge. He did not address the question of whether a state of war existed when Casey was shot, leaving that question for the jurors to decide.[47]

The jurors retired at four o'clock to deliberate.[48] While they deliberated, Living Bear walked the corridors in agony. At ten o'clock that evening, the jury sent for Judge Shiras and asked him to reread a portion of the charge against Plenty Horses. At nine o'clock the next morning, Thursday, April 30, the jury foreman reported that the jurors were unable to agree on the verdict. Shiras ordered them to continue deliberating. At noon, the jurors still had not reached a consensus. Shiras sent for them. "Have you reached a verdict?" he asked. The foreman replied, "We have not, your Honor." Shiras discharged the jury and announced that the verdict was contested. He remanded Plenty Horses back to jail to await a retrial on May 25.[49]

Realizing that another trial meant the judge was not going to immediately order his son's execution, Living Bear broke down in tears of relief and joy.[50] He soon returned to his tepee in No Water's village and undoubtedly shared his firsthand account of the trial and that no decision was made as to Plenty Horses's fate. Living Bear would have also shared with them his fear that upon retrial, Plenty Horses would be found guilty and hanged. Of course, every member of No Water's village, including Two Sticks, would have believed that Plenty Horses was justified in killing Casey, and the mere thought of him being hanged would have deepened their anger toward white men, an anger that could be quenched only by getting revenge.

❈ 8 ❈

PLENTY HORSES'S
SECOND TRIAL

Judge Shiras and Judge Edgerton were again on the bench for Plenty Horses's retrial. George Nock and David Powers continued to represent the defense. Their spirits were buoyed by more than 150 letters and telegrams from people in the East, proffering help and encouraging words.[1] U.S. Attorney William Sterling headed up the prosecution and was again assisted by Charles Howard of Redfield and army captain John G. Ballance. In preparing for the second trial, Sterling went to Chicago and called upon General Miles, commander of the Division of the Missouri, headquartered at Fort Sheridan. Sterling asked Miles to come to Sioux Falls and give testimony to refute the war theory the defense team was sure to invoke. Miles declined, hinting that it would belittle his Indian campaign and place him in an unfavorable light before the American people.[2] Sterling's visit with Miles had an unintended, deleterious effect. It alerted the general that the prosecution expected the defense to invoke the "at war" argument to acquit Plenty Horses and was strategizing ways to discredit it. Forewarned is forearmed, and he was.

Prospective jurors were summoned to Sioux Falls on Saturday, May 23, two days before the second trial was scheduled to commence. Jury selection began at 9:30 that morning. Seventy-five citizens were in the venire. By noon, thirty had been questioned but only seven selected. It took the rest of the day to impanel a jury.[3] The jurors were W. B. Windsor, Brown County; Christian Adams, Brookings County; C. Ingersoll, Marshall County; J. E. McKoane, Edmunds

County; George Kennan, Codington County; John Doonan, Edmunds County; A. M. Starks, Sully County; B. B. Potter, Walworth County; W. S. Fassett, Campbell County; William Breen, Potter County; S. N. Palmer, Clay County; and Edger Dean, Lincoln County—all East River men.[4]

When the trial commenced on Monday morning, May 25, the courtroom was packed. U.S. Deputy Marshal Frank Keyes and another deputy marshal were at the door, admitting some and turning away others until the room filled to capacity.[5] Plenty Horses sat at the railing wearing a shirt of sunset red brought to radiance by a silk handkerchief of bright yellow, likely the one given to him by his father a month earlier. Whereas Plenty Horses's clothes were eye-catching, his face was stoic and expressionless.

Living Bear, Plenty Horses's father, was noticeably absent. That was surprising because U.S. Deputy Marshal George Bartlett had left Sioux Falls a week earlier with orders to go to Pine Ridge, serve Living Bear a subpoena, and escort him back to Sioux Falls. A telegram was sent to Pine Ridge asking whether Living Bear was en route to Sioux Falls. Philip Wells replied that Living Bear was in an Indian village twenty miles away from the agency and no one had seen Bartlett.[6]

Sterling opened the case for the prosecution. He informed the jurors that the state would prove beyond a reasonable doubt that Plenty Horses had coldbloodedly and without cause murdered Casey. He promised to provide evidence that Plenty Horses had never joined the Ghost Dance movement and had no direct involvement in the battle at Wounded Knee.[7] In short, Sterling's opening remarks started the second trial down the same path the first trial had taken.

The prosecution's first witness was Rock Road, one of Casey's Cheyenne scouts. William Rowland, a half-blood Cheyenne and sergeant in Casey's detachment, interpreted. Rock Road testified that early on the morning of January 7, he, White Moon, and Casey had started for No Water's village. About four miles from the hostile encampment, which Rock Road erroneously identified as Red Cloud's camp, they came upon a party of Indians. Broken Arm and Plenty Horses, both of whom could speak English, broke off from the group and rode up to greet Casey and his scouts. Casey shook hands with them. As they were talking, Bear That Lays Down came riding down the White Clay Creek road from the direction of the hostile encampment. At Casey's request, Broken Arm asked Bear That Lays Down to take a message to Red Cloud. While they waited for a response, Casey directed Rock Road to return to the soldiers' camp on the west bank of White River.[8]

George Nock cross-examined Rock Road, getting him to admit that he did not remember whether at the last trial he had testified that he was afraid to go into Red Cloud's camp. Rock Road replied that if he had testified to that effect, it was not true. He would not have been afraid to go with Casey. He was armed and Casey had forewarned him there might be trouble. Upon cross-examination by Sterling, Rock Road stated that he did not like Plenty Horses because he had killed Casey. With that, court was adjourned until two o'clock.[9]

When court resumed that afternoon, the audience was as large as ever, including the usual sprinkling of well-dressed women escorted to front seats by the obliging deputy marshals. White Moon was the next witness, and again William Rowland interpreted. The first part of White Moon's testimony was almost identical to Rock Road's, but his testimony was particularly important because he was one of five people sitting on their horses close by Casey when the officer was killed.

In cross-examination the defense tried to break down White Moon's testimony. "Upon returning to the soldier camp, did you tell [Americus] Thompson that you did not know who shot Casey as the man who shot him was painted?"

"No. I did not."

"Did you tell Thompson, or say in his presence, that you fired two shots at the man who killed Casey?"

"I did not."

"Did you say in his presence that you regretted not killing the party who shot Casey?"

"I think not."

"Do you know a man by the name of William Craven?"

"I do not."[10]

Attorneys make mistakes and this was one. White Moon almost certainly knew Craven, at least by sight. Both of them were with the soldiers bivouacked at Camp Leavenworth on the west bank of White River. However, no one in the camp would have called the civilian scout "William Craven." He was known simply as "Gus" to both whites and Indians. At Camp Leavenworth it is likely that only officers were referred to by their surnames.

At three-thirty that afternoon, Dr. B. L. Ten Eyck was called to the witness stand. Ten Eyck testified as to the wound that caused Casey's death. Court was then adjourned until the next morning, May 26.[11]

That evening Sterling and his prosecution team plotted their courtroom strategy for Tuesday. They intended to put Captain Frank D. Baldwin of the

Fifth Infantry on the stand. He was General Miles's aide-de-camp during the Indian unrest of 1890–91. But after the prosecuting attorneys privately interviewed Baldwin, they decided not to have him testify.[12]

Court resumed on Tuesday, May 26, at exactly nine o'clock. The prosecution's first witness was Broken Arm, an elderly Oglala with streaks of gray in his long black hair. He was a former member of the Indian police at Pine Ridge. Broken Arm was present when Casey was killed. He related that while the six men sat on their horses, Peter Richard and Casey brought the heads of their horses close together and talked. When asked about the positions of the six men, he requested paper and pencil. He drew these marks:

Each mark showed the relative positions of the six men. The top two marks represented Broken Arm and White Moon. The set of horizontal marks were for Peter Richard and Bear That Lays Down. The third set was for Plenty Horses and Casey.

Broken Arm related that as Richard and Casey talked, Plenty Horses backed up his horse so that he was directly behind Casey. Lifting his rifle until of the end of the barrel was not three feet away from the back of Casey's head, Plenty Horses fired. Broken Arm saw the soldier fall from his horse and watched as Plenty Horses rode quickly toward No Water's village.[13] Broken Arm related that after the shooting he went to the body, took from it a pistol, turned the body on its back, and returned to No Water's camp.

A defense attorney cross-examined Broken Arm, asking questions designed to show that at the time of Casey's death and in the preceding days, Broken Arm had drawn rations from the War Department. That line of questioning was not productive because Broken Arm knew only that he got rations; he did not know who issued him a ration ticket. In his cross-examination, the defense attorney tilled more fertile ground by asking Broken Arm why the chiefs told Casey to return to the soldiers' encampment. Broken Arm said that Red Cloud advised the lieutenant not to come into No Water's village because the young Indians were excited and there might be danger.[14]

At eleven-fifteen that morning Bear That Lays Down, the messenger dispatched to No Water's village, took the stand. He said he was not a ghost dancer and was not in sympathy with the hostiles but was in their camp because he couldn't safely get away. He also stated that his wife and Plenty Horses's mother were sisters, making him Plenty Horses's uncle. Bear That Lays Down related that he rode to No Water's camp and delivered Casey's message and that Peter Richard accompanied him when he rode back with Red Cloud's reply. Upon cross-examination, the defense strengthened its case by asking Bear That Lays Down if he was painted at the time.

"Yes."

"Why?"

"Because every day I expected to die." Court was adjourned until one-thirty.[15]

Peter Richard was the first witness that afternoon. He was the man who brought the message from Red Cloud to Casey. Richard stated, "I told Casey that Red Cloud said he [Casey] had better go back. A lot of the young Indians at the camp are crazy." Richard also related his recollection of Plenty Horses shooting Casey.[16]

Thomas Flood, the official interpreter at Pine Ridge, was the prosecution's final witness. Flood testified that Plenty Horses spoke English fluently. In its cross-examination, the defense established that whereas Plenty Horses could speak English, with but few exceptions he spoke the Sioux language. At that, the prosecution rested its case.[17]

David Powers opened the case for the defense. He announced that the defense would make no effort to disprove Casey came to his death at the hands of the defendant, Plenty Horses. Instead, the defense would present evidence showing that in Plenty Horses's mind he was justified in killing Casey. "Plenty Horses is a savage," Powers told the court. "If he went before his God this very hour, he would go without a twinge of guilt and without a thought of having done a wrong."[18] Powers told the jurors that the defense had evidence to show that two years before, Sioux men, women, and children were starving because of the government's failure to keep its treaties and furnish proper supplies: "We shall show that the Indians continued in a starving condition until hostilities broke out.... They committed no outrages until they heard soldiers were coming to exterminate them, which they took as a declaration of war. Even then the Indians made no move until five or six Indians were shot down by whites in cold blood, one of them a cousin of the defendant."[19]

Powers did not elaborate on his assertion that "five or six Indians were shot down by whites in cold blood." Nor did he give any details about the killing of Plenty Horses's cousin, presumably referring to White Horse, who was killed during the foiled raid on the Daly-Torkelson Ranch. For its part, the prosecution wisely did not ask the defense to elaborate on its claim that five or six Indians had been shot down by whites in cold blood or to provide evidence that one of them was Plenty Horses's cousin. After all, the prosecution had nothing to gain by exploring those issues.

"We will show you," Powers told the jury on Tuesday afternoon, May 26, "that the day after the battle at Wounded Knee, Plenty Horses was at the Mission fight, riding in the front ranks with a battle axe." Powers also claimed that while Plenty Horses and Casey were riding together, Casey dropped a remark from which the prisoner inferred that the Indian camp was to be attacked and its members killed. "Place the responsibility of Casey's blood where it belongs; and not upon this deluded child of the forest, but upon the damnable system of robbery and treaty violations that brought it about."[20]

The first witness for the defense was American Horse, the dignified Oglala chief known around Lakota campfires for his eloquence. American Horse approached the witness stand with a dark scowl on his face and a red fan in his hand. Power's first question to him was, "What was the condition of the Sioux before the trouble arose?" Sterling vigorously objected, arguing that the question was too broad. The court agreed, reasoning that if such a vast field of inquiry was pursued, it would open up the whole range of dealings between the whites and Indians since the time of Columbus. Powers then limited his questions to the effect of the Messiah craze on the Sioux. American Horse's testimony wrapped up on Tuesday at four-thirty. Court was adjourned for the day.[21]

When court convened Wednesday morning, May 27, the defense team put Robert Pugh on the witness stand. He was an old-timer at Pine Ridge, his first wife being Emily Janis, a mixed-blood and something of a firebrand. Now, in 1891, Pugh was married to another Oglala woman. The couple had several children of their own and were also rearing several adopted Indian children. In the early days of McGillycuddy's tenure at Pine Ridge, Pugh served as the head teacher at a day school. Under Indian agent Hugh Gallagher, he was the issue clerk, but not long after Daniel Royer arrived, Pugh was demoted to warehouse clerk.

When put on the witness stand, Pugh testified that on January 15, 1891, the War Department took responsibility for issuing rations and issued them to all Indians, both "hostile" and "friendly." Before that the hostiles had not received rations since sometime in November. Pugh confirmed that Plenty Horses was a member of Two Strike's band, thereby including him in the group of Indians designated as hostiles. Having observed the Ghost Dance, Pugh described it in detail. He said that ghost dancers believed that those who didn't participate would be crushed and those who took part would eventually inherit the earth.

Sterling cross-examined Pugh. In response to the prosecuting attorney's questions, Pugh acknowledged that he did not know whether Plenty Horses engaged in the Ghost Dance. He also related under cross-examination that the Indians who went into the badlands killed cattle belonging to whites and friendly Indians.[22]

The defense's next witness was Captain Baldwin, a member of General Miles's staff. He did not come to testify for the prosecution. Rather, Miles had sent him to Sioux Falls to support the defense's claim that a state of war existed at the time Plenty Horses killed Casey. As soon as Baldwin was sworn in as a witness, Powers asked, "Captain Baldwin, how many dead Indians did you see [at Wounded Knee]?"

Sterling jumped to his feet to object: "There is nothing to show that the Indians who fought at Wounded Knee had anything to do with or were known by this defendant. They belonged to different tribes." Judge Shiras overruled Sterling's objection.

"Over a hundred," Baldwin replied.

Powers continued: "Did you see any dead soldiers?"

"No."

"How many soldiers were killed?"

"There were forty-nine."

"What garb were the dead Indians dressed in?" Powers asked.

"They all had on their war or ghost shirts."

"Would you consider the affair at Wounded Knee a battle?"

Sterling again objected to the question because it called for speculation. The objection was sustained.

"How was the army fixed for guns and ammunition?" Powers asked.

"They possessed the equipment necessary to conduct a war."

"When did the [hostile] Indians come in [to the agency]?"

"January 15. There were four thousand of them in all."

"What did they do?"

"They surrendered as prisoners of war."

"Was Plenty Horses one of the prisoners of war?"

Again, Sterling jumped to his feet to object to the question. Powers countered, "We propose to show that this Indian in the prisoner's box was arrested as a prisoner of war and that General Miles refused pointblank to surrender him to the civil authorities except under certain conditions."

"Conditions, sir," Judge Edgerton asked with a frown on his face. "What conditions? The prisoner was arrested by the order of this Court!"

"I have seen," Powers replied, "the official correspondence that passed between General Miles, the Secretary of War, and the Secretary of the Interior. In that correspondence General Miles positively refused to surrender Plenty Horses unless the Interior Department agreed to exercise its power to secure the conviction of the murderers of Few Tails."[23]

"Conditions, sir!" shrieked Edgerton again as he pounded his fist on his desk. "I want you to understand that the defendant was arrested upon my order. This Court has not been put under any conditions by General Miles."

"But . . ."

"The Court has made no conditions with General Miles," Edgerton interrupted, "and he is in no position to make them with this Court."

"But your Honor . . ."

"The Court," Edgerton roared, "will not discuss this matter further."

Baldwin continued his testimony. He stated that Casey's duties on January 7 were merely to keep the commanding officer posted as to the movements of the enemy."[24]

"He was a spy, was he not?" Powers asked.

"There is no such thing as a spy in the army. We call it reconnoitering."

"Was he overstepping his authority as a scout when he asked for a council with the chiefs?"

"Yes."[25]

The prosecution waived its right to cross-examine, and Baldwin stepped down from the witness stand.

William McGaa, a resident of Pine Ridge and an interpreter, took the stand. He described the battle at the gates of Drexel Mission, saying that he left the fight at the time the soldiers retreated. He did not know whether the Indians were shooting, but he knew bullets were coming from their direction.[26]

He Dog was the next witness. He was in No Water's camp with Red Cloud and Two Strike. He related that Two Strike's band, of which Plenty Horses was a member, participated in the skirmish near Drexel Mission. He Dog also described the fortifications at No Water's camp, saying the defenses were put up to protect the Indians from the soldiers.[27]

"Do you remember the day Casey was killed?" attorney Powers asked.

"Yes."

"On the day before the killing were there any wounded Indians in your camp?"

"Yes, they came in night and day by twos and threes. Among them were many women and children." The galley of spectators gasped audibly.

The defense rested.[28]

The prosecution recalled Broken Arm to ask him about the fortifications around No Water's camp. He reported that the village was well fortified. The statement did not help the prosecution's case.

E. P. White, the stenographer from Plenty Horses's first trial, testified next. He produced his notes of Rock Road's testimony during the first trial. In that trial Rock Road said he was afraid to go to the hostile camp, which was inconsistent with his testimony at this retrial. White's notes also revealed that White Moon's testimony was not always consistent from the first trial to the second.[29]

The stenographer was followed on the witness stand by Gus Craven. He was living with his mixed-blood wife, Jessie, and their children at the confluence of Indian Creek and the Cheyenne River when the Messiah craze erupted. Colonel Eugene Carr had recruited him as a scout. It was Craven who found Clown lying near death behind his tent at Camp Leavenworth on the morning of January 18, 1891.

By putting Craven on the stand, the prosecution had scored a success in that his testimony markedly diminished the veracity of White Moon's testimony. After all, how could White Moon not know who killed Casey yet claim he shot twice at Casey's murderer. The prosecution then reviewed written records showing that the testimony White Moon gave at the second trial was inconsistent with his testimony at the first trial.[30]

William Thompson, better known as Americus, was the next person on the stand. Like Craven, Thompson was a local settler recruited by Carr as a guide during the Messiah craze. Thompson testified that he was present when White Moon told Craven about Casey being killed and that he had heard the story pretty much as Craven had related it in his testimony.[31]

The defense team's next witness was Woman Dress, a government scout. Woman Dress related that he saw the bodies of Big Foot's band at Wounded Knee and he knew Plenty Horses was a member of Two Strike's band.[32]

Red Shirt, a good-looking Indian with a high forehead, bright eyes, and a fine physique, was the last witness of the day. Red Shirt had served as a government scout during the Messiah craze. He related that almost the entire Brulé tribe was at No Water's camp on the day Casey was killed. With that, court was adjourned for the day.[33]

Court was scheduled to resume at nine o'clock the next morning, May 28, but it did not. Living Bear was to be the defense's next witness, but he had not arrived from Pine Ridge. No one could explain his absence. U.S. Deputy Marshal George Bartlett had left for Pine Ridge on Monday, May 18, taking the train to Sioux City and, supposedly, on to Rushville and from there traveling by horse and buggy to Pine Ridge. He was to serve Living Bear with a subpoena and bring him back to Sioux Falls. When neither Living Bear nor Bartlett appeared in court, an inquiry was launched. A reliable source claimed that Bartlett was seen in Sioux City the previous day, May 27.[34]

While spectators jostled for a place to sit in the crowded courtroom on the morning of May 29, White Moon went shopping for a knife. At noon, he returned to the Merchants Hotel and went to the interpreter's unoccupied room. Shortly after entering the room, White Moon opened the two-and-one-half-inch blade of his newly bought pocket knife and thrust it clear to the hilt into the base of his neck. Bleeding freely, he fell onto a bed. When White Moon was found, Dr. C. H. Files was called. The doctor removed the knife and put pressure on the wound until the blood coagulated, foiling the attempted suicide.[35]

Why did White Moon attempt to kill himself? He might have attempted suicide because it had been revealed in court that the story he told to Gus Craven about Casey's killing was inconsistent with his courtroom testimony and that inconsistency might be grounds for acquitting Plenty Horses. It is also plausible that White Moon attempted suicide because the mere sight of Plenty Horses alive and well made the Cheyenne scout feel that he had fallen short of the Indians' honor code by failing to immediately kill Plenty Horses back on that fateful day of January 7.[36]

While White Moon was lying on a hotel bed bleeding profusely, Plenty Horses's trial continued. The defense offered notes from General Miles's field reports that provided four pieces of crucial evidence:

- Miles stated that Casey was reconnoitering to discern the force at No Water's camp.
- He regarded Plenty Horses to be a prisoner of war by forbidding delivery of the defendant to the civil authorities until a promise to indict Few Tails's killers was forthcoming.

- The general recognized Plenty Horses as a prisoner of war by directing him to be fed by the War Department.
- Miles noted that when Sydney Coleman arrested Plenty Horses, he acted without papers of any kind or other authority.

With that, Judge Edgerton gaveled the court into recess, saying it would reconvene at one-thirty.[37]

When court reconvened that afternoon, the room was filled to capacity and beyond. Those who could not gain access peered through the windows. When Judge Shiras entered the courtroom, all respectfully rose. Something about the judge's countenance so silenced the audience that a falling pin would have created a disturbance.

In a clear, resolute, and authoritative voice, Shiras announced, "There is no need of going further with this case. What I shall say is the opinion of this Court, but not of my colleague [Judge Edgerton]. It is said upon my own responsibility." The judge explained that the guilt or innocence of the accused, Plenty Horses, turned upon the question as to whether a state of war existed at the time of Casey's death. "In the opinion of the Court, it has been shown beyond a doubt that such a state of war did exist. . . . If [it did] not, it would be hard to justify the killing of the Indians at Wounded Knee. . . . Had Lt. Casey shot Plenty Horses, the officer would not have been arraigned on the charge of murder." While not specifically stating it, Shiras's implication was clear. If Casey would not have been indicted for killing Plenty Horses, Plenty Horses should not have been indicted for killing Casey. "Killing Casey was a cruel act, but it was an act of war; and it therefore is the duty of the court to order a verdict of not guilty."[38]

The audience cheered. Applause erupted. Disbelief could be read on Sterling's face. There was only person in the courtroom absent of any emotion—Plenty Horses. He stood awkwardly and expressionlessly as young women surrounded him and put their arms on his shoulder. It took Judge Edgerton and Marshal Cyrus Fry several minutes to establish order.[39]

Defense attorney Powers led the shy young Indian back to the hotel lobby, where he spent several hours signing autographs for young women and other well-wishers A number of women each paid Plenty Horses a dollar for his signature, which they intended to preserve as mementoes. Several women brought him flowers.[40]

A reporter later asked S. N. Palmer, one of the jurors, what the outcome would have been had the case gone to the jurors. Palmer replied that the jury

Participants in Plenty Horses's second trial. Front row, left to right: Tom Flood, Living Bear, Plenty Horses, Bear That Lays Down; second row, left to right, sitting: Pete Richard, Broken Arm, Jack Red Cloud, He Dog, Philip Wells; standing: W. B. Sterling, J. G. Ballance, William Rowland, White Moon, F. C. Fry, Chris Matthiessen, Rock Road, William Thompson, George P. Nock, D. E. Powers. (South Dakota State Historical Society.)

would not have been out over fifteen minutes and the verdict would have been manslaughter.[41]

The next day Plenty Horses and the other Indians from Pine Ridge boarded the afternoon train bound for Sioux City and then west to Pine Ridge. David Powers was there to see Plenty Horses off. As the train departed, a reporter asked Powers for his thoughts as to Plenty Horses's motive for killing Casey. "If I could, I would. [However], he has told me that since his cousin's death [that of White Horse, the young Indian killed by cowboys at the Daly-Torkelson Ranch on December 11, 1890[42]] his heart has been bad." Powers told the reporter that Plenty Horses would not live long because he had consumption.[43] (Consumption was the name given at the time for a condition now known as pulmonary tuberculosis.)

Postscript: George Nock sent a letter to Charles Penney, the acting Indian agent at Pine Ridge, on June 6, 1891, informing him that a "party in Chicago" would like to have Plenty Horses travel in an exhibition. Penney replied that permission could be granted only by the commissioner of Indian affairs and the commanding general of Military Division of the Missouri.[44] Either permission was never sought or it was not granted. Perhaps Plenty Horses was not interested. However, he was with Buffalo Bill's Wild West Show at the World's Fair in Chicago. He did not die of consumption as Powers predicted. In 1910 Plenty Horses was a farmer on the Pine Ridge Reservation, living with his second wife, Susie, and several stepchildren.[45] He died in 1933.

❊ 9 ❊

FRONTIER JUSTICE

In 1891 the nascent state of South Dakota was unified in name only. The south-flowing Missouri River divided the state into two nearly equal-size but distinctly different parts, East River and West River. The differences between East River South Dakota and West River South Dakota were (and still are) many.

One hundred million years ago, a large inland sea—the Cretaceous Sea—covered all of present-day South Dakota. Roughly sixty million years ago, the land in the area now known as the Black Hills and farther west began a gradual uplift—the Laramide orogeny. The climate got progressively drier. The inland sea gradually became shallow and marshy. In time, roughly thirty million years ago, land emerged. The land was composed of sediment laid down on the bottom of the inland sea. The base layer was shale—Pierre shale. On top of the shale was a thick layer of claylike soil, locally known as gumbo. The best and in many places the only use of gumbo is for growing grass.

Thirty thousand years ago (the Wisconsin Ice Age), an ice sheet one hundred to two hundred feet thick reshaped East River. The glacier slowly slid south, leveling the land as it went. Roughly fifteen thousand years ago, the North American climate began to warm. As the temperature rose, the glacial meltwater formed the Missouri River. The ice sheet slowly retreated north, leaving behind several feet of rich, plant-loving table-flat soil.

The different East River–West River topographies created distinctly different weather. On average, East River is blessed with twenty-three inches of rain during the growing season. The rain comes reliably. Even in a "dry" year, the rich soil east of the Missouri River sees sufficient rainfall for crops. While the East River climate could not be characterized as moist, it is corn-loving humid.

In contrast, West River is dry country. The average yearly rainfall is fifteen inches, but the amount varies considerably from year to year. Occasionally it rains less than seven inches per year. The rainfall also varies widely from place to place, with no predictable pattern. Some summers thunderstorms dump four or more inches of rain on a few square miles in a matter of minutes, creating flash floods that carve deep gullies and dry-wash creeks into the landscape. Other summers, it seldom rains. The grass withers and goes dormant, the first step to dying. When several dry years follow in succession, as often happens, West River becomes arid.

In the early 1800s, men of science and learning ventured west. Among other things, they drew maps that were fairly complete up to the 100th meridian. Beyond that, only major topographic features, like the courses of rivers and mountain ranges, were recorded. The explorers found the land west of the 100th meridian, which included all of West River, so arid that they penciled it in on their maps as "The Great American Desert." Edwin Jones, the geographer for Major Stephen Long's exploratory expedition in 1832, reported the land west of the 100th meridian is "almost wholly unfit for cultivation and uninhabitable by people depending upon agriculture for their subsistence. It will prove an insuperable obstacle to settling the country."[1]

Just as the geology determined the weather, the weather selected the people. West River was so arid and the gumbo so unproductive that the government did not hesitate in 1868 to allocate all of it to the Lakota Sioux.[2] The too-thick-to-drink and too-thin-to-plow Missouri River provided a buffer between the Lakota who inhabited West River country and whites who settled East River.

East River's fecund topsoil spooned the Great Dakota Boom of 1878–79. Thousands of homesteaders arrived to sink their plows, their aspirations, and their hopes into the land. With few exceptions the homesteaders were northern European immigrants. Scandinavians were drawn to the northeast corner of the East River country, German-Russians homesteaded in the northwest part, and Czechs settled in the southwest corner of East River. The immigrants were large-framed stout people—men who could walk all day holding horse-drawn plows between their strong arms and women who could effortlessly carry a five-gallon milk pail in each hand from the milking shed to the house. The

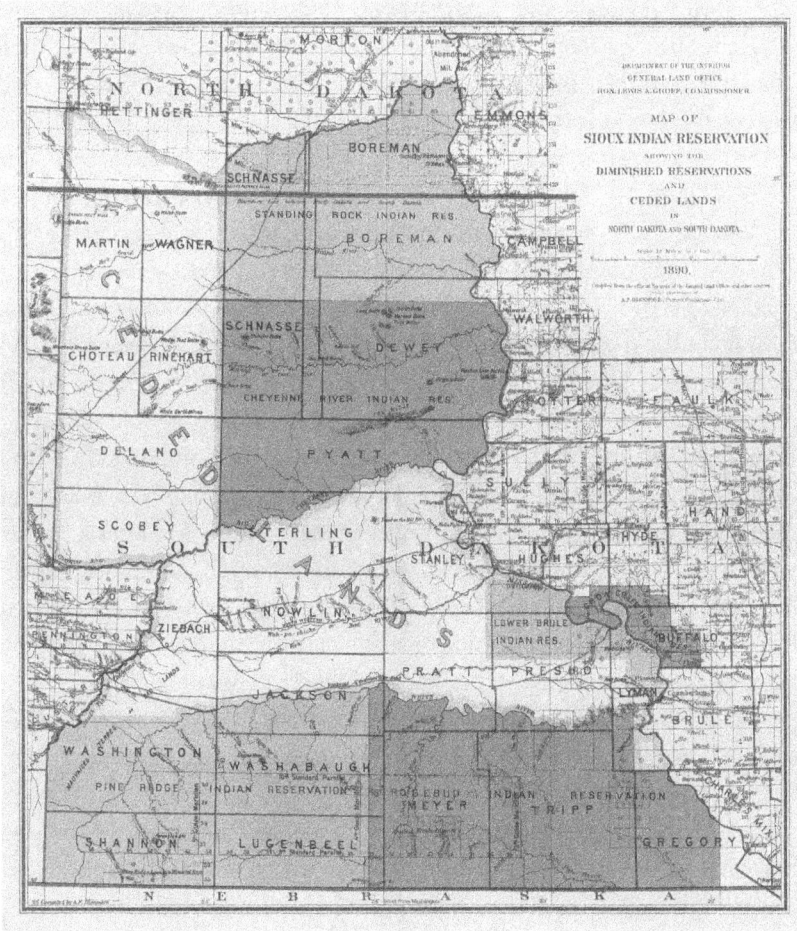

Sioux land, showing the diminished reservations and ceded lands. (South Dakota State Historical Society.)

northern Europeans brought with them community-binding religion and an appreciation for the uplifting benefits of education. Churches and rural schoolhouses—the seeds of social order and conformity—dotted East River's horizontal landscape.

The weather and soil of the West River country similarly selected its people and they were of a different ilk. The first white men to live west of the Missouri River were fur traders, many of whom cohabited with Indian women. These men were locally and historically known as "squawmen." When the government established the Great Sioux Reservation in 1868, officials enrolled everyone eligible to draw rations as full-blood Lakota. They included the Caucasian squawmen and their mixed-blood children, forever blurring the distinction between full-blood and mixed-blood Lakota.

The next white men who settled West River looked at the rear ends of herds of Texas longhorns for a month and choked down a lot of trail dust before they arrived. They were a wiry lot, most standing about five feet, eight inches and weighing about 160 pounds. They could do anything and everything that could be done from the back of a horse and not much else if they could help it. Many of them were runaways who left home in their early teens and put distance between themselves and what they were running from by hiring out to drive Texas longhorns, often called mosshorns, north to be sold as beef for reservation-confined Indians. Other drovers were ex-Confederate soldiers whose homes and families had been destroyed by the Civil War. A few had ridden with William Quantrill's guerrillas. If they went back to Missouri, they risked having their hides nailed to a barn door. Many cowboys were known only by descriptive nicknames—Slim, Tex, or perhaps Dusty—which implied they were running from something or someone, often the law. Those who gave their full names were the most suspicious. Likely they were using aliases. If a too-nosy acquaintance asked a prying question, a drover punctuated his fierce independence with a curled-lip reply: "Mind yur own business, Mister, if ya know what's good for ya."

After a trip or two up the Great Western Cattle Trail, many drovers decided they had had enough adventure and they stayed up north. The industrious ones rounded up enough mavericks on the open range to get in the cattle business, but most continued being forty-dollar-a-month cowboys working for one of the large cattle syndicates owned by titled men from Europe. A few of the ex-drovers stole cattle and horses or, like Cornelius Donahue (alias Lame Johnny), robbed stagecoaches.[3]

Another immigration of whites arrived in West River in 1876. They sneaked into the Black Hills when it still belonged to the Sioux. Like moths drawn to a flame, they were drawn by the siren's call of gold. Simply being in West River made every one of them a lawbreaker and they knew it. To them, defying the government and trespassing onto Lakota land was a badge of honor. They were the sharp tip of the spear of Manifest Destiny and proud of it. A '76er's penultimate distinction was claiming he had to fight off Indians to get to the Black Hills. That honor was bested only by the pioneers, as they called themselves, who could boast that they had to kill an Indian or two to get to Deadwood, the newest Eldorado.

After Herbert Welsh, secretary of the Indian Rights Association, spent an evening in Pierre socializing with some of the town's citizens, he pretty much said all that needed to be said about the mind-set of West River folk: "The air which western men affect toward the eastern sentimentalism is rather one of condescension due, I suspect, to the assumption of superior knowledge. . . . The residents of frontier towns often exhibit a curious ignorance or affect ignorance of facts and conditions existing on a neighboring reservation."[4]

The differences between East River and West River explain why weeks went by and no one was arrested for the murder of Few Tails, prompting General Nelson Miles to refuse to release Plenty Horses to civilian authorities until they indicted Few Tails's killers for murder.[5] Those behind-the-scenes negotiations took several months to complete. While they were transpiring, the public did not see any effort being made to indict the men who had killed Few Tails. By mid-May 1891, four months had passed since William Sterling had promised charges would be brought against the white men who murdered Few Tails, but still no one had been arrested. Wanting justice, Herbert Welsh sent a scathing letter to New York City's *Evening World*: "Has any attempt been made on the part of the local authorities to bring these white murderers to justice? After weeks of correspondence on the subject, not the slightest. The Indian Office in Washington has offered to provide the local authorities with the witnesses in the case, and yet they do not stir. The Attorney General of the United States, to whom I wrote begging that the Federal Government would aid in the matter, has instructed the District Attorney of South Dakota to assist the local authorities, but nothing is done."[6] The Indian Rights Association purchased five hundred copies of the letter describing the "cold-blooded murder" and sent it to newspapers across the country.[7]

Welsh's public criticism of Meade County authorities and the political pressure exerted by the U.S. attorney for South Dakota finally forced Meade County state's attorney Alex McCall to convene a grand jury, which met on May 14. Henry A. Carpenter was the jury foreman. Witnesses were Alfred Turton, Benjamin M. Oliver, Sheridan Quinn, Oscar Kausche, Frank Marshall, David Quinn, One Feather, Clown, Red Owl, Otter Robe, and Philip Wells. Clown was the most compelling witness. Based largely on her testimony, the grand jury indicted Peter Culbertson, Nelson Culbertson, Andrew Culbertson, Alva Marvin, and Julius "James" Juelfs for the murder of Few Tails.[8]

That very day, Meade County sheriff Valentine M. Beaver was furnished warrants for the arrest of the indicted men. On Tuesday, May 19, Sheriff Beaver made the thirty-mile trip from Sturgis to the Culbertsons' ranch to inform the men that they had been indicted for the murder of Few Tails. He ordered them to remand themselves to the Meade County Jail. The alleged murderers made no resistance, expressing their belief they would have no trouble justifying the killing of Few Tails.[9] The next day four of the five indicted men appeared in court and pleaded not guilty. Andrew Culbertson was the missing man. At the time the indictments were served, he was away on a horse roundup and a messenger was dispatched for him.[10]

Andrew Culbertson turned himself in on May 25. He was served with a warrant and jailed. Juelfs, a well-to-do cattleman and a respected resident of Meade County, was allowed to post bail and return to his ranch. The trial was scheduled for June 23.[11]

While the three Culbertson brothers and Alva Marvin languished in jail, Plenty Horses's second trial reached its conclusion—not guilty. Acquitting an Indian who had killed a white man chaffed at the sensibilities of West River folk. C. C. Moody, editor of the *Sturgis Weekly Record*, expressed their sentiments: "I have lived out West too long to advocate the conviction of whites for killing an Indian when the court has condoned an Indian's murder of a white man."[12] William Sterling, the lead attorney in the government's prosecution of Plenty Horses, also believed that Plenty Horses's acquittal would make it unlikely that a Meade County jury would find the killers of Few Tails guilty of murder.[13] The *Omaha Daily Bee* countered that sentiment: "The people of South Dakota have an excellent opportunity to prove to the eastern philanthropists that western people are not the enemies of the peaceable Indian they have been represented to be.... It will do South Dakota's reputation great harm to acquit [the culprits] if the evidence shows them guilty."[14]

The trial got under way on Monday, June 22. Defense attorneys were Sturgis lawyers Charles Polk, Thomas E. Harvey, Ralph Kirk, and Wesley Stuart, assisted by W. H. Parker of Deadwood. The prosecution team was headed by Alex McCall, state's attorney for Meade County. He was assisted by U.S. District Attorney William Sterling and Robert Dollard, the attorney general for South Dakota. Judge Charles Thomas presided. A venire of twenty-four Meade County men sat in the courtroom, waiting to learn which of them would be selected as jurors. Twelve potential jurors were interviewed that day and eleven were dismissed for stated bias against Indians or presumed bias. The judge ordered

Sheriff Beaver to have another venire of twenty-three potential jurors in the courtroom at ten o'clock the next morning. Court was adjourned for the day.

Thomas gaveled the court to session the next morning, June 23. People in the courtroom had barely taken their seats when Sterling announced that the state wished to submit a nolle prosequi with regard to the charges against James Juelfs. Thomas accepted the petition and the murder charge against Juelfs was dropped.[15] The defense attorneys were shocked and leery. They feared the prosecution had struck a deal with Juelfs to drop the charges against him in exchange for him turning state's evidence. While Juelfs had not agreed to testify against the indicted men, it nonetheless was a smart tactic for the prosecution because Juelfs was a well-to-do, influential citizen. It would be hard, if not impossible, to get a Meade County jury to convict him of murdering anyone, much less an Indian.

The rest of the day was devoted to impaneling a jury. One potential juror was asked if he held the opinion that there were no good Indians except dead ones. He replied, "That is about the size of it." Another potential juror stated that he did not believe that any Indian ever born was guilty of telling the truth. At the end of the day, Thomas issued a venire for thirty more potential jurors.[16]

On Wednesday, June 24, jury selection continued, and it was time-consuming. Each potential juror was put on the witness stand and swore voir dire, a pledge to tell the truth. He was questioned by both the prosecution and the defense. Forty-eight potential jurors were examined that day. As adjournment time approached, Thomas ordered the sheriff to secure a venire of fifteen more potential jurors.[17]

As the trial resumed on Thursday, June 25—its fourth day—a full jury still had not been impaneled. It was only after the defense team exhausted its quota of sixteen preemptory challenges and sixty-five potential jurors were examined that a jury was selected. All but two jurors were Meade County farmers or ranchers.[18]

Late in the morning of June 25, Sterling stated the prosecution's case, promising to provide the evidence needed to convict the four men of murder. Philip Wells was sworn in to interpret for the prosecution. George Carson was sworn in to provide a similar service for the defense. The court recessed for lunch.

When court reconvened at two o'clock that afternoon, Sterling gave notice that the prosecution had subpoenaed two more Indians from Pine Ridge and that U. S. Deputy Marshal Chris Mattheissen had been dispatched to find them and bring them to Sturgis. Sterling also made a correction to the official record. Previously filed court documents stated that only Few Tails and One Feather were at the scene on January 11 when Few Tails was killed. Sterling requested the court record be changed to reflect that five Indians were at the scene.

With that, the prosecution called its first witness: Few Tails's wife, Clown.[19] She took the stand before a packed courtroom, including a large number of Indians from Pine Ridge who came to see justice done.[20] Clown started her testimony by identifying Andrew Culbertson as one of the men who visited the Indians at their camp on the evening before the attack. She then related in riveting detail the attack, the killing of her husband, and her escape. Taking her testimony was slow because the questions put to her had to be translated from English into Lakota and her answers translated into English.[21] Clown was on the witness stand for four hours. It was late in the afternoon when she finished her testimony. Court then adjourned for the day.[22]

When court convened on Friday, June 26, the defense cross-examined Clown. Try as the defense attorney might, he could not shake Clown's testimony. The prosecution's next witness was Alfred Turton, a rancher from Lower Alkali Creek. He testified as to a conversation between himself and Abe "Squire" Jones. Turton said that Jones told him he had visited with the Culbertsons on the evening before the attack on Few Tails and heard them say that the Indians should be killed. However, the credibility of Turton's testimony became suspect when he was unable to look over the spectators in the courtroom and identify Squire Jones.[23]

The prosecution then called John Porter. Porter testified that he, too, was with the Culbertsons the night before the killing and listened to them plot how they would attack the Indians. Oscar Kausche, an area rancher, also testified. He recalled seeing Few Tails and One Feather and their wagons on the day of January 10, but he did not see any other Indians. Court was then adjourned until Monday morning.[24]

On Monday morning, June 29, the two Indians the prosecution expected to arrive from the reservation during the weekend were not in the courtroom. The prosecution's fallback position was to recall Clown. She reiterated much of the evidence given in her opening testimony, but also brought out several new facts damaging to the defendants. As she was about to step down from the stand, Sterling ask Clown to show the wounds inflicted on her that fateful morning of January 11. As she bared her chest and exposed the scars from the bullet wound, an audible gasp went up from the spectators in the courtroom.[25]

As a time-stalling maneuver while waiting for the arrival of their witnesses from the reservation, the prosecution recalled John Porter. His testimony did not bring any new information to light. At that, the prosecution rested its case, with the court's assurance that it could continue when the expected witnesses arrived.

C. C. Polk rose to state the defense's case. He told the jurors the defense would present evidence that conclusively proved that a band of a dozen or more Indians had attempted to steal the Culbertsons' and Juelfs's horses on the morning of January 11. When caught in the act, the Indians opened fire on the ranchers when they attempted to retrieve their animals. The indicted men returned the fire and that is how and why Few Tails was killed. It was, the defense contended, a matter of self-defense, plain and simple. Court recessed until 12:45 p.m.[26]

When court resumed that afternoon, the defense put three of the four indicted men on the witness stand to testify on their own behalf. In turn, August "Pete" Culbertson, Alva Marvin, and Nelson Culbertson took the stand, and each told the same story. Their story was that on the morning of January 11, they discovered a band of ten to fifteen Indians attempting to drive off thirty horses belonging to the Culbertson brothers and James Juelfs. The Culbertson brothers, James Juelfs, and Alva Marvin armed themselves and set out to retrieve their property. When they were within a hundred yards of the Indians, they demanded the horses. Instead of releasing the ranchers' animals, the Indians fired on them, wounding Pete Culbertson in the hand.[27]

The prosecution cross-examined each of the indicted witnesses, but each held firm to their concocted story. However, the prosecution got Andrew Culbertson to admit that he had been arrested in Bon Homme County for horse stealing in 1882 but was acquitted through a technicality.[28] If the jurors had heard the whole story, their hearts would have been hardened against Andrew Culbertson. The whole story was that Andrew Culbertson, Kid Wade, Ephraim Weatherwax, and Charles Fitch stole horses from H. Steel's ranch near Pickerel Lake. They trailed the horses south to the Tyndall area and tried to sell them. Suspicions were aroused. The men were arrested and put in the flimsy Bon Homme County Jail, from which they escaped. While on the run, Weatherwax thought it prudent to perfect his fast draw. In the process of learning to be a fast-draw gunman, Weatherwax pulled the trigger a little too soon and shot himself in the leg with his Colt .45, fracturing the tibia and fibula. His partner in crime, Charles Fitch, took Weatherwax to the hospital at Fort Niobrara, where the post surgeon amputated Weatherwax's leg below the knee. The other two on-the-lam criminals, Andrew Culbertson and Kid Wade, were soon thereafter recaptured in the Fort Niobrara area and brought back to Bon Homme County for trial.[29]

In succession, the defense put John Netland and James Juelfs on the witness stand. They were neighboring ranchers who joined the chase of One Feather and his family. Netland and Juelfs related the same story the three indicted men had told the jurors earlier that afternoon.[30] Juelfs delivered some of the most damaging testimony against the prosecution when he reported that the rifles used in the fight with Few Tails were issued to the settlers by Governor Mellette so they could protect themselves from marauding Indians and that Fort Meade soldiers had notified him that the Indians were on the warpath. While that evidence was circumstantial, it supported the defense's claim the indicted men were simply defending themselves and their property. With that, court adjourned for the day.[31]

On Tuesday morning, June 30, the defense continued its parade of witnesses. In succession, Frank Sands, Thomas Miller, Clarence Horton, Sherman Bumper, and Edward Steel testified.[32] Each gave testimony that was consistent with the indicted men's story. At noon, court recessed.[33]

When court reconvened at one-thirty, the defense put Squire Jones and then V. P. Shoun on the stand. Both had joined the chase when they heard the rifle shots reverberate over the frozen prairie. Adolph Rundquist, Joseph Timmons, Lucius B. Judson, and David Quinn also testified. They repeated the story about the Culbertsons catching Indians stealing their horses and having to shoot at them in self-defense. George M. Baldwin, a soldier detailed to carry mail between Fort Meade and Cheyenne Camp, took the stand. Baldwin testified that on January 11 he had left his mail route and followed a band of twelve or fifteen hostile Indians nearly a mile before they fired on him.[34]

The defense had subpoenaed Captain Frank Baldwin, the army officer who had testified at Plenty Horses's trial that war existed at the time the Indian killed Casey. The attorneys expected Baldwin would testify that a state of war existed at the time and place Few Tails was killed; but when Baldwin informed the defense lawyers that he would not so testify, they did not put him on the witness stand.[35] At four-thirty that afternoon, the last of the defense witnesses stepped down from the stand. Court was adjourned for the day.[36]

Court convened at nine o'clock sharp on Wednesday, July 1. It was the prosecution's opportunity for rebuttal. They called Clown to the witness stand for a third time. Her testimony brought out a few new facts damaging to the defense.[37] Joseph Timmons, Frank Bradford, and Valentine Schwab testified that they did not see any Indians other than the families of Few Tails and One Feather on the day of the killing. John McAbe and Joseph Wagner, two soldiers from Troop I of the Eighth Cavalry, also testified that they did not see any other Indians in the area at the time Few Tails was killed. Court recessed for noon.[38]

The train from Rushville arrived in Sturgis late that morning. Matthiessen; One Feather; his wife, Red Owl; and their daughter, Otter Robe, debarked. The prosecution's key witnesses had arrived. When court resumed at two o'clock that afternoon, the prosecution's first witness was George W. Ladd, the county surveyor. Ladd told of accompanying Sheriff V. M. Beaver to the site where Few Tails had been killed and of making a detailed map of the crime scene and immediate area, which was shared with the jurors. Beaver was then called to the witness stand. He told of his meticulous examination of the site where Few Tails was killed and the surrounding area. Beaver related that the tracks he examined showed that Few Tails and One Feather were the only Indians at the scene of the killing. Beaver also stated that Few Tails's body was still in the wagon box and that the Indian had been fatally shot just below the left eye. The sheriff concluded his testimony by saying that the evidence found at the scene showed that Few Tails had been killed without the slightest provocation.[39]

The prosecution put One Feather on the stand. His testimony was taken slowly because the attorney's questions had to be translated into Lakota and One Feather's answers translated into English. Nonetheless, One Feather's testimony was clear and straightforward, undoubtedly sending chills down the backs of the four indicted men. One Feather's version of how Few Tails was killed on the morning of January 11 collaborated Clown's account of the ambush. Following One Feather's riveting testimony, Red Owl was brought into the courtroom and put on the witness stand. She confirmed everything One Feather had just told the jury. Otter Robe was the next witness and she, too, testified that the two Indian families had been ambushed. Clement Davis, an assistant farmer from Pine Ridge, was the next witness. He vouched for the honesty of One Feather, Clown, and Red Owl. The state rested. The defense recalled Thomas Miller and James Juelfs and then it too rested.[40]

On Thursday, July 2, Sterling made a lengthy closing argument for the state. He was followed by Thomas E. Harvey, who made an impassioned closing argument for the defense. Court took recess until one-thirty. After the recess, Polk and Parker finished their closing arguments for the defense.[41]

Judge Thomas issued his instructions to the jury. In part, the instructions read:

(2nd)

I charge you that if the Indians who have testified on behalf of the prosecution . . . in conjunction with other Indians or without the assistance of other Indians, gathered or rounded up horses belonging to the defendants and James Juelfs, as witnesses on behalf of defendants testified they did with the intention of stealing them . . . the defendants had the right to and were authorized by law to retain possession of them; and if the defendants while in the act of taking them from the Indians, as has been testified to in this case, the Indians or either of them fired at the defendants or either of them while thus engaged, they had the right and were justified . . . in returning the fire of the Indians. And if any of the Indians were killed while engaged in shooting at the defendants . . . the killing was justified . . . [as] self-defense, and they are entitled to a verdict of acquittal at your hands.

(3rd)

As to the danger mentioned in the preceding instruction and the necessity of the shooting mentioned therein, the defendants under the law were themselves permitted to judge; nobody else could judge for them. . . . If you shall find the defendants did honestly believe and had fair reason to believe their lives were in imminent danger . . . they are not responsible for so doing unless such force . . . was so disproportionate to the requirements of the occasion as to show wantonness or a malicious purpose to injure the deceased.

And in judging of the necessity to use such force as is claimed was used by the defendants, you may take into consideration testimony as to the existence, if such is the fact shown by the evidence of an Indian war or an Indian outbreak at that time, And whether the defendants had been informed and honestly believed that such a state of war existed and that said Indians belonged to said hostile band or tribe of Indians.

The danger mentioned in the preceding instruction need not be real. It is sufficient if it was only apparent, and the defendants had reason to believe, and honestly believed it was real, and shot, as it is alleged they shot, under the honest belief that they could only avert such danger by shooting as they did.[42]

Thomas's instructions to the jurors gave several avenues for concluding that the defendants were not guilty. With the guidelines in hand, the jury went into deliberation at five o'clock. On the first ballot, eleven of the jurors voted that the defendants were not guilty. After a quick reconsideration of the evidence, a second ballot was taken. Again, eleven jurors voted that the defendants were not guilty. More discussion followed and a third ballot was taken. After convening for only two hours, the twelve Meade County residents returned with a verdict. Their verdict was not guilty.[43]

Like everyone else who attended the trial, C. C. Moody, editor of the *Sturgis Weekly Record*, knew beyond a shadow of a doubt that Few Tails had been murdered. However, he was a businessman. Like every other West River newspaperman, he sold papers by confirming and supporting the biases and prejudices of his readers. Not surprisingly, his summary of the trial was what his readers wanted to believe: "Thus ends one of the greatest farces that Meade County has ever experienced. Probably not one man in a thousand has thought for a moment that these men should even have been arrested—much less placed on trial. But the outside pressure has been such that nothing would do but to haul them up, keep them in jail for months, and finally bring them before a court of justice—for what? Simply for killing an Indian that with others was engaged in stealing horses."[44]

❧ 10 ❧

FOR WHAT, SIMPLY KILLING AN INDIAN?

Another killing with racial overtones—the fourth that year west of the Missouri River—happened on December 29, 1891. Exactly one year after the Wounded Knee Massacre, a white man beat and kicked an Indian to death.[1]

The white man was Devine Albert Whipple, better known as Jack. At the age of eleven, young Jack ran away from his home in Cattaraugus County, New York. He made his way via the Ohio and Mississippi Rivers to New Orleans and eventually Texas. At the age of eighteen he made it to Dakota Territory with a cattle drive. During the next six years, Whipple choked down the dust roiled up by three herds of cattle he helped trail from Texas, first to the Spotted Tail Agency in Nebraska and later to its new location, Rosebud. Following the discovery of gold in the Black Hills, Whipple stopped being a drover and took up freighting on the Sidney–Black Hills Trail. On June 10, 1881, he married Sally Kelly, a part-Indian woman and half sister of the prominent Brulé chief Hollow Horn Bear.[2] The Whipple family initially lived with the Brulé and drew rations at the Rosebud Agency. During this time Whipple had charge of the trail-gaunt cattle driven up from Texas as they fattened on the reservation's protein-rich grass.[3] In the fall of 1891, forty-two-year-old Jack Whipple, Sally, and their children moved to a small ranch near Stearns on the north bank of White River, putting them across the river from the Rosebud Reservation. The main headquarters for the ranch was a log cabin. It was said that prior to the Whipples taking possession, someone had died in the cabin under mysterious circumstances. Being superstitious, Sally told Jack that before she and the children would move into the cabin, he had to whitewash the inside walls. Even then, she occasionally had Jack go outside in the dark of night and shoot his pistol into the air to scare away evil spirits.[4] Whipple's personality and character were such that his white neighbors in the Stearns area regarded him as a "hard man."[5]

The alleged homicide took place in Whipple's cabin. The dead Indian went by the name of Lays On His Mother-In-Law,[6] which was not likely his birth name. Lakota youth, particularly males, were often renamed as they advanced toward manhood. The renaming usually described some event or characteristic. As for Lays On His Mother-In-Law, the name suggests its own explanation. It is a surprising explanation because Lakota custom forbade a married man to be alone with his mother-in-law.

Two days after Jack Whipple killed Lays On His Mother-In-Law, he sent a letter to George Wright, the Indian agent for Rosebud, informing the agent of the man's death:

White River, S. Dak.
Dec. 31, 1891
Mr. George Wright
U.S. Indian Agent
Dear Sir:
An Indian staying with me died in his bed last night, and was carried away by his friends this morning.
Respectfully,
Jack Whipple[7]

Whipple sent the letter because he knew word of the killing would spread across the reservation with wind-blown speed, and it was certain to be heard by Indian police, who would report what they heard to their boss, the Indian agent. Clearly, Whipple wanted to plant misinformation in the Indian agent's mind before others brought him a more incriminating story. In doing so Whipple was counting on the same bias against Indians that resulted in a white jury acquitting the Culbertsons and Marvin of the murder of Few Tails. Whipple was also counting on the "us against them" and the "civilized man against the pagan Indian" sentiment still alive on the frontier when he and other white settlers in the Stearns community circulated the story that "the Indian girded up his loins and went to a bungalow three miles from Whipple's cabin. There, he procured a beer bottle full of alcohol. This he poured into his system without any reduction, which so surprised his stomach that it refused to perform its regular functions. His heart knocked off work, and he was picked up dead the following morning."[8]

However, neither Whipple's letter to Wright nor the story he and his friends circulated about how Lays On His Mother-In-Law had died worked. They did not work because there was, and still is, a phenomenon on the reservations known as the "moccasin telegraph," the quick and mysterious spreading of news among people separated from each other by considerable distances. It was likely the moccasin telegraph that informed Wright that Lays On His Mother-In-Law had not "died in his bed last night." Rather, Whipple had killed him.

The Indian agent sent A. Judson Morris, the agency physician, to locate Lays On His Mother-In-Law's grave, exhume the coffin, and perform an autopsy on a man who had been buried for five days. Morris took with him four Indian police; Thomas Flood, the agency interpreter; and an unnamed agency farmer. They found Lays On His Mother-In-Law's grave on the south side of the White River, in the northwest corner of the reservation. The coffin was exhumed and the body removed.

Morris found an extensive bruise on the back of Lays On His Mother-In-Law's head, involving the entire occipital region. His neck was dislocated at the second vertebra. Prior to the man's death, his chest had been beaten or pounded on until the skin turned a bruised color. The region around his navel had a large purple spot or bruise as if made by the heel of a boot. The thumb on Lays On His Mother-In-Law's right hand had been bitten off or cut off at the second joint.[9]

The autopsy confirmed the rumor that Lays On His Mother-In-Law had been murdered. Investigating further, Wright learned there were witnesses to the killing. One of them was Attack Him, also known as Julio, a 21-year-old full-blood enrolled in the Brulé tribe and reputedly the murdered man's brother.[10]

On January 15, 1892, Wright had Attack Him brought into the agency for a deposition.

> State of South Dakota, County of Meyer, Rosebud Agency.
> Attack Him or Julio, a full blood Indian being duly sworn according to law deposes and says: That he belongs to the Rosebud Agency; that in December 1891 he worked for Jack Whipple, a White man with Indian wife, who lived near the mouth of Black Pipe creek on the north side

of White River; that on December 30, 1891, while at Whipple's house, Thomas Larvie, his wife, and a white man known to him as "Jim" came there in a wagon. Larvie left his wife there and accompanied by an Indian named "Grandmother" [the Indian the newspapers called Lays On His Mother-In-Law,] who also worked for Whipple, and Jack Whipple, who went on horseback, departed for a store [in Stearns] about 3 miles distant [upriver]; he, the deponent, remained at the house [Whipple's house]. About noon the four parties above named returned, all drunk. They stopped and unloaded packages from the wagon and all, except himself, went into Whipple's house. Soon after "Jim" came out to where he was, locked arms with him and took him towards the house. When near the door, "Jim" told the others to give the deponent whiskey. Whipple came toward him with a bottle. The deponent broke loose and ran away. "Jim" and "Grandmother" came after him, calling to him that unless he returned they would give him no liquor in [the] future. After some time the deponent returned and stepped [in] back of the house and soon all came out. Larvie and his wife, "Jim" and "Grandmother" getting into the wagon. Whipple said to "Grandmother" "you don't live down there," and pushed him off the wagon. Grandmother then grabbed hold of the deponent; That he, deponent, carried Grandmother into the house, laid him on a bed and covered him; and ran away and hid. Whipple followed them into the house and immediately caught hold of Grandmother and raised him from the bed and pounded the back of his neck against the wall, saying, "this man is trying [pretending] to be drunk;" then grabbed him about the abdomen with both hands and shook him; then struck him several times with his fists. Grandmother meanwhile lying on the bed and crying out, "Brother, leave me alone," during which time deponent endeavored to make Whipple desist. Deponent then ran outside, being frightened and looking several times saw Whipple throwing chairs over to where Grandmother laid, who was then stretched out and laying quiet. About that time a white man named "Curry" came up; deponent started to run away; Whipple calling to him to return. He saw that Whipple was angry and started back. When Whipple returned to the house, he again started to run away; Whipple again came out, calling to him and asking where he was going, saying he would kill him anyway. He [the deponent] replied that he was looking for a gun Whipple had lost. Deponent then went to the

stable, got a horse, and went to Thomas Larvie's, whom he told of the trouble and asked him to come and help him before Whipple killed Grandmother. Larvie said, "Let them have it out." Larvie and "Jim" soon afterward got horses and all went back; they went into the house and deponent stopped at the stable watching; he saw Whipple pulling and jerking his wife. Whipple saw deponent and called to him, to which the deponent replied he would come as soon as he stalled the horses. On the way to the house, he met Whipple with a revolver in his hand, who said when [the deponent] approached him, "You have no cause" and raised the revolver and snapped it at him [meaning that when Whipple pulled the trigger, there was no bullet in the chamber]. He then raised the revolver to strike him [the deponent]. Larvie came out and got in between them, and stopped Whipple. Deponent then told Whipple he was going to feed the horses, which he [Whipple] directed him to do and then return to the house. [The deponent] went to the stable [and] saddled a horse and saw the four men [who would have included Whipple] going toward Curry's house. Deponent then went into Whipple's house and saw Grandmother was still alive; he got his overcoat, went to the stable, got his horse, and went to the [indecipherable] creek. That the next morning, he went to Whipple's house and while there, Whipple came on horseback, his horse much ragged [meaning it had been ridden hard]; that Whipple told the deponent to go back and attend to his work; that the Indian "Grandmother" was dead. [Whipple] also told the deponent to tell "Broncho Bill," the dead man's brother, that he [could have] four of Whipple's horses. That on arrival at Whipple's house, he found the body; that Whipple's wife asked him to deny any knowing of the killing. Two days later Thomas Larvie came there and [told the deponent] he was a relative of Whipple's and asked him to deny it, as they had an agreement to tell one story which was that the Indian had died from the effects of alcohol and that a bottle had been found on his body in bed. Whipple's wife told the deponent Whipple had instructed her not to let him [the deponent] go away as he might make trouble.
Witnesses:
ATTACK HIM, his X
FRANK MULLER
GEO. E. BARTLETT
Sworn to and ascribed before me on this 15th day of January 1892.

J. GEO. WRIGHT
U.S. Indian Agent
I hereby certify that I interpreted the foregoing affidavit to Attack Him in the presence of the above named witnesses before which he acknowledged the same to be correct statement of facts.

I further certify that I am satisfied he fully understood the nature of the above affidavit and the contents thereof.
THOMAS FLOOD
Interpreter[11]

The deposition convinced Wright that Jack Whipple had murdered "Grandmother," also known as Lays On His Mother-In-Law. Yet two months went by and Whipple was not arrested. The Indians on the Pine Ridge and Rosebud Reservations became irate. Some resumed ghost dancing. Wright worried that the Indian unrest would ignite violence, but, legally speaking, his hands were tied. The murder had occurred off the reservation, where the federal government had no authority.

Knowing something had to be done to terminate the Indians' growing unrest, Wright conspired with U.S. District Attorney William Sterling and U.S. Marshal Cyrus Fry to have Whipple arrested.[12] Even though the three of them knew the murder had occurred outside the federal government's jurisdiction, a complaint against Whipple was sworn to by Sterling. A warrant for Whipple's arrest was issued by U.S. Commissioner F. R. Grant of Huron and placed in the hands of Fry.[13] U.S. Deputy Marshal George Bartlett was ordered to arrest Jack Whipple. He did so on March 10, 1892, two and one-half months after the murder, and transported Whipple to Deadwood, where he was jailed.[14]

Not knowing the hearing would not be held immediately, Wright arranged for key witnesses to be in Deadwood on March 11. Accordingly, Morris, the government physician who had done the autopsy on Lays On His Mother-In-Law; Tom Larvie and Yellow Eyes, half-bloods; and a full-blood Indian known as Jumbo were in Deadwood on March 11 for the hearing.[15] When it was announced the hearing would not be held until thirteen days later, they returned to Rosebud.

Whipple was arraigned before John Burns, U.S. commissioner of the District Court of Western South Dakota, on Friday, March 11, and given until Saturday morning to enter a plea. Whipple hired Henry Frawley, a Deadwood attorney, to defend him. With the approval of his attorney, Whipple pleaded not guilty, claiming that Lays On His Mother-In-Law had died from an overdose of whiskey. Whipple was released on his own recognizance pending a hearing set for March 25 or later.[16]

As the time approached for Burns to hear the case against Whipple, Fry wired Wright that it was not necessary to have witnesses go to Deadwood for the hearing.[17] After all, what was the point? Lays On His Mother-In-Law had been killed off the reservation; the federal government did not have jurisdiction.

Nonetheless, on March 28 Whipple was brought before Burns.[18] By then Burns had read Attack Him's deposition and Morris's autopsy report. The commissioner was confident that Whipple was guilty of murder, but because Lays On His Mother-In-Law did not die on the Rosebud Reservation, Burns knew he had no authority to indict Whipple on the charge of murder. Jackson County, which was attached to Pennington County for judicial purposes, had jurisdiction.[19] Burns invited Pennington County state's attorney Charles Brown to attend the preliminary hearing. Brown did not acknowledge the invitation and was not in the Deadwood courtroom when Whipple was brought before the U.S. commissioner.[20]

Burns sent an urgent telegram to Brown, offering to have Whipple delivered to Pennington County authorities for prosecution. Brown informed Burns that he was not sending anyone to Deadwood to take custody of Jack Whipple as he had no interest in pressing charges against the alleged murderer. "The killing occurred one hundred miles east of Rapid City," Brown pointed out in his response to Burns. "Witnesses would have to travel for two days to reach the courthouse, and that would entail a considerable expense in travel, lodging, and meals. Furthermore, the trial would be a waste of taxpayers' money as it would be impossible to get a Pennington County jury to convict a white man for killing an Indian."[21]

When a newspaper reporter sought out Brown for an explanation, the thoroughly West River attorney replied with what he knew his constituents would find palpable: "I have never refused to prosecute the case, but on the contrary have been ready and willing to do so whenever a complaint shall be made in the regular way. No information against Whipple has ever been laid before a Pennington County magistrate or before our grand jury which convened on March 19 and is still in session. I will myself lay the matter before the grand jury on the opening of court on April 5th, when, no doubt, that body will do what justice may require."[22]

Upon learning that Whipple was discharged from jail and that Pennington County authorities declined to prosecute, the editors of several East River newspapers expressed their outrage: "This declaration is keenly resented by all the better class of people of the state.... The crime was a cold-blooded one, and the evidence against Whipple is strong enough to convict."[23]

Several West River newspapers jumped to attorney Brown's defense. "The disgusting sentimentalists that prate of Pennington County's indifference to the rights of the Indians should be sat down upon. Pennington County justice is just the same for white, black, and colored, but when a useless Indian dies of delirious tremens, eastern philanthropists need to not expect the county to go to an immense expense to prove eventually that he was not murdered."[24]

Nonetheless, the foreman of the grand jury for the Circuit Court of the Seventh Judicial District in and for Pennington County felt the pressure. On April 9 the grand jurors discussed whether to bring an indictment against Jack Whipple for murder:

> It has come to our notice that a crime had been committed on the borders of the Sioux reservation and presumably in Jackson County, being one of the unorganized counties of the ceded Sioux reservation. The witnesses in this case are Indians in the custody of the United States, at the Rosebud agency, distant in a round about way of about 250 miles from Rapid City. We are also informed that it requires considerable correspondence with the United States government and the agent at the agency to get permits for these witnesses and an interpreter to come before the grand jury, all of which would take more time than the present grand jury can devote to the matter. The foreman of the grand jury and the district attorney have consulted with a member of the Indian Rights Association, and the member, in behalf of said organization, has volunteered to do the necessary correspondence and secure the necessary witnesses here before the next grand jury without any cost to Pennington County. We therefore recommend that the case be investigated by the next grand jury.[25]

Every informed person knew that Pennington County authorities were announcing that Jack Whipple would never be indicted for the murder of Lays On His Mother-In-Law.

The Brulé Sioux were incensed that yet again a white man could murder an Indian and get away with it. They resumed ghost dancing and, in the opinion of some, looked for another excuse to stage an outbreak.[26] About this time

Valentine McGillycuddy was passing through Chicago. On March 28 he called upon General Nelson Miles, commander of the Division of the Missouri, and informed him the Indians on Rosebud were incensed that Jack Whipple had pounded one of their kinsmen to death and the authorities had released the murderer from jail. McGillycuddy told Miles that given the level of the Indians' anger, trouble might be expected at the Rosebud and other agencies.[27] Miles went through the proper channels to bring the killing of Lays On His Mother-In-Law to the attention of John Noble, secretary of the interior, but no further legal action was taken against Whipple. It is possible that state officials did not want to again defame their state's reputation by putting a white man on trial for the murder of an Indian and then seeing him acquitted.

But the ordeal did not end there. When it appeared that no legal action was going to be taken against Whipple, rumors surfaced that Lays On His Mother-In-Law's brother (probably a half brother) had taken a vow to kill Jack Whipple.[28] The supposed revenge-seeking Indian was Wets His Lips, also known as Broncho Bill, a moniker Wets His Lips acquired by his exhibits of skillful bronc riding in Buffalo Bill's Wild West Show.

When Jack Whipple heard that Wets His Lips intended to kill him, Whipple hatched a plan. At Whipple's urging, two cowboys offered Wets His Lips a steer to feed his hungry family. Wets His Lips accepted the animal and butchered it, not knowing the steer belonged to Mott & DeLancy Brothers and was not the cowboys' critter to give away. As soon as the steer was killed and butchered, Whipple arranged for Wets His Lips to be arrested for grand larceny.[29] U.S. Deputy Marshal Frank Keyes arrested Broncho Bill on March 26 and took him to the Hughes County Jail in Pierre.[30] He appeared before a U.S. commissioner the next day and was indicted on the charge of stealing cattle.[31]

George Wright was convinced that Whipple had conspired to get Wet His Lips arrested and jailed, thereby securing Whipple's protection. Wright also surmised that the Indians knew Whipple was behind the scheme. The agent concluded that if Wets His Lips was imprisoned, there was no telling what measures the Indians would take to get revenge. In an attempt to avert a catastrophic outcome, Wright went to Pierre, posted the two hundred dollars bail, and returned with Wet His Lips to the Rosebud Reservation. Wright also retained on Wets His Lips's behalf the services of George P. Nock, the defense attorney who had secured Plenty Horses's acquittal.[32]

As the date for the trial approached, Nock wrote to Wright: "I shall be obliged to leave for Pierre on Monday . . . in order to follow out the instructions of Judge Edgerton ... and shall commence the trial of Wets His Lips if all of the witnesses are there and ready Tuesday."[33]

Judge Alonzo Edgerton gaveled the federal court to order on the morning of May 13. The prosecution called its first witness: Jack Whipple. When it was time for the defense to present its case, Nock put Wets His Lips on the stand.[34] He testified that on March 1, the day of the alleged crime, he was physically ill to the point that it would have been impossible for him to commit the crime.[35] After hearing the evidence, the jury deliberated. Two jurors believed that Wets His Lips was guilty, but the other ten voted for acquittal, making it a contested outcome. Edgerton ordered a retrial.

However, there was no retrial. Sterling, who had earlier conspired with Wright to have Whipple arrested, decided the state would not further prosecute the case.[36]

The murder of Lays On His Mother-in-Law and the resultant legal proceedings against Jack Whipple and then Wets His Lips would have been followed closely by the Lakota, especially the Brulé in No Water's village, Two Sticks being among them. After all, both the murdered Indian and Two Sticks were Brulé, and they likely knew each other. Failure of white men in positions of power to convict Whipple likely further fueled Two Sticks's desire for revenge.

✢ 11 ✢

PINE RIDGE, 1891

A TIME OF GLOOM

When the Lakota agreed in the summer of 1889 to cede nine million acres, the government transported selected chiefs and headmen to the nation's capital to formally and symbolically sign the Sioux Bill. The Indian delegation used the occasion to meet with Secretary of the Interior John Noble on December 18, 1889, and lay some pressing concerns before him.[1] Among other requests, the delegates appealed for more rations. Their request fell on a closed mind at least partly because sixteen days earlier, Assistant Commissioner of Indian Affairs Robert Belt had penned a letter to Noble:

> Special Agent A. T. Lea has been engaged for some months among the Indians of the Pine Ridge Agency. He has had special facilities and opportunities for observing and learning the exact condition of the Pine Ridge Sioux Indians. I am satisfied that his report has not been made without a full knowledge of the facts stated by him and a clear conviction that the Department should be properly informed of their situation. I think he is better informed on this subject than the military officers who only see the Indians as they are gathered in camps around the agency away from their homes. Lea's statements are entitled to the fullest weight and credit, and they confirm the position that has heretofore been asserted by this office: These Indians are not in a starving condition, though many

of them suffer from hunger more from their improvident habits than from any lack of sufficient food."[2]

C. P. Jordan, the chief clerk at Rosebud, saw it otherwise. In a confidential letter to General Miles, possibly never sent for fear of reprisal should the content become public knowledge, Jordan shared his assessment of Special Agent A. T. Lea: "He is a cynical, eccentric, and nervous individual. [The] man often remarked that the Indians were overfed. On one occasion he saw a liberal allowance of dried beef in the lodge of an old woman who was keeping it for Indian families; [and] he remarked, 'Look at that—thousands of pounds of beef rotting.' Prior to his departure for Pine Ridge . . . and his usual reference to overfed Indians, Lea stated 'I will stir the animals up . . .' As if to ease his conscience for unaccountable misrepresentation of the conditions of the Indians . . . he published in the papers a statement that the Indians had not been suffering for want of food."[3]

Lea's report gave Noble justification to deny the Lakota's request for more rations, but then he did not need one. The Interior Department wanted to keep the Indians' rations meager with the expectation it would force them to take up 320-acre allotments, plow fields, grow crops, and raise livestock. That expectation was based on a mixture of ignorance, indifference, and an unwillingness to listen to those who knew better. As was commonly said by people familiar with the Lakota reservations, "You can raise just as much wheat on a pine floor as you can on the Sioux Reservation. Nothing grows there but a rank prairie grass and there are acres which are absolutely bare."[4] Less poetically, the director of the U.S. Geological Survey, a branch of the Interior Department, would have said the same thing if only someone had asked. But no one in Washington wanted to hear from John Wesley Powell, the man who, at the time, knew the livability of the American West better than any person alive. Nor was it likely they had read his *Report on the Lands of the Arid Region*. In that report, Powell advised policy makers, planners, and anyone who would listen—and no one with influence did—that in the arid West, a stock farmer (rancher) needed a minimum of four sections (2,560 acres) with access to live water to make a go of it. The bureaucrats who crafted the Sioux Bill did not care that it was then [and still is] impossible for a family to make a living off 320 acres of West River land. Despite all the commissioners' hollow promises, the Sioux Bill had nothing to do with helping the Lakota develop a viable economy that would support self-sufficiency and everything to do with getting their land.

The reduction in rations was doubly painful for the Oglala because it was a reminder that the government had told them yet another lie, and yet again they had believed the lie. Specifically, they remembered when Chief Hollow Horn Bear had pointedly asked the Sioux Bill commissioners in the summer of 1889 whether the beef ration would be sustained at the same level if they signed the Sioux Bill. The commissioners knew that three months earlier Congress had passed an appropriations bill that reduced the beef ration for fiscal year 1890. Yet Senator William Warner replied, "The intention of the Great Father is that every member of your families shall receive three pounds of beef on the hoof a day." General Crook echoed Warner's assurance. "The beef ration will remain the same because it is in the law."[5] Only a few months after the government got the land it wanted, it reduced the Lakota's beef and other rations.[6]

Even the weather conspired against the Oglala. The reservation had seen little moisture in 1886. The rains had again been sparse in 1887 and 1888. In 1889 rain was a stranger, but a frequent visitor was hot wind that turned the prairie grasses to chaff. Anthrax killed large numbers of the Oglala's cattle and horses. Grasshoppers ate anything and everything green, including the Indians' gardens. Potatoes, which nearly always were a good crop, produced too little to be worth the effort it took to dig them. The seemingly endless drought compelled the Indians to depend for subsistence entirely on what was issued to them by the government, and that was meager.[7] The drought continued into 1891.[8]

The effects of meager, inadequate rations combined with drought left the Indians seriously malnourished, the effect of which could be seen in their faces. "Their appearance shocked me," Elaine Goodale related. "Many displayed gaunt forms, lackluster faces and sad, deep-sunken eyes."[9] The malnutrition hit the very old and very young the hardest. John Sweeney, the teacher at the Medicine Root Creek School, confided to a reporter that the children brought their lunch to school in little beaded sacks. He opened several of these "lunch baskets" and found that each contained only a small piece of jerked beef and a hard biscuit made mostly of lard. "The children would get very hungry ... during recess [they] would dig out chipmunks and prairie dogs, which they cooked and ate." Sweeney fed many of the hungry little ones, using a considerable part of his salary to feed them.[10]

Another misery visited on the Oglala at this time was unemployment. There were no jobs, even though the Sioux Bill commissioners had held out the expectation that more Indians would be employed on the reservations. In the summer council of 1889, William McGaa, a mixed-blood, started the discussion, saying, "You told us the time will come when we must make our own living by the sweat of our brow. We believe that to be true. But how can those who have been educated in the mechanics and other branches make a living when the white man is preferred above us for all positions at the agencies and draw their pay from the money that belongs to the Indians under former treaties? There are among us competent blacksmiths, carpenters, chief herders and farmers. Still these jobs are denied us and given to white men no more competent and who feel no interest in our welfare." Chief American Horse added his voice: "There is something like fifteen positions on this reservation. I hope [our people] will be given these positions so the money will be left here without being sent out to somebody else [meaning white men]."[11]

Commissioner Charles Foster was initially put off by what he saw as the Indians' attempt to derail the commissioners' sole objective—getting the Oglala to agree to cede the coveted land. But as Foster listened, he saw a way to use the Oglala's desire for jobs to get them to sign the Sioux Bill: "We will write a report to the Great Father and we will say to him that on a certain page you will find the complaint made by American Horse. We think that what American Horse said about this [jobs for Indians] is right, and we will recommend that his views be adopted." When the Oglala bit on the bait, Foster set the hook. "[But] if we fail to get your consent [to the Sioux Bill] who do you suppose is going to read what we say? But if we succeed, the Great Father will read what we say, and every just complaint you have made will be redressed."[12] Foster's assurances gave the Oglala every reason to believe that when the Sioux Bill became law, many reservation jobs would be filled by Indians.

The promised jobs never appeared, in large part because duplicitous bureaucrats in the Bureau of Indian Affairs believed that trying to get the "inherently lazy Indians to work by giving them paying jobs was a waste of money; and it would also necessitate the erection of buildings, such as a wheelwright shop or a blacksmith shop, that would be abandoned in a few years."[13]

At this time it was painfully apparent to the Oglala that the white authorities were striving mightily to put an end to the Lakota's traditional culture. The elders could remember when the Lakota were nomadic hunter-gatherers who claimed everything south to north from the North Platte River to the Yellowstone River and east to west from the Missouri River to the Bighorn Mountains, approximately 134,000 square miles.[14] In 1891, only twenty-four years later, the Oglala found themselves confined to a mere 4,922 square miles, which held such a dearth of wild game and edible plants that they were completely dependent on biweekly issues of government rations. The men were too embarrassed to stand in line for government handouts. That became women's work, stripping the men of their traditional role as providers. Moreover, they could not set foot outside the boundary of Pine Ridge without a written pass from the agent.[15] This edict came as a surprise to the Lakota. There was nothing mentioned in any treaty they had signed that restricted their movement. Nonetheless, the government now confined them to their small reservation. The authorities did not restrict the Lakota's movements because it was a matter of law or specified by treaty; they did it because they could. The confinement cut into the heart of what the Lakota cherished. They were a visiting people, always going from one Lakota band to the next to visit, to trade, to hear the latest, and to stay connected. Travel was also genetically important. The Lakota understood the importance of genetic diversity. During their visits to different bands, young maidens invariably caught the wandering eyes of young men. Courtship and marriage often followed, ensuring the continuance of the tribe's vitality. All of that ended when the government sequestered the Oglala and other Lakota on their own reservations. The Lakota came to call it their corral period.

The formerly nomadic Oglala were forced to pitch their tepees in semipermanent, isolated villages located near spring-fed creeks that furnished water for dogs, horses, cattle, and themselves. Each village's sanitation facility was an open latrine. During heavy downpours the latrines overflowed, putting human waste in the creek. During the long, cold Dakota winters, the Oglala warmed themselves as best they could by an open fire in the middle of their tepees, but in a nearly treeless prairie, the wood supply around the villages soon dwindled, forcing them to go farther and farther for fuel or else shiver in their cold tepees. They knew the forced living conditions promoted the spread of infectious diseases that were killing them by the score, but they were powerless to do anything about it.

Another systemic problem facing them was greed—the greed of unscrupulous whites, both government employees and others, who ruthlessly exploited the Oglala while higher-level government bureaucrats turned a blind eye. The whites exploited the Oglala by stealing rations and annuities, diverting government money intended for subsistence items to their own pockets, illegally grazing thousands of cattle on the reservation, and selling goods to the reservation-confined Oglala at exorbitant prices. To exploit the Indians, it was necessary to subjugate them. The whites often used U.S. soldiers, or at least the threat of the military, to keep the Oglala in check.

In particular, white ranchers egregiously exploited the Oglala. Each winter they trampled on the Indians' rights by illegally pushing thousands of their cattle onto Pine Ridge to graze on the Indians' protein-rich "unused" grass. When winter abated, cattlemen from three states gathered at the Harney Hotel in Rapid City to plan the spring roundup. Like a well-organized army, cowboys came onto the reservation, gathered their cattle, and left without paying a grazing fee. The first organized roundup on Pine Ridge occurred in the spring of 1882.[16] Thereafter, reservation roundups were conducted twice a year. There was a spring roundup to brand the calves and a fall roundup to gather the marketable animals. "Boss Cowman" Ed Lemmon admitted that in the 1880s he ranged ten thousand head on the reservation. Between roundups, the ranchers hired the toughest cowboys to patrol their stock on the reservation.[17]

Senator Richard Pettigrew was also an exploiter of the Oglala, but he did not exploit them to put money in his own pocket. He did it to put money in the pockets of loyal South Dakota Republicans, trusting they would then vote for him. Under his patronage practices, seasoned agency employees comfortably meshed into the Lakota culture were dismissed and replaced with new employees, many of whom came to cheat the Oglala out of their rations and annuities and also to defraud the government. Captain Charles Penney, the acting Indian agent at Pine Ridge, bitterly complained about the deleterious effects of Pettigrew's patronage practices: "The appointment of employees at the agency on account of political influence or bias tends to cripple the service and put it out of the power of the agent to secure the best service possible. I have had occasion to discharge an additional farmer for incompetency, and was positively required to reinstate him; and I understand that his reinstatement was brought about through political influence. This state of affairs cannot be productive of anything but inefficiency and poor service. It should be stopped and only capacity and ability should be regarded as fit qualifications for employment."[18] His complaints were to no avail. Pettigrew's political power, cunning, and duplicity assured continuance of patronage practices.

The Oglala were also thoroughly disillusioned by the unfilled promises of educating their children. As far back as 1868 they had been told that if their children learned to read and write, they could be like white people and gets jobs and support themselves. In 1889 the Sioux Bill commissioners again led the

Oglala to believe that education would put their children on the white man's road to comfortable lives. Commissioner Foster told them, "[T]he Great Father is anxious that you should enter upon a road of prosperity. Your daughters shall be educated to teach your children in your schools, instead of sending for the daughters of white men to come here and teach your schools for you. The money paid out to these teachers will be kept here among you, spent here and used for the benefit of your people instead of being carried away. Your sons, like the sons of white men, shall be taught how to farm so that instead of the Great Father sending farmers here, your sons shall take their places."[19]

Believing that, Oglala parents had sent more than one hundred of their children to the Carlisle Indian Industrial School, Hampton Normal and Agricultural Institute, Haskell Indian School, and other off-reservation boarding schools. When the children returned to the reservation, they found themselves no better off than before and jobless. After his six-day tour of the Pine Ridge Reservation in 1892, Theodore Roosevelt concluded: "It is a cruel thing to educate a boy to do something which he cannot find to do on the reservation and turn him back to work out his own fate in a tepee. It is much harder on girls. If a girl is educated at Carlisle or elsewhere and is then put back in her old life of the tepee, the transaction can only be regarded as a piece of deliberate cruelty. It is only too probable that she will fail. The girls are not educated to the degree that would make them competent to fill the positions of teachers, positions which they are especially anxious to fill. Rather, they have been educated just enough to make them discontent to be house maids."[20]

Plenty Horses, the Brulé who shot Edward Casey, delivered a telling indictment of sending Indian children to off-reservation boarding schools: "I was at Carlisle five years. When I came back, there was no chance to get employment. There was nothing for me to do whereby I could earn my board and clothes, but also no opportunity to learn more and remain with the whites."[21]

During this dark time the Oglala learned of yet another government betrayal. They discovered that rather than receiving cash for the nine million acres ceded to the government, the U.S. Treasury would use their money to pay white men to build their schools and white teachers to educate their children, and for harrows and plows purchased from eastern contractors at inflated prices and built of such inferior materials that they broke upon any serious use.[22]

In these years it was all but impossible for an Indian to get a money-earning job on the reservation, and there were only two ways to get a job off the reservation. One way was to join a Wild West show, such as Buffalo Bill Cody's or Colonel Alveren Allen's. However, those jobs were seasonal and the wages were meager. Agent Hugh Gallagher at Pine Ridge grieved for the Oglala who joined a Wild West show: "The injury done to them is irreparable and will prove a curse to these people for many generations to come. These people [the hiring agents who secured the Indians] are engaged in the occupation of stealing Indians for the shows at so much per head. They deserve a term in the penitentiary. Cody and Saulsbury took away from this agency in the spring of 1890 seventy-two healthy young men to travel with the Wild West Show. Five of them died among strangers in a strange land [Europe] while seven others have been sent home owing to their shattered health, rendering them unfit for further service."[23]

Herbert Welsh of the Indian Rights Association agreed with Gallagher.[24] The complaints lodged by Gallagher and Welsh were heard by Commissioner of Indian Affairs Thomas Morgan, and he held an inquiry. No Neck and Black Heart, two Lakota who had traveled with Buffalo Bill Cody's Wild West Show, were taken to Washington, D.C., to testify. To Morgan's chagrin, the two men did not relate the tale of woe the inquiry board expected to hear. Instead, No Neck said that while in the show he was fed well. "That is why I am getting fat. It is only when I get back to the reservation that I am getting poor. But if the Great Father wants me to stop, I will; but until then that is the way I get money."[25]

The accumulative effects of insufficient rations, forced confinement to the reservation, exploitation by whites, the hollow promises of education, and no jobs had the Oglala living, such as it was, in endless misery. Out of desperation, the Oglala chiefs and headmen met with General Miles in January 1891 to request permission to go to Washington, D.C., and lay their grievances before the Great Father. Permission was granted, not only for the Oglala but also for a delegation of Lakota chiefs and headmen from all parties to the Sioux Bill.[26]

Secretary Noble greeted the thirty-nine Lakota delegates and ushered them into his office on February 7, 1891. Also waiting for them were Morgan, Secretary of War Redfield Proctor, and others prominent in their work with Indians. Noble opened the meeting on a charitable note: "There has been trouble [recently] and you have come again to say what you think proper as the causes of the trouble, and to make any further complaints you see fit. . . . The Secretary is here to tell you he has kept his word, but if there is anything more he can do through friendship for the Sioux, he is ready to do it." Noble then named six Lakota chiefs who could each speak, telling them to keep the comments brief. Their interpreter, Louis Rencoutre, said that the arrangement was not satisfactory, as at least one delegate from each agency should be given a chance to speak. His concern was ignored.[27]

John Grass spoke first. He said the delegates came to Washington to determine the path to their future. He believed that putting their children in school and following the teachings of Christianity was going down the right road. American Horse was the next speaker. He pleaded that the jobs on the reservations be filled by Indians, not white men: "At the agencies the white men are so numerous that they fairly trample on us Indians." When the chief tried to raise additional concerns, Noble reminded him to keep his remarks brief. American Horse quipped, "Then can I come often?" Noble heard the delegates out, but he promised nothing.[28]

For the next two mornings the delegates met with Morgan. Others knew, but the Indian delegates did not, that Morgan had served under Benjamin Harrison, then a general, during the Civil War, rising to the rank of lieutenant general. After the war, Morgan had attended a Baptist theological seminary, briefly served as a small-town pastor in Nebraska, served as principal of the Nebraska State Normal School for two years, and then taught homiletics and ecclesiastical history at a Baptist Theological Seminary in Chicago. When his former commander became president, Morgan presented his education credentials and asked to be appointed secretary of education. Instead, Harrison offered him the top job in the Bureau of Indian Affairs. Morgan accepted, although he had no previous experience with Indians or an understanding of their culture.[29] As commissioner of Indian affairs, Morgan was hardly enlightened. He believed tribal relations should be broken up, Indian socialism destroyed, and the English language universally adopted. "The Indians must conform to the white man's ways peacefully if they will or forcibly if they must."[30]

Robert Pugh, a longtime agency employee with a Lakota wife and mixed-blood children, met Morgan when he paid a courtesy visit to Pine Ridge in October 1892.[31] Pugh concluded that Morgan was a preacher filled with more religious zeal than sound judgment, who did not realize the importance of creature comforts as the foundation for religious conversion. "Instead of meat, he gave them religious tracts. When told the Indians were hungry, he inquired as to what kind of religious reading would be best for them."[32] Morgan could be of no help to malnourished, continuously lied-to Indians.

Morgan told the Sioux delegates that he wanted to hear from them but that he had no power to make laws, nor any food or money to give them, except what Congress provided. He also told them he had heard all that was necessary with regard to the past and wanted to hear only about their plans for the future.[33] In other words, they were not to talk about their insufficient rations, malnutrition, rampant illnesses, exploitation, and other things contributing to their ever-worsening misery.

After meeting with Noble and then privately with Morgan, the delegates knew that neither man was going to help. Therefore they anticipated their upcoming meeting with the Great Father, who according to the Sioux Bill commissioners was compassionate and caring. "He [regards] you as his children,"[34] the commissioners had said. "He says that every member of your families . . . shall receive three pounds of beef on the hoof per day[35] . . . and he [wishes] that your daughters be educated to become school teachers in your schools."[36] Based on what the Sioux Bill commissioners had told them about their Great Father, the delegates were confident the Great Father would listen to their concerns, be sympathetic, and take specific actions to ameliorate their plight.

At one o'clock on February 12 the Sioux delegates were ushered into the East Room of the White House for a meeting with the Great Father. There were many spectators waiting for them to arrive, including a number of women who had themselves invited simply for the entertainment of seeing real Indians. After a short wait, President Harrison made his entrance. He greeted the delegates with words that opened not-yet-healed emotional wounds: "It has been a great grief to me," he told them in a scolding tone (the Reverend C. E. Cook from Pine Ridge translated), "that some of the people represented by you have recently acted badly, having gone upon the warpath. . . . You must not expect that you and your children will always be fed by the government . . . without you working yourselves. . . . You must each take your allotment and endeavor the best you can to earn your living."[37]

After Harrison finished his short address, each delegate was presented to him. As instructed, no one said anything to the president. Instead, each delegate shook the Great Father's hand and bowed.[38]

After the meeting with Harrison, the delegates conferred privately. Big Road said, "We did not willingly go on the warpath. We were driven [to it] for want of the necessities of life." American Horse: "He can talk. It does us no good." Captain Sword: "Why did he not show us a little compassion for the loss of our many men, women, and children slaughtered by the soldiers?" Young Man Afraid of His Horses: "He said that this money, food, and annuities were given to us. This is not so. It was in exchange for our lands we sold [to them]."[39]

Some of the Sioux delegation of 1891. Front row, left to right: High Hawk, Fire Lightning, Little Wound, Two Strike, Young Man Afraid of His Horses, Spotted Elk, Big Road; second row, left to right: F. B. Lewis, He Dog, Spotted Horse, American Horse, George Sword, Louis Shangreaux, Bat Pourier; back row, left to right: Zephier, Hump, High Pipe, Fast Thunder, Charles S. Cook, P. T. Johnson. (South Dakota State Historical Society.)

The delegates left the Capitol feeling they had been treated like schoolchildren. As American Horse departed, he announced his intent to resign as a chief.[40] Presumably, he did not want the responsibility of being a leader who was powerless to help his suffering kinsmen. The other delegates also could not hide their disappointment.

As the delegates passed through Chicago, one of them told a reporter that the distress on the reservations was such that another uprising was likely as soon as the grass turned green. A newspaper published the story under the alarming headline "Will They Rebel."[41] The delegate who spawned the story knew there was no Indian uprising in the offing. However, he was sufficiently worldly to understand the effectiveness of public pressure. Sure enough, the implied threat was picked up by newspapers across the country and retold. One newspaper gave the details of how the Indian uprising would unfold: "The Brulé and Ogallala will start the trouble and they will be quickly joined by Standing Rock and Cheyenne River warriors . . . the Yanktonais, a renegade tribe of all the bands of the Sioux, will doubtless come down from the Poplar

River, so it may also be expected that the Shoshones, the Grosventres, the Crees, the Snakes, and the bands from the Cheyenne and the Arapahoes will join the war party."⁴² The story was picked up by newspapers from coast to coast and reprinted under such alarming headings as "Sulky Redskins,"⁴³ "Danger of another outbreak,"⁴⁴ and "The Sioux Indians have started on war path again."⁴⁵

After reading a few of these articles, Father Francis Craft, who had been a missionary to the Lakota from 1883 to 1891, wrote a letter to Eugene McAuliffe of Providence, Rhode Island, expressing his assessment of the ongoing Indian unrest. McAuliffe passed the letter to an eastern newspaper, which printed part of it: "The [root] causes of the trouble still exist . . . and I am heartily sick and tired of witnessing miseries that I cannot correct, and share the suffering of the unfortunate Indians and brave soldiers who are forced into conflict and slandered by the cowardly politicians who slaughtered them."⁴⁶ When Craft's article came to the attention of officials within the Bureau of Indian Affairs, they denounced him as a confirmed nuisance who ought to harness his mouth.⁴⁷

Fortuitously, at this bleak time, Special Agent James Cooper came to Pine Ridge and Rosebud in April 1891 to determine those eligible to receive compensation for ponies the army had taken from them in 1876. That the Indians should be paid for horses stolen from them was prescribed in Section 27 of the 1889 Sioux Bill⁴⁸ as an inducement to get them to sign. A month later, May 19, Cooper arrived in Rushville, Nebraska, and lodged in the Commercial Hotel. That afternoon he notified the acting Indian agent: "I just received a telegram that thirty thousand will arrive for me tonight which makes forty thousand to go the agency tomorrow. Will you please send ten policemen."⁴⁹ It would have been expeditious to convey this request to the acting Indian agent via a telegram, but telegrams were not confidential. To make sure that lurking-about road agents did not hear about the cash destined for Pine Ridge, Cooper put his request in a letter. He likely folded it into an envelope, scrawled his signature over the seal, and paid a reliable courier to hand it to the acting Indian agent. The next day Cooper was at Pine Ridge doling out money to sixty-two claimants and a few days later to the thirty-two at Rosebud.⁵⁰

While Cooper was promising a very small percentage of the Oglala and Brulé that they would receive a one-time payment for their previously confiscated horses, General Miles dispatched Captain Frank D. Baldwin to the Lakota reservations to assess the extent of unrest. After Baldwin completed his investigation, he passed through Pierre, where, as government officials were wont to do, he assured a newspaper reporter that "he found the Indians at the different agencies in the most peaceful mood."⁵¹ That assessment was for public consumption. He then sought a private audience with Governor Mellette and advised him to restrict the sale of arms and ammunition to Indians.⁵² On Baldwin's advice, Mellette issued a proclamation on April 2 with instructions that it should be posted in a conspicuous place.

A Proclamation

The attention of all good citizens is hereby called to the penalties provided against selling arms and ammunition to Indians within the State of South Dakota. Its strict enforcement by means of the severest penalties is urged upon States Attorneys and those especially charged with the enforcement of law and order. The person, who for gain, will furnish arms and ammunition to an Indian under the existing circumstance within the state should be considered an enemy of society and punished to the full extent of the law. The Indians have no possible use for arms. They are attempting by every way to secure them. If they succeed, trouble is sure to result, ultimately. If the officers will do their duty and can have the support of all good citizens, a public calamity to the state and to the frontier settlers can be avoided.⁵³

A few months later, Captain Charles Penney, newly-appointed acting agent at Pine Ridge, penned a letter to the commissioner of Indian affairs, advising him that "the effect of the recent outbreak [the Indian uprising of 1890 generally and the Wounded Knee Massacre specifically] is bad and has left their hearts sore and bitter. The memory of the loss of their kinfolk and friends still rankles and is an ever-present source of discontent, which may break out whenever the needed spark is applied."⁵⁴

On March 9, 1891, Congress held out the promise of jobs for at least some young Lakota males by passing General Order No. 28. It authorized the enlistment of three thousand Indians in cavalry and infantry regiments (except those composed of black soldiers) stationed west of the Mississippi River. General John M. Schofield, commander of the army, ballyhooed the order. "Enlisting the Indians as scouts in the army will avoid future trouble."⁵⁵ Young Sioux men signed on primarily because they had no food, no horses, no blankets, and little clothing. They were willing to do anything that would bring them food and shelter.

Many of the Lakota men who tried to enlist were turned away because they could not pass the medical examination. Many had scrofula or erysipelas[56]—types of tuberculosis readily spread among malnourished people living in unsanitary conditions. There was no treatment and most infected Indians suffered slow, painful deaths.

In announcing General Order No. 28, Schofield made one small and possibly intentional error of fact. He said the Indians would be enrolled as "scouts." The days when scouts were needed to locate the enemy were past. If the Indians were lucky, the lieutenant who came to their reservation was recruiting for a cavalry company. If the Indians were unlucky, the lieutenant was recruiting for an infantry company. The young Oglala men at Pine Ridge were unlucky. When First Lieutenant John Kinzie of the Eighth Infantry arrived in Pine Ridge on May 12, 1891, to recruit soldiers, he tried to enlist young men into an infantry company at thirteen dollars a month. Only a small number were willing to join a military unit that walked everywhere.[57] The few Oglala who signed up quickly became disillusioned with military life. Whereas their commitment was for five years, all of them took early discharge and mustered out in May 1894. By 1895 the experiment of recruiting Indians into the army was over.[58]

The cloud of gloom hanging over Pine Ridge was reflected in Captain Penney's official report to the commissioner of Indian affairs in 1891. It painted a dismal picture: "The Indian police are inefficient and unreliable, and would prove an utter and complete failure in case of an emergency." Penney thought even less of the Court of Indian Offenses: "I have made no appointments to the Court of Indian Offenses for the reason that it does not appear that any real good can result from such a court. Indian judges would not be granted any respect by the Indians, nor would they, in my opinion, merit any such respect. The Indians are not, in any sense, judicially minded." His report concluded with this ominous observation: "The sparks of dissatisfaction have been smothered, but the fire is not quenched."[59]

Penney's conclusion that the Oglala were incapable of providing law and order among themselves revealed his ignorance of the Lakota. Long before the appearance of white men in their lands, the Lakota efficiently and effectively maintained law and order by relying on *akicitas*. Among other duties, akicitas policed camp moves, regulated buffalo hunts, and enforced tribal laws and customs. When dealing with lawbreakers, akicitas were the judges and jurors. When circumstances warranted, they meted out harsh punishment.

Penney's opinion of the Indian police differed sharply from the experiences of his predecessors. When Valentine McGillycuddy became the Indian agent for Pine Ridge on March 10, 1879, he expanded the police force from four men to a company of fifty. He did that by filling the ranks with akicitas. He put two or more akicitas from every band of Oglala on the police force. The chosen akicitas were middle-aged family men, well-known and highly regarded among their kinsmen for bravery and integrity. McGillycuddy's Indian police effectively maintained law and order among six thousand Indians while dressed in everyday clothes and unarmed. They did not even carry pistols. Their only visible signs of authority were badges pinned to their jackets. That was enough.[60] McGillycuddy's successor, Colonel Hugh Gallagher, also thought highly of the Indian police. In his last annual report, Gallagher wrote, "[T]he police have maintained throughout this year the high point of efficiency reached by them in years past. They are valuable aides to the agent and all deserve honorable mention for their many sacrifices made in the discharge of duty."[61]

But in 1891 the Indian police were so demoralized that Captain Penney considered them to be well-nigh useless.[62] In his annual report, Penney wrote, "The U.S. Marshal Service is increasingly called upon to take the lead in arresting Indians who break the law, clamping them in handcuffs, and hauling them off to federal court in Deadwood. It has a most wholesome effect upon these Indians as they have a healthy dread of going over the road to Deadwood."[63]

In the spring of 1891, the Oglala experienced yet another heartache, a particularly excruciating one. The mass grave where the bodies of the Lakota men, women, and children killed at Wounded Knee had been stacked like cordwood was open and unenclosed.[64] Magpies, crows, turkey vultures, and coyotes were gorging on their kinsmen's corpses.

The pervasive gloom on Pine Ridge in 1891 was too much for Penney. After only seven months as acting Indian agent, he asked to be relieved of his duties. Shortly before his departure he wrote, "[The Oglala] seem to be fenced in with no future and nothing to do but draw and eat their rations and then die."[65]

⚜ 12 ⚜

PINE RIDGE, 1892

A YEAR OF RESISTANCE

Captain George LeRoy Brown arrived at Pine Ridge in December 1891 to take up the duties of acting Indian agent.[1] In the preceding twelve months, the Oglala and reservation employees had seen three agents come and go—Daniel Royer, Captain Francis Pierce, and Captain Penney. Stability was needed.

Soon after taking up his duties, Brown toured his domain, traveling to the far-flung villages scattered throughout the reservation's 4,690 square miles. He found the Oglala to be "a very suspicious people."[2] In January and only two months into the job, the first of many problems came to his attention. He was told the Oglala were enraged that a white man, Jack Whipple, had killed an Indian and was not immediately arrested. Weeks went by before Whipple was jailed, but the court with legal jurisdiction (Pennington County) declined to try him for murder. In April, an anxious Brown wrote to Agent George Wright at Rosebud: "What will be done with Jack Whipple?"[3]

Another problem was not long in coming, and it would prove to be intractable. On August 2, 1892, Brown received a tersely worded telegram from Commissioner Morgan: "If Indians from other agencies arrive at your agency without permission, you are to send them immediately back to their agency."[4]

At the time there were a number of Indians from other Lakota reservations at Pine Ridge. They were drawn to No Water's village of malcontents like iron filings to a magnet. Among the interlopers were Bear Eagle and his followers, Miniconjou from the Cheyenne River Reservation. They arrived at No Water's village in November 1891. Upon arriving, they went straight to the acting agent, Charles Penney. Bear Eagle informed Penney that he and his band wanted to relocate to Pine Ridge because they were discontent with their treatment on the Cheyenne River Reservation. Penney was sympathetic; he reported to authorities that "dissatisfaction with management of the Cheyenne River Reservation [under Agent Perain Palmer] manifested by all visitors from Cheyenne River inclines me to believe that there is some ground for the complaint."[5] Penney instructed Bear Eagle to make application for transfer to Pine Ridge, and he wired Bear Eagle's request to Commissioner Morgan, adding that in his opinion the Indians meant no mischief.[6]

In response, Robert Belt, acting commissioner of Indian affairs, recommended to the secretary of the interior that the inspector at the Cheyenne River Agency be instructed to investigate Bear Eagle's complaints and submit a report. Secretary Noble approved the recommendation. Belt urged Penney to encourage Bear Eagle to return to the Cheyenne River Agency so that his concerns could be investigated.[7] Bear Eagle did not go back, but the matter was not diligently pursued, likely because Penney asked to be relieved at Pine Ridge and the issue was not a high priority for the incoming agent, George LeRoy Brown. In the meantime, Bear Eagle and his band had aligned themselves with Moccasin Top, an ardent ghost dancer during the Messiah craze who reputedly was still ghost dancing in the summer of 1892, albeit covertly.[8]

Having been given a directive from Commissioner Morgan to remove unauthorized arrivals from Pine Ridge, Brown had no alternative but to comply. He sent Thunder Bull, the captain of his Indian police, and Thunder Bear, a first lieutenant, to No Water's village on August 4 with orders to bring Moccasin Top into the agency.[9] Presumably Brown wanted to order Moccasin Top to inform Bear Eagle and his band that they were no longer welcome in his camp and also to question Moccasin Top about reports that some in his band had butchered cattle belonging to the beef contractor Ike Humphrey.

As directed, the Indian police went to No Water's village, found Moccasin Top, and conveyed Brown's order for him to come to the agency. Moccasin Top said he couldn't come in.[10]

Thunder Bull and his detachment of Indian police were surely back at the agency by mid-afternoon, but a day passed before he reported to Captain Brown that Moccasin Top had refused to come in. When Brown learned of Moccasin Top's defiance, he increased the size of Thunder Bull's detachment and on August 6 sent him back to No Water's village on the same mission. Moccasin Top again refused, saying he would die first.[11]

On August 8 Brown dispatched Sergeant Guy Belt and six Indian police to bring in Moccasin Top. When Belt and his detachment of Indian police approached No Water's village, Moccasin Top and nine of his followers grabbed their Winchesters and ran into the bushes along White Clay Creek. As the Indian police rode into the village, Little Wolf, Moccasin Top's father, hailed them. Little Wolf told Belt that Moccasin Top and other men had gone in the bushes. Little Wolf informed the Indian police that they could go get them if they were prepared to take the consequences.[12]

Disobedience to the Indian police had never happened during Valentine McGillycuddy's eight years as Indian agent or during Hugh Gallagher's four. Clearly, the Indian police had lost the moral authority that previously enabled them to maintain law and order on the reservation.

Upon returning to the agency, Belt lied to Brown. He told Brown that Moccasin Top was no longer at No Water's village and had gone to the Cheyenne River Reservation.[13] It is likely that Belt gave Brown misleading information to avoid further encounters with Moccasin Top that would needlessly put lives at risk. Quite possibly, Belt also believed that if Moccasin Top came into the agency, he would be locked in the guardhouse, inflaming an already tense situation. Regardless of Belt's reason for lying to Captain Brown, one thing was clear: the Indian police were unwilling to support Brown. They also had such little regard for the Indian agent that they lied to him when it seemed prudent to do so.

At this time, Can Nopa Uhah took Moccasin Top and his followers into the Broken Arrow Band, giving them the additional protection of more warriors with guns.[14]

Brown eventually learned that Moccasin Top was still at No Water's village, and he ordered an even larger force of Indian police to go to the village and bring him in. The Indian police returned the next day and reported that Moccasin Top had no intention of coming into the agency. During this encounter, Bear Eagle, the Miniconjou from the Cheyenne River Reservation, gave the Indian police a message to deliver to Brown. Bear Eagle wanted Brown to know that his brother was Big Foot, the Miniconjou chief killed at Wounded Knee, and that if Brown tried to remove Bear Eagle from Pine Ridge, he would die as Big Foot had died—fighting. The Indian police also told Brown that the Indians in No Water's village were frenetically ghost dancing.[15]

Upon learning of Bear Eagle's threat, Brown wrote Commissioner Morgan:

> It has been reported to me by the police that the Bear Eagle band of renegade Cheyenne River and Rosebud Indians have been killing beef cattle belonging to the contractor, which are being held on White River near the mouth of White Clay Creek, and that they resisted arrest by taking to the ravines with their guns. The police claim that these Indians are fully armed and that Moccasin Top put on his Ghost Shirt and went to the hills, defying the police. Bear Eagle is with this band. I sent today a police force sufficient to arrest this party, but have previously sent word to them, through Young Man Afraid, that they had better come in peaceably to the Agency in obedience to instructions. This will be the third message that has been sent them and I consider that the exigencies of the case now demand that these Indians shall be compelled to obey instructions.[16]

The implication was obvious. The Indian police had no ability to control the lawless malcontents in No Water's village, and Brown's threat was equally clear. He wanted soldiers to come onto the reservation and arrest Moccasin Top and Bear Eagle. Remembering what happened the last time an Indian agent had brought soldiers onto Pine Ridge to control unruly Indians, Morgan did not respond to Brown's request.

Brown then tried to shift the blame for the lawless Indians to No Water and two other chiefs, who were at the time visiting their Shoshone friends in Wyoming: "I think that if permission should be granted these Indians to leave, they should be distinctly given to understand that they will be held responsible for those whom they leave behind."[17]

Having taken the stance that the Moccasin Top's and Bear Eagle's lawlessness was No Water's problem, Brown did not make any more attempts to bring in Moccasin Top or remove Bear Eagle. After all, an important guest was coming. Brown wanted it to appear as if everything was going smoothly on the reservation and he was in absolute control.

The important guest was Theodore Roosevelt, who was on a committee of three that had oversight of the United States Civil Service Commission. At the time, Civil Service Commission rules did not cover employees on Indian reservations. Many in the capital saw extending civil service to the Indian reservations as the best way to end the havoc visited on many reservations, particularly Pine Ridge, caused by the partisan appointments of unqualified persons.[18]

Roosevelt arrived at Pine Ridge during the last week of August 1892. Brown personally guided him on a six-day tour of the reservation, covering 250 miles in a light, horse-drawn wagon. Brown charmed Roosevelt with stories of his tours of duty on the frontier during the Indian wars, his three-year stint as commandant at the Hampton Institute, and his days at Delaware College. Roosevelt was suitably impressed. He wrote in his report: "Captain Brown is a man of wide experience in Indian affairs, evidently deeply and intelligently interested in the welfare of Indians under him, striving earnestly and with all his heart to advance them on the road toward civilization.... No one could be with him as long as I was and see the Indians with him without realizing that he is thoroughly devoted to his work and is laboring with an eye single to the public good. I cannot speak too highly in his praise. He is the exact type of Indian agent whom we most need."[19] Clearly, Brown was a smooth talker.

Roosevelt no sooner left Pine Ridge than Short Bull and Kicking Bear arrived. They had been gone from the reservation since January 26, 1891, when General Miles left Pine Ridge via special train for Fort Sheridan, headquarters of the Division of the Missouri, and took with him twenty-five leaders of the Messiah craze.[20] He intended to confine the rabble-rousers at Fort Sheridan long enough for the unrest on Pine Ridge to dissipate. As Miles's luck would have it, William F. "Buffalo Bill" Cody almost immediately asked the general for permission to employ the prisoners in his Wild West Show, which was about to debark on a European tour.[21] This struck Miles as a good solution. The instigators of the Messiah craze would be humbled by a trip across the Atlantic in a big steamboat and educated about the powers of white people as they craned their heads to look up at cathedral spires reaching high into the sky. At the very least, the renegades would be Cody's problem.

Short Bull's European tour went well for him until February 1892. The troupe was then in Glasgow, Scotland, a damp, windy land at all times and especially bone-chilling in the dead of winter. Short Bull got deathly sick and became partially paralyzed. His chest muscles were so weak that he could hardly breathe. Consulting physicians expected him to die.[22] But he did not. On March 4 twenty-four Lakota, including Kicking Bear and Short Bull, set sail from Scotland for America aboard the SS *Corean*. When the ship berthed at Brooklyn Harbor on March 18, a corporal and three privates went aboard and took charge of the former ghost dancers. Twelve of them were escorted directly back to Pine Ridge. The other twelve were taken to Fort Sheridan.[23]

Two months later, nine of the Indian prisoners at Fort Sheridan pledged they would not take up ghost dancing if they were returned to Pine Ridge, and they were escorted back. Short Bull, a fermenter of the Messiah craze, was held at Fort Sheridan until the first week in September, when he was returned to Pine Ridge.[24]

Later, Kicking Bear was personally escorted from Fort Sheridan to Pine Ridge by Captain Frank Baldwin. Wearing a black sombrero and dressed in store-bought clothes, Kicking Bear arrived at Pine Ridge on Monday, September 12. Short Bull, Young Man Afraid of His Horses, American Horse, and other Oglala notables were waiting to greet him. They held a corn dance in Kicking Bear's honor. A few days later, Kicking Bear joined Short Bull as a resident of No Water's village.[25] Government officials hoped a trip across the ocean and a tour of several European countries had mollified the two old warriors. Being a realist, Kicking Bear gave them assurances that he was a changed man and told a newspaper reporter, "I have promised to go on the war path no more. I want peace."[26]

However, he and Short Bull soon had the malcontents frenetically ghost dancing. If they needed a reason for ghost dancing, the Bureau of Indian Affairs supplied it by giving the Oglala rations that were rotten and spoiled.[27]

While the malcontents ghost danced, Brown initiated a questionable transaction. On September 27 he requested that the Bureau of Indian Affairs send him $26,000 in cash with which to make an emergency purchase of cattle from individual Indians.[28] The request departed from government policy designed to ensure against fraud in the cattle-buying process. The policy stated that when a beef contractor delivered cattle, Lieutenant Guy Preston from Fort Robinson was to be present to certify accuracy.

Retrospectively, it is difficult to identify the circumstances that warranted Brown's request to purchase cattle directly from individual Indians. A month earlier, Bartlett Richards, who had a big ranch in Nebraska, had brought a large delivery of beef cattle to the agency.[29] On November 2, Ike Humphrey delivered 225 head of cattle to the agency for the beef ration.[30] Moreover, Brown wired Humphrey on November 7 to cancel an upcoming delivery of cattle, notifying the beef contractor that "we do not need cattle from you on 14 November."[31]

Robert Belt questioned Brown's request to buy cattle directly from individual Indians: "If the necessity for early purchase of beef from Indians existed, why did you delay your request until September 27?"[32]

Buying cattle directly from Indians had been done before. In 1891 Cheyenne River Indian agent Perain Palmer and his chief clerk, George Shoenfelt, who was also his in son-in-law, had bought cattle directly from Indians. It was alleged that they paid the Indians a fraction of the market value, billed the government the market price, and pocketed the difference.[33] Brown's unwarranted request to make an emergency purchase of cattle directly from Indians suggests he was using the same playbook.

It was now fall and time to bring the needed rations and annuities to Pine Ridge to sustain the Oglala through the upcoming winter. Baking powder was unloaded at Rushville by the hundreds of pounds. Lumber arrived by the thousands of board feet; coal arrived by the ton. Thousands of bushels of corn were delivered. It fell to Indian freighters to get the supplies from Rushville to the agency, twenty-three miles to the north.

The freighting did not go smoothly. J. E. West, the station clerk at Rushville for the Fremont, Elkhorn and Missouri Valley Railroad, notified Brown on November 14 that one hundred thousand pounds of flour had arrived, but because storage capacity was exhausted, the flour could not be unloaded.[34] (Most likely the railroad billed the Bureau of Indian Affairs for tied-up freight cars.) That same week, West notified Brown of another transportation problem: "Please inform me about the transportation of the lumber now here."[35] Brown informed E. C. Harris, division superintendent of the Missouri Valley and Elkhorn Railroad, that "being restricted to Indian freighters it is impossible to have any given number of them at the railroad [terminal] at a certain date to move freight, their movements being slow at best and uncertain at all times."[36] Harris replied, "I will see what can be done toward extending the present warehouse. But if the capacity were doubled, the same trouble would exist unless the freight is moved more promptly than at present."[37]

The problem Brown experienced with his Indian freighters was in sharp contrast to the assessment Agent Hugh Gallagher had made of his Indian freighters three years earlier: "With regard to freighting, this work the Indians have performed in a perfectly satisfactory manner, no loss or injury to goods resulting from their transportation."[38] That same year, 1889, Dr. Charles McChesney, the agent for the Cheyenne River Agency, reported, "During the past year the Indians have transported from Fort Pierre to the agency [a distance of thirty-eight miles] without loss or damage, all of their annuity goods and supplies, as well as all school supplies; and from the boat landing, about four miles from the agency, all of their flour."[39]

Why did the Indian freighters working for Gallagher do such excellent work but those same Indian freighters working for Brown prove so undependable? The answer lies in the relationship Gallagher and McChesney had with their Indian wards. Both were honest men. During their tenures as Indian agents, there was not one allegation that they had lined their pockets with ill-gotten gain obtained by cheating the Indians out of their annuities and rations or defrauding the government. American Horse's assessment of Gallagher shared with the Crook Commission in 1889 attests to the Oglala's regard for him: "Our agent here is a very good man, and we are pleased with him and respect him."[40] The Indians' high regard for McChesney was reflected in the steady progress they made, without a ripple of unrest, during his four-year tenure as agent at the Cheyenne Agency. The contrasting unreliability and slowness of the Indian freighters at Pine Ridge suggests that they were cagily doing their best to frustrate Brown and undermine his dictatorial, iron-fisted control. In that they were at least moderately successful.

That fall the Indian unrest at Pine Ridge became public knowledge on the western frontier when a Rapid City newspaper informed its readers: "[T]he Indians are dancing again and the Indian police were unable to bring in the renegade Moccasin Top."[41] As always, newspapers across the country reported word of unrest on Pine Ridge and used it as grist for articles intended to increase sales. On September 20 the story about unrest and lawlessness on Pine Ridge was reprinted in newspapers across the country, including the *Evening Herald* of Shenandoah, Pennsylvania; *Lincoln Evening Call* of Lincoln, Nebraska; *Dakota Farmers' Leader* of Canton, South Dakota; *Waterbury Evening Democrat* of Waterbury, Connecticut; and *Wilmington Daily Republican* of Wilmington, Delaware.[42]

The implication that Indians were the cause of the tension on the Dakota frontier ruffled the feathers of Captain Frank Baldwin, who had just returned from assessing the extent of the Indian unrest and its causes. Baldwin felt it was incumbent upon him to inform the public where the blame for the unrest really lay: "If the Indians at Pine Ridge go on the war path again, it will be the fault of Indian Commissioner Morgan. The bacon furnished them is rotten and nothing has ever been done in season [meaning the rations and annuities often arrived late]. The government is to blame. Morgan simply refuses to listen to any complaints the Indians make and the contractors have no checks placed on them.... All of the Indians cherish no bad feelings against the whites, but the meat [they have been given] would have made any white man ready to fight the Indian Commissioner."[43]

Morgan was quick to defend himself, saying that Baldwin's claim about rotten meat was not true.[44] Morgan's driving mission to reduce the Indians' rations in the belief that it would motivate them to become self-sufficient and less of a drain on white taxpayers seemed to close his ears to concerns of people like Craft and Baldwin with firsthand knowledge of the conditions on Pine Ridge. Morgan's ideological blinders were even more inexplicable in that he had, at that time, not set foot on the Pine Ridge Reservation.

The alarming talk of dangerous Indian unrest on the Pine Ridge Reservation fed on itself; newspaper coverage of the problems and Indian unrest increased. It reached a fever pitch on October 10 when the *Omaha Daily Bee* published a lengthy front-page article under the headline "Inclined to Give Trouble." The article was based on an interview with Valentine McGillycuddy. The former Indian agent had just come from a visit to Pine Ridge, where he had sought out a number of his old Indian friends to get their assessments of the situation. McGillycuddy found his Indian friends extremely reticent to talk, which only prompted him to probe deeper. McGillycuddy shared his conclusions:

> I don't wish to pose as an alarmist, but the situation at Pine Ridge is not at all satisfactory at present; and there are no immediate prospects of its improving. The Indians are sullen... and unless something is done to counteract this, there is danger of trouble next spring.... The messiah spirit is not dead and the whites must not depend on the statement that the Indians are no longer considering the promises made by old Sitting Bull and the other medicine men who led the trouble two years ago.... The most significant thing of all is the fact that there have been communications between the various tribes of a secret and apparently important nature during the summer. No Water was on secret mission to the Crows and old Red Cloud had just returned from Wyoming, where he went in hopes of meeting a delegation of the Utes.[45]

The alarming article was reprinted in newspapers from coast to coast, including the *Chicago Tribune, Inter Ocean, New York Times, Los Angeles Herald,* and *Saint Paul Globe.*[46]

George Bartlett also believed there were ominous signs of unrest among the Oglala. He shared his opinion with a reporter for the *Sioux City Herald*:

> I do not think that McGillycuddy exaggerated in the least when he told what the situation is on the reservation. I have been on the reservation eighteen years in one capacity or another, and I think I understand the Sioux pretty thoroughly. I know that the Indians on the reservation are more than anxious to engage in the ghost dancing again. The only reason they do not dance is because they are afraid to start. All they need is an impulsive fellow to start them. Once started, they would be like a flock of sheep and the Indians would commence dancing all over the reservation. . . . If once the Indians get to dancing, they will go from the dance to open hostilities. . . . Despite the denial of the agent, I know there is imminent danger of an outbreak. There are hundreds of ghost shirts among the Indians and all that is keeping them from engaging in the dance is fear of the consequences. They are very much dissatisfied. . . . I know the [Indian] police cannot be depended on. Half of them lean toward the Indians in sentiment and will undoubtedly join the hostiles. . . . The trouble, I think, is with Agent Brown at Pine Ridge. He knows nothing of Indians and nothing of how to deal with them."[47]

Bartlett's concern about an Indian outbreak was reprinted by the *Evening World* of New York City under the inflammatory headline "Talk of a Sioux Outbreak."[48]

When the newspaper articles came to Brown's attention, he immediately wrote to Commissioner Morgan, denying that trouble was brewing on the reservation.[49] That Morgan made no intervention suggests that Brown's assurance there was no unrest at Pine Ridge was exactly what the commissioner wanted to believe.

In spite of Brown's denial and effort to convince his superiors that there was no unrest at his agency, dissatisfaction and anger were rampant. How long would it be until the Oglala's passive resistance erupted in bloodshed?

⚔ 13 ⚔

NO WATER AND HIS CAMP OF MALCONTENTS

When the calendar rolled over to 1892, bureaucrats in Washington pushed concerns about an Indian outbreak on the Sioux reservations to the backs of their minds. They convinced themselves that all was calm on the Lakota reservations. It was, but with one exception—No Water's village.

In 1892 the malcontents in No Water's village were defiant and beyond the pale of the Indian police—untouchable. Despite Captain Brown's efforts, Moccasin Top and his followers were still ghost dancing and Bear Eagle and his band of hotheads from the Cheyenne River Reservation continued to pitch their lodges in No Water's village. Can Nopa Uhah and his Broken Arrow band also resided in No Water's village.[1]

As nearly as can be determined, No Water was born in 1840 along the North Platte River into a family of considerable influence. His older brother was Black Twin, a skilled orator and a man of growing importance. As a young man, No Water was a contemporary of Crazy Horse, and the two were rivals for the attention of Black Buffalo Women, a sixteen-year-old Lakota maiden. When Red Cloud sent out word that he would lead a horse-thieving party against the Crow, he picked No Water and Crazy Horse, among others, to join him. Not far into the journey, No Water complained of great pain in a tooth. Because his medicine was the two canine teeth of the grizzly bear, No Water interpreted his toothache as a warning that he should not go on this horse-stealing trip, which was likely to entail a skirmish with the Crow. He went back to the Oglala

No Water's village. From *Illustrated American*, January 24, 1891.

camp. When Crazy Horse and the others returned from their raid on the Crow, they found No Water had married Black Buffalo Woman, Red Cloud's niece.[2]

Crazy Horse was despondent over the marriage and refused to honor it. During the next several years, he spent increasing amounts of time in No Water's camp, publicly displaying his affection for No Water's young wife. Crazy Horse's father tried to dissuade his son from showing such obvious attention to Black Buffalo Woman. However, Crazy Horse could not be dissuaded. After all, by Lakota custom a wife could leave her lodge anytime she wished.

And that is what happened. Early one day Black Buffalo Woman put her three children out among relatives and in the bright sun of the morning rode away from the encampment with Crazy Horse. On the second evening, the eloped couple came upon a small band of Oglala camped along a timber-lined creek in the Slim Buttes area. They were invited to stay. The couple and their hosts had just finished the evening meal when the tepee flap was suddenly torn back. No Water stood before them. He aimed his pistol at Crazy Horse, who reached for his knife and started to stand. As he did, No Water fired. The bullet tore through Crazy Horse's upper jaw and he fell across the fire. No Water immediately fled, believing he had killed Crazy Horse, but he hadn't.

Black Buffalo Woman was soon back in No Water's lodge, and No Water gave three horses to Crazy Horse's father in retribution. According to Lakota custom, all animosities were then to be set aside. However, the gift of three horses did not placate Crazy Horse. He wanted revenge. Sensing that, No Water and Black Buffalo Woman departed and moved a considerable distance to live with another band of Oglala.

Sometime later Crazy Horse saw from a distance two Oglala men skinning a buffalo. He slowly rode his horse toward them. One of the men was Moccasin Top; the other was No Water. Upon recognizing Crazy Horse, No Water jumped on his horse and fled. When Crazy Horse learned that the fleeing man was No Water, he started after him. Crazy Horse chased No Water mile after mile, gradually gaining on him. Ahead was the Yellowstone River, swollen bank full by the June rise. Crazy Horse was certain that he had cornered No Water against the raging river. However, No Water chose possible drowning to doing combat with Crazy Horse. He plunged his horse into the ice-cold water, reached the north shore, and escaped.[3]

No Water did not return to his former lodge. Instead, he moved south to pitch his tepee with Chief Big Mouth and the Loafer band, who lived like beggars near Fort Laramie. For several years No Water stayed with the Loafer band, under the implicit protection of the American flag that flew over Fort Laramie. As for Crazy Horse, from 1866 to 1868, he, Young Man Afraid of His Horses, He Dog, Big Road, and Man Who Carries the Sword aligned with Red Cloud in a successful war that forced the army to remove the military forts strategically placed along the Bozeman Trail.[4]

That year, 1868, the U.S. government and the Lakota negotiated the Fort Laramie Treaty, which, among other things, established the Great Sioux Reservation. East to west, it ran from the Missouri River to the west-facing slope of the Black Hills. South to north, it went from the Nebraska border to the Cannonball River, a total of approximately thirty-five thousand square miles.[5] Article 16 of the treaty specified "that the country north of the North Platte River and west to the summits of the Big Horn Mountains shall be held and considered to be unceded Indian Territory [upon which] no white person or persons shall be permitted to settle upon or occupy . . . or pass through without the consent of the Indians."[6] Five agencies were established on the Great Sioux Reservation as distribution stations for treaty-promised rations and annuities. Most of the Indians, including Red Cloud's band and Spotted Tail's band, settled into semipermanent camps. However, a few Lakota rejected agency life and moved to the unceded Indian territory, preferring to continue their nomadic hunter-gatherer life. Crazy Horse and his band were among them. That made it convenient and indeed possible for No Water to move with the Loafer band when they left Fort Laramie and went north to pitch their lodges near the newly established Red Cloud Agency, along the headwaters of the White River and only a few miles northeast of Fort Robinson. No Water was living at the Red Cloud Agency in June 1876 when Crazy Horse and the allied Indians wiped out Lieutenant Colonel George Armstrong Custer and nearly all the Seventh Cavalry.

The next time No Water saw Crazy Horse was on May 6, 1877. He was among the gawkers when Crazy Horse and the 150 warriors in his band, followed by some seven hundred women and children, rode into Fort Robinson to "surrender." From Fort Robinson, the band went downriver a few miles to pitch their tepees at the Red Cloud Agency. Crazy Horse was camped there only a short time when he heard a rumor that soldiers were coming for him.[7] Accompanied by Shell Boy and Kicking Bear, Crazy Horse and his wife, Black Shawl, fled upriver toward Spotted Tail's camp. Believing Crazy Horse was escaping back to the unceded Indian territory, an army officer gave No Water encouragement and permission to lead twenty-five armed Indian scouts in pursuit. They chased Crazy Horse, Black Shawl, and the two warriors for forty miles. It was said that No Water killed two horses in his futile attempt to catch and presumably kill Crazy Horse. However, Crazy Horse and Black Shawl reached Touch the Clouds's village safely. Touch the Clouds and his warriors jumped on their horses and chased No Water and his party until they passed through the stockade door at the adjacent Fort Sheridan. The next day, September 5, Crazy Horse was killed.[8]

In 1879 the Red Cloud Agency was moved northeast to White Clay Creek and renamed the Pine Ridge Agency. No Water was then a chief in his own right, with 285 people in his Hogan Yute Sni (Don't Eat Fish) band.[9] They settled along the south bank of White Clay Creek, fifteen miles downstream from the agency.

In the summer of 1889 the Crook Commission came to Pine Ridge for thirteen days, doing all they could to entice adult male Lakota to sign the Sioux Bill. Many Indians addressed the council during those tense days. No Water addressed the council only once, saying, "I never get up and make many speeches. There is my father, the agent, over there. He knows that I never come around and talk to him very much." No Water went on to make two points. He reminded the commissioners that they promised not to pressure the Oglala to sign the agreement, but simply to explain it. His second point was more direct: "I hope that we will not any of us lose our ration tickets on account of this."[10]

When the Messiah craze erupted on the Pine Ridge Reservation in the summer of 1890, several thousand Indians gathered at No Water's village to take part in the Ghost Dance. When the ghost dancers sought refuge on Stronghold Table, No Water stayed put, making sure not to be regarded as a hostile while simultaneously not doing anything that might suggest alignment with the friendlies.

On December 29, 1890, the day of the Wounded Knee Massacre, four thousand frightened Lakota streamed down White Clay Creek to No Water's village. Many of them were still there in 1893. The government marginalized the Indians in No Water's village by referring to them as "malcontents." As boss farmer of the White Clay District, Philip Wells had responsibility for the residents of No Water's village, including the Indians in the Broken Arrow band, whom he considered to be outlaws. He was tipped off by friendly Indians that some in Can Nopa Uhah's band daily looked for an opportunity to kill him. In the presence of any adult male from this band, Wells kept his right hand inside his coat as if fingering a pistol. "The Indians knew I was ready to draw my gun and in that way I bluffed them. But I was as afraid of them as they were of me."[11]

In the fall of 1892, No Water was the head of the village in name only. The real leader was forty-three-year-old Short Bull, who had all the qualifications. Short Bull had been a warrior at the Battle of the Little Bighorn. In the fall of 1889, the Lakota had selected him to be one of their eleven emissaries to journey to Pyramid Lake and learn Wovoka's teachings about the second coming of the Messiah. Short Bull brought back Wovoka's teachings and soon had hundreds of Brulé in Chief Lip's isolated camp at the mouth of Pass Creek ghost dancing.[12] He and Two Strike rendezvoused near the confluence of Grass Creek and White River and then took refuge on the nearly impenetrable Stronghold Table. They departed Stronghold for the agency on December 27, but hearing the sounds of battle coming from Wounded Knee Creek on the morning of December 29, the hostiles retreated to No Water's village and stayed there until surrendering on January 15.

Short Bull was one of the twenty-six Indians singled out by General Miles for incarceration at Fort Sheridan near Chicago.[13] Being hauled away to Fort Sheridan only added to Short Bull's credentials. He was at Fort Sheridan only a short time before going with Buffalo Bill's Wild West Show on a European tour. In contrast to most of the Indians on the reservation, who had never been more than one hundred miles from Pine Ridge, Short Bull was a worldly man. He had seen the big eastern cities, traveled across the huge ocean in a steamboat, toured Europe, and even been introduced in one of Queen Victoria's drawing rooms wearing a shirt made of scalps, presumably of men—both white and Indian—he had killed in battle.[14] When Father Florentine Digmann met Short Bull, he was impressed: "[Short Bull] was well-built and had vivacious eyes. He was witty, level-headed, smart, amiable, social and conscious of his dignity—all the qualities of a leader."[15]

An explanation of No Water's village would not be complete without mentioning a place called the "halfway camp," so named because of its location fifteen miles from the western border of the reservation and roughly fifteen miles from the agency headquarters. The dugout and the adjacent corrals had been erected as early as 1886.[16] A succession of government herders stayed there while holding large herds of cattle close by, making it convenient to drive a couple hundred head into Pine Ridge every fifteen days for the beef issue. At the time it was built, the halfway camp was a convenience. But after several thousand malcontents flocked to No Water's village following the fighting at Wounded Knee, it became problematic to have the beef contractor's men living only a quarter mile up White Clay Creek from No Water's village of malcontents and within sight of Can Nopa Uhah's band of outlaws.

As 1893 commenced, the halfway camp and the white cowboys responsible for cattle belonging to white ranchers were a daily reminder to the malnourished, hungry Indians of the injustice forced upon them—thousands of cattle feeding on Lakota grass that could not be touched by Indians. In short, the halfway camp and what it represented was a ready-to-explode powder keg.

⋈ 14 ⋊

THE BROWN-EASTMAN DISPUTE

Valentine T. McGillycuddy, the mercurial former Indian agent at Pine Ridge, was also concerned about Indian unrest in 1892, and he knew how to engage the levers of power. As McGillycuddy passed through Chicago on March 28, he called on General Nelson Miles and informed him that the Rosebud and Pine Ridge Indians were aroused to a high state of excitement. They were again ghost dancing and looking for an excuse for an outbreak.[1]

Albeit slowly, the U.S. government was moving to placate the Oglala and the Brulé in the best way it knew how—with money. Special Agent James Cooper was concluding his yearlong task of ascertaining who among the friendlies had legitimate claims for losses suffered during the Messiah craze. The money for these claims would come from the Indian Depredations Act, which dated back to 1796 and thereafter was included in every annual appropriation until 1920. The original act enabled whites to petition the court for financial compensation for property damage done to them by marauding Indians.[2] For the government, it was a winning hand. Putting money in the hands of white settlers curried their goodwill and, hopefully, their votes, and without additional cost to the government because the money was deducted from funds in the U.S. Treasury already allocated to Indians.

At the urging of Secretary of the Interior John Noble and Commissioner of Indian Affairs Thomas Morgan, Congress put a provision in the Depredations Act of March 3, 1891, to allocate one hundred thousand dollars for the friendly

Indians on the Cheyenne River, Lower Brulé, Pine Ridge, Rosebud, Standing Rock, and Tongue River Reservations who had incurred depredations as the result of the Indian unrest of 1890. A total of 754 residents submitted claims amounting to $201,456.64.[3] By the end of March 1892, Cooper had traveled to each reservation, completed his investigations, and left for Washington with the 150-pound bundle of claims and supporting evidence.[4] After approval by Morgan, Noble signed the order to release the funds on April 11, 1892. Cooper was to act as disbursing agent.

Cooper had rejected ten claimants because they belonged to the hostile faction and determined that claims totaling $110,976.58 could be substantiated. That amount was reduced by 10 percent per claimant to bring the payments within the one hundred thousand dollars appropriated by Congress. It was further reduced by 1.5 percent when expenses incurred in investigating and then dispersing the money were deducted. The final amount allocated to the residents of the six reservations was $97,708.90, with $80,000 slated for the claimants on the Pine Ridge Reservation.[5]

Cooper arrived back in Pine Ridge in April 1892 ready to distribute the money. A day or two before Cooper began the distribution, James A. Finlay, the post trader, had in his possession the names of the claimants and how much money each was going to receive. He then allowed each claimant credit at his trading post up to the amount the Indian would receive a few days later.[6]

Not everyone thought that paying "friendly" Indians for depredations committed by "hostile" Indians was a good idea. Months after the money had been dispersed, acting Indian agent George LeRoy Brown made it known that he disapproved of paying the friendly Oglala for losses suffered during the Messiah craze. In a letter to Commissioner Morgan, he wrote: "The Indians have been saying among themselves that it was about time for them to start another outbreak inasmuch as the money that they recently received from the government for their claims had about given out. They are convinced that by creating trouble on the reservation they would be able to collect damages from the government."[7] That might have been Brown's honest assessment, but it also indicated his management style. During his tenure at Pine Ridge, Brown found ways to avoid taking responsibility for any problems, real or anticipated.

Cooper allocated four days for the dispersal to Pine Ridge residents. Each recipient was told to be at the agency on a specific day and stand in line outside the agency building. When the door opened, each claimant entered the building and walked down a narrow passageway to a small table. Two men sat behind the table. One was a man by the name of Black, Special Agent Cooper's brother-in-law; the other was Finlay. The Indians knew Finlay well and they didn't like him. Anything they bought at his trading store cost two or three times more than the same item sold for in Rushville, but for an Indian, Rushville might as well have been a hundred miles away. They could not go there without a written pass from Captain Brown. Finlay was at the table for one reason and one reason only: to make sure that any recipient owing money at the trading post had that amount deducted from the reimbursement.

Black then handed the claimant a slip of paper showing the amount of cash he was to receive. The recipient took the voucher to another table twenty feet away, where James D. Hyde, Brown's brother-in-law, was seated.[8]

One has to wonder why Brown's brother-in-law was in charge of handing out the money. He was not, then or later, an agency employee. Rather, James Hyde, the oldest of Mary Hyde Brown's four brothers, was at the time a store clerk living in Saint Louis with his wife and two children. Had he come 550 miles upriver by steamboat and then 250 miles by rail to visit his sister and was simply conveniently handy? Or had he been solicited to come to Pine Ridge and offered a tidy financial incentive to disperse the money to the claimants? At any rate, Hyde looked at the amount of the voucher and had the Indian sign a receipt; those who were illiterate were to "touch the pen." Hyde then gave the recipient the money. Whereas several people witnessed Black determine the amount of money due the Indian, no one was delegated to witness Hyde hand out the money. When the money was awarded, an Indian policeman quickly showed the recipient out through another door and onto the street.[9] The entire allocation process and the personnel in charge had the appearance of being organized from beginning to end to enable deception and fraud.

When the claimants had been given their money and were back on the street, many of them paused to consider what had just transpired. Some believed they had been shortchanged. They took their concerns to educated friends—some Indian, some white—gathered in the street to watch this boredom-breaking event. The voluntary consultants found that in almost each case the claimant had been cheated out of 10 to 15 percent of the money owed. Several of the interlocutors took their concerns about possible shortchanging to Special Agent Cooper. He curtly told them the Indians had either made a mistake about the amount of money they were to receive or had lost some of the money.[10]

A few of the Indians who believed they had been shortchanged and also some of their advocates shared their concerns with Dr. Charles Eastman, the post physician and also a Santee Sioux. Eastman brought the matter to Brown's attention. When Cooper was made aware of the accusations against him, he too requested that Brown investigate. After interviewing a selection of claimants, Brown announced that there was no evidence that any of them had received a cent less than was due them.[11]

Eastman was suspicious of Brown's conclusion because the acting Indian agent refused to permit him or any of the Indians' advocates to sit in on Brown's investigative interviews. Eastman also believed it was not within the Indian agent's authority to investigate charges made against a federal employee not under his supervision. Eastman wrote a letter to Commissioner Morgan, stating his concerns and asking for an independent investigation.[12]

When Brown learned that Eastman had written Morgan about the Indians possibly being shortchanged and also questioning his authority to conduct an investigation, the Indian agent was livid. He sought out Eastman and reprimanded the doctor for not bringing his concerns directly to him, the acting agent. He also beseeched Eastman to rescind his call for an inquiry. Eastman refused. "I was," Eastman later related, "determined to do all in my power to secure justice for those poor, helpless people who had been shortchanged."[13]

Morgan dispatched Benjamin H. Miller, an inspector for the Indian Service and a Quaker, to investigate. First he met with Eastman and Brown for a joint discussion of the matter. Brown began the meeting by framing the issue as if it was Eastman's credibility that was being questioned. Addressing Eastman, Brown said, "In the very start I wanted to defend you, if I could."[14]

Eastman replied that he was not accusing Brown of fraud. Rather, in his opinion, the matter was beyond Brown's hands and should have been investigated at a higher level. Eastman also wanted Miller to understand that he did not incite these suspicions among the Indian claimants; he was simply reporting concerns some of the claimants and their advocates had brought to him.

Each man laid out his position. Brown told Miller that no one other than Eastman had mentioned a word to him about being shortchanged, including the Indians themselves. Eastman reiterated to Miller that he did not start the rumors. He simply listened to the people, both whites and Indians, who sought him out and told him their concerns. All he wanted was an impartial investigation by a properly authorized employee of the Bureau of Indian Affairs.

At that point, Miller dropped a bombshell: "I was ordered to come here and look into this very matter and then I received orders to drop it."[15] It can be surmised that the order to drop the investigation did not come from Commissioner Morgan, who had ordered the inquiry, but rather from Secretary Noble.

Despite learning that Miller had been ordered to drop the inquiry, Brown and Eastman pressed Miller to investigate, but for different reasons. Eastman wanted Miller to investigate whether Cooper had defrauded the Indian claimants. Brown wanted Miller to investigate and clear him of the implied accusation that he had not properly conducted his inquiry.[16]

Capitulating to the pressure from Brown and Eastman, Miller engaged Herbert Good Boy, a young Oglala recently returned from the Carlisle Industrial Indian School, to be his interpreter. Because of the necessity of translating all of Miller's inquiries into Lakota and the Indians' answers into English, taking the testimony was laborious and time-consuming. Miller conducted the first interview on the morning of August 29 and completed the last one on September 9. During those twelve days, he interviewed one hundred claimants. Miller concluded that the claimants had been shorted approximately ten thousand dollars. He sent his report to Washington without letting either Brown or Eastman know its contents.[17]

Eleven days after Miller conducted his last interview, Brown received a short letter from Eastman, notifying him that Eastman's government-issued horse was lame and had been lame for a year.[18] Upon receipt of Eastman's letter, Brown passed it on to Morgan, along with a request for authorization to purchase a horse for Eastman.[19] That would be the last cordial exchange between Brown and Eastman.

When Morgan passed Miller's report on to Noble, he refused to accept the conclusion, offering up the thinly veiled justification that the interpreter, whom he mistakenly called Weston, was totally incompetent.[20] That was an interesting excuse for dismissing Miller's report. After all, Noble was not present at Miller's interviews with the Indian claimants, and even if he had been, Noble did not speak Lakota and would not have known whether the interpreter was incompetent. However, Noble used the contrived charge of incompetence as an excuse to send Special Agent James H. Cisney to Pine Ridge with instructions to conduct another investigation.

While the agency awaited Cisney's arrival, a letter from Eastman to Miller came into Brown's possession. It is surmised that in the letter Eastman reiterated his concerns that Cooper had shortchanged the Indian claimants and also that Brown did not have the authority to investigate the alleged fraud. Brown passed

Eastman's letter on to Morgan with the request that Eastman be transferred to some other agency.[21] The fight was on.

Brown fired the first salvo. On October 15 he wrote to Morgan, reporting Eastman for abusing the government-issued horses in his care: "The condition of these horses has been noted by me from time to time as becoming rapidly worse, [as] indicated by their appearance, reckless use, [and] want of proper care.... In accordance with my best judgement, Charles A. Eastman, Agency Physician, is alone at fault."[22]

Ten days later Brown attempted to recruit the temporary services of Dr. James Davis, a physician from nearby Rushville, but was unsuccessful because the sought-after doctor was unable to travel. Brown belatedly notified Eastman of his recruitment efforts, writing "the request for a physician was made after being informed by your wife that you were unable to attend to your official duties on account of illness."[23]

When Cisney arrived at Pine Ridge on November 11 to commence his investigation, the animosity between Eastman and Brown was palpable. As an employee who reported directly to the secretary of the interior, Cisney knew his role. He had played it a year earlier at the Cheyenne River Reservation, where he had investigated fraud charges against Agent Perain Palmer and, despite considerable evidence, exonerated him.[24] Cisney now came to Pine Ridge to vindicate Cooper and, by implication, Brown.

The circumstances at Pine Ridge made it easy for Cisney to get the evidence he needed to exculpate Cooper and Brown. In 1892 an Indian agent was a dictator. He had almost total control over the Indians on the reservation; there was almost no limit to an agent's power. An Oglala could not leave the reservation without a pass signed by Brown. When very important people, specifically Theodore Roosevelt and then Herbert Welsh, had toured the reservation in August of that year, Brown ordered all Indians under the age of fifty to cut off their long hair—to look "civilized." Any male who refused to comply was denied rations, stripped of his job if he had one, and made ineligible for any job that might develop.[25] Brown also had the power to deny rations to Indians who did not send their children to school. He helped gather up Indian children and send them to Captain Richard H. Pratt at the Carlisle Indian Industrial School, despite parental objections and their emotional remonstrations. An Indian could not kill and butcher his own beef without written authorization from the Indian agent. A man and woman could not marry without his permission; nor could they divorce without his consent.

As the acting Indian agent, Brown had dictatorial powers and he wielded them often.

Special Agent Cisney conducted his investigation as if it were a court trial. During the course of thirty days, he put selected Oglala claimants on the witness stand and grilled them with questions. All the claimants took the witness stand knowing that first Brown and then Miller had previously held formal inquiries to investigate whether the claimants had been shortchanged. That they were now testifying to Cisney made it apparent to them that their previous testimony had been discarded. By word of mouth, they also knew that Brown was insistent that no claimant had been shortchanged. Though most of the Oglala claimants were illiterate, they were not fools. As Brown sat in on the court-like proceedings, closely listening and watching, Cisney got the testimony he needed to exonerate Cooper and, by implication, Brown.[26]

Cisney had no sooner completed his courtroom investigation than Brown ramped up his attack on Eastman. He sent Cisney a five-page letter wherein he accused Eastman of insubordination. "I have the honor to submit herewith the following statement, to wit: The relations between myself and C. A. Eastman, Agency Physician, have been strained on account of the Doctor's insubordination and disrespectful conduct towards me, as Agent." Brown concluded the letter by accusing Eastman of medical incompetence: "I have made allowance at all times on account of the fact that he was an Indian, although his age being 35 years and having had exceptional educational advantages would lead one to think that he would be able to perform his duties without such allowance being made."[27]

As the dispute between Brown and Eastman intensified, Eastman's wife, Elaine, inserted herself into the fray in the worst possible way. She wrote an article for the *New York Evening Post* implying that Brown was incompetent and had questionable ethics.[28] Making the Brown–Eastman dispute public did not help her husband's cause. Rather, it turned up the heat. Herbert Welsh, whom Brown had personally guided on a four-day tour of the reservation in September 1892, jumped to Brown's defense by writing newspaper articles supportive of Brown.[29]

When Elaine Eastman's article came to Captain Brown's attention, he enclosed a copy of it in a letter to Cisney and asked him to include it in his report to Noble.[30] Brown also began to intentionally and maliciously hamper Eastman's ability to do his medical work, including not adequately equipping the hospital, locking up the doctor's private stock of medicines, and sending Eastman to the far corners of the reservation to see ill patients, who upon

Eastman's arrival proved to be perfectly healthy.[31] The animosity and mistrust between the two men reached the point that Brown refused to speak to Eastman without a witness present because "either his knowledge of the English language is utterly at fault or he willfully misstates facts." For his part, Eastman kept up the fight in Washington by contacting his influential friends and otherwise making considerable efforts to prove the Indian claimants had been defrauded.[32]

Morgan attempted to end the dispute by offering Eastman a position at Fort Lewis, Colorado, or some other agency.[33] Eastman replied that he would accept a position at the Indian school at Flandreau.[34] But before the position could be formally offered, Eastman informed Morgan that he had changed his mind.[35] While Eastman's letter declining the position was en route to Washington, Morgan wired Brown: "You are advised of the transfer of Dr. Eastman to the position of physician at the Flandreau School."[36]

While those exchanges were transpiring, Noble instructed Cisney to return to Pine Ridge and investigate the strained relationship between Brown and Eastman.[37] While Cisney's investigation was nearing completion, someone—likely Brown or his clerk, George Comer—informed the *Chadron Democrat* that "Dr. Eastman and wife Elaine Goodale and the principal of the Indian schools at Pine Ridge [probably meaning Superintendent James Meteer] have been discharged for sending out sensational reports to the effect that the Indians were preparing for an outbreak."[38] There was no basis for the story, suggesting that it was intentionally planted in an attempt to prompt their dismissals.

When Cisney completed his investigation, he shared his findings and conclusions with Brown. Brown immediately wired Morgan to suggest that he ask Noble to order Cisney to return to Washington with all the papers about the case.[39] Brown waited two days for Morgan to reply. When he did not, on December 20 Brown sent a letter to Cisney, asking him to arrange for Noble to officially request Cisney to appear before him and explain his written report about the strained relation between the agency physician and Brown and also the conduct of certain employees who, on the witness stand, had expressed their opinion that the investigation was a whitewash.

Knowing that Cisney's investigation supported Brown, Eastman asked Morgan for a thirty-day leave. Morgan approved the request,[41] but Eastman did not immediately depart.

On December 24 Brown wired Morgan yet another request for Eastman to be transferred.[42] Morgan responded: "Dr. Eastman will not be transferred but retained in service."[43]

Brown was incensed that Morgan would not do his bidding. Disregarding that it was Christmas Day, Brown sent yet another telegram, a particularly strident one, asking if Morgan had revoked his order transferring Eastman to Flandreau. "If so, can't he be transferred elsewhere without delay and authority granted me to employ a physician temporarily?"[44] No reply was forthcoming from Morgan's office on Christmas or, not surprisingly, the day after. In a move that can only be described as desperate, Brown wired Morgan yet another appeal: "I earnestly request that this matter be brought to the attention of the Secretary of the Interior. I consider it in the best interest of public service that he [Eastman] be transferred."[45] Again, Morgan did not reply. At that, an anxious and frustrated Brown ceased following the chain of command. He decided that if Morgan would not remove Eastman from Pine Ridge, maybe Noble would. With that intent, Brown forwarded a copy of Morgan's telegram, which denied Brown's request to transfer Eastman, to Cisney. Brown added, "I earnestly request this matter be brought to the attention of the Secretary of the Interior. I consider it to be in the best interest of public service that he [Eastman] be transferred."[46]

At this time Noble was being pressured by Welsh, spokesperson of the politically powerful Indian Rights Association, to support Brown. Noble wired Cisney: "Hurry the report on Eastman case which is immediately needed."[47] The next day, December 28, Cisney replied: "Report and evidence in Eastman case mailed today."[48]

On January 1 Eastman slipped off the reservation without notifying Brown. Upon learning that Eastman had left his duty post without notifying the acting Indian agent, Cisney wired the information to Noble, adding, "Eastman should be dismissed without further notice."[49] The next day Brown sent a similar telegram to Morgan.[50]

The problem became further complicated when a man by the name of Hutson arrived at Pine Ridge, claiming to have been employed by Eastman as a substitute in his temporary absence. Brown reported in his telegram to Morgan that Hutson refused to accredit himself as a practicing physician. The agent concluded the telegram by requesting authorization to employ a capable physician as a temporary agency physician.[51] Brown followed that telegram with another that was direct and to the point: "Dr. Eastman's action in leaving the reservation without reporting to me . . . as well as his previous conduct justifies in my opinion his immediate removal."[52]

At that point, it was clear to Morgan that Eastman had ramped up his disagreements with Brown into a personal vendetta and then overplayed his hand. Worse yet, the dispute between Eastman and Brown had entered the public domain and it could no longer be handled internally. Looking for a way to gently deal with Eastman, Morgan solicited the help of Frank Wood, Eastman's benefactor and life coach while in medical school.

The telegraph wire in and out of Pine Ridge began to hum. The first telegram was from Morgan, asking Brown to ascertain the whereabouts of Eastman. Brown wired back that he had asked the hospital steward as to Eastman's whereabouts and was told that, according to Elaine Eastman, her husband was at the Cataract Hotel in Sioux Falls but that she was not sure a communication sent there would reach him.[53] That information apparently got passed through channels to Wood. He enlisted the help of U.S. Marshal Cyrus Fry, whose office was in Sioux Falls, asking him to locate Eastman.[54] Fry wired back that Eastman's whereabouts were unknown.[55]

Morgan decided it was necessary to make the Eastmans aware that their situation was dire. He did that by wiring a rather terse missive to Elaine Eastman: "The President directs Doctor Eastman to report here to see the Secretary of the Interior. Communicate with him and advise me by wire if you have reached him."[56] Wood wired that same message to Eastman: "By direction of the President, you will report to the Secretary of the Interior."[57]

Recognizing the urgency, Elaine Eastman wired her husband in Flandreau: "Received telegram from Commissioner. President directs you to report to the Secretary of the Interior."[58] The next day, January 8, Eastman wired Morgan: "Will leave for Washington tomorrow."[59]

At this sensitive time, Eastman sent a lengthy article to the *Omaha Daily Bee*, detailing how the Indians were shortchanged in the distribution of their depredation money. His article appeared on the front page of its January 8 paper.[60] That very day the newspaper story was brought to Brown's attention. He immediately wired Morgan, notifying him of the article and asking him to "take proper action."[61] Brown also began a word-of-mouth search for a new agency physician.[62]

Eastman's brother, the Reverend John Eastman, pastor of the Sioux Presbyterian Church at Flandreau, joined him on the trip to Washington, D.C. Upon arriving, they took lodging at the National Hotel.[63] During the next several days Eastman laid his case before Senators Henry Dawes and George Hoar, Commissioner Morgan, and Secretary Noble. All were noncommittal; Eastman left for home without a definitive answer.

While Eastman was in Washington, his wife sent an article to the *Springfield* (Massachusetts) *Republican* for publication. In part, it read: "Dr. Eastman

Dr. Charles A. Eastman. (South Dakota State Historical Society.)

Elaine Goodale Eastman. (South Dakota State Historical Society.)

and I demand a full and fair examination of the conduct of the acting agent, and also that of the inspector. . . . It now remains to be seen whether one can speak the truth upon an Indian agency and survive."[64] That article sealed the couple's fate.

Upon returning to Pine Ridge on January 23, Eastman told Brown that he had no positive orders and therefore expected to resume his work as agency physician. Brown wanted to know from his superiors whether he was ordered to place Eastman on duty.[65]

Cisney, who was still at Pine Ridge, wired news of Eastman's return to his boss, Noble, adding that in the best interest of the service, Eastman should not be allowed to return to duty. "Brown and Eastman cannot work together."[66]

Cisney's telegram convinced Noble that enough was enough. He could not wait for Morgan to act definitively. The next day, January 25, Noble sent Brown a drama-ending telegram: "Have sustained you. . . . Dr. Eastman is suspended and will be sent elsewhere. . . . Exercise your authority firmly but quietly. Let Indians and others know you have my approval and will be sustained."[67]

Morgan wired Eastman: "The Secretary directs you to be transferred unless you wish to resign. Must decide at once."[68] Eastman immediately wired back: "I prefer to resign."[69]

After being forced out of Pine Ridge, Charles and Elaine Eastman and their one-year-old daughter, Dora, moved to Minneapolis. He opened an office and hung out his shingle, but patients were few and far between. In 1893 white people were not ready to believe an Indian could be a skilled, highly competent physician. After three decades, during which they reared six children and were under financial strain, Dr. and Mrs. Eastman separated. Later in life Charles Eastman built a small cabin on the eastern shore of Lake Huron and lived there alone, with little social contact. When winter came each year, he retreated to Detroit to the home of his only son. He died there in January 1939.[70]

✣ 15 ✣

LOOKING AT THE BROWN-EASTMAN DISPUTE THROUGH OTHERS' EYES

When assessing a person's character, a wise person is suspicious of vitriolic debasements uttered by a known adversary. Applying that cautionary note to Eastman's criticisms of Brown in 1892, one wonders whether at the time there were others at Pine Ridge who believed him to be dishonest and deceitful and questioned his competence.

One person in a good position to have an opinion as to Brown's character was George Bartlett. He had seventeen years' experience working on or near the reservation and served as U.S. deputy marshal on Pine Ridge during much of Brown's tenure.

Bartlett was born on August 25, 1858, in New Haven, Connecticut. At the age of sixteen he moved west with his parents to Sioux City, Iowa. A year later he went to the Yankton Agency and clerked in a trading store until the siren sound of gold reached his young ears. In August 1876 he left Yankton, Dakota Territory, with a party bound for the Black Hills.[1] Their guide was the legendary Louis Shangreaux, a one-time army scout of Lakota and French ancestry. The party traversed along the northern border of Nebraska and avoided drawing the army's suspicions by putting up a pretense of looking for homesteads in the Nebraska sandhills. At a point near present-day Gordon, Nebraska, they turned north toward the Black Hills and immediately trespassed onto the Great Sioux Reservation. Early one morning a party of warlike Sioux approached their circled wagons. Shangreaux talked to them in their native language. Recognizing him, the Indians left without attacking.[2]

Upon reaching the new goldfield, Bartlett located several claims near Deadwood in Two-Bit Gulch. In 1879 John B. Marshall, the U.S. marshal for Dakota Territory, appointed Bartlett deputy U.S. marshal, a job he kept for the next fourteen years. In 1883 Bartlett married Catherine Carroll and started a trading store/post office at the Indian village on upper Wounded Knee Creek.[3] The couple parted ways in 1886.[4]

On September 7, 1890, U.S. Marshal Cyrus Fry assigned Bartlett to be U.S. deputy marshal for the Pine Ridge and Rosebud Reservations.[5] It was a good choice. At a time when every frontiersman considered himself a good shot with a rifle, Bartlett was regarded as a crack shot, as testified by his ability to unfailingly put a hole in a silver dollar thrown into the air.[6] He spoke passable Lakota and knew the two reservations like the back of his hand. He also knew the Indians and they knew him. The *Daily Deadwood Pioneer Times* lauded his appointment.[7]

Not long after Brown became acting Indian agent at Pine Ridge, Bartlett began to suspect that Brown and some of his employees were cheating the Indians out of their rations and annuities. Specifically, Bartlett began collecting evidence that Brown's chief clerk, George P. Comer, was defrauding the government; but Bartlett too openly shared his suspicions and apparently word got back to Brown. On February 23, 1892, Brown wrote to Commissioner Morgan, requesting that Bartlett be terminated as U.S. deputy marshal and not be allowed to set foot on the Pine Ridge Reservation.[8] When Bartlett was not removed, Brown wrote to U.S. Special Inspector Benjamin Miller, complaining about Bartlett's continuing presence on the reservation and using innuendo to smear Bartlett's character: "I am enclosing newspaper clippings which appeared in the *Omaha Bee* under the date of July 26, 1892 . . . with the request that you take such action as will protect the Indian Service against employing a man who has the character that the correspondence will show Geo. E. Bartlett has."[9] The enclosed article from the *Omaha Bee* was not a defamation of Bartlett's character. It merely related that Bartlett was back from Washington, D.C., where he had consulted with the South Dakota congressional delegation about taking seventy Sioux to the upcoming Chicago World's Fair in 1893 and having some of them set up a display of a typical Indian village and others set up an adjacent "civilized" village, so by contrast the public could see how far the Sioux had advanced.[10]

When Brown's effort to remove Bartlett was again disregarded, a clever plan was hatched. Likely at Brown's urging, George Comer accused Bartlett of stealing horses from the Indians and filed charges with the U.S. attorney for the District of South Dakota, William Sterling.[11] Although no evidence that Bartlett had stolen anyone's horses was uncovered, he was suspended as U.S. deputy marshal and removed from Pine Ridge.[12] Senator Richard Pettigrew jumped to Bartlett's defense, saying that an accusation was not sufficient grounds for suspending Bartlett. Sterling reconsidered and Bartlett was reinstated.[13]

Brown continued his vendetta against Bartlett and despite no evidence of malfeasance brought sufficient pressure to bear that in November 1892 Cyrus Fry terminated Bartlett as a deputy marshal,[14] removing another of Brown's accusers from Pine Ridge.

Bartlett did not go quietly. He let it be known that, in his opinion, Brown wanted him removed because he knew too much: "I was a little too attentive to duty and certain Indian officials feared I was learning too much about [their] shady transactions."[15]

Another person at Pine Ridge whom Brown singled out for retribution was the Reverend James H. Meteer. In early 1891, at the age of fifty-six, Meteer was hired as superintendent of the government boarding school at Pine Ridge for the munificent salary of seventeen hundred dollars a year—not much, even in 1891. His wife, Jane, was installed as matron of the school at an annual salary of $720.[16]

It likely was Meteer whom the defrauded Indian claimants sought out upon suspecting they had been shortchanged. That would explain why a few weeks later Brown lodged an accusation against Meteer. In a letter to Miller, Brown related that Meteer "has made certain charges against me personally, including a charge of shaking and kicking two of his boys."[17] Brown later wrote another letter to Miller critical of Meteer. In that letter, Brown related that someone (whom Brown conveniently did not name) came to him and reported that while Meteer and his wife rode the train to Hot Springs, Meteer was overheard making negative comments about Brown's mistreatment of two Indian boys. Brown concluded the letter by asking Miller to support "transferring Meteer and his wife in accordance with my request."[18] In response to the request to transfer the Meteers, Morgan replied: "Your request for Mr. and Mrs. Meteer to be transferred was disapproved. Re-nominate them immediately."[19] Being a person who did not like to have his will thwarted, Brown made it a point to inform Commissioner Morgan that transferring Meteer and his wife "would be in the best interest of the service."[20]

Brown likely did not know that Meteer and Morgan were friends of long standing. They were both Indiana boys. During the Civil War, then General Thomas Morgan commanded the first brigade of colored troops of the Army of the Cumberland. Brevet Captain James Meteer served in his brigade. In December 1891, four officers of that brigade met in Lincoln, Nebraska, to renew their friendship and reminisce about scenes and triumphs of their war experiences. A few days later Meteer and Morgan traveled together to Lawrence, Kansas, to attend a meeting of Indian teachers from all parts of the West.[21]

Brown continued to make things so difficult for the Meteers that six months later Meteer appealed to Morgan for a transfer. Without asking Meteer to explain why he wanted a transfer, Morgan wired back: "I will offer you desirable transfer by mail today.[22] Two weeks later, Meteer notified Morgan that he accepted the transfer.[23] Brown was pleased. Another of his accusers had been dispatched.

The Eastmans, George Bartlett, and the Meteers were not the only ones at Pine Ridge who disapproved of Brown's management style. So did Father Florentine Digmann. Digmann was born in Heiligenstadt, Germany, in 1846 and moved to Austria in 1872 to finish his studies in a Jesuit seminary. Digmann, a Jesuit brother, and three nuns arrived at the Rosebud Agency in 1886 to establish the Saint Francis Mission. Being a polyglot, he quickly became fluent in Lakota.[24]

In 1891 Digmann replaced the recently departed Father Francis Craft at the Holy Rosary Mission, formerly known as the Drexel Mission. One of Digmann's challenges was keeping the mission solvent. To do that, Digmann needed to fill the mission's boarding school to capacity with students because with each came a government stipend. To bring in more students, Digmann solicited Brown's assistance. In response, Brown gave Digmann a list of students in the Wounded Knee District whose parents were anxious for their children to attend the mission's boarding school. However, when Digmann went to Wounded Knee to gather up the children on Brown's list, he found only one child. "All the rest [of the parents] wanted to send their children to the day school."[25]

When Digmann informed Brown that the promised Indian children were nowhere to be found, Brown said he would personally go to the Wounded Knee District with the priest and produce the students. On the specified day, Digmann went to the agent's office at the appointed time and waited. When

Father Florentine Digmann and unidentified man wearing chief's costume. (Courtesy of Red Cloud Indian School and Marquette University. Holy Rosary Mission–Red Cloud Indian School Records. ID: MUA_HRM_RCIS_0083.)

Brown arrived, he declined to go with Father Digmann, citing threatening weather as an excuse. However, he again promised to talk to the Indian parents. A few days later, Digmann was at the agent's office at the scheduled time to learn the result of Brown's promised talk with the parents. Again, he waited for Brown. When the agent arrived, he walked past Digmann as if the priest weren't there and went directly into his office. Digmann attempted to follow him, but Brown slammed the door in the priest's face. Acting on the priest's behalf, the interpreter knocked on the office door. Brown did not answer. The interpreter advised Digmann to enter the office via another door. Quietly and slowly opening the door, Digmann saw that Brown was not busy; but as soon as Brown saw Digmann, he rushed to his desk and opened some letters. After waiting a few minutes and continuing to be ignored, Digmann broached the critical issue, "What did the Indians [the parents] say?" he asked.

Turning to the interpreter, Brown said, "Louie, didn't the supervisor of the schools want just three children [for the mission's boarding school]?" At that obvious dodge, Digmann confronted Brown. "There are eight hundred on the reserve of school age who are not in school." Rather than answer the implied question, Brown went into the adjoining room and shut the door. Ignoring Brown's less than subtle clue to leave, Digmann stayed and waited, and waited. When Brown eventually came back, he passed by Digmann without acknowledging him and addressed his clerk, "Call the parents of these children. I want to talk to them." And he left the building.[26]

Digmann was relentless in his efforts to get more Indian children in his boarding school. When he continued pressing the Indian agent for students, Brown, feeling frustrated and possibly embarrassed, let the truth slip out, "I was sent here to keep the Indians quiet. To force [their] children to [attend] school would excite them."[27]

Not surprisingly and even predictably, when Brown reported to Morgan and indirectly to Congress about his success at promoting the education of Indian children, he painted a rosy but patently false picture: "One of the prime factors in the work of the uplifting of the Indian is education, and I have devoted a good deal of time and attention to encouraging and helping in this development of the school work being done upon this reservation, and the results have in the main been very gratifying."[28]

Will Hughes, who came to the reservation in 1889 to work for his uncle, W. C. Smoot, the boss farmer for the Medicine Root District, was young but observant. Hughes learned that his uncle did not think highly of Brown. Hughes soon was of the same opinion: "Captain Brown did not understand the Indians very well and didn't get on well with people."[29]

Philip Wells, an agency employee who kept a low profile, had both the experience and knowledge needed to make a well-informed assessment of Captain Brown. Wells was born on December 5, 1850, on the shore of Lake Pepin, Minnesota. His mother, Jane, was one-fourth Santee Sioux. His father, James, was a fur trader. Philip was the eighth of their ten children. Dakota, the dialect of the Eastern Sioux, was spoken in their home.[30] In 1875, at the age of twenty-five, Wells went to Sioux City, Iowa, a gathering place for men wanting to go to the newfound goldfields in the Black Hills and strike it rich. But they faced one problem—getting there. The Black Hills belonged to the Sioux, and in 1875 the government was committed to keeping whites out. Wells hired out that summer at the munificent wage of $150 a month to help gold seekers evade the army patrols ranging out of Fort Randall. That summer Wells successfully guided several parties of gold seekers to the Black Hills. His success was due, in part, to knowing the right person in the right place at the right time. To wit: Philip's older brother, army scout William "Wallace" Wells, was assigned to lead patrols to apprehend trespassing gold seekers.[31]

The next year, 1876, Philip Wells was at Fort Lincoln near present-day Mandan, North Dakota, serving as an interpreter for Lieutenant Colonel George A. Custer. In early June he and several others were ordered to deliver a dispatch to a cavalry detachment camped in the vicinity of Bear Butte at the northern edge of the Black Hills. On the way back to Fort Lincoln, Wells and his men were attacked by a war party of Sioux. They took up a defensive position behind some large boulders on a steep hill. The Indians captured their horses and departed. Forced to walk two hundred miles back to Fort Lincoln, Wells missed the opportunity to accompany Custer and the Seventh Cavalry to the fate that awaited them on June 25, 1876, at the Battle of the Little Bighorn.[32]

Destiny had other plans for Philip Wells. Being fluent in French, German, Ojibwa, Winnebago, English, Lakota, and the sign language of the Plains Indians, Wells was involved in important events that shaped the unfolding history of the West. Among them were working as an interpreter at Fort Buford when it served as a prison camp for Sitting Bull and Gall; supervising twenty-eight hundred Indians from the Standing Rock Agency in 1883 on the last great buffalo hunt; serving as an interpreter at trials in South Dakota involving Indians; and being at Wounded Knee as Colonel James W. Forsyth's interpreter on the morning of December 29, 1890. An Indian would have killed Wells that morning had it not been for the scout's catlike quickness and strength. Nonetheless, the Indian nearly sliced off Wells's nose.[33]

As boss farmer for the White Clay District, one of five districts on the Pine Ridge Reservation, Wells had responsibilities far beyond teaching the Indians agricultural skills. He was the day-to-day assistant agent for his assigned district, which included the most malcontent, unruly, and renegade Indians in the West. The position gave Wells a good vantage point from which to observe Brown, and what he saw dismayed him. In his autobiography, written near the end of his ninety-six years, Wells related that "unscrupulous men existed on many of the reservations at the time. One of the rings controlled the Pine Ridge Agency, and Captain Brown was a rubber stamp for the vicious ring."[34] Wells found the men sent by the War Department as Indian agents to be the least desirable in character. In his opinion, the army sent poor officers to the backwater of a reservation and considered it "good riddance." Wells considered Brown to be one of them.[35] At the time, Wells kept his assessment of Brown to himself because he had Sioux blood in his veins, a Caucasian spouse, and a young family to support.

Additional evidence there was a vicious Indian ring at Pine Ridge came from Brown's trusted employee George P. Comer, the chief clerk. In October 1892 Comer sent J. E. West, the station clerk at Rushville for the Fremont, Elkhorn and Missouri Valley Railroad, a cryptic telegram: "Keep your eye on [Cyrus] Fry. He is drawing nigh and will make you sigh."[36]

To fully understand the Brown–Eastman dispute, it is necessary look beyond the opinions of those who lived and worked at Pine Ridge and also the findings of various official investigations. The formative experiences of the antagonists—Captain George LeRoy Brown and Dr. Charles Eastman and his wife, Elaine, must be considered.

As for Brown, the formative experiences that influenced his management of Pine Ridge began the day he entered the U.S. Military Academy (West Point). It was the fall of 1868 and Republicans were trying to get Ulysses Grant elected president. Their campaign theme was "Let us have peace." Like most slogans, this one could be interpreted to mean whatever was foremost in one's mind. Many believed the slogan referenced the requisite tone and tenor for ongoing reconstruction of the war-torn South. Some believed the slogan alluded to the nation's history of relentless and bloody warfare against Indians. In keeping with the latter interpretation, shortly after taking office, Grant announced his "peace policy." He believed that for too long the government had used warfare to force the Indians to cede more and more land, and it was time to adopt a more enlightened approach. Henceforth, Indians were to be regarded as "wards of the nation" and treated as such. Among other measures to achieve that end, Grant established a ten-member Board of Indian Commissioners and gave them broad powers, including oversight of the Department of Indian Affairs and authority to replace corrupt Indian agents with Christian missionaries and to "civilize" the Indians by parceling out to various religious orders a monopoly to proselytize on designated reservations.

Grant's peace policy immediately encountered opposition, including that of the highest-ranking military officer, General William T. Sherman. Sherman believed it was still necessary to use force against Indians when warranted, and in Sherman's eyes, force was often warranted.

Throughout his four years at the Military Academy, Cadet George Brown would have been at least a passive participant in academic discussions as to whose strategy was best—Grant's peace policy or Sherman's advocacy of warfare when warranted. It does not require much speculation to believe that when the cadets at West Point discussed this quandary, there were snickers in the classroom whenever the idea of peaceful relations with the Indians was voiced.

When Brown graduated from the Military Academy in the class of 1872, he was commissioned as a second lieutenant, with his first assignment at Fort Concho, Texas, where soldiers occasionally skirmished with small parties of Indians.[37] While Brown was at Fort Concho, word arrived that Custer and most of the Seventh Cavalry had been killed during a battle with the Sioux in eastern Montana Territory. The dead included Lieutenant Henry Moore Harrington, a fellow cadet with Brown in the class of 1872. Another classmate at West Point, George Wallace, was killed by the Lakota at Wounded Knee just two years before Brown became the acting Indian agent at Pine Ridge.[38] These deaths undoubtedly sparked within Brown a dislike and possibly even hatred, at least temporarily, of the Sioux.

Brown was later transferred to Dakota Territory. He was one of the officers among the five companies of the Eleventh Infantry crowding the deck of the *Nellie Peck* on September 4, 1876, when the steamboat arrived at the Cheyenne River Agency, the home of a significant number of the Indians who had participated in the Battle of the Little Bighorn and recently slipped back to the agency to get rations and annuities. It was a heady time to be an army officer on the frontier. Six weeks earlier, on July 22, control of the Lakota agencies had been transferred from the Department of the Interior to the Department of War.

The Eleventh Infantry's mission at the Cheyenne River Agency was to put Fast Bull, Touch the Clouds, Kicking Bear, Hump, and other Lakota chiefs and headmen on notice that their June 25 victory at the Battle of the Little Bighorn was not the beginning of their power; it was the end. To make that point, in October General Philip Sheridan, commander of the Division of the Missouri, ordered that the Indians at the Cheyenne River Agency be forced to surrender their guns and give up most of their horses.[39] Brown was on the cutting edge of the sword that emasculated the Lakota warriors drawing rations at the Cheyenne Agency.

In 1881 Brown was transferred to the Hampton Normal and Agricultural Institute in Hampton, Virginia, where he served as commandant of students. The institute was mostly for black youths, but there were also 140 Indian children at the school. After Hampton, Brown did another tour of duty in Dakota Territory before becoming commandant of students at Delaware College.

When Brown became acting Indian agent at Pine Ridge in November 1891, President Grant's belief that it was time to look after "our Indian wards" had morphed into "our Indian problem." It was a problem no one knew how to solve, and the government gave up trying. Its unarticulated fallback position was to give the Indians just enough rations and annuities to keep the unrest on the reservations from fermenting into a headline-grabbing Indian uprising. Brown understood that. As he told Digmann, "I was sent here to keep the Indians quiet."[40]

Precedence supported Brown's primary responsibility as he saw it. The bureaucrats and politicians in Washington, D.C., had made it clear that an Indian agent who could keep the Indians quiet was more highly valued than an honest one. Their handling of fraud charges brought against Valentine McGillycuddy was a case in point.

In August 1882 a petition from the Indians at Pine Ridge was placed on the desk of Merritt L. Joslyn, assistant secretary of the Department of the Interior. The petitioners asked that McGillycuddy be removed as Indian agent. Joslyn dispatched Special Inspector W. J. Pollock to Pine Ridge with instructions to take temporary control of the agency and investigate.[41] After taking testimony from a good many residents of Pine Ridge, both whites and Indians, Pollock concluded that McGillycuddy was supplementing his meager annual salary of twenty-two hundred dollars by stealing rations, overweighing and hence overcharging for beef cattle, and filing false receipts to the tune of one hundred thousand dollars annually.[42] When Pollock finished his report, he showed it to McGillycuddy, who made a written confession and wrote a letter of resignation.[43]

Upon receiving Pollock's report, Interior Secretary Henry Teller wired the inspector that he was suspended from the investigation by order of the president. Teller then dispatched Special Agent Eddy Townsend to Pine Ridge to conduct a second investigation.[44] Townsend investigated and sent his report to Hiram Price, commissioner of Indian Affairs. The report stated that there was substantial evidence that McGillycuddy had indeed defrauded the government. Price read Townsend's report and immediately confined it to the darkness of a locked desk drawer, from which it never emerged to see the light of day.

When McGillycuddy's letter of resignation came to Teller's attention, the secretary refused to accept it.[45] After all, McGillycuddy was keeping Red Cloud, the man who had driven the army from the Bozeman Trail, in check and was almost daily eroding the chief's power and influence. Teller believed that only one man could single-handedly accomplish that, and that man was Valentine McGillycuddy. Evidence of fraud be damned. McGillycuddy was the man Teller wanted and needed at Pine Ridge.

A decade later the Department of Indian Affairs was still overlooking evidence of fraud as long as the agent kept Indian unrest at a low simmer. Such was the case with Parain Palmer and his chief clerk, George Shoenfelt. When they were accused of defrauding the government, Secretary of the Interior John Noble dispatched Special Agent James Cisney to investigate. Cisney arrived at the Cheyenne River Agency in October 1891. Despite considerable evidence of fraud, he wrote a report that exonerated Palmer and Shoenfelt.[46]

Yet the department's response was much different when Captain Charles Penney, acting Indian agent at Pine Ridge, notified authorities that there was considerable unrest among the Indians at the Cheyenne River Reservation and that he believed it was largely due to Palmer's mismanagement. Noble had the concern investigated.[47] Before a calendar month passed, Palmer and Shoenfelt resigned, no doubt under pressure.

Compared to those two insistences of fraud, so systemic that it amounted to organized crime, Eastman's complaint that the Indian claimants at Pine Ridge had been, in total, possibly cheated out of eight thousand dollars hardly seemed worth the bother. Furthermore, if the allegation was true, it was a victimless crime. After all, was it really of much concern if a claimant's unexpected windfall was to be $500 and he was handed only $450? Then there was the big picture. If Eastman's charges of fraud were substantiated, it would ruin the career of James Cooper, a heretofore loyal government servant. It would also be a black mark against Thomas Morgan and John Noble; and it would be rich fodder for whoever was Benjamin Harrison's competitor in the upcoming election. Many in the nation's capital were likely thinking, "Please, Dr. Eastman, let it go!"

Letting it go was not within Charles Eastman's makeup. In 1858 he was born in a buffalo-hide tepee along the shore of the Minnesota River. His birth name was Hakadah (the Pitiful Last). Hakadah was four years old when the Dakota War of 1862 erupted. He, his mother, and his siblings escaped to Canada. When Hakadah reached adolescence and was renamed Ohiyesa (the Winner), he had long believed his father had been hanged along with thirty-seven other Indians in retribution for their roles in the Dakota War. It made sense to Ohiyesa when his elders instructed him to "never spare a white man from the United States,"[48] meaning if he should come across a white man from the United States, kill him.

When Ohiyesa was fifteen, his father, Wak-anhdi Ota, unexpectedly appeared in their camp in the Canadian wilds. He had converted to Christianity, become a proponent of education, and taken the surname of his wife's father, Eastman. He took his son with him back to his 160-acre farm near Flandreau, Dakota Territory, and renamed him Charles Eastman.

When Charles was sixteen and still not speaking or understanding English, he enrolled in the Santee Training School. He quickly absorbed new information and understandings and was hungry to learn more. With encouragement and support from compassionate teachers, in succession he attended and graduated from Beloit College and Dartmouth. In 1887 he entered the Medical School of Boston University. Ramrod-straight, tall, and strikingly handsome, Eastman lived with and was supported by Frank Wood and his wife while attending medical school. Wood was a successful merchant, a trustee of Wellesley College, and a founding member of the Boston Indian Citizens Committee. As a beneficiary of the family's friendship and connections, Eastman met and conversed with such luminaries as Ralph Waldo Emerson, Francis Parkman, Henry Longfellow, and Matthew Arnold. In October 1890, Wood invited his protégé to the eighth annual Indian conference at Lake Mohonk, New York. Wood proudly introduced Eastman as "a splendid illustration of the development the Indian is capable of."[49] For the Indian rights activists at Lake Mohonk that fall, Eastman was the *glacage sur le gateau* (icing on the cake).

Passionately feeling a commitment to help his kinsmen, Eastman accepted a position as the physician at Pine Ridge. He arrived in November 1890 and was well received, particularly by the Oglala. However, trouble was in the air. When the massacre unfolded along Wounded Knee Creek, scores of Indian women and children, bleeding profusely from the bullets of large-caliber rifles that had ripped into and often through their bodies, were brought into Pine Ridge in such numbers that the pews were moved from the mission chapel, converting it into a hospital. Eastman saved some of the wounded, but many died. On the third day after the massacre, Eastman and a number of volunteers, most being Indians, went to the battlefield. He counted eighty bodies in one cluster. "It took all of my nerve to keep my composure in the face of this spectacle.... All of this was a severe ordeal to one who had so recently put all his faith in the Christian love and lofty ideals of the white man."[50]

Whether Eastman had a measure of animosity against Brown because of his military background, the ruthless slaughter at Wounded Knee by soldiers, and what Brown's military credentials represented pursuant to the treatment of the Sioux cannot be gleaned from Eastman's writings. However, that Brown was racially biased against Eastman is without question. In a letter to Special Agent Cisney, Brown wrote, "I have made allowance at all times on account of the fact that he [Eastman] is an Indian, although his age being 35 years and having had exceptional education advantages would lead one to think that he would be able to perform his duties without such allowance being made."[51] At another time Brown informed his superiors that he refused to speak to Eastman without a witness being present because "either his knowledge of the English language is utterly at fault or he willfully misstates facts."[52] That is an interesting assessment from a man who graduated from college ranked forty-eighth in a class of fifty-seven against a man who graduated at the head of his class from one of the best medical schools in the country.

Elaine Goodale Eastman's role in the dispute must also be considered. She was a child prodigy who read fluently by age three and was reared in a privileged Massachusetts family. At the tender age of fourteen, her first book of poetry was published, launching her literary career. In 1883 Elaine Goodale accepted a teaching position at the Hampton Normal and Agricultural Institute and was attached to the portion of the boarding school that served Indian children. That year she became a founding member of the Women's National Indian Rights Association. In 1885 she and a female colleague adventurously went to the Lower Brulé Reservation as teachers. Goodale soon parlayed her experiences at Lower Brulé into being a paid lecturer for the association and gave lectures up and down the East Coast about the plight of the pitiful Sioux.

In that capacity she met Thomas J. Morgan, the newly appointed commissioner of Indian affairs. Morgan was so impressed with Goodale's accomplishments, her understanding of Indian culture, and her enthusiasm that he created the office of supervisor of education for Indians in the two Dakotas and offered her the job. She accepted, moved to Pine Ridge in the fall of 1890, and began her work. That was when and where she met Charles Eastman.[53]

When two like-minded souls intertwine their lives, it often is a benefit to both, but not always. The marriage of Charles Eastman and Elaine Goodale on June 18, 1891, was a case of not always. They both had strong feelings not only about the historical injustices done to Indians but also about the injustices occurring in front of their eyes. Because of their education and positions, both felt obligated to right the wrongs, especially the wrongs happening right outside their door, one being the purported shortchanging of the Indian claimants. When their attempt to right that wrong mushroomed into a dispute with Brown, Elaine supported her husband and encouraged him to be a staunch advocate for the Indians' cause. That was the mistake of an overly idealistic, supportive spouse. What Charles needed from his wife was not encouragement but a thoughtful, dispassionate analysis of the situation. In particular, he did not need her using her literary credentials and abilities to publish articles in the *New York Evening Post* and the *Springfield Republican* that stopped just short of accusing the commissioner of Indian affairs and the secretary of the interior of incompetence in the misguided, naive belief that the articles would unleash a tidal wave of public opinion that would compel the government to adopt a more compassionate posture toward the Oglala. By 1892 being an Indian rights activist was no longer fashionable, and the few remaining activists had little influence.

By the end of January 1893, Charles and Elaine Eastman were gone. So too were Brown critics Bartlett and the Meteers. So how would the Oglala fare under the management of a military Indian agent whom bureaucrats retained because he was keeping the simmering Indian unrest from erupting into a headline-grabbing incident?

⚔ 16 ⚔

CAN NOPA UHAH'S CRIME

Ike Humphrey and Ed Stenger were West River men. By the mid-1880s each was well-to-do, if not downright wealthy. Stenger was sole owner and proprietor of the Glendale Hotel in Hermosa. Humphrey arrived in the Black Hills in 1877, briefly prospected for gold, but switched to logging and running a sawmill and later to raising horses.[1] In 1887 Humphrey and Stenger formed a partnership and purchased the Z-Bell Ranch near the mouth of Battle Creek.[2]

They soon built the ranch up to nine thousand acres. In 1890 they brought in eleven thousand sheep from Oregon and two thousand steers. Under the terms of their partnership, Stenger was responsible for managing thousands of acres of irrigated land on the Z-Bell Ranch and Humphrey managed the cattle and took care of the beef contract with the Pine Ridge Agency. Humphrey and Stenger also had seven-eighths ownership in the Spokane Mine, a hard-rock mine located a few miles northeast of where the Custer Expedition had discovered gold in 1874.[3] Humphrey and Stenger were among the contractors in 1891 who furnished beef to Pine Ridge, delivering their first herd of three-year-old spayed heifers in April. They were at the mouth of White Clay Creek when a messenger from Acting Indian Agent Charles Penney met them. The messenger advised Humphrey and his cowboys not to proceed farther because there were two camps of hostile Indians between them and the agency. The cowboys went into camp for two weeks, during which time not a single Indian visited them, which was unusual. However, they often saw Indians watching them from a distant ridge. After two weeks a messenger arrived with instructions for them to proceed up White Clay Creek to the agency. En route, they met numerous small bands of Indians, many of whom they knew. The Indians were hungry, and many were afoot because February snow had covered the overgrazed prairie so deep that a great many of their horses had starved to death.[4]

In June 1892 Humphrey and Stenger secured the beef contract at Pine Ridge for fiscal year 1893, which began the next month. The contract called for the delivery of 3,750,000 pounds of beef on-the-hoof at the price of $3.30 per hundred pounds.[5] (That computes to $123,750 in 1892 dollars, equivalent to $3,207,227 in 2018.)

After making a few fifty-five-mile cattle drives from the Z-Bell Ranch to the agency, Humphrey asked Captain Brown for permission to graze four thousand head of cattle on the reservation, making it easier for him to deliver 270 beeves to the agency every twenty days. Permission was granted.[6] Humphrey grazed the cattle near No Water's village and moved three cowboys into a dugout known as the halfway camp to look after the livestock.

The halfway camp wasn't much—a twenty-by-twenty-foot dugout built into the west side of a hill at the confluence of Hill-in-the-Woods Creek and White Clay Creek. The dugout was barely big enough to accommodate two single beds, a bunk bed, a cooking stove, a small table and a few chairs. Less than a stone's throw away was an east-facing stable large enough for four horses. The stable opened up to a small corral with a gate at the south end leading to a five-acre feed corral.[7]

The presence of Humphrey's four thousand cattle grazing for free on reservation grass was an affront and an irritant to the malcontents in No Water's village. Humphrey and Stenger were getting rich while they starved. To some of the constantly hungry, malnourished residents in No Water's village, the cattle were an irresistible temptation. It was not long before Humphrey reported to Brown that Moccasin Top and his followers had killed nine head of Z-Bell cattle.[8] The implication was that Brown should do something about it, but he didn't because by then Brown knew he had no control over Moccasin Top and his followers.

However, Humphrey, being a take-charge West River rancher, spent increasing amounts of time on the reservation,[9] so much time that in November he notified the postmaster in Rapid City to forward his mail to Pine Ridge.[10]

On or near the first of February 1893, word reached Brown that Indians from No Water's village had killed yet another Z-Bell critter. In response,

Brown ordered Sergeant Joe Bush to take a detachment of six Indian police to No Water's camp and arrest the man or men who had killed the steer.[11] Bush and the Indian police rode into No Water's camp mid-morning on February 2, and Bush did as custom demanded. He sought out the man in charge of the camp and made his needs known. "I have come," Bush likely said to No Water, "for the men who killed the Z-Bell cow. Captain Brown wants to talk to them." Traditionally, No Water would have handed over the wanted men to the Indian police, but he didn't.

There are several explanations for why No Water did not comply. One was that Joe Bush was not an Oglala; he was a Brulé from Rosebud, where he had previously been a government herder. That a Brulé was recently made a sergeant of the Indian police for Pine Ridge indicates that no qualified Oglala with enough respect among his people to do the job would take the position. No Water had an even more compelling reason for not handing over the cattle thieves. The Oglala were malnourished because of poor quality, insufficient rations and reduced beef issues.[12] No Water likely chastised Bush for coming to his village to arrest a man for killing a white man's cow so he could feed his hungry children. "Go back to the agency," No Water probably told Joe Bush, "and find something important to do." As Joe Bush and his Indian police left, Hollow Wood and No Flesh fired shots over their heads.[13]

As Philip Wells observed, "the Indians were ... beginning to satisfy their craving of hunger by slaughtering cattle found at large on the reservation. ... [The] evil had been put in motion by faithless administrative orders creating a whirlwind [that soon was] beyond control."[14]

The Indian policemen's attempt to arrest braves in No Water's village for simply killing and butchering one of Humphrey's four thousand beeves angered the Indians in Can Nopa Uhah's Broken Arrow band. On the evening of February 2 they recklessly talked about getting revenge on the cowboys who tried to have one of their band arrested. Their talk of revenge was out of proportion to what had taken place. No one had been arrested and the Indian police had been forcibly rebuffed. From all perspectives, it looked like a coup for the malcontents. Clearly, the talk of revenge had deeper roots.

While the young men in Can Nopa Uhah's Broken Arrow band were working themselves into a frenzy, a mile farther down White Clay Creek, Philip Wells, his family, and his visiting brother, Orman, retired for the night. As the Wells family slept, men in the Broken Arrow band put war paint on their faces and ghost danced themselves into a frenzied rage.[15]

About midnight Philip Wells stepped out his log cabin, possibly to check on the horses in his corral. As Wells stood in the dark trying to determine whether lightly falling snow was the harbinger of a blizzard, a crack pierced the stillness. It sounded like a gunshot. But could it have been, Wells wondered, merely the cracking of ice on White Clay Creek in response to the wave of cold air that had suddenly come down from the north? He wasn't sure. Standing silently, Wells waited to hear what other sounds the night air might bring. It brought nothing.

Wells walked back to the cabin, barred the door, and quietly, so as not to wake his wife and children, slipped into bed. He was nearly asleep when the sound of footsteps running toward his cabin jolted him wide awake. There was a sharp, demanding knock at the door. It was Peter Richard, the same mixed-blood who saw Plenty Horses shoot Lieutenant Casey, his Lakota wife, and their three children. Wells opened the door and the Richard family rushed in. Breathlessly, Peter Richard announced that men from Two Sticks's band had just killed four cowboys at the halfway camp.[16]

Soon after daybreak, No Water sent several men to guard Wells's wife and property so that the Fox, as the Indians called Wells, could investigate the crime. He was accompanied by Peter Richard; Eagle Louse, an Indian from No Water's camp; and his visiting brother Orman, the agency interpreter at Fort Yates, North Dakota. The halfway camp was only a mile from Wells's cabin, so the men walked.[17]

They found four dead men in the dugout. Wells recognized two of them. One was Rodney Royce; the other was Emanuel Bennett. They were the cowboys Ike Humphrey had stationed at the halfway camp to look after the Z-Bell cattle grazing on reservation grass.

Neither Wells nor anyone in the group recognized the other two bodies. In time, it was learned that one of the dead youngsters was James Bacon, age sixteen, and the other was William Kelly, age fifteen. They were farm boys whose parents lived just across the Nebraska line. Taking advantage of the unseasonable warmth of a fifty-degree day, the boys had ventured onto the Pine Ridge Reservation in search of missing horses. It was not by chance that the boys rode twenty-six miles north in search of their horses. Every rancher knows horses are content to stay week after week in an area no bigger than a few hundred acres as long as they have grass, water, and protection to block winter winds. It was strange, at least strange under normal circumstances, that the boys rode north in search of missing horses. In the Dakotas the prevailing winter wind comes sharp and biting out of the northwest, and horses turn their tails to it. The farm boys knew there was no chance the horses had wandered twenty-six miles northwest. They rode that far on the hunch that lawless Indians in No Water's village had stolen the horses. After looking over the horse herd grazing near No Water's village, the boys had stopped at the halfway camp, expecting to be greeted with customary western hospitality. As was anticipated, Royce and Bennett put two more plates on the table that evening and made up the bunk bed in the southeast corner adjacent to the door.

Outside the cabin Wells saw four sets of tracks in the freshly fallen snow, leading to the corral. The tracks indicated that after the Indians had killed the four white men, they took the horses in the corral and led them to No Water's village. The tracks also told Wells that the men were killed by four Indians—all members of Can Nopa Uhah's Broken Arrow band.[18]

When the investigation was complete, Eagle Louse rode into the agency to inform Brown that four white men had been killed at the halfway camp during the night. He had seen their bodies.[19]

Brown immediately sent out a flurry of telegrams. His first wire was to Ike Humphrey: "Four men found on White River above Hidden Butte dead in dugout at your ranch."[20]

Humphrey had spent the evening of February 2 at the Evans Hotel in Hot Springs. The next day he continued on to Pine Ridge.[21] Brown's telegram was likely waiting for Humphrey when he debarked the train at Rushville. Brown then wired Commissioner of Indian Affairs Thomas Morgan: "Three men found dead and one mortally wounded at beef contractor's ranch on White River. Killed last night. Every effort is being made to arrest murderers. Do not anticipate further trouble. Indians so far seem to condemn the act."[22] The telegram was typical of Brown. The facts were not accurate, the action taken was overstated, and the conclusion reached was overly positive. Brown's next telegram was to Colonel Caleb Carlton, the commanding officer at Fort Meade, with whom he shared the same misleading assurances he had given to Morgan; he also added: "The murderers believed to be Indians that have gone north toward the Cheyenne River or Tongue River. Have scouts out scouring the reservation for them. Anticipate no further trouble."[23] Brown's assertion that the murderers had fled toward the Cheyenne River or anywhere else was without foundation. To say the murderers had fled the reservation and then to conclude that he did not anticipate any further trouble was a contradiction from which Carlton may have surmised that Brown's control over the situation was tenuous. Carlton notified Lieutenants Joseph Byron and George Kirkpatrick of the Third Cavalry to prepare to deploy Troop L, Indians recruited from the Cheyenne River Reservation, to the mouth of French Creek.[24]

Brown wanted everyone, including his superiors, believing that he had everything under control. To do that, he sent out assurances without having accurate information. In actuality, four white men were killed at the halfway camp, not three, and no one was wounded; there were no reports that the perpetrators had fled the reservation; and as of February 3 no effort had been made to arrest the alleged murderers. In fact, Brown had little knowledge of what was transpiring in and around No Water's village.

Brown also did not know that early Friday morning, February 3, an Indian had told Frank Galigo, a mixed-blood who lived not far from No Water's camp, of the killings. Upon confirming the information, Galigo and the Indian struck out horseback on a forty-mile ride, much of it through the badlands, to give the tragic news to the foreman of the Z-Bell Ranch, Charles Swartz. Swartz put the reins of a fast horse in a cowboy's hands and told him to cover the twenty-two miles to Hermosa as fast as possible and inform Ed Stenger of the killings. He then asked the Z-Bell cowboys for volunteers to go with him to the halfway camp. Every cowboy stepped up. Despite the hour, Swartz and his heavily armed men left at once for the murder site, arriving in the middle of the night. They struck matches and cautiously entered the dugout. The flickering light revealed two dead men on the floor and two more men dead in their bunks. Overcoats concealed their faces. The cowboys looked around and saw that the dugout had been looted. There was nothing more they could do. Fearing a full-scale war might be about to erupt on the reservation, Swartz and his cowboys hastily set out for Buffalo Gap.[25]

That same day, Friday, February 3, Young Man Afraid of His Horses and He Dog, a son-in-law of Chief Red Cloud, learned of the killings. The two influential Indians immediately went to see Brown. They told Brown that if the Indian police went to No Water's village to arrest the murder suspects, there would be a fight. Blood would be shed and the agent was apt to lose control of the reservation. Soldiers would again be brought in, just like in 1890. Wanting to avoid another Wounded Knee Massacre, Young Man Afraid of His Horses and He Dog volunteered to go to No Water's village and peaceably bring in the wanted men. Brown rebuffed their offer; he did not want it to appear that he was unable to control his reservation.[26]

On Saturday, two days after the murders, Brown ordered Bush to take a squad of twelve Indian police to the halfway camp, retrieve the bodies, and then go to No Water's camp and arrest the murder suspects. Clark Bacon, father of one of the murdered youths, went along.[27] When Bush reached the halfway camp, he came upon Ike Humphrey and three Z-Bell cowboys—Charlie Edgerton, Paul McClelland, and Francis Roush—loading the frozen bodies into a wagon.[28] Approaching Bush, Humphrey said, "Two of these dead men worked for me. I'd like to take care of them. The other two are farm kids from Nebraska. I'd like permission to take them into Hermosa where I'll put their bodies on the train bound for Chadron and send a man along to see that James is delivered to Mr. Bacon and the other boy's body is given to his parents." Bush granted the request.[29] A few days later Humphrey shipped Rodney Royce's body to Royce's brother in Bellwood, Nebraska. Emanuel Bennett's remains were shipped to his family at Breckenridge, Missouri.[30]

Bush and the Indian police went on to No Water's village. Having seen the Indian police arrive at the halfway camp, Two Sticks had directed those in his band who had committed the murders to load their possessions into a wagon and flee. First Eagle, Two Sticks's eldest son; Fights With, also Two Sticks's son; Two-Two, Two Sticks's nephew; and White Face Horse were about to take flight when Bush called out that he wanted to talk to No Water. The young men in the Broken Arrow band answered Bush with a volley of lead.

The Indian police returned the gunfire. Bush shot Two Sticks. The bullet plowed through his chest and he fell to the ground. Believing his father had been killed, First Eagle became enraged and charged the Indian police. They shot him dead. White Face Horse broke for the timber along White Clay Creek. As he reached the trees, Sitting Bear, an Indian policeman, took aim and fired. White Face Horse fell into a clump of heavy brush. Seeing their friends being shot, other men in No Water's village picked up guns and started shooting at the Indian police. In the face of the intense gunfire, the police retreated. A number of Indians from No Water's village pursued the Indian police and likely would have killed some or even all of them had not Young Man Afraid of His Horses and a number of his young braves daringly ridden their horses between the two groups of combatants.[31]

When the Indian police returned to the agency, they had no prisoners. The most positive picture they could paint for Brown was that First Eagle, one of the murder suspects, was dead; Two Sticks was probably dead; and White Face Horse was seriously, if not mortally, wounded. This information did not mitigate the harsh reality that the Indian police were unable to enforce the law on the reservation. The situation was exactly as Young Man Afraid of His Horses and He Dog had foreseen, feared, and tried to prevent. Brown had a crisis on his hands.

To manage the crisis, Brown censored all telegrams sent out of the agency, trying to prevent word of the killings from spreading across the frontier and allowing him to portray to the outside world that he was master of the situation.[32] Accordingly, Brown wired Carlton at Fort Meade on February 4 that the "police detachment under First Sergeant Joe Bush have killed the four murderers. Everything is quiet." He sent a similar misleading telegram to the secretary of the interior.[33]

The same day Brown sent the "all is well" telegrams, he wired a request to the commissioner of Indian affairs for authority to increase the police force from fifty to eighty. Acting Indian Affairs Commissioner Robert Belt approved the request. However, Commissioner Morgan was back in the office the next day and countermanded the permission because it could not be paid for except by a special act of Congress.[34] The denial forced Brown to share the seriousness of the situation with Morgan: "The cause of the trouble not yet determined. . . . Two Sticks' party came out of the sweat lodge and declared their intention to go on the warpath as the time had come for the extermination of whites. Increase of police force to eighty is imperative."[35] James Cisney, the special agent who accounted directly to the secretary of the interior, was at Pine Ridge at the time. He beseeched Secretary Noble to authorize the increase in the Indian police force for at least the balance of the month.[36] Noble approved the request, but asking for a 62 percent increase in the number of Indian police alerted the higher-ups that the situation at Pine Ridge was serious and potentially more explosive than Brown had previously claimed. Orders came down from the Department of War that cavalry troops at Fort Meade were to move into position at the western border of the Pine Ridge Reservation.[37] The Ninth Cavalry at Fort Robinson, forty-five miles to the south, was put on alert and readied for immediate deployment.[38]

Before Brown censored all the telegrams coming out of Pine Ridge, James Finlay, the post trader at Pine Ridge, wired the *Omaha Daily Bee* that four white men had been killed in a skirmish between malcontents and Indian police. Upon reading the telegram, a reporter for the *Omaha Bee* sought out officers of the Department of the Platte for confirmation. He found General John R. Brooke and his staff at a photography gallery. None of them had heard anything about the killings on Pine Ridge; Brooke told the reporter that he was certain there was no foundation for it. However, he dispatched Colonel M. V. Sheridan, assistant adjutant general for the Department of the Platte, to headquarters with the directive to wire Brown and inquire whether there was any truth to the rumor.[39] Brown replied by wire, confirming that four men had been murdered, but he concluded the missive with another of his inaccurate assurances.[40]

In 1893 when a telegram was sent, telegraph machines along the line clicked out the message, creating a conduit for any telegram to become public knowledge. When newspaper reporters heard rumors that unrest on the Pine Ridge Reservation had resulted in bloodshed, they searched for anything and everything that might be grist for the mill. The *Record-Union, Salt Lake Herald, New York Tribune, Helena Independent, Indianapolis Journal, Washington Bee, National Tribune, Alexandria Gazette, Fort Worth Gazette*,[41] and scores of other newspapers splashed the news of the murders under such attention-grabbing headlines as "An Uprising Is Feared"[42] and "They Were White."[43]

A reporter for the *Minneapolis Tribune* sought out Charles Eastman, the former physician at Pine Ridge, who had only recently arrived in Minneapolis. Eastman, still smarting from his dispute with Brown, related a story about the situation on Pine Ridge that sold newspapers. He said the schism between these two factions—the malcontents and the progressives—was so deep and so contentious that it would lead to an outbreak. According to Eastman, the schism had many components, one being that after the unrest of 1890 the progressives were not thanked for the part they had played in the suppression of the unrest, which included risking their lives; and that many progressives were openly saying they would never again help the government against their own people. According to Eastman, another driving force for the unrest was the progressives' sympathy for the injustices inflicted upon the malcontents, which "can be seen on every hand; and the authorities know it, but will not acknowledge it. Young Man Afraid of His Horses professes friendship with the whites, but at heart he is sympathetic with the others [the malcontents]. . . . Even George Swords [sic] . . . one of the most powerful men of the agency is in sympathy with the Indians and has said that in case of a revolt he would stand off and not help the whites."[44]

The *Saint Paul Globe* ran a front-page article under the heading "Butchered by Reds." The paper devoted two columns to the situation at Pine Ridge, much of which was false, including a story that "the cowboys brought on their own killing by returning from town in a drunken condition and with a good supply of whiskey and then proceeded to mistreat an Indian and fire their revolvers at him." The fearmongering article also related that Indians had raided three cattle ranches lying west of the Cheyenne River, driving off many cattle and killing one cowboy, and that hostile Indians had secretly set up a winter camp in one of the most inaccessible parts of the badlands, "where they can defy the United States army until late in the summer."[45]

Newspapers on and near the Dakota frontier also printed stories about the killings laced with inaccuracies. The *Custer Chronicle* told its readers that "the four men were murdered while sleeping, their bodies being literally riddled with bullets. Several of them were otherwise mutilated, having arms broken and their bodies slashed with knives."[46] The *Chronicle* went on to report that there were "wild rumors of another outbreak of the Pine Ridge Agency Indians and a wholesale massacre of cattlemen and ranchers has struck terror to the hearts of the citizens of southwestern Dakota."[47]

The *Omaha Daily Bee* published a letter said to be from Clark Bacon, father of James Bacon:

> I would like to set you right in this. Upon hearing the report of the murder, I and James Kelly, older brother of William, went at once to the Pine Ridge, where the agent, Captain Brown, called in the Indian police who had seen the bodies. In the accompaniment of Indian police, we went to the scene of the murders. There we found four dead bodies. Two were our boys and two were strangers to us. We moved the bodies to the nearby ranch of Philip Wells. At Mr. Wells' house on the night of the murders were his visiting brother and Peter Richard. They saw Indians watching the house, but did not know how many there were. To deceive the Indians, they crawled out a back window and slipped around so they could walk in the front way, thus making it appear that there were a larger number of white men in the house. There were five dirty plates on the table [in the dugout] the next day, which shows the Indians had been fed and then, each picking his man, fired at their victims. At ten o'clock the next morning an Indian policeman found my son James still alive, and made a bed for him and built a fire. At 12 o'clock Mr. Wells went after him with a team and found him dead . . . there was blood all around the woodpile, showing that James had been out [of the dugout] after wood. When we dressed him for burial, we found he had been shot three times to the head and once in the right arm.[48]

Almost nothing in the article was true.

The *Sioux Falls Argus Leader* fanned the flames of panic by printing that an unnamed government official (probably George Bartlett) from the Pine Ridge Indian Reservation covertly informed the paper that "matters on the reservation are in a much more serious condition than is indicated by the dispatches.... The murders were the result of ghost dancing.... When the weather moderates there will almost certainly be an outbreak."[49]

The inaccurate, inflammatory newspaper articles had their effect. William J. Thornby, a rancher bordering the reservation, went into Hermosa to see what could be done about having a couple of companies of cavalry from Fort Meade stationed at the mouth of Battle Creek.[50] Thornby had the distinction of being a pioneer, having walked from Cheyenne, Wyoming, to the Black Hills in 1877, when Indian attacks were commonplace. In 1887 he earned the appellation "Colonel" by becoming a member of territorial governor Louis Church's staff. Now, in 1893, he was a member of the South Dakota State Senate.[51] Thornby's credentials made him a man of importance, whom authorities dismissed at their peril. On March 18, Thornby wrote a letter to General Brooke, commander of the Department of the Platte, asking that one or two companies of soldiers be placed at the confluence of Battle Creek and the Cheyenne River to protect the settlers from marauding Indians.[52] Of course, Thornby did not mention that he had a ranch on Battle Creek and that it would fatten his pocketbook if soldiers, whose stomachs demanded beef and whose horses needed hay, were stationed in the area. Thornby's request was bumped up the chain of command to Daniel S. Lamont, secretary of war. Lamont informed Thornby that placing a company of soldiers at the mouth of Battle Creek made about as much sense as ringing the southern and northern borders of the Pine Ridge Reservation with a line of military posts.[53]

The whites living on the perimeter of the Pine Ridge Reservation were not the only ones alarmed by the murder of the four white men. So were the progressive Indians. Luther Standing Bear, a Carlisle graduate, was teaching school on the reservation and also operating a small general store. One evening Henry Twiss rode his horse to the school. Greatly excited, he informed Standing Bear that Two Sticks and his sons had killed some cowboys and were headed that way. According to Twiss, the murderers said they were going to kill all the white people they could. Twiss reasoned that because Standing Bear dressed in civilized clothes, Two Sticks might mistake him for a white man and kill him. The following morning things got worse. Some Indians came to Standing Bear and said white men had warned them that if any more trouble started, they would kill all the Indians. Standing Bear told them they should move their belongings to his place: "If the soldiers come, I will try to explain to them; but if the soldiers refuse to listen we will fight them to the finish."[54]

Four days after the cowboys were killed, three of the murder suspects were still in No Water's village of malcontents, and the Indian police were powerless to arrest them. Despite all Brown's bluster and assurances, the truth was that his control of the reservation did not extend beyond the perimeter of the agency's headquarters.

⋆ 17 ⋆

CATCHING THE CULPRITS

Fortuitously for all concerned, the temperature plummeted Sunday night. Starting the next morning, February 6, a two-day blizzard with heavy snow and strong wind swept across the northern plains, stopping all travel.[1] During the blizzard, no troops left Fort Meade for the reservation, no settlers organized home guards or solicited Governor Mellette for guns and ammunition, and residents of No Water's village huddled around warming fires in their tepees. During a lull in the blizzard, Bear Louse, a nephew of Young Man Afraid of His Horses, and Short Bull, the medicine man, secured Mark Red Elk (also known as Fights With) and Two Two and moved them to Young Man Afraid of His Horses's village.[2]

Within hours of the storm abating on February 8, Young Man Afraid of His Horses and his braves took the two murder suspects to the agency. To dissuade the malcontents from No Water's village from attempting a rescue, Young Man Afraid of His Horses and his braves formed a large square and rode the ten miles to the agency with the two wanted men in the middle of the square. He told Captain Brown that White Face Horse was seriously wounded and that Two Sticks was expected to die before sundown.[3]

Agent Brown notified his superiors that two of the murder suspects were in his custody.[4] At Brown's urging, the *Black Hills Weekly Times* informed its readers that "the parties of wrong doing have been properly punished, three having been killed and two are now in the hands of the U.S. court at

Deadwood. . . . Everything is quiet here."[5] Of course, Brown did not mention that it was Young Man Afraid of His Horses who brought in the two murder suspects. He wanted the citizens of South Dakota and the rest of the country to believe that on the Pine Ridge Reservation, he and his Indian police were the law and order.

As soon as Fights With and Two Two were locked in the agency guardhouse, Brown wired U.S. Marshal Cyrus Fry, telling him to be at Rushville the next morning to take custody of the prisoners.[6] Fry's office was in Sioux Falls and his assistant, U.S. Deputy Marshal Chris Matthiessen, operated out of Deadwood, making it impossible for either of them to be in Rushville by the next morning, and Brown knew that. Brown likely made the unrealistic request so that if the prisoners escaped, he could claim it was not his fault.

When neither Fry nor Matthiessen was in Rushville the next morning, Brown wired the adjutant general for the Department of the Platte, asking for authorization to have Lieutenant John H. Gardner of the Ninth Cavalry at Fort Robinson transport the two suspects to Deadwood.[7] Permission was granted.[8] Friday morning, February 10, Gardner arrived to take custody of the prisoners. Out of concern that malcontents might try to free Fights With and Two Two, Brown solicited George J. Jarchow, proprietor of the hotel at the agency; Frank Young, storekeeper at Manderson; and George Comer, chief clerk for the agency, to accompany Gardner and his prisoners the twenty-three precarious miles to Rushville and assigned Lieutenant Thunder Bear, Sergeant Joe Bush, Sergeant Blunt Horn, Sergeant Sitting Bear, Two Lance, Black Elk, Black Heart, Red Owl, Dog Chief, Catch Bear, Yellow Shield, White Hat, No Ears, and Gets Thrown From His Horse Three Times to escort them.[9]

While Fry and Mattheissen waited at Rushville that evening to take custody of the prisoners, they heard that a vigilante mob, friends of Rodney Royce and Emanuel Bennett, intended to board the train when it stopped at Hermosa, relieve Fry of his prisoners, and hang them. Believing there might be some truth to the rumor, Fry received permission from Brown for Gardner and the fourteen Indian police to board the evening train and accompany the marshals and their two prisoners all the way to the Lawrence County Jail in Deadwood.[10]

As the train pulled into Hermosa for a brief stop, a glance out the passenger car window revealed a large crowd waiting at the depot. Fry pulled down the window blinds of the coach and locked the doors. Stationing Matthiessen at one door, he went to the other door and stepped out. The crowd wanted to see the prisoners, but Fry told them he would not allow admittance to anyone under any circumstances and the crowd melted away. However, the train ride to Deadwood did not go without mishap. At one point on the trip, Fights With attempted to strangle himself with a handkerchief but was thwarted in the attempt. A short time later he tried to commit suicide by swallowing a large button.[11]

Soon after Fights With and Two Two were incarcerated in the Lawrence County Jail, a grand jury met and indicted each of them on the charge of murder. Granville G. Bennett and John H. Burns presented themselves as attorneys for the defendants.[12]

The Indian police officers' return trip by train from Deadwood back to Rushville did not go smoothly. At Hermosa a group of cowboys boarded the train and harassed and threatened the Indian police.[13]

Matthiessen's next assignment was to arrest White Face Horse and Two Sticks and transport them to Deadwood. Possibly because Matthiessen knew it would be difficult to extract them from No Water's village of malcontents, he allowed John Burns to accompany him to the reservation.[14] Burns likely gave the young, inexperienced marshal several reasons for tagging along. For starters, Burns was the self-appointed attorney for Two Two and Fights With. Burns likely also claimed that he personally knew many of the influential Indians in No Water's camp—which he did not—and that he was on good terms with them—which he was not.

John Burns was a bona fide but quixotic lawyer with a penchant for seeing where the limelight was shining and finding a way to step into it. At the age of twenty-six, Burns had arrived in Deadwood in the summer of 1876 when the newly born town, if it could be called that, was raw and raging.[15] Burns had a lawyer's penchant for inserting himself into any situation where there lurked the possibility of making a dollar or adding to his envisioned prestige. A pamphlet published in 1881 by the Deadwood Board of Trade listed him as an attorney, one of forty-eight in a town of only thirty-seven hundred people. Over the years the Deadwood newspapers variously referred to him as Judge Burns, Colonel Burns, Commissioner Burns, and every other appellation used on the frontier to connote the appearance of power and influence.

During the Sioux uprising of 1890, Burns dressed himself in buckskin and sallied out of Deadwood for the Pine Ridge Reservation, stopping in Rapid City long enough to attend a meeting of its home guard. Claiming to be a seasoned Indian fighter, Burns excited the men in attendance with his supposed eyewitness account of Sioux atrocities during the Minnesota uprising of 1862.

He proceeded to the Pine Ridge Agency and gained admittance by presenting himself as the *Deadwood Pioneer*'s "war correspondent."[16] Once at Pine Ridge, he took on the role of self-appointed peacemaker. After visiting with a couple of Indians, he returned to the Black Hills and went on the lecture circuit, telling paying audiences about the latest news from the front and the details of the Ghost Dance.[17]

Burns's credibility as a peacemaker suffered when an Oglala named Fishing Skunk shared his assessment of John Burns with the editor of the *Hot Springs Star*. "I want to write to you about Judge Burns," Fishing Skunk wrote in December 1890. "Burns came down here saying that he loved the Indians and he wanted to make peace. But what was the use? We had no trouble with Burns . . . only with the government. . . . All of his foolish talk is no good."[18] Ike Scholfield, editor of the *Buffalo Gap Republic*, also poked fun at Burns's pretentious posturing. From time to time, Scholfield punctuated his paper with little quips about Burns: "Judge Burns heap big man. Much talk. Run fast. Much scared.—Two Strikes."[19] When the Messiah craze was extinguished and there was no more glory to be squeezed out of it, Burns sent a letter to Governor Mellette: "I hereby place at the disposal of my state and country my services in the event of war with Chile. I can place at your disposal a troop of cowboys almost instantly."[20]

It likely was Burns's self-aggrandizing manner that persuaded Matthiessen to let the attorney accompany him to Pine Ridge. They arrived at the agency on Thursday, March 24. Early the next morning the deputy marshal and Burns went No Water's village to arrest Two Sticks and White Face Horse. Despite Burns's presence, eloquence, and self-claimed esteem by the Indians, Chief No Water informed them that Two Sticks and White Face Horse were gravely ill from their bullet wounds and if moved would likely die. No Water also reminded Matthiessen, "You have two of Two Sticks' party in jail at Deadwood. That is enough. We will not surrender the wounded men until you send back those two boys."[21]

When Matthiessen informed Brown that No Water would not permit him to arrest either of the two wanted men, Brown summoned Joe Bush. Brown told Bush that in the morning he and a squad of Indian police were to go to No Water's village and bring in the two fugitives. While Matthiessen and Burns waited at the agency for the Indian police to bring in the fugitives, Burns passed the time talking and boasting. His eloquence and especially his loquaciousness were not universally appreciated. Brown ordered Burns off the reservation.[22]

The Indian police were no more successful then Matthiessen and Burns. When they got to No Water's village and announced their intent to arrest Two Sticks and White Face Horse, shots were fired over their heads and they were forced to retreat. The Indian police again returned to the agency empty-handed and embarrassed.[23]

Matthiessen's inability to arrest Two Sticks and White Face Horse, coupled with the second forced retreat of the Indian police from No Water's village, provided additional evidence that Brown's control did not extend past the perimeter of the agency headquarters. How long could that continue before the secretary of the interior and secretary of war concluded that it was necessary to send in troops?

The possibility of troops coming onto the reservation worried Young Man Afraid of His Horses and He Dog. They were certain that bringing troops onto the reservation at this tension-filled time would set off another wave of unrest, likely resulting in more bloodshed. To prevent that from happening, some unknown progressive Indians loyal to Young Man Afraid of His Horses did what the Indian police could not accomplish. They went to No Water's village and took custody of No Water, Hollow Wood, and No Flesh, moving them a few miles up White Clay Creek to George Sword's village. Sword, the former captain of the Indian police, sent word to Brown that he was holding the three men in his village.[24] On March 29, Matthiessen arrived at Pine Ridge, took the wanted men into custody, and transported them to the Pennington County Jail. They were held there awaiting further instructions from the court.[25]

When the court's instructions came, they were for Matthiessen to board the eastbound train on April 1 and transport his three prisoners to the Minnehaha County Jail in Sioux Falls. They were held there pending trial during the spring session of federal court.[26]

That Hollow Wood and No Flesh shot over the heads of the Indian police underscored how deeply Oglala society was fissured in 1893. On one side of the chasm were the malcontents, who saw themselves as upholders of Lakota culture and tradition. On the other side were the progressives, who believed the Lakota could survive only if they found a way to live in the white man's world. In 1893 Hollow Wood and No Flesh found themselves aligned with the malcontents, but that had not always been the case. In 1879 they had been handpicked by Valentine McGillycuddy, with the concurrence of Young Man Afraid of His Horses and George Sword, to be members of the original Pine Ridge police force. Now, in 1893, they shot over the heads of the Indian police, most of whom they knew personally.[27] The fissure among the Oglala had grown into a chasm.

When No Water arrived at the Minnehaha County Jail on April 2, he was sick; each day he got progressively worse. At his grand jury trial on April 5, he sat in the courtroom with his hat over his eyes. When asked about his role in sheltering Two Sticks, through an interpreter No Water merely said, "My heart was bad." That was sufficient for the jurors to indict him on the charge of resisting an officer of the law. No Flesh and Hollow Wood were indicted on the same charge.[28]

After the grand jury trial, No Water's health continued to worsen. Four days later, on April 9, Judge Elmer Dundy signed an order transferring him to the Central House. That evening fifty-three-year-old No Water died of pneumonia. On the morning of April 10, the Reverend James Trimble of the Episcopal church conducted a brief service at Fuller's Mortuary, followed by burial at Mount Pleasant Cemetery, Sioux Falls.[29] That he was not brought back to Pine Ridge for burial underscores the negative opinion others had of No Water. Young Man Afraid of His Horses and George Sword, influential leaders among the Oglala, apparently did not request the Indian agent to have No Water's body returned to Pine Ridge. Why would they? Both shared the honor of being shirt wearers with Crazy Horse, the man No Water once attempted to kill.

No Flesh and Hollow Wood were released on their own recognizance and ordered to be in Deadwood for the fall term of the federal court.[30] Cyrus Fry escorted them back to Pine Ridge.[31]

The removal of No Water, No Flesh, and Hollow Wood from the malcontents' camp enabled Young Man Afraid of His Horses to take custody of Two Sticks and White Face Horse and lodge them in his camp five miles farther up White Clay Creek. Both had life-threatening gunshot wounds, rendering them too weak to be moved any farther.[32]

Several days later Two Sticks was sufficiently strong that Young Man Afraid of His Horses took the wanted man into the agency. Instead of handing him to the Indian police, who likely would have put him in the guardhouse, Young Man Afraid of His Horses took Two Sticks to the agency hospital.[33] Dr. Z. T. Daniel determined that Two Sticks had been shot through the right shoulder. He cleaned the severely infected wound and kept Two Sticks in the hospital for a month, during which time he was constantly guarded by two Indian police.[34]

With Fights With and Two Two in jail and Two Sticks under guard in the agency hospital, there was only one fugitive at large—White Face Horse. Authorities assumed he was in Young Man Afraid of His Horses's village and that as soon as he was well enough to be moved he would be brought to the agency. Steeled by that belief, the authorities waited patiently for White Face Horse to gain enough strength to be moved. It would be an endlessly long wait.

On April 5, Fights With, then incarcerated in the Lawrence County Jail, received a letter written in Lakota from someone at Pine Ridge. Upon reading the letter, Fights With broke down and openly cried, as did Two Two. They refused food all that day. The next day Fights With asked to talk to a newspaper reporter. He told the reporter that the letter had brought him terrible news. It informed him that while White Face Horse lay near death, a medicine man gave him a concoction of roots and herbs to ease his pain. Instead of easing the pain, the medicine increased the pain. The medicine man had no sooner left the tepee than White Face Horse grabbed his revolver, placed the muzzle to his right temple, and pulled the trigger. The ball entered just above his ear, tearing a big hole and scattering his brains all over the tepee.[35]

That presumably brought the search for the culprits to an end, but when White Face Horse's body was not produced, authorities began to question whether he had indeed committed suicide. The story then changed. It was said that he had mounted a horse and ridden alone into an isolated, rugged section of the badlands and there committed suicide.[36] According to the people telling that story, the location of his remains was unknown, but that was not surprising because the badlands are remote, rugged, and laced with dead-end canyons.

Believing the second suicide story to be plausible, people turned their attention back to Two Sticks. During his monthlong recuperation in the agency hospital, he gave a lengthy account of the killings to a newspaper reporter: "I had nothing to do with the killing of the white men," he said. "My son [First Eagle] that was killed by the Indian police was the cause of all of the trouble. I made a mistake at this time: my heart was bad. . . . I am crying, and I am sorry that I done it. . . . This trouble I had nothing to do with it, but my boys made me do it. . . . My boy that is dead killed three of the white men and White Face Horse [who was also presumed to be dead or at least fatally wounded] was the other one. I don't know when we first talked about killing the white men. . . . I told them the night we started that they had better not kill any white men, but if you want to kill them go do it, and we will all die together."[37]

Two Sticks seated beside Indian police sergeant Joe Bush, 1893. The two men standing are U.S. Marshal Cyrus Fry and U.S. Deputy Marshal Chris Matthiessen.

Was the interview a denial, as when Two Sticks said, "I had nothing to with it." Or was it a confession, as when Two Sticks said, "[M]y boys made me do it." The best way to address that question is to consider the context. Two Sticks did not speak English and the reporter did not speak Lakota, which means someone translated everything Two Sticks said from Lakota to English. It was unusual in 1893 to find a person who was sufficiently fluent in both languages to be a good translator. The inconsistencies of the interview, as it was reported, and the disparity between what Two Sticks was quoted as saying and what would eventually become known about the killings suggest that either the interpreter was not up to the task or that Two Sticks was not telling the truth—perhaps both.

When Two Sticks sufficiently recovered, Matthiessen came for him. Concerned that malcontents might try to rescue Two Sticks as he was transported from the agency to the railroad depot in Rushville, Matthiessen swore in George J. Jarchow, proprietor of the hotel at the agency, and a man named Bennett as special deputies and had them accompany Matthiessen and his prisoner to Deadwood. The trio secreted Two Sticks off the reservation on April 29. Upon arriving in Deadwood, Two Sticks was so weak that he had to be carried from the train and put in a carriage. At the jail, doctors named Rogers and Howe examined him. They found that the .44-caliber bullet fired from a Winchester had plowed through Two Sticks's shoulder and left a gaping hole. He had no use of his right arm. Almost all of his right shoulder, extending from his breast around to his shoulder blade, was gangrenous. The gangrene was gradually moving toward his right lung. The doctors concluded that Two Sticks's death was imminent.[38]

A month later the Deadwood newspapers announced the death of a man whose name often appeared in the state's newspapers in connection with the four men murdered at Humphrey's halfway camp, but it was not the long-anticipated death of Two Sticks.

On Saturday, May 27, 1893, Matthiessen returned to Deadwood from Hill City on an early morning freight train. At three-thirty that morning he entered the hotel room he was sharing with Fry and found Fry lying on his bed and gasping. In a whisper, Fry asked for a glass of water. Believing Fry was merely indisposed, Matthiessen did not summon a doctor. When Phillips & Burroughs Drugstore opened several hours later, Matthiessen went there and asked Joe Shaller, the prescription clerk, to come take a look at Fry and determine if there was any medication that might help him feel better. Shaller recognized that Fry was dangerously ill and summoned Dr. Rogers.

By then Fry was drifting in and out of consciousness. Rogers concluded that Fry had somehow ingested a poison. He administered several remedies that often reverse the effects of poison, but to no avail. Rogers then summoned his medical colleagues, doctors named Howe, Paddock, and Conrad. A little later doctors named Freeman, Bowman, and Dickinson were also brought in for consultation. All known remedies were applied, but none of them, including a strong electric shock, worked. At 6:40 that evening, Fry died. He was forty-three years of age.[39]

An investigation revealed that on Friday evening, Fry had a severe headache and sharp pain in his side. He went to Deetken's Drugstore, purchased three ten-grain packets of antipyrine, and took two. It was also learned Fry had heart problems and Bright's disease, a chronic inflammation of the kidneys. The physicians concluded that the antipyrine had caused those organs to fail, resulting in his death.[40]

Fry's death came as a shock even to his close friends, but he apparently knew that premature death was only a matter of time. He had a twenty thousand dollar life insurance policy with the Northwestern Bank of Milwaukee, ten thousand dollars of which had been taken out on December 26, 1892. The remaining half had been taken out on April 27, 1893, only a month before his death. Fry also had a ten thousand dollar policy with Masonic Aid of Chicago, five thousand dollars with New York Life, and three thousand dollars with Mutual Life of New York. Whether Fry kept his health problems from his wife is unknown.[41]

The marshal's body was shipped back to Vermillion, where hundreds of people attended the funeral service. The Vermillion newspaper published a three-column obituary lauding the man, his service to the larger community, and his friendship.[42]

A new U.S. marshal was needed for South Dakota. Senator Pettigrew looked around for a deserving loyal Republican and found one in Otto Peemiller of Yankton County. In the general election of October 1, 1889, Peemiller had lost the bid to be South Dakota's first secretary of state by a narrow margin. Pettigrew used his patronage privilege to slide Peemiller into the U.S. marshal position. At that time deputy marshals served at the marshal's pleasure. Nonetheless, Peemiller temporarily retained Chris Matthiessen and Frank Fry, Cyrus Fry's younger brother.[43]

Spring had now tiptoed to summer. The feared Indian outbreak was largely forgotten. After all, First Eagle had been shot dead. White Face Horse had committed suicide, and Two Two, Fights With, and Two Sticks were in the Deadwood jail waiting to be tried for murder. It was anticipated that during the fall session of the U.S. district court they would be found guilty of murder and hanged. The frontier was ready to turn its attention to opportunities appearing on the horizon.

⹋ 18 ⹋

THE FRONTIER PEERS INTO THE TWENTIETH CENTURY

In the late spring of 1893, South Dakotans focused their attention on two happenings well beyond the state's borders, but with profound effects on the state. One of them began quietly enough, something like the tremor of a distant earthquake. On February 23 the Philadelphia and Reading Railroad reported that it was bankrupt.[1] As word spread, people rushed to take their money out of banks, causing a run on bank deposits. Panic ensued and a credit crunch rippled through the economy. Many Europeans who had invested heavily in the stocks of American companies, primarily railroads, sold their stock in exchange for gold, which left America for Europe by the shipload. The statutory limit for the U.S. Treasury's minimum amount of gold reserves was soon breached and a series of bank failures followed. That in turn led to business failures and a nationwide depression lasting four years. Before the depression was over, five hundred banks and fifteen thousand businesses had failed; the unemployment rate shot up to 25 percent. At that time the government did not see itself as having any responsibility for people's welfare. Thousands faced starvation.[2]

The nationwide depression stopped the planned extension to the Black Hills of both the Chicago Northwestern Railroad from Pierre and the Milwaukee from Chamberlain, and it severely hampered South Dakota's ability to recover from the previous four years of drought. The depression also mitigated South Dakotans' attention to the upcoming World's Fair awarded to Chicago in 1890.

With the four hundredth anniversary of Columbus "discovering" America, it seemed fitting to give the Chicago World's Fair its official nom de plume—the Columbian Exposition. The planners and promoters expected the Columbian Exposition to surpass all previous World Fairs in size, with 633 acres of dazzling grandeur. They envisioned a fair that would introduce the world to the coming twentieth century, a century in which the Industrial Revolution, scientific breakthroughs, and new inventions would reshape the world. The themes were technology, science, government, aesthetics, and progress in human relations. They wanted the fair to showcase the United States as a great industrial power and thereby announce the passing of leadership from the Old World to the New.

The Columbian Exposition, or the White City as it was popularly known, opened on May 1 and closed on October 31. During those six months, twelve million spectators attended.[3] The countless wonderful things to see and experience included a moving sidewalk and a Ferris wheel. Two exhibits were particularly riveting. One was a cannon whose barrel weighed almost two and one-half tons and could shoot a two-thousand-pound shell thirteen miles.[4] Frontiersman who saw it may have recalled that only seventeen years earlier, Lieutenant Colonel George A. Custer and the Seventh Cavalry had been armed with only breech-loading single-shot .45-caliber rifles. They likely thought, "If only Custer would have had such firepower." Fairgoers from the hot plains of South Dakota were amazed to step into the coolness of a large exhibit hall where a machine kept the building at a comfortable temperature.[5] While those inventions were impressive, they paled in comparison to the Electric Building. The Electric Building housed the most novel and brilliant exhibits of the exposition. There were neon lights, powerful search lights that dissolved darkness, electric-powered generators, row upon row of incandescent lights, and electric motors powerful enough to move trains. Outdoors, several electric generators powered the 8,000 arc lights and 130,000 incandescent lamps that lit the fair's buildings and walkways. The most transformative exhibit in the Electric Building was a display of George Westinghouse and Nikola Tesla's machine that generated alternating current, which would soon electrify the country.[6]

William F. "Buffalo Bill" Cody and his Wild West Show were also there—almost. Cody had applied to the World Fair committee for his show to be one of the attractions. Approval was initially given but then rescinded. Promoters wanted the fair to be a prescient view of the future. A show reminding fairgoers of the past and glorifying the subjugation of American Indians did not fit the theme.

However, Buffalo Bill, ever the showman-entrepreneur, was not to be denied. He leased fourteen acres near the main entrance and constructed stands to seat eighteen thousand spectators. Cody contracted with seventy-four men and women from the Pine Ridge Reservation to perform. Short Bull, Kicking Bear, and Two Strike—leaders of the Messiah craze of 1890—along with Plenty Horses were drawing cards.[7] All fairgoers visiting or even passing by the Wild West Show likely reflected on America's historical relationship with Indians as they walked toward a jaw-dropping glimpse of its future.

Like every large fair, the Columbian Exposition had its sideshows. The one that got the most attention was, quite literally, a horse race. Not just any horse race, but a thousand-mile horse race that began as a hoax. The jokester was John G. Maher, clerk of court for Dawes County, Nebraska, and a stringer for a few eastern newspapers, which occasionally published his stories about the latest happenings on the frontier. Some of the stories he sent to the newspapers were tongue-in-cheek hoaxes, written to titillate and remind easterners that there really was a place called Nebraska. The idea of a horse race from Chadron to Chicago was just another of Maher's attention-getting stories. To his astonishment, letters began pouring in from across the country asking for more information. The publicity potential was too tempting to pass up.

Doers and shakers of the little town of Chadron, population sixteen hundred and declining, decided to turn the hoax into reality. A committee meeting was held on March 20, 1893, to make arrangements. A. C. Putman was named president of the committee and N. H. Weir corresponding secretary.[8]

The committee set the rules for the race:

- This race shall be open to the world. No horses barred.
- No rider will be allowed more than two horses.
- Rider with saddle and blanket shall weigh not less than 150 pounds. Saddle with blanket shall weigh not less than thirty pounds.
- Each rider will be provided with a route map on day of start.
- All horses will be branded with special race brand the day before starting.
- Every rider will be required to register at points designated by committee.
- Entrance fee shall be $25 payable at Bank of Chadron as follows: $10 on or before May 1; $15 on or before June 1, when all entries close.
- The start will be made from Hotel Blaine, Chadron, Nebraska, on June 13, 1893, the signal being a pistol shot.
- The first prize of $1,000 will be handed to the winner at Chicago.[9]

It was anticipated that the prize money would attract twenty to thirty contestants. However, when the newly established Humane Society of America announced that it intended to prevent the race from being held, many potential riders did not proceed with making arrangements. After negotiation, the Humane Society agreed not to oppose the race on the condition that at three checkpoints in Nebraska, seven in Iowa, and three in Illinois, its representatives could examine each horse and determine if it was fit to continue.[10]

June 13 was an exciting day in Chadron. The regimental band of the Ninth Cavalry from nearby Fort Robinson played while a crowd of thirty-five hundred spectators, more than twice the town's population, lined the streets. Each rider was mounted on one horse and led another. With a map of the route in their pockets, riders waited for a signal to start. Standing on the balcony of the Blaine Hotel, Jim Hartzel called down: "Boys, the hour is now arrived for the cowboy race from Chadron to Chicago to start. I trust you will take good care of your horses and I know you will conduct yourselves as gentlemen and uphold the good name of Chadron and the State of Nebraska." With that, Hartzel fired his pistol into the air.[11]

The race was on! A few riders nudged their horses into a trot, but most of them left town at a walk. It was a long, long way to Chicago.

There were nine riders: Emmett Albright of Crawford, Nebraska; John Berry riding horses owned by Jack Hale of Sturgis, South Dakota; Joe Campbell of Denver, Colorado (with only one horse); Dave Douglas of Hemingford, Nebraska; Joe Gillespie of Coxville, Nebraska; George Jones of Whitewood, South Dakota; Doc Middleton of Chadron; Charles Smith of Hot Springs, South Dakota; and James Stephens of Ness City, Kansas.[12] Whereas Berry was a rider, the rules committee forbade him from being a contestant because he had helped lay out the route of the race. The committee decided that Berry's knowledge of the route gave him an unfair advantage.[13] For those making side bets, most of the money was on Berry. The *Black Hills Weekly Times* opined, "He has almost lived in the saddle and on the plains a greater part of his life. He is accustomed to long horseback journeys and knows pretty near what a horse can stand. If necessary, he can walk fifty miles and make as good time as a horse."[14]

The crowd's favorite was Doc Middleton, a forty-two-year-old outlaw. He was neither a doctor nor a Middleton, his birth name being James M. Reilly. As a thirteen-year-old, Reilly was indicted for the theft of a horse, making him a wanted man on the run. In 1876 Middleton, like many who came to West River country, hired on to drive cattle north from Texas to the Sioux reservation.

Having eluded the law in Texas and changed his name, Middleton used the change in geography to slip on the vestiges of a law-abiding citizen and became a freighter on the Sidney–Black Hills Trail. On January 13, 1877, he went to a dance in Sidney. The six-foot-tall, 150-pound cowboy with brown wavy hair attracted the attention of a young woman who had come to the dance on the arm of Private James Keefe. A fight erupted between the two men; Middleton shot and killed the soldier. He was again on the run.[15]

Doc Middleton then became a horse thief, at least a horse thief in a serious way. Initially he stole loosely tended horses belonging to Indians on the Red Cloud Agency and the adjacent Spotted Tail Agency because civil authorities had no jurisdiction over reservation Indians and government officials weren't much interested in chasing white men who stole Indians' horses. Before long Middleton expanded his business to stealing horses from large ranches. Again, it was a fairly safe occupation. The lowly homesteaders trying to eke out a living on quarter sections of sandhills had a good deal of animosity against ranchers who grazed their livestock on "free" government land and ran roughshod over the rights of homesteaders. Middleton befriended the homesteaders, sometimes giving a destitute family a horse or two—always a stolen horse. He became something of a sandhills Robin Hood. His motto was "travel fast, travel light and travel friendly."[16]

Middleton was apprehended in 1879 and sentenced to five years. As a model prisoner, he served only three years and nine months. In 1893 he was living in Chadron with his third wife and their two children.[17]

As Doc Middleton mounted his horse on June 13, 1893, hundreds of people surrounded him. All tried to shake his hand and bid him Godspeed. His wife and two little children threaded their way through the crowd. Upon seeing them, Middleton reached down and pulled first one child and then the other up into his saddle. He kissed them and then leaned down and kissed his wife. He was the last rider to leave town. As his horse walked down the street, he remarked, "Boys, I am the last now but may be the first at Chicago."[18]

The riders advanced toward Chicago at the rate of fifty-five to sixty miles a day, covering four miles an hour during the heat of the day but doubling the pace in cooler evening air. Two hundred miles into the race, Dave Douglas dropped out at Atkinson, Nebraska. The horses did not play out; the rider did.[19]

Six days into the race, the leader arrived in Covington, Nebraska, at 7:25 in the evening, having traveled four hundred miles. Not surprisingly it was Doc Middleton. However, at that point Middleton's luck played out. One of his horses went lame because it had been improperly shod in Chadron. (Horseshoe nails are designed such that upon being hammered into the hoof, a bevel causes the nail to turn outward. If the bevel is inadvertently or intentionally reversed, the nail goes into the live part of the hoof. That may have been why Middleton's horse went lame.)

Joe Gillespie and J. H. Stephens were not far behind Middleton. All three racers crossed the Missouri River on the same ferry to reach Sioux City, Iowa. Humane Society officers waiting on the far shore examined the horses and were satisfied with each animal's condition. Fifteen hundred people accompanied the riders to the Union Hotel, where they had been preregistered by Secretary Weir. The horses were stabled and given a generous amount of oats. At nine-thirty that evening, John Berry arrived at Covington, where he stayed the night. On Tuesday morning Gillespie and Stephens left Sioux City a few minutes past six. At that point, the oddsmakers were favoring Gillespie. He had ridden the same horse most of the way across Nebraska and did not expect to change mounts until near the Illinois line. Then he would make it to the finish on what he considered to be his best and fastest horse.

Back at Covington, John Berry, Emmett Albright, and Charles Smith registered at the Union Depot Hotel for the night. They gave their horses a long rest and did not cross the river to Sioux City until nine-thirty Tuesday morning. All three left Sioux City at eleven o'clock. Middleton was several hours behind them.

It took the riders five days to cross Iowa. As they rode the eight-hundred-mile width of the state, Doc Middleton's lone horse gradually became slower and slower. At or near Dubuque, he realized it was pointless to push any harder on the horse's endurance. He slowed his horse to a walk, rested frequently, and, for competitive purposes, dropped out of the race. Only seven riders continued on to Illinois, with two checkpoints remaining between them and the finish line.

The winner of the Chadron–Chicago horse race crossed the finish line at nine-thirty on the morning of June 27. After riding 1,040 miles in thirteen days and sixteen hours, John Berry was the first to reach the gate of Buffalo Bill's Wild West Show and was guided to Colonel Cody's tent. A half dozen of his western friends fairly lifted the little man from his saddle. "Please take care of my horses" was the first thing he said. A dozen men gathered about the horse and in a few seconds removed the saddle and bridle. At each limb a man rubbed the horse with liniment while others brought water and a sponge to rinse the horse's mouth and bathe his legs with cool water. Cody stepped forward to greet Berry and shake his hand. "You are the first man in. You are all right, John. You are all right!"

Two hours later Emmett Albright rode in at a gallop, making a dramatic entrance by sharply reining up his horse. Since Berry was not officially registered for the race, it could have been concluded that Albright was the winner and could rightfully claim the prize money, or so it initially appeared. It was later learned that after registering at the DeKalb checkpoint, Albright had ridden to Dixon, Iowa, loaded his horses into a boxcar, and shipped them to Chicago under the name of J. Johnson.[20]

A large crowd gathered at the entrance to Buffalo Bill's Wild West Show to await the next riders. At one o'clock Joe Gillespie came down the street on a trot, waving his sombrero to cheering spectators. At exactly 1:31 p.m. he jumped from his horse and shook Buffalo Bill's hand. Charles Smith arrived at 1:47 p.m., looking every bit a cowboy with his wide-brimmed white hat and enormous spurs. His horses showed no signs of disuse. George Jones arrived the next morning, June 28. James Stephens and then Joe Campbell came in the following morning. Later and without fanfare, Doc Middleton reached the entrance gate.[21]

The prize money was distributed widely. Buffalo Bill's purse of $500 was divvied among all the riders who reached Chicago: John Berry, $175; Joe Gillespie, $50; Charles Smith, $75; George Jones, $75; James Stephens, $50; Doc Middleton, $25; Emmett Albright, $25; and Joe Campbell, $25. The Chadron committee's purse of $1,000 was also spread among all the riders who reached Chicago: $200 to Joe Gillespie; $200 to Charles Smith; $187.50 to George Jones; $187.50 to James Stephens; $75 to Emmett Albright; $75 to Joe Campbell; and $75 to Doc Middleton. In addition, Cody awarded John Berry a saddle donated by Montgomery, Ward and Company and gave a Colt pistol to Joe Gillespie.[22]

With the one-thousand-mile horse race over, South Dakotans shifted their attention from the anachronistic sideshow to the main event, the fair itself. The state's connections with Chicago were extensive. Chicago was South Dakota's commercial link to the rest of the country. All four railroads coming into South Dakota started in Chicago. Pierre passengers could board the Chicago Northwestern train for a seven-hundred-mile ride to Chicago. The Chicago, Milwaukee, and St. Paul Railroad entered South Dakota at Sioux Falls, the state's largest "city," and ran arrow straight to its terminus at Chamberlain on the east bank of the Missouri River. Not to be outdone, the Fremont, Elkhorn and Missouri Valley, a subsidiary of Chicago Northwestern, pushed its rails from Sioux City west along the northern border of Nebraska, turned north, and ceremoniously puffed into Rapid City on July 5, 1886. In 1890 the railroad extended its tracks to Belle Fourche, which within a few years became the world's largest livestock shipping point, with twenty-five hundred carloads of cattle loaded for market each month at the peak of shipping season. Not to be left out, the Chicago Burlington and Quincy Railroad carved its tracks from Edgemont at the southern end of the Black Hills along their rocky spine, reaching Deadwood in January 1891.[23]

However, there was an obstacle that made it difficult for South Dakotans to throw their full support behind the World's Fair, and it was huge—the state was in the grip of a severe drought. In 1890 grain planted in the usually productive eastern half of the state withered in the fields. When crops failed, farmers failed. Thousands of agrarian families abandoned the land and left. They were the lucky ones. They had a place to go and the means to get there. The truly destitute remained on foreclosed farms so worthless that no one came to evict them. Governor Arthur Mellette drove his buggy throughout the drought-stricken land, visiting farm families to hear of their heart-wrenching plights firsthand. When the drought continued into the next year, he appealed to citizens of the large communities for assistance, but the usually well-to-do merchants showed him long lists of agrarian creditors who would never be able to settle their debts. Donations were meager. Mellette then took his appeals to eastern cities.[24] He vowed that all the money given would go directly to help feed the needy, and he used thirty-six hundred dollars of his own money to cover the incurred expenses. The response was generous; even the king of Sweden contributed.[25] South Dakota received nearly forty thousand dollars in relief supplies, and most actual suffering by the citizens of South Dakota was averted.[26]

In Mellette's eyes, these years of drought and despair made it particularly important for South Dakota to have a presence at the Chicago World's Fair. He saw the fair as an opportunity to counter the image of South Dakota as a place to go broke and urged the 1891 legislature to allocate money for promoting the state, including a building in which to exhibit South Dakota's mining and agricultural resources. His appeal was poignant: "Coming as it does to our very door, [the fair will] bring hither the brightest representatives from all the nations of the earth. Our new state with her matchless resources cannot afford to deny herself its benefits."[27] But the state's coffers were empty. The 1891 legislature did not allocate one penny to promote South Dakota at the upcoming fair.

Mellette's recourse was to name an official South Dakota World's Fair Commission. For the rest of 1891 the commissioners promoted the cause throughout the state. They set their sights on raising eighty thousand dollars to cover the cost of constructing a South Dakota Building and producing impressive displays of the state's mineral resources, agricultural products, dairy interests, stock raising, horticulture, soils, geology, art, manufacturing, building materials, artesian power, irrigation, and other vital interests in hopes of attracting people and investors to the state. The commissioners were not universally acclaimed for their hard work. Some citizens accused the commissioners of using the money raised to line their own pockets. In the face of the accusations, all the commissioners resigned. Mellette appointed a reconstituted and expanded commission, and the work went on.[28]

At a women's convention at Yankton in May 1891, women protested the unfairness of all the commissioners being men and formed their own commission, which Mellette acknowledged. Both commissions worked closely with citizen groups around the state to collect money and plan the South Dakota Building and its exhibits. By August 1892, the two commissions had raised enough money to begin construction of the South Dakota Building. The plans called for a two-story building with twelve thousand square feet of floor space.[29]

By then Mellette's term had expired. In his inaugural address on January 3, 1893, Charles H. Sheldon, the new governor, requested that legislators make a suitable appropriation to complete the exhibits already begun and reimburse those citizens who had expended their own funds for the South Dakota Building. Just months before the fair was scheduled to open, the legislature came through with an allocation of sixty thousand dollars.[30]

The South Dakota Building sat just inside the gate on Fifty-Seventh Street, a prime location directly in the path of all visitors who used that entrance. A large crowd gathered at eleven o'clock on the morning on July 12 for the dedication. Prior to the formal dedication, "Buffalo Bill" Cody arrived with his entire entourage in tow. As his cowboy band played, Cody dismounted from his big white horse and paid his respects to Governor Sheldon. The Reverend F. D. Newhouse of Huron opened with an invocation, after which Thomas H. Brown, executive commissioner of the men's fund-raising committee, presented the governor with the keys to the building. Sheldon made a few opening remarks extolling the state's rich soil, mild climate, mineral deposits, and timber reserves. Helen Barker of Huron, manager of the women's fund-raising committee, related the work the women of the state had done for the South Dakota Building and its exhibits. Judge C. S. Palmer of Sioux Falls delivered an oration, promoting the state with such remarks as, "Do you wish to become identified with men broadened by contact with western civilization, yet poised by principles transfused from sturdy New England stock? Go to South Dakota!"[31] The last speaker was William Sterling,[32] and the audience included many Oglala, including Rocky Bear, No Neck, High Bear, and Plenty Horses—the man Sterling had once tried to convict for murder.[33]

As a coming-out party, the dedication of the South Dakota Building was a huge success. William Brown, editor of the *Turner County Herald*, opined that "any person who can take in the world's fair and does not do so makes a great mistake, and they will sure regret it as long as they live."[34] The Fremont, Elkhorn and Missouri Valley Railroad did its part in encouraging West River citizens to attend the World's Fair. Beginning in May, the railroad advertised reduced rates to Chicago.[35]

Some 19,684 South Dakotans signed the guest register in the South Dakota Building.[36] Anybody who wanted to be somebody in South Dakota went to the World's Fair.

That same day, over at the Art Institute on the fairgrounds, Frederick Jackson Turner addressed the American History Association. His talk was entitled "The Significance of the Frontier in American History," with the thesis that the history of America was largely shaped by a continually advancing frontier. Turner told the audience that in its westward expansion, the frontier was always on the outer edge of the wave—the meeting point between savagery and civilization. Each frontier was a new field of opportunity and a gate of escape from the bondage of the past, a scorn of older society and impatience with its restraints.[37]

After delineating the characteristics of a "frontier" and explaining how the frontier shaped America's history, Jackson went on to explain what constituted a frontier. One necessity was free land. Other characteristics were the lack of effective government, which created a void filled by individuals who were at times antisocial; geographic isolation; and a dearth of institutions, such as schools and churches, that were the conveyance of social conformity.

Jackson concluded his talk by pointing out that all the elements that constituted a frontier were gone. There was no more "free" land. The entire country had been parceled into states that promulgated laws and had the ability to enforce them. The landscape was punctuated with churches, and there was a school in every town. He saved his profound conclusion to the last sentence: "[T]he frontier is gone."[38]

An event the very next day underscored that the frontier was, indeed, gone. At two o'clock on the afternoon of July 13, a young Indian, a member of Young Man Afraid of His Horses's band, came riding down the hill north of the Pine Ridge Agency as hard as his horse could run. Grief-stricken, he dashed into the issue house and announced in a loud voice that Young Man Afraid of His Horses was dead. Robert Pugh, the issue clerk, discounted the preposterous announcement. After all, Young Man Afraid of His Horses was known to be more than one hundred miles from Pine Ridge on his way to visit his Northern Cheyenne and Crow friends.[39]

A few hours later on that same day, July 13, a telegram arrived at Pine Ridge. It stated that at noon on July 13, while on his way to visit his Northern Cheyenne and Crow friends, Young Man Afraid of His Horses had suffered a massive heart attack and fallen from his horse.[40] The Oglala's peacemaker and protector of his people was dead.

Captain Charles Penney wired the news to Commissioner of Indian Affairs Thomas Morgan with the recommendation that the chief's body be properly prepared and brought to Pine Ridge for burial among his people at the expense of the Indian Bureau.[41] That was done.

A newspaper reporter aptly summed up Young Man Afraid of His Horses's life: "Many a white man, whose deeds have been less valorous, has had his memory kept green by monuments. Young Man Afraid of His Horses [went] to the happy hunting ground unwritten and unsung."[42]

The frontier was indeed gone. Well, almost. The last living vestiges of the Dakota frontier were still awaiting justice to be served. As much as South Dakota's citizens would have liked, they could not step into the twentieth century until these three Indians were tried for their Ghost Dance–fueled murder of four cowboys.

☆ 19 ☆

THE WHEELS OF JUSTICE TURN SLOWLY

While South Dakotans were preparing for the World's Fair and then taking in its sights, three impactful events unfolded. Although disparate, each had implications pursuant to the murder of the four cowboys. The first event occurred on July 9, 1893, when Captain George LeRoy Brown was replaced at Pine Ridge by Captain Charles Penney, quite possibly because Brown had been unable to keep the Indian unrest out of the headlines. It was Penney's second tour at Pine Ridge. In his annual report, he wrote, "[T]here is little to note in the way of improvement among the Indians. They are still the same shiftless, improvident people, and withal careless and happy, patient under hardships and with a faithful trust in the future that is exasperating."[1]

The second event—a surprise revelation—was that White Face Horse had not committed suicide. Rather, he had mounted a horse and ridden two hundred crow-fly miles northeast to the Standing Rock Reservation.[2] How he could have done that begs for an explanation.

White Face Horse did not disappear from No Water's village. Rather, he disappeared from the village of a chief whom the authorities considered their ally—Young Man Afraid of His Horses.[3] White Face Horse's bullet wound was far too severe for him to quietly slip out of a tepee in the dark of night and steal away unnoticed. Beyond a doubt, someone provided a horse and someone helped him get on the horse, but even more was needed. Riding two hundred miles horseback across freshly thawed, soggy prairie would be daunting for a healthy man. A severely wounded man on death's doorstep could not have made that trip alone. At least one person went with White Face Horse, and that person had to be leading a well-provisioned pack horse. They could not have left without Young Man Afraid of His Horses's knowledge and, more importantly, his approval.

Why did Young Man Afraid of His Horses allow White Face Horse, an alleged murderer and a wanted man, to flee his village? One explanation is that, as Dr. Charles Eastman claimed, Young Man Afraid of His Horses sympathized with the malcontents.[4] His empathy was understandable. After all, many of the disastrous events visited upon Indians in No Water's village occurred simply because they had killed a few of Ike Humphrey's four thousand steers to feed their starving families. Another plausible explanation is that Young Man Afraid of His Horses expected White Face Horse would never make it alive to Standing Rock. He likely thought that someplace in the isolated badlands, White Face Horse would die with dignity and be spared the humiliation of being hanged at the end of a white man's rope.

After a journey of several months, White Face Horse made it to the Standing Rock Reservation. However, that did not guarantee his escape from justice. In 1893 there were few secrets in West River country. Whereas the area was large and a mixture of whites and Indians was lightly sprinkled on the landscape, a well-patterned tapestry was woven into their daily lives. Anything, even the slightest thing, be it natural or human, that altered the rhythm of life was noticed, including a few new horses showing up in an Indian village's remuda. The keen-eyed observer would have examined the surrounding prairie and discovered a straight line of bent-over grass, telling the direction from which the visitors had come. The distance between the horses' hoof prints would have told whether the visitors came from near or far. In short, someone noticed.

It was not surprising, indeed it was inevitable, that word reached U.S. Marshal Otto Peemiller that White Face Horse was alive and on the Standing Rock Reservation. On August 1, 1893, Peemiller wrote to Indian Agent James McLaughlin: "I am informed that there is an Indian by the name of White Face Horse . . . at or on your reservation and under your controll [sic]. Will you kindly inform me if this is so and if you will hold him for me?[5]

Peemiller's request could not have been placed on the desk of a more competent Indian agent. By 1893 McLaughlin had been an Indian agent for seventeen years and in charge of Standing Rock for twelve. There, he implemented what today might be called shared governance. He placed an Indian in charge of each of the agency's twenty-five subdistricts; directed a force of efficient, loyal Indian police; and lightly oversaw an Indian-run tribal court. During his many years as an Indian agent, no administration, be it Republican or Democrat, made any effort to remove him.

As was characteristic of McLaughlin, he had the information Peemiller wanted and immediately responded: "An Indian answering the description given arrived on this reservation about two weeks ago, coming from the Pine Ridge Agency. He gave one of the Indians of this agency, who was visiting Pine Ridge, a pony to bring him here and is now living with his father on this reservation in South Dakota, about thirty miles south directly opposite La Grace. I can secure him for you at any time, but think it best to say nothing about the matter until you arrive here. Wire me further regarding it."[6] The referenced Indian village was across the Missouri River from La Grace and near the confluence of Oak Creek and the Missouri River, just down the hill from the Saint Elizabeth Mission.

In a second letter to McLaughlin, Peemiller wrote, "By the way the strange Indian came onto your Agency it undoubtedly is White Face Horse. If you will kindly try and find out if it really is him or not and whether he is in condition to be transported or not, it will be a great favor to me."[7]

At McLaughlin's direction, the Indian police then took custody of White Face Horse and took him to the agency. The rifle shot that felled him in February and blew away his kneecap had turned his leg gangrenous. Believing White Face Horse was at death's door, the police transported him to the agency hospital and put him in the care of Dr. James Brewster.

In late August, Deputy U.S. Marshal Frank Fry went to Fort Yates to arrest White Face Horse and take him back to South Dakota to stand trial. However, Brewster refused to allow his patient to be moved, saying that White Face Horse was too weak to be transported and that it was only a matter of time before gangrene killed him.[8] Fry left without the alleged murderer, but not without misgivings tinged with resentment: "I find," he wrote to McLaughlin upon his return to South Dakota, "that White Face Horse is liable to lie about his condition. He had it given out that he was dead before he left Pine Ridge."[9]

Two months later Fry again contacted McLaughlin to learn whether White Face Horse was sufficiently recovered to be transported. McLaughlin replied that White Face Horse's leg had been amputated at the thigh on October 10. "When [he is] able to be removed I will notify you."[10] White Face Horse remained in the hospital and under the care of the Sisters of Charity for several weeks.[11]

On November 1, 1893, McLaughlin notified Peemiller that "White Face Horse was recently discharged from the hospital and allowed to go live with his uncle, Grasping Eagle, who lives in the South Dakota portion of the Standing Rock Reservation. In the Doctor's judgment, the Indian should not be taken from his uncle's to make a long journey (until fifteen days from now) as the limb although healed nicely is yet quite tender, susceptible to cold, and would be easily injured."[12] The missive likely frustrated Peemiller, who was anxious to take custody of White Face Horse, but he acquiesced to the advice. McLaughlin had a sterling reputation within the Indian Department and his influence stretched all the way to Washington, D.C. One disregarded McLaughlin's instructions at his own peril.

On December 15, Jacob Tschetter, deputy U.S. marshal for South Dakota, sent a letter to McLaughlin requesting an update on White Face Horse's health.[13] McLaughlin informed Tschetter that White Face Horse was now able to go about on crutches and no doubt could be removed without injury to his leg.[14] Deputy U.S. Marshal Martin Cogley of Flandreau, South Dakota, made a similar inquiry on January 3, 1894, and McLaughlin assured Cogley that White Face Horse could be safely transported.[15] However, no U.S. marshal arrived to take custody of White Face Horse. After all, 130 miles of open, wind-swept prairie lay between the Standing Rock Agency and Pierre, the nearest point in South Dakota where the suspect could be securely jailed. It would take a team and wagon at least three long days to make the trip, and then only if the prairie was snow-free and the weather uncommonly favorable. Everyone on the frontier understood that there was no telling whether a several-day blizzard with thirty-below temperatures and a twenty-mile-per-hour wind would sweep down out of Canada midway into the trip. If it did, the marshal and his prisoner would likely freeze to death. White Face Horse could wait.

During his convalescence, White Face Horse converted to the Catholic faith. To attest to the sincerity of his conversion, he sent his ghost shirt to McLaughlin.[16]

But sympathy, religious conversion, and sincerity could not protect White Face Horse from the long arm of the law. In early February 1894, Cogley arrived at Standing Rock, took custody of White Face Horse, and transported him by team and wagon to Gettysburg, South Dakota. Along the way the prisoner did not give the marshal any trouble other than "he eat too much." Cogley borrowed a fur coat and blankets to keep his prisoner from freezing to death.[17] On February 16 White Face Horse was arraigned before Commissioner Ben Hoover at Gettysburg and then taken to the Hughes County Jail in Pierre.[18]

A grand jury met in Pierre on March 31, 1894, to consider the charges against White Face Horse. On hand to testify to his guilt were five Indian police officers: Joe Bush, Thunder Bear, Bear House, Henry Moore, and John Coitter.[19] After they related how White Face Horse and others had tried to kill them on February 4, 1893, rather than submit to arrest, the jurors quickly returned three indictments against him for murder. He pleaded not guilty.[20] During the last week of April, Alfred Coe, based in Pierre and the official interpreter for U.S. district court, was called upon to help a physician determine whether White Face Horse could survive being transported to the Lawrence County Jail in Deadwood and thus be available for the spring session of the federal court.[21] The physician determined that White Face Horse was too sick to be moved, so sick that some worried he would cheat the gallows.[22]

The third impactful event was a series of prairie fires that swept over the Pine Ridge Reservation during the summer of 1893, burning four-fifths it.[23] The fires were not the result of lightning strikes; they were intentionally set by Indians.[24] Whether the fires were arson or justifiable depended on one's point of view. White ranchers considered the fires to be arson because they destroyed winter grazing for their cattle. From the Indians' perspective, destroying the winter grazing for white ranchers' trespassing cattle was justified.

When the prairie fires had burned most of the grass on the Pine Ridge Reservation and the fourth consecutive hot, dry summer receded, the frontier's attention was grabbed by legal proceedings in Deadwood. On October 14, 1893, U.S. Deputy Marshal Chris Matthiessen served four indictments against Two Sticks for murder and three indictments each against Fights With and Kills the Two (Two Two).[25] The wheels of justice began turning.

On Sunday, October 22, 1893, the Fremont, Elkhorn and Missouri Valley train chugged into Deadwood with Judge Alonzo J. Edgerton aboard. He came to convene the fall term of the U.S. court for the District of South Dakota. With Edgerton on the train were U.S. District Attorney Ezra Miller and his assistant, Charles Howard; U.S. Deputy Marshal Frank Fry; U.S. Marshal Otto Peemiller; and Charles Mellette, son of ex-governor Arthur Mellette and newly appointed clerk of the U.S. district court. O. S. Pender, clerk of the U.S. Eighth Circuit Court of Appeals, had arrived previously.[26] A bevy of newspaper reporters was waiting for them. The town was also bursting at the seams with spectators,

150 witnesses, and 103 potential jurors.[27] The flood of people put smiles on the faces of Deadwood's businessmen and the town's numerous "upstairs girls."[28]

Court got under way shortly before two o'clock on Monday, at which time Judge Edgerton stated that he would try jury cases first so that jurors could return home in time to cast their ballots in the upcoming election. He announced his intention of clearing both civil and criminal calendars before final adjournment, an ambitious goal.[29] To help reach that goal, two cases were cleared from the calendar on Tuesday morning when District Attorney Ezra Miller entered nolle prosequi on behalf of Hollow Wood and No Flesh, the men who had earlier shot over the heads of the Indian police.[30]

Two Sticks was brought before Judge Edgerton that same day. After the charges against him were explained, Two Sticks's attorney, William McLaughlin, pleaded not guilty on behalf of his client and reported that he was ready to proceed with the trial. However, Miller moved for a continuance because he was not prepared to prosecute the case.[31] That left Edgerton no choice but to continue Two Sticks's case until the next term of court in Deadwood. The judge released Two Sticks and told the old chief that he could return home but needed to understand that if he tried to flee the reservation, he would be jailed again. Edgerton was likely surprised when Two Sticks said he would like to remain in jail because it was warm and there was plenty to eat. His request was not granted, and he reluctantly went back to Pine Ridge.[32]

After reviewing the twenty-five cases on the court docket, Edgerton concluded that he had time to deal with only four or five of them. Finding the U.S. district attorney unprepared to prosecute Two Two, Edgerton ordered the young Indian released from jail and allowed to return to the reservation.[33]

One of the first cases tried was that of Fights With, also called Iwicakeze, his Lakota name. Fights With, the nineteen-year-old son of Two Sticks, had been indicted for murder. His court-appointed defense attorneys were John Burns and Granville G. Bennett.[34]

Bennett was a man of considerable distinction and high regard in South Dakota and well beyond the state's borders. He was admitted to the Iowa Bar in 1859 and served in both houses of the Iowa legislature. After service in the Civil War, in 1872 he and his family moved to Vermillion, Dakota Territory. Territorial governor John L. Pennington appointed Bennett a federal judge in 1875 and assigned him to the Black Hills region.[35] Throughout his legal career, his ethics were beyond reproach. One example of refused temptation makes the point: during his time as a federal judge, a friend and owner in the

Homestake Mine offered to sell him two thousand shares of Homestake stock. When Bennett replied that he did not have the money to buy two shares of stock let alone two thousand, the friend said the company would be glad to carry his two thousand shares for him as long as might be necessary. The offer was tempting. Everyone in the Black Hills knew that Homestake had tapped into the mother lode, and it was only a matter of time before money would begin to flow to the shareholders. But Bennett declined. He could envision the day when a lawsuit involving Homestake would come to his court, and he did not want owning stock in the company to bias his decision. In 1879 Bennett was elected Dakota Territory delegate to Congress, a position he lost two years later to Richard Pettigrew in a hotly contested election.[36] Bennett was six feet tall, handsome, and distinguished looking. Some thought it was the Irish in him that coated his tongue with silver, making him one of the resplendent lights of the Deadwood Bar.[37]

Fights With's other attorney was John Burns. He was as different from Granville Bennett as two men can be. One of Burns's first concerns was getting paid for his legal services. He sent word to Fights With's relatives that his fee would be two horses. Upon learning the offer was accepted, Burns wrote to John Shangreau, a mixed-blood residing on the reservation, asking him to go see Fights With's people, deliver the letter, and get the two horses. Burns told Shangreau to hold the horses until he came for them or to sell them if a buyer could be found.[38]

Not wanting to run afoul of the Pine Ridge Indian agent, Shangreau showed Burns's letter to Captain Brown. Brown sent a tersely worded letter to Burns: "Your attention is invited to the fact that the law and regulations governing an Indian Agency does not permit any person or persons to go upon the Indian reservation making contracts with Indians, driving off their stock and selling them without first obtaining authority from the proper officers of the Indian Department." Still smarting from the embarrassment of being duped into believing that White Face Horse had committed suicide, Brown reprimanded Burns for his presumed role in permitting "the two Indians now at Deadwood [in jail] to write directly to their own people using the Indian dialect [the Lakota language] as they are the most ruthless and unruly Indians on the reservation."[39]

In the days before Fights With was to be tried, Burns made it publicly known "that we cannot get justice for our Indian clients from a Deadwood jury owing to the bitter feelings against the red man."[40] Porter Warner, editor of the *Black Hills Daily Times*, vehemently objected, claiming "our people have no prejudice against the Indians."[41]

Burns's claim that Fights With could not get a fair trial because of the frontier's bias against Indians became a moot point when, like so many others, he was not tried that fall because Ezra Miller, a Democrat newly appointed as district attorney, was not prepared to prosecute. At that, the Republican-oriented *Rapid City Journal* opined, "He [Miller] apparently has no conception of his duties and as a consequence every case is continued just as fast as it is called from the calendar. This is an outrage. The expense of bringing the court to Deadwood will not fall much below $20,000."[42] That was quite the insult, and it likely explains why members of the Deadwood Bar presented Miller with an elegant gold-headed cane. At the presentation, General A. R. Z. Dawson, a civil war veteran and clerk of the U.S. circuit court, gave a laudatory speech honoring Miller.[43]

Some viewed the hoopla about honoring Miller as being downright embarrassing to Judge Edgerton. There was not a more distinguished man in the courtroom than he. His storied service dated back thirty-one years to when, in 1862, he had raised a company of men and gone with them to Saint Paul to muster into the Union Army, rising to the rank of brevet brigadier general. After the war Edgerton was a U.S. senator for Minnesota. Later he was appointed chief justice of the Dakota Territory and was chair of the constitutional convention that met in 1885 to promote statehood. Upon South Dakota's admission to the Union, he was appointed U.S. district judge.[44] In the fall of 1893 Edgerton's failing health foreshadowed the end of his career, not to mention his life, and it was deemed appropriate to acknowledge his service. As the court session drew to a close, Charlie Howard, assistant district attorney, approached the bench and presented Edgerton with a handsome and costly watch chain with beautiful pieces of rose quartz showing large nuggets of gold. The chain was a present from the grand jurors, the petit jurors, and clerks. Edgerton graciously accepted the gift, saying that he had always strived to do his duty without fear or favor, to punish the guilty and protect the innocent, and he acknowledged that at times he might have appeared harsh.[45]

When November 1893 arrived, nine months had passed since the four white men were murdered at the halfway camp. Justice had not been served on any of the alleged murderers. White Face Horse remained at Standing Rock recuperating from the amputation of his leg. Two Two and Two Sticks were back on Pine Ridge under their own recognizance, and Fights With had been remanded to the Lawrence County Jail to await the spring term of federal court in Deadwood. Justice was moving slowly.

The frontier settlers looked forward with anticipation to the spring session of the U.S. district court, scheduled to convene in Deadwood during the second week of May. Deadwood welcomed Edgerton when he arrived Sunday, May 7, 1894.[46] One of the first cases was that of Fights With on the charge of murder, but there was no trial. On the advice of his attorneys, Burns and Bennett, Fights With withdrew his plea of not guilty and pleaded guilty to manslaughter. Edgerton fined him one hundred dollars and sentenced him to three years in prison.[47]

Two Two, also known as Kills the Two, was the next case on the docket. The day before the trial was to commence, John Burns, the counsel for the defense, informed Edgerton that he was not able to prepare for the trial because Two Two did not speak English and neither Burns nor Bennett spoke Lakota. Edgerton was not sympathetic. He assigned Albert Coe, the court interpreter, to assist the attorneys on Monday and told the defense team that the trial would commence first thing Tuesday morning.[48]

The jury was selected Tuesday morning, freeing the afternoon for the prosecution to begin making its case against Two Two.[49] District Attorney Ezra Miller began the proceeding by informing the jury that the prosecution had a witness who would testify that Two Two had confessed to his role in the murder of the four white men. That witness was George Comer, chief clerk for the Pine Ridge Agency.[50] Defense attorney Burns objected, saying that the confession, if it really happened, was made in the Sioux language and that Comer could neither understand nor speak that language sufficiently to interpret whatever Two Two might have said. Edgerton told Comer to take the witness stand. A rigorous grilling of Comer's understanding of Lakota ensued, and the court determined that Comer knew only enough Lakota to transact ordinary store business. With that, the court ruled he was an incompetent witness.

At that point Comer confided that he had not personally heard Two Two make the confession. Rather, he had been informed by Louis Menard, the official interpreter at Pine Ridge, that Two Two had confessed. The prosecution requested that a telegram be sent to Menard to confirm that Two Two had confessed. Burns again objected, pointing out that the law required the prosecution to share its intended witnesses with the defense ten days prior to the commencement of the trial and that Menard's name was not on the list. The court sustained Burns's objection.[51]

The prosecution, believing that Comer's testimony would be sufficient, had no other witnesses. Clearly, Miller, then almost one year into the new job, was still struggling.

At that point Edgerton informed the jury that no evidence that proved the defendant guilty had been given. He therefore ordered the jury not to leave the jury box to deliberate and instead to immediately arrive at a verdict of not guilty.

The trial suddenly went from interesting to bizarre. Disregarding Edgerton's directive, the jurors asked for permission to retire and talk the matter over. After deliberating a short time, they came back into the courtroom to announce their position. The jury foreman informed the court that the jurors could not conscientiously bring back a verdict of not guilty.[52]

Edgerton, not a man known for equanimity, again ordered the jurors to arrive at a verdict of not guilty. The jurors again refused. Edgerton thunderously reprimanded them, saying that in his twenty-six years on the bench, his judgment had never before been questioned.[53]

After the trial, one of the jurors confided to a newspaper reporter that the jurors were not willing to declare an Indian not guilty simply because a technicality had prevented incriminating evidence from being presented. Porter Warner, proprietor of the *Daily Deadwood Pioneer Times*, opined, "A jury of Black Hills men are not going to give an Indian the best of it. They remember distinctly the days of '74, '75, '76."[54] Two Two was released on his own recognizance and went back to Pine Ridge[55] with the understanding that he could be reindicted.[56]

Elsewhere and five months later, the blindfolded lady with the scale was persistent. On October 6, 1894, Hughes County sheriff Ben Ash and U.S. Deputy Marshal Martin Cogley took custody of White Face Horse and transported him from the Hughes County Jail to the Lawrence County Jail in time for the fall session of the federal court.[57]

Judge Edgerton was scheduled to be on the bench, but he was an old man. The wear and tear on his sixty-seven-year-old body did not permit him to preside when the fall term of the federal court convened in Deadwood. His replacement was Elmer S. Dundy.[58] Attorneys defending indicted Indians were undoubtedly pleased. In 1879 Dundy had presided over the trial of Standing Bear, a Ponca chief arrested for leading members of his tribe from Indian Territory (Oklahoma) back to their traditional home near the confluence of the Niobrara and Missouri Rivers. As that trial reached its conclusion, Dundy permitted Standing Bear to speak. "[My] hand is not the color of yours," he said, "but if I prick it, blood will flow and I shall feel pain. The blood is the same color as yours. God made me, and I am a man." His argument persuaded Dundy that the government did not have authority to arrest Standing Bear because, as he explained his decision, "an Indian is a person."[59] Two Two, White Face Horse, and Two Sticks would be tried in the courtroom of a judge presumably without prejudice toward Indians.

In anticipation of the upcoming trials, fifty Indians traveled overland from Pine Ridge to Deadwood and camped near the D&D smelter.[60] A few days later the Fremont, Elkhorn and Missouri Valley train pulled into Deadwood and more Oglala men, women, and children debarked. They, too, camped near the D&D smelter. Among them were several prominent men, including Indian policemen Thunder Bear and Joe Bush.[61] Some came to Deadwood because they were subpoenaed witnesses; others came to provide moral support for their relatives slated for trial. A few were curious spectators. Attired in their traditional clothing, the Indians made a colorful sight as they went about Deadwood's businesses and streets.

On October 7, Judge Dundy and a host of court luminaries and their wives arrived in Hot Springs, a resort town nationally known for its hot springs and the elegant four-story Evans Hotel, constructed of red sandstone. Debarking the train were Ezra Miller from Elk Point and his wife; Assistant U.S. District Attorney S. B. Buskirk from Sioux Falls and his wife; O. S. Pender, clerk of the circuit court; Charles E. Mellette, clerk of the U.S. district court; U.S. Marshal Otto Peemiller from Yankton and his wife; U.S. Deputy Marshal F. Bieglemeier; Fred Buchanan, court bailiff; U.S. Deputy Marshal Martin Cogley; and Sheriff Ben Ash of Hughes County and his wife.[62] The notables' sightseeing that day included an excursion to Wind Cave. The next morning they walked across the street from the Evans Hotel and boarded the B&M train; their destination was Deadwood.[63]

When the B&M train arrived at the Deadwood depot, Elmer Dundy gingerly stepped onto the platform. While bear hunting the previous week in the Bighorns, the sixty-four-year-old judge had severely strained his back. He limped to his suite of rooms in the Keystone Hotel.

About nine o'clock Tuesday evening, October 9, Dundy suddenly became ill. He had severe chills and the blood in his limbs appeared to cease circulating. His arm and leg muscles were vigorously massaged for an hour, which restored the circulation and normal body warmth. He then fell into a deep slumber.[64]

The first day of court was scheduled to start the next day, Wednesday, October 10. It did not because Judge Dundy was still incapacitated. That evening he was in such excruciating back pain that it took all his effort merely to sit up in bed,[65] rendering him unable to attend a reception that evening in his honor at the Olympic Club.[66]

To further aggravate the judge, he was told that neither Two Sticks nor Two Two had reported to the Lawrence County Jail. The two alleged murderers were again fugitives from justice. Who knew what it would take to get them back into custody? Dundy issued a capias for Two Sticks and Two Two and placed it in the hands of U.S. Deputy Marshal J. P. Walters.[67] Walters promptly went after the men, but he did not have to go far. He found them in Hot Springs; they were on their way to Deadwood.[68]

Monday morning, October 15, Judge Dundy took the bench. His condition was perceptibly improved, but not his patience.[69] There were more cases on the court docket than could be adjudicated in the allotted time. Some were serious offenses; others were not. Among those alleged of committing less serious crimes were ranchers indicted for pasturing cattle on the reservation. Dundy dismissed the indictments against nearly all of them, including, as the *Hot Springs Star* reported, "Solomon Sharp, a poor but honest old granger. [He has] been laying in jail for the last four months, will now be set at liberty and can go to his home and family. It is a shame that he had to suffer thus on account of cattle straying over the line a little to get a few mouthfuls of grass that otherwise would never have been eaten."[70] Ranchers Eugene Powell, Edgar Cummings, and Joseph Powell were also tried, having been indicted for stealing Indians' cattle on the reservation. They pleaded guilty. Dundy fined each of them ten dollars and sentenced them to twenty days in jail,[71] making the crime of stealing the Indians' cattle little more than a misdemeanor and fairly profitable.

With the judge feeling better, social festivities resumed. On Monday evening U.S. Marshal Peemiller and his wife hosted a banquet for twenty-four people in the dining room of the Keystone Hotel, locally known as the Deadwood Club. After two large bowls of spiked punch were emptied, the food consumed, and cigars passed around, it was time to award tokens of esteem.[72] The court officers presented Ezra Miller's wife with a dozen Deadwood souvenir silver spoons and a handsome watch chain made of gold nuggets with a crystal locket filled with gold dust. Van Buskirk's wife received a silver coffee set and tray and a Black Hills gold broach. Ash's wife was honored with a silver ice cream set. The time was then opportune for Colonel William Steele to give a flowery speech and, on behalf of court officials in attendance, present Judge Dundy with a beautiful watch chain made of gold nuggets fastened together by small gold rings.[73]

The next day, Tuesday, Dundy was on the bench. His first case involved Eagle Louse, the man who had accompanied Philip Wells on the morning of February 3, when the boss farmer had gone to examine the murder scene. Eagle Louse was on trial because fourteen months later, April 24, 1894, to be specific, he killed had Thunder Hawk.[74]

A jury was secured and Eagle Louse's trial commenced. Testifying on his own behalf, Eagle Louse said he and Thunder Hawk were neighbors, but there had been "bad blood" between them for years. On the day of the killing they were both on horseback and met on the prairie. Harsh words regarding ownership of some cattle were exchanged. Thunder Hawk dismounted and started for Eagle Louse, saying that he intended to "put some ears on him." Eagle Louse drew his Winchester. As he did, the gun accidentally went off, but Thunder Hawk kept coming at him. Eagle Louse quickly levered another cartridge into the rifle's chamber and fired. The bullet struck Thunder Hawk in the chest and killed him instantly. Eagle Louse immediately went into the agency, reported the incident, and gave himself up.[75]

At that point in the trial, Eagle Louse's attorneys, Walter Anderson and Matthew Anderson, advised him to plead guilty to manslaughter. Dundy sentenced Eagle Louse to six months in the Lawrence County Jail.[76]

The trial of Two Two was called the following day, Wednesday, October 17. On the advice of his attorneys, Bennett and Burns, eighteen-year-old Two Two pleaded guilty to manslaughter. Dundy sentenced him to five years in prison.[77]

The next alleged murderer to be tried was White Face Horse, age twenty-two. At the request of William Benoist, the mixed-blood interpreter at the Cheyenne River Agency, Pierre attorney Thomas Drake agreed to defend the alleged murderer, apparently with the understanding that Benoist would solicit nearby Indians (most likely members of the Crow Eagle band, who had allotments along Bad River) to pay the attorney's fees.[78]

White Face Horse's trial began on Wednesday. Jury selection took up the morning. The jurors were John F. Wood, Frank Kellar, James Tuplin, Julius Rebasmen, George Parker, Owen Walsh, W. E. Lowe, W. H. Whealen, Ben Hurley, N. E. Franklin, Peter Lee, and William Martin.[79] When the jurors were seated, Judge Dundy asked White Face Horse to enter a plea. He pleaded

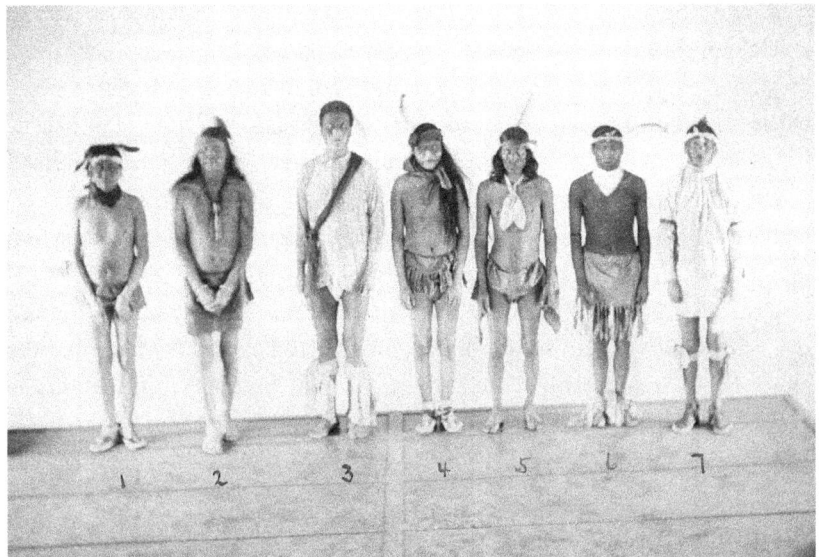

Indians held in the Lawrence County Jail in October 1894, with the exception of Two Sticks and White Face Horse, who was still recovering from the amputation of his leg. Those of interest to this story are number 5: Eagle Louse, among the first to visit the crime scene on the morning of February 3, 1893; number 6: Fights With (also known as Mark Red Elk), Two Sticks's son; and number 7: Two Two (also known as Kills the Two). (Courtesy Deadwood History, Inc., Adams Museum Collection, Deadwood.)

not guilty. White Face Horse told the court that he had attended the Santee Industrial School for four years but had never learned to speak English. At the school he was known as George Fields, but among his own people he was called Ptay Ptessau Hacksilau.[80]

The interpreter at White Face Horse's trial and later at Two Sticks's was Alfred Coe. Born in Vermillion, Dakota Territory, in 1867 to Charles and Jeanette Coe, he traced his Indian blood to his great-grandmother, a full-blood Sioux, which made him, genetically speaking, one-eighth Indian. When Alfred was eight, his father died and the family moved to the Yankton Reservation. There, Alfred attended the Presbyterian day school run by the church for the benefit of Indian children. His mother died three years later, and he went to the Normal Industrial Training School, a boarding school on the Santee Reservation. During his childhood years at those schools, his classmates and friends were Sioux, and he learned to speak fluent Dakota. From there, Coe attended Pierre College. To support himself, he got a job as a court interpreter.[81]

Most of the witnesses at White Face Horse's trial were Indians who did not speak English. Coe had to translate every question asked and every reply given, making the testimony tedious to obtain and laborious to follow. By three-thirty in the afternoon, little had been accomplished. Frustrated at the slow pace of the proceedings, Ezra Miller and defense attorney Thomas Drake huddled briefly and spoke in whispers. Upon concluding their private conference, Drake asked the judge to adjourn court until the next morning, assuring him that it would expedite the trial.[82]

It did. On the morning of October 19, White Face Horse changed his plea from not guilty of murder to guilty of manslaughter. Miller accepted the plea.[83] Dundy fined White Face Horse five hundred dollars, ordered him to pay court costs, and sentenced him to five years in prison.[84] White Face Horse and Two Two were later transferred to the South Dakota State Penitentiary at Sioux Falls.[85]

The three Indians who pleaded guilty to manslaughter for the killing of the four white cowboys expected to serve their relatively short prison sentences and, upon being released, return to Pine Ridge to resume their lives, but fate intervened. On June 20, 1895, Fights With died of scrofula, a common disease among the Indians, associated with tubercle bacilli. He was twenty years old.[86] Two Two died on February 25, 1896, at the age of twenty-one. His death was attributed to consumption. In November 1895, White Face Horse was placed in the prison hospital. By May 1896 he was emaciated and weak, coughing and occasionally expectorating mouthfuls of blood.[87] In that late stage of tuberculosis, he could not have survived much longer, although the exact date of his death is now buried under the dust of history.

❖ 20 ❖

TWO STICKS'S TRIAL

Two Sticks's defense attorney was William L. McLaughlin. He graduated from Georgetown Law School in 1884 and returned to Deadwood to join his father, Daniel, in the practice of law.[1] Like most of the other forty-six attorneys in the town of thirty-one hundred, they specialized in litigation over mining claims.

Because Fights With, Two Two, and White Face Horse had successfully plea-bargained the charge of murder down to manslaughter, McLaughlin offered the same plea bargain on behalf of his client. U.S. District Attorney Ezra Miller refused.[2] He wanted Two Sticks tried for murder and, if found guilty, punished accordingly. A recent change in state law gave Miller reason to be confident of obtaining a conviction. Previously, jurors for federal court sessions held in South Dakota were selected from a statewide pool. Roughly 90 percent of the population lived east of the Missouri River. Thus every jury was predominantly composed of men who did not see Indians as archenemies. The new law changed that by stipulating that when federal court was held in Deadwood, jurors would be drawn exclusively from a pool of West River men.[3]

Geographically speaking, West River was a huge area—forty thousand square miles. However, in 1894 nearly a quarter of the area was allotted to five Indian reservations, whose Lakota occupants were not citizens and thus ineligible to serve as jurors. With the exception of Fort Pierre and its immediate vicinity, there were likely fewer than five hundred potential jurors living on the sagebrush-covered prairie bordering the Black Hills. The majority of whites in the West River area lived in the Black Hills or in its evening shadow, and the bulk of them were congregated within ten miles of George Hearst's Homestake Mine. Lead, the site of Homestake, had a population of 4,129. Two miles down the gulch sat Deadwood; its population had dwindled to 4,205 souls. Rapid City, the third most populated town in the Black Hills, could boast only 1,887 denizens. The remaining "towns" were little more than dots on a map.[4] The venire of fifty men summoned to the courtroom on October 23 as potential jurors for Two Sticks's trial could have come from anyplace west of the Missouri River. Indeed, an attorney committed to providing the best possible defense for his Indian client would have seen to it that at least some of them had firsthand knowledge of Indians. He would have wanted the jury pool to include men such as John Farnham, Connie Utterback, Mike Dunn, Guy Trimble, Charley Gallagher, Narcisse Narcelle, Scotty Philip, John Nelson, and others who were married to Sioux women and who understood and spoke Lakota.

Instead, the venire consisted of men who lived in and around Deadwood and Lead. On the morning of October 23, twelve were selected as jurors. One was N. E. Franklin, who had arrived during the peak of the gold rush. In 1879 he and a man by the name of Gottstein obtained gold flakes the easy way—as wholesale liquor dealers they extracted it from the pokes of men who stood knee-deep in ice-cold water staring to see color in the bottom of their mining pans.[5] By 1894 Franklin had sold the liquor business and was the owner and proprietor of the Palace Pharmacy. He was also the outgoing chief of the Deadwood Fire Department.[6] Another jurist was Barney Hurley, the ace pitcher on Deadwood's baseball team, which had beat its archrival, Lead, that summer by the humbling score of 22–2.[7] Hurley upheld his civic responsibilities by being a member of South Deadwood Hose Co. No. 1.[8] W. A. "Will" Ickes had arrived in Deadwood in 1876 with his gold-seeking father, steadfast mother, and older brother.[9] In June 1894 Ickes became Deadwood's city auditor.[10] Scott Notley lived in Lead. A Republican, he was seeking to be elected in November to the town board.[11] Former Iowan George Parker, age forty-six, had arrived in Deadwood in 1892 and found work as a handyman.[12] That summer he bid thirty dollars and secured a contract to paint the roof of the city hall.[13] W. A. "Tex" Rankin lived in Lead. He was a partner in a brick business that had gone bankrupt that spring during the nationwide depression; he saw his company's tangible assets sold on the steps of the county courthouse.[14] Rankin also was the first assistant on the Deadwood Fire Department.[15] Bryan Rossiter was foreman of the Cyanide Mining Company. He had been instrumental in constructing a cyanide plant that extracted 95 percent of the gold from pulverized ore.[16] Joseph Schwing was a partner in a Deadwood mercantile store,[17] treasurer of the Deadwood Fire Department[18] and a member of the school board.[19] A few days before Two Sticks's trial, he was appointed by the county commissioners to monitor the upcoming November election.[20] Frank Smith operated the Sheridan Fuel and Feed Store, where customers bought coal shipped in by rail from Sheridan and Rock Springs, Wyoming.[21] Noah "James" Tuplin had stepped off the Bismarck stagecoach in 1879 and planted himself in Deadwood.[22] In time, he and J. A. Johnson established the Pine Street Lumber Yard. When the business went bankrupt in the spring of 1894, their tangible assets were sold on the courthouse steps.[23] Louis Werthheimer and his older brother operated the M. J. Werthheimer and Bro. mercantile store, a long-standing and profitable Deadwood business.[24] The twelfth jurist was Julius Rebsamen, who operated one of Deadwood's many saloons.[25] Rebsamen was also secretary for the Creston Mining Company[26] and the Prospectors Protective Association.[27] The other eleven jurists selected him to be jury foreman.[28]

As a group, the twelve were stalwart citizens of the Lead–Deadwood area. However, not one of them had two cents' worth of knowledge about Indians or their conditions on the Pine Ridge Reservation except for the diatribes they read in the Black Hills newspapers or heard on the street. For them, an Indian was a curiosity.

The jury was impaneled by noon on October 23. Right after lunch recess, the prosecution team went to work, led by District Attorney Miller. He was assisted by Charles Brown, former state's attorney for Pennington County, and Thomas Drake, the Pierre attorney who had defended Fights With a year earlier. In his opening argument, Miller informed the jury that the prosecution would produce witnesses who had heard Two Sticks order the four young Indian men to kill the cowboys. The prosecution also promised to provide evidence that placed Two Sticks at the scene of the murders.[29]

The prosecution's first witness was Philip Wells. Wells was called to the stand to review for the jurors a map, drawn to scale by William Lewis, of the crime scene area and the plan of the dugout where the four white men were killed.[30] Wells likely pointed out that Lewis had mistakenly identified White Clay Creek as White River. (The map shows Wells's cabin at the lower edge; the dugout, stable, and feed corral in the center; and several lodges farther down

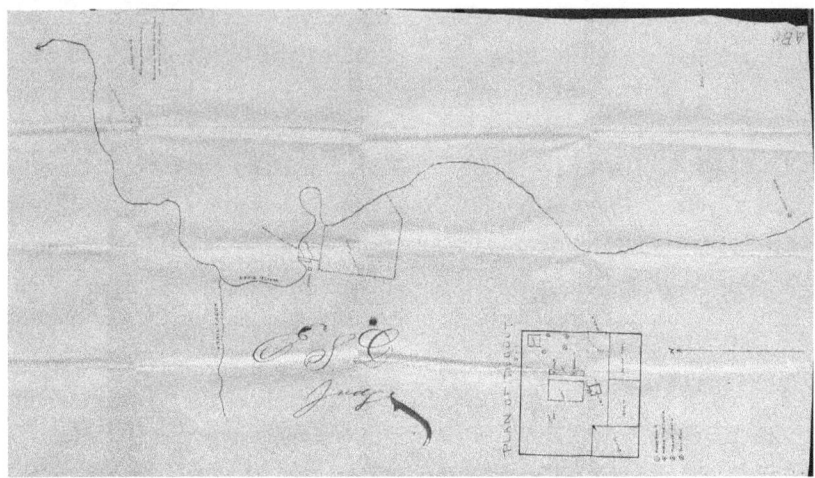

Drawing of White Clay Creek area. (U.S. National Archives, Kansas City.)

the creek. Wells's cabin was reportedly one mile south and the Indian lodges one-half mile northeast of the halfway camp.)

It is interesting that William Lewis's drawing of the dugout included the names of First Eagle, White Face Horse, Fights With, and Two Two. Philip Wells, who had tracked the murderers back to their lodges, likely supplied the names. It is noteworthy that there was no mention of Two Sticks's attorney, William McLaughlin, calling the court's attention to the fact that Two Sticks's name was not listed.

Miller's next witness was Clark Bacon, father of the murdered James Bacon. Clark Bacon told the jury about accompanying Sergeant Joe Bush and a detachment of Indian police to the dugout on the morning of February 4 and related how he watched as Ike Humphrey and his Z-Bell cowboys loaded his son's frozen, lifeless body into a wagon.[31] Nothing in Bacon's testimony implicated Two Sticks, but that was not Miller's intent. The shrewd attorney wanted to begin the trial by raising the jurors' ire against Two Sticks, and what better way to do that than have them hear a grieving father describe the horror of looking upon the body of a son killed by Indians.

A succession of Oglala was then called upon to testify. None of them spoke English, necessitating Albert Coe, the official interpreter, to translate all questions asked and all responses given, which made the oral evidence hard to extract and laborious to follow.[32] Eagle Louse was the first Oglala to testify. He was escorted to the courtroom from his jail cell, having eight days earlier

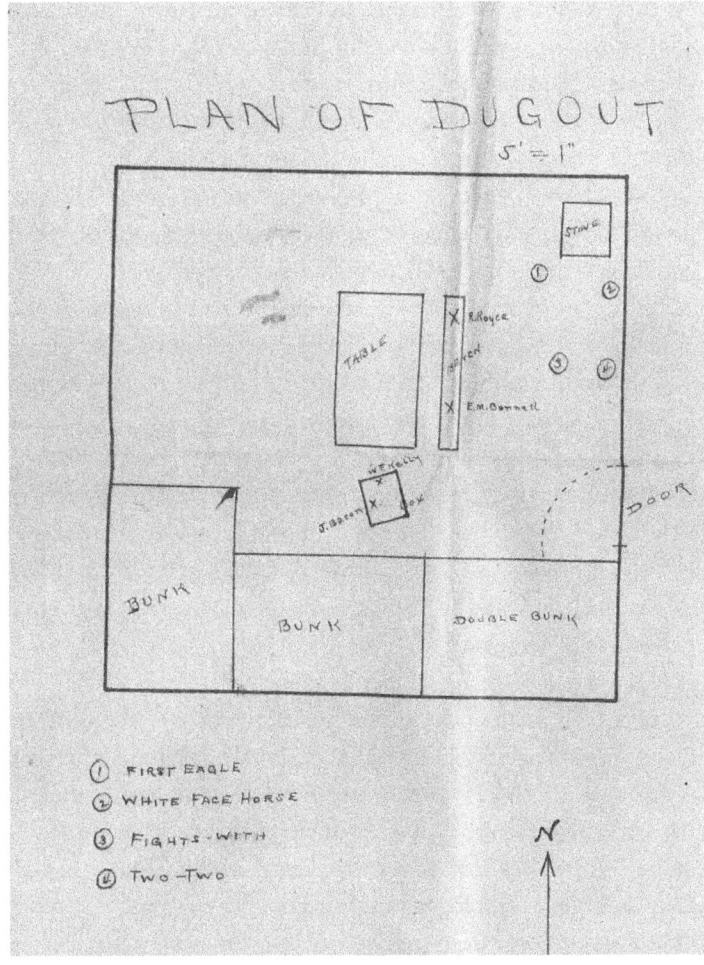

Drawing of the halfway camp dugout. (U.S. National Archives, Kansas City.)

pleaded guilty to manslaughter, a crime unrelated to the Two Sticks case. Eagle Louse told the court about the position of the bodies of the dead men when he, Philip Wells, and others went to the crime scene on the morning of February 3, 1893. His testimony confirmed that four white men had been killed in the dugout, but it did not shed any light on Two Sticks's role, if any, in the murders.[33]

Lob, a resident of No Water's village, testified. He told the court that on the night of February 2, Bear Eagle told him there had been trouble at the cowboys' camp.[34] Lob immediately went to Two Sticks's tepee to learn more about it. There he found First Eagle and White Face Horse. First Eagle, who was cleaning his gun, said, "I killed one of the cowboys." White Face Horse said he had also killed one of the cowboys; he too was cleaning his gun.[35] Lob's testimony implied that First Eagle and White Face each shot one or more of the white men in the dugout, but his testimony did not implicate Two Sticks.

An Indian whom newspaper reporters identified as Comes Crawling was called to the witness stand. He testified that on the afternoon of February 2, 1893, Two Sticks stirred up the Broken Arrow band, urging them to get even with the cowboys for trying to have them arrested for killing a white rancher's beef. Comes Crawling said that Two Sticks gathered guns and ammunition that afternoon and distributed them to some of his young men and boasted that his boys were going to kill the cowboys.[36]

Comes Crawling was the first witness to connect Two Sticks with the murders of the four cowboys, but nothing in his testimony suggested that Two Sticks had killed anyone in the dugout or that he was at the scene of the killings.[37] Nonetheless, as Comes Crawling stepped down from the witness stand, Miller likely believed he had scored an important point with the jurors: Two Sticks was the instigator!

On Wednesday morning, October 24, the courtroom was again crowded with spectators. They attentively listened as White Face Horse's wife told the court that Two Two, Fights With, and her husband had left their lodges on the night of February 2 with their guns and gone up the creek toward the cowboys' camp. They had on ghost shirts made of unbleached muslin with designs made of red paint. White Face Horse had on a war blanket.[38] They returned when the moon was high, and each was mounted on a horse—a bay, a black, and a gray—that she had never seen before. They took off saddles that she also had never seen before.[39] All of them went into White Face Horse's tepee, and she heard them laughing. Early the next morning, Two Two and Fights With went to the cowboys' camp and brought back a nickel clock and three saddles. On the morning of February 4, she heard Two Sticks order Two Two, Fights With, First Eagle, and White Face Horse to pack up their things and pull out. The Indians hitched the black and gray horses (likely the stolen horses) to a wagon.[40] Her testimony, which was internally consistent and logical, did not include anything that put Two Sticks at the halfway camp on the night the cowboys were killed.

The prosecution then called Fights With's wife to the stand. She gave her name as Fat Woman, which Judge Elmer Dundy thought was a misnomer because she was about as big around as a fence post and, as a newspaper reporter described her, as straight up and down as a yard of pump water. Fat Woman related that she lived in Two Sticks's tepee and was his daughter-in-law.[41]

Fat Woman was a reluctant witness, always slow to answer the prosecuting attorney's questions and sometimes responding to the attorney's questions with maddening silence. Even Coe, the interpreter, lost patience. In a fit of desperation, Judge Dundy resorted to intimidation. He told her to answer the questions or he'd put her in jail.[42] The threat worked. As Fat Woman was being questioned, Two Sticks skewered her with wicked looks.[43] Fat Woman eventually admitted that she was afraid to testify.[44]

However, in response to direct questions by the prosecuting attorney, she revealed that on the night of the murders, Two Sticks put on his cartridge belt and started up the creek in the direction of the halfway camp, a half mile away. White Face Horse, Two Two, First Eagle, and Fights With followed him.[45] They all had guns. White Face Horse had a "plenty shooter," the Indians' term for a level-action Winchester rifle, and the other men had single-shot rifles. They were all wearing their ghost shirts. She did not know how long they were gone. She and Two Sticks's wife, who was blind, and her two children stayed in the tepee.[46] Two Sticks came back first, leading four horses she had not seen before.[47] As the men entered the tepee, White Face Horse said, "My cousins are cowards, so I whipped them across the face." It was reported to her that First Eagle and White Face Horse shot several of the cowboys. She also heard Two Sticks say, "I put it into one of them."[48]

Fat Woman was the first witness to place Two Sticks at the murder scene. She also told the jurors that Two Sticks claimed to have killed one of the cowboys. As Fat Woman left the witness stand, the prosecution believed it had presented the evidence the jurors needed to convict Two Sticks of murder.

D. M. Underwood was the next witness. As a cowboy for Z-Bell Ranch, he was one of three men assigned to the halfway camp. However, Underwood was not at the dugout the night the four men were murdered. Upon returning to the halfway camp and learning that his friends had been killed, he went to No Water's village and discovered the carcasses of two horses belonging to Rodney Royce and Emanuel Bennett. Underwood presumed that the guilty men had killed the horses to hide evidence of their involvement.[49] A more plausible explanation is that the horses were hitched to the wagon into which the alleged murderers were loading their belongings on the morning of February 4, 1893, and the horses were shot in the intense gunfire that erupted when the Indian police suddenly arrived.

CHAPTER 20

When court convened Thursday morning, October 26, the first witness was White Face Horse. He related that at the time of the killings, he was camped with Two Sticks and his band about a half mile down the creek from the cowboy camp.[50] He related that several men in Two Sticks's band entered the sweat house the evening of February 2. As they left the sweat house, he heard Two Sticks say he was going to kill the cowboys. First Eagle said that if they could kill the three white men, all the people would join them.[51] White Face Horse related that later that evening, Fights With, Two Two, and First Eagle told him they were going to go see some girls and wanted him to go along. White Face Horse claimed that he did not know what the others intended until they got to the cabin of the cowboys. He saw a light inside, but he could not see any men. Two Sticks's sons (First Eagle and Fights With) ran off the cowboys' horses and then went into the cabin. White Face Horse then saw Two Sticks come out of the stable; he saw Two Sticks and Two Two go into the cabin. However, White Face Horse did not go into the cabin but looked through the door. He saw Two Sticks point a gun at a man inside and shoot. He then heard a lot of shooting. White Face Horse concluded his testimony by saying, "I took no part in the firing."[52]

The necessity of translating the prosecuting attorney's questions into Lakota and translating the answers into English was tedious and so time-consuming that White Face Horse was on the witness stand all morning. As he testified, it became apparent that he knew a fair amount of English, because he occasionally got so excited that he animatedly answered questions while they were still being translated.[53]

White Face Horse's testimony was troublesome for several reasons. It was implausible that First Eagle and Fights With had run off the cowboys' horses and then gone into the dugout. Every horseman knows—and all the jurors were horsemen—that at the entrance of unfamiliar men into a corral, horses whinny in alarm and shy, making them difficult to catch. The horses' natural inclinations would have been intensified because of the differences in the dress and smell of unfamiliar Indians compared to familiar white cowboys. As for "running off" with the cowboys' horses, nothing would wake a cowboy faster than the sound of horses' hooves striking frozen, flint-hard ground. The final and telling inconsistency was that, according to White Face Horse, First Eagle and Fights With had led the cowboys' horses away, an implied trek of a half mile back to their tepees, and then returned to the dugout. That sequence of events was not plausible. Individuals bent on killing men would do the killing first so as not to be caught stealing horses and shot. The final hard-to-believe part of White Face Horse's testimony was his claim of innocence: "I took no part in the firing." Because much of White Face Horse's testimony was implausible, jurors likely disregarded it, with one possible exception. They might have believed White Face Horse when he testified that Two Sticks was at the scene of the murders and was seen firing his gun at the white men.[54]

The prosecution's next witness was Two Two, Two Sticks's eighteen-year-old nephew. He testified that on the evening of the killings he, First Eagle, Fights With, and White Face Horse had gone up the creek toward the cowboys' dugout. First Eagle, Fights With, and White Face Horse had guns, but he was unarmed. Two Two told the court that the four of them knocked on the cowboys' door and were invited in. They sat down by the stove and smoked some cigarettes the cowboys offered. Two Two then got up to leave. As he opened the door, he saw First Eagle point his gun and fire three shots. As he stepped out the door, he saw White Face Horse point his gun and he heard another shot.

What was important about Two Two's testimony was what he did not say. He did not say that Two Sticks was at the murder scene—just the opposite. Two Two testified that he did not see Two Sticks at the halfway camp.[55]

Two Two's testimony was not consistent with the accounting of the murders just related by White Face Horse. The jurors surely noted, and likely also found it interesting, that Two Two put the blame for the killings on First Eagle, who was conveniently dead, and on White Face Horse; and that Two Two claimed he was not in the cabin when the cowboys were killed. Two Two's testimony also lacked credibility. The dugout was only four hundred square feet, and in that small space there were two beds, one bunk bed, a table, a bench, a stove, and a wood box. There would not have been room for eight men. Furthermore, Royce and Bennett considered the men of the Broken Arrow band to be lawless renegades who killed Z-Bell cattle. Royce was so concerned about his safety that he asked another Z-Bell cowboy, Charley Edgerton, to purchase a pistol for him and bring it the next time he brought supplies to the halfway camp.[56] Royce and Bennett would not have allowed four young, armed Oglala men to enter the dugout.

The testimony of Two Two and White Face Horse differed sharply from the account related years later by Charley Edgerton. Edgerton occasionally told what he witnessed when he and other Z-Bell cowboys had accompanied Charles Swartz to the murder scene on the evening of February 3, 1893. In the retelling, Edgerton said they found the four men dead in their beds. James Bacon, William Kelly, and Emanuel Bennett had died in their sleep, having been hit in the head with a heavy object like an ax. The fourth man, Rodney Royce, had died with his hand over his head, as if to ward off a blow. There was a bullet hole through his hand and into his forehead,[57] explaining the one sharp "crack" Wells had heard while standing outside his cabin on the night of February 2.

When Two Two completed his testimony, the prosecution rested its case. It was time for the defense to prove that Two Sticks was not at the murder scene. Defense attorney McLaughlin began his testimony by introducing as evidence an almanac showing the times the sun set and the moon rose on the night of the murder. If there was a point to be made by that evidence, not one reporter at the trial conveyed it to newspaper readers.

As his first witness, McLaughlin called Albert Coe, the interpreter, to the stand. He asked Coe questions designed to show that Fat Woman was not of sound mind. Why McLaughlin believed that Coe had any knowledge about Fat Woman's state of mind is unclear. After all, Coe lived in Pierre and had never seen Fat Woman prior to the trial. Not surprisingly, the prosecution objected to the questions, and the court sustained the objection.[58]

The defense's next witness was Thomas Two Sticks, a young son of Two Sticks's who gave his age as thirteen.[59] He was enrolled in the Holy Rosary School, where all classes were taught in English,[60] yet Albert Coe was called upon to translate. Upon being put under oath, Thomas made it known that he did not understand anything about this ceremony of taking an oath. McLaughlin, a staunch Catholic, explained the oath-taking process in religious terms, telling young Thomas that if he lied or told a falsehood he would be punished by God in the hereafter.[61] Judge Dundy explained the implications of the oath in terms an adolescent boy could understand: "Lie to me and you will be arrested at once and jailed." Dundy asked Thomas if he understood that. The boy nodded.[62]

Thomas Two Sticks testified that he was in his mother's lodge on the night in question. Thomas related that Two Sticks, his mother, White Face Horse's wife, and Lob were in the tepee. Thomas said that when he went to bed, Two Sticks also retired. He did not know of Two Sticks leaving the tepee that night.[63] Thomas's alibi for his father likely rang hollow for the jurors because Lob had earlier testified that he went to Two Sticks's tepee upon hearing that there had been an incident at the halfway camp.

McLaughlin wanted to put Two Sticks's wife on the stand. However, the court would not allow her to testify, ruling that as Two Sticks's wife, she was, Judge Dundy said, "an incompetent witness."[64]

After putting only two witnesses on the stand, McLaughlin called his last witness—Two Sticks. "I knew nothing of the killings of the cowboys," Two Sticks related, "until my sons woke me that night and told me of the terrible thing they had done." Two Sticks also offered an alibi. He stated that late on the afternoon of February 2, 1893, he had gone to visit Pawnee, who lived farther down the creek and in the opposite direction of the halfway camp. Here, the judge interrupted Two Sticks's testimony. Addressing Two Sticks's attorney, Dundy asked, "Why, Mr. McLaughlin, didn't you issue a subpoena for Pawnee?" McLaughlin replied that he had no opportunity to talk with Two Sticks until after the trial opened, and he did not know anything about Two Sticks visiting Pawnee until it was too late to serve notice to the prosecution.[65] That was a weak excuse. McLaughlin became Two Sticks's defense attorney shortly after the Oglala was incarcerated in the Lawrence County Jail in the spring of 1893. Two Sticks was in jail from June until October, giving McLaughlin more than sufficient time and opportunity to interview his client. The first thing a competent attorney would ask his client: "Do you have an alibi who can testify that you could not have been at the murder scene that night?" Obviously, McLaughlin had not asked his client that critically important question. Furthermore, when Judge Alonzo Edgerton was deciding which cases to try in the fall of 1893, McLaughlin informed the court that he was ready to go to trial.

Two Sticks concluded his testimony by saying that he had never been to the cowboys' camp and had never seen the cowboys, either dead or alive.[66]

At that, the defense attorney rested his case without putting Philip Wells on the stand. It was a perplexing oversight. After all, Wells was the well-known and highly regarded boss farmer for White Clay District. Whatever he said on the stand would have credibility with the jurors, and as one of the first people at the murder scene on the morning of February 3, 1893, Wells had interesting testimony that would have shed light on Two Sticks's guilt or innocence. But McLaughlin did not call Wells to testify about the tracks he saw that morning in the freshly fallen snow.

Miller made the closing argument for the prosecution, and McLaughlin did the same for the defense.[67] Judge Dundy then gave the jury their instructions, telling them:

[T]he defendant, Two Sticks, is charged with the killing of one Bacon . . . and before you can find a verdict of guilty of murder, you must be satisfied beyond a reasonable doubt that the defendant either killed the said Bacon or he was present at the time Bacon was killed by someone else, and was assisting and aiding the person who killed said Bacon at the time of the killing. Unless one of these states of facts is proved to your satisfaction beyond a reasonable doubt, your verdict in this case should be not guilty. If you believe from the evidence that the defendant, Two Sticks, did not go to the cowboys' camp on the night of the second of February or go to the vicinity of the camp, then your verdict should be not guilty.

If you believe from the evidence that the defendant Two Sticks aided, abetted, or assisted either White Face Horse, First Eagle, Fights With, or Two Two, or all of them in preparing in any way to kill the said Bacon, but was not actually present at the time of the killing nor was so near that he might have rendered assistance to them in case it should have been needed, then he might be what is termed an accessary before the fact to the crime of murder, but he would not be guilty of the crime charged against him in this indictment and could not be punished in this proceeding for such acts, and your verdict in this case should be not guilty.[68]

The jurors' charge was clear. For a verdict of guilty they needed to be convinced by the evidence that Two Sticks was at least present when the four white men were murdered and that he had either killed James Bacon or he aided the other Indians in killing the young white man.

With those instructions in mind, the jury went out at four-thirty on Monday afternoon, October 29, to consider the evidence and arrive at a verdict. They deliberated for eighteen hours. At ten o'clock Monday morning, October 30, the foreman informed Judge Dundy that the jury had reached a verdict. The judge invited the jurors into the courtroom. As a packed courtroom listened, Dundy asked the jury foreman to announce the verdict. The foreman replied, "The jury finds Two Sticks guilty..."[69]

At that, McLaughlin ponderously rose to his feet. "Your Honor," he said to Judge Dundy, "I intend to prepare an appeal for a new trial." The court granted McLaughlin twenty-five days to prepare and present a brief stating the grounds for a new trial.[70]

When court convened the next day, Tuesday, at ten o'clock, Judge Dundy announced his sentence. "Two Sticks," Dundy informed the old man, "you are to be hanged by the neck until dead. The execution will take place on Friday, December 28th."[71]

Upon being asked if he had anything to say, Two Sticks replied, "I do not consider myself as doing anything [wrong] but even for that I am to be executed, and I am glad that I am to be executed for my people. [As] I have said before, I am an old man, and I am rather anxious for it. I do not want to suffer any more in this life."[72]

As Judge Dundy departed from Deadwood, he was presented with a gold-headed cane, a gift from the twelve jurists for Two Sticks's trial.[73] It is likely the expensive gift was presented not so much as an expression of their esteem for his comportment during the trial but more to ensure that the influential judge left town with positive sentiments regarding Deadwood and its citizens.

A month and a half later, the editor of the *Black Hills Daily Times* sought out McLaughlin to ask if his appeal for a retrial had been successful. McLaughlin curtly replied, "It is a matter of considerable expense to prepare a transcript of the proceedings and to write a brief of the trial stating the reasons for an appeal. The relatives and friends of Two Sticks do not appear to be much concerned in the matter; at least [they] have not made an effort to furnish the funds."[74]

The hanging was on.

⊰ 21 ⊱

THE HANGING

When Father Florentine Digmann learned that Philip Wells was going to Deadwood on a business trip, he asked the boss farmer to go to the Lawrence County Jail and call on Two Sticks. "Earlier I had offered to baptize Two Sticks," Digmann informed Wells, "and he refused. Maybe now that he is about to meet his maker, he will reconsider. Please do me the favor of asking him."[1]

Father Digmann was not offering to baptize Two Sticks because they were friends or, as best as can be determined, even acquaintances prior to his arrest. Rather, as soon as Indian Agent Hugh Gallagher allowed Catholic clergy to have a presence on Pine Ridge in 1886, the priests saw it as their mission to baptize every Indian in the belief that it saved a person's soul from spending eternity in the hot fires of hell and damnation.[2]

Wells informed Digmann that he was reluctant to ask Two Sticks if he wanted to be baptized because "the old Indian is apt to think that baptism will save him from death." Digmann hastily wrote a letter Wells could read to Two Sticks, making it clear that there was nothing the priest could do that would save him from being hanged.[3]

On Monday, December 3, Wells visited Two Sticks in his jail cell. Wells read Digmann's letter to the prisoner and underscored the point of the letter by saying, "The Blackbeard can do nothing for you but prepare you for a happy death." Two Sticks answered, "I expect nothing from him to get free, but I want to be baptized and lie down like a man."[4]

Upon learning that Two Sticks was amenable to being baptized, Digmann wrote to Bishop Martin Marty, requesting permission for the trip but also requesting that another priest be assigned to go, because "I am currently crippled with rheumatism." Marty wired back: "Sorry for your having rheumatism, but you have to go."[5]

While Digmann was preparing for the trip, an important package arrived in Deadwood on December 18 by express mail. The package was addressed to U.S. Marshal Otto Peemiller. Inside was a uniquely constructed rope, the one that would be used to hang Two Sticks.[6]

A few days later, December 22, U.S. Deputy Marshal Walters received a telegram from Peemiller: "Deputy Marshal Beiglemeir will arrive in Deadwood Monday. Have Tuplin ready to do carpenter work." Accordingly, James Tuplin, one of the jurors who had voted to convict Two Sticks, commenced construction of the scaffold on Tuesday, Christmas Day.[7]

Digmann presented himself to Walters on December 23. "The sheriff received me very kindly," Digmann noted in his daily diary, "but he had orders not to let anyone see the sentenced Indian who could speak Sioux without a witness being present." U.S. Deputy Marshal Frank Beiglemeir intervened. He told Digmann that he could disregard Walters's order and see Two Sticks as often and for as long as needed and could speak with him alone.[8]

"Two Sticks was very glad to see me," Digmann reported. "He was in his cell or 'cage' as they called it. There were quite a number of iron cages separated from each other by iron plates. Upon my arrival, Two Sticks, who had behaved himself well, was allowed to leave his cage and walk free outside the cells where there was a small table and a couple of chairs." The two pulled up chairs at the table, and Digmann gave Two Sticks instructions about the Catholic faith.[9]

In addition to Two Sticks, there were two full-bloods and one mixed-blood in the jail. The mixed-blood had read to Two Sticks everything written about him in the newspapers, including an article purporting the possibility of another trial to wash him clean of the crime for which he had been sentenced to hang. Digmann believed that the mixed-blood shared the possibility of another trial with Two Sticks out of compassion for the old man and to keep him in good humor. "However, I thought it was cruel and certainly not the way to dispose Two Sticks for a sincere conversion. As long as he had hope for this life, I feared he would not settle his accounts honestly with God. In fact, in my first talk with him, I found he had hope yet, not through my intercession but because his lawyer and others had told him he might get another hearing. So I went to his attorney, Mr. McLaughlin, who was a Catholic and a graduate of Georgetown University, and begged him to speak plainly to the poor old man and tell him that there was no hope for him in this world and he should get ready to die a good death. McLaughlin did so. Two Sticks took the information with resignation and again asked to see me."[10]

On the afternoon of December 27, Ezra Miller and Marshal Beiglemeir went to the jail yard to inspect construction of the gallows. Two Sticks went to the little west-facing window of the jail and with a grim face peered down on them. As he watched, Beiglemeir tried the trapdoor and a piece of wood broke and fell to the ground.

At three o'clock that afternoon, Father Digmann, accompanied by Father Matthew Traynor of Deadwood, went to the jail to perform the baptism ceremony. Two Sticks was baptized into the Catholic faith under the name of John.[11]

On the day scheduled for the execution, December 28, Digmann went to the jail early in the morning to comfort the sixty-two-year-old man. Digmann was there when at nine-thirty, U.S. Marshal Peemiller and other officials came for Two Sticks. After Peemiller read the death warrant, Beiglemeir tried to strap Two Sticks's hands behind him, but scar tissue from the massive bullet wound suffered nearly two years earlier would not allow his right arm to come back very far. Laying the strap on a chair, Beiglemeir went to find a suitable rope. Two Sticks grabbed the strap, put it around his neck, and handed the loose end to Eagle Louse, who was in the neighboring cell. "Pull it, pull it," Two Sticks called out to Eagle Louse. But Eagle Louse did not pull the strap. So Two Sticks grabbed hold and gave it a hard jerk.[12] Peemiller forced his hand inside the makeshift noose and made him let go of the strap.[13]

When a rope was found, Two Sticks's arms were pinioned behind him and he was led outside. The sun had risen over the east ridge of Deadwood Gulch, bathing the gallows in bright light and warming the crowd of curious spectators that had been gathering since eight o'clock that morning to watch the hanging.[14]

The gallows stood in the center of the forty-by-sixty-foot area between the jailhouse and the stable that was enclosed by a fence sixteen feet high. Ex-deputy marshal Chris Matthiessen stood at the narrow gate. At nine-thirty he opened the gate and allowed the two hundred men with personalized admission tickets to enter.[15] Among those attending were Ike Humphrey, Ed Stenger, and

D. M. Underwood. In addition to those admitted at the gate, a large number of uninvited spectators watched from the stable roof.

It was rumored that many Oglala and Brulé were gathered at Pine Ridge to protest the hanging of Two Sticks.[16] Specifically, it was said that Lob, Leaves, Sheep Knife, and Bear Eagle had gone among the hostiles along Grass Creek and No Water's village and persuaded about one hundred to travel overland to Deadwood and make a public demonstration. Officials believed there was no basis for the rumor because, among other reasons, no Indian could leave the reservation without a pass from the Indian agent.[17] The officials were correct. The Indians in No Water's village accepted the inevitable. Their spokesman sent Two Sticks a letter of support, which arrived the day before his execution, and concluded with an assurance that the tribe would honor him on his last day on earth.

> Chief Two Sticks,
> On the day of your departure your band will kill a dog and one old horse in commemoration of this day, and there shall be carved on the old cottonwood tree near your tipi on the White River the words:
> CHIEF TWO STICKS
> CIVILIZED WANNICA
> I shake hands with you,
> His Fight
> Hemia Yelo[18]

As Two Sticks climbed the steps to the gallows, he examined the construction carefully. Finding it solid and well constructed, he said "Was-te" (Good). When he reached the top of the platform, Beiglemeir tied a rope around his legs. As Two Sticks's legs were being bound together, he sang his Lakota death song—"Aici-lowanpi" the Sioux call it. He sang it over and over until Digmann finally said, "Henala!" (Enough). Peemiller pulled a black cap over Two Sticks's head and put the hangman's noose around his neck. Stepping back, at 10:38 Peemiller signaled his deputy to open the trapdoor. Dutifully, Beiglemeir pulled on the lever to spring the trapdoor, but under the weight of Two Sticks's 165 pounds, the iron pin refused to move. So Beiglemeir gave a hard pull, resulting in a loud, ear-piercing screech. The trapdoor fell away. Two Sticks hit the end of his seven-foot, six-inch drop with a loud thud.[19]

For a few moments there was no movement. Then a muscular contraction drew up Two Sticks's legs. A few seconds later another contraction curled his shoulders forward—then another contraction and still more. It was some time before Two Sticks's body hung still and seemingly lifeless. But when Dr. H. A. L. von Wedelstaedt took his pulse, he found the chief's heart was still beating. The pulse lasted another five minutes. At forty-nine minutes past ten on the morning of December 28, 1894, Two Sticks's heart beat for the last time. The rope was removed from around the dead man's neck; his body was placed in a coffin and taken to the undertaking establishment of S. R. Smith. In the next few hours a great many curious people went to the mortuary to view the body.[20]

At two-thirty that afternoon, Digmann and Traynor went to Smith's mortuary and claimed Two Sticks's body. They took it up the side of the mountain to where a little shelf of land afforded space for the Catholic cemetery. Father Digmann had baptized Two Sticks on Christmas Day and had also administered the last rites. God might have forgiven Two Sticks, but the parishioners of Saint Ambrose Catholic Church did not. Two Sticks was buried outside the perimeter of the Catholic cemetery in an unmarked and now, 125 years later, unknown grave.

The day after the execution the *Rapid City Journal* gave the details of Two Sticks's execution under a front-page headline reading, "A Good Indian." The article concluded by saying that hanging Two Sticks "[made] him the last good Indian to visit the Black Hills."[21]

By calling Two Sticks "a good Indian," Joseph Gossage, editor of the *Rapid City Journal*, was not implying that Two Sticks was innocent of the crime for which he had been tried, convicted, and hanged. Rather, Gossage was using the phrase "good Indian" in the parlance of the time—a time when the extermination of Indians was unofficial U.S. Army policy and, in the reputed words of General Philip Sheridan, "The only good Indian is a dead Indian."[22]

Today, more than a century after Two Sticks was hanged, we can view Joseph Gossage's pronouncement that Two Sticks was the "last good Indian" from a different perspective. In the days following the execution, many who had attended the trial or followed the proceedings in the newspapers realized the guilty verdict was based almost entirely on Fat Woman's testimony; they shared Digmann's assessment that it was a "judicial hanging."[23] A few wizened people realized that Two Sticks's hanging was emblematic and also symptomatic of the government's half century of dishonesty with the Lakota.

Two Sticks's execution ushered in a change in government policies regarding the Lakota, and it also saw the frontier adopt a more understanding and sympathetic attitude toward Indians. One of the important changes occurred in 1897 when the Bureau of Indian Affairs stopped allowing white ranchers to regard the reservation as their "south pasture."[24] Instead, white ranchers were assessed a dollar for every bovine gathered up in reservation roundups, with the money going to feed and clothe the Indians.[25] On the Pine Ridge Reservation, white cowboys were no longer permitted to come onto the reservation to conduct roundups. Instead, Oglala cowboys gathered the cattle, took every maverick (an animal with no brand) as compensation, and met the white ranchers' throwback wagons at designated points on the border of the reservation.[26]

There were other subtle but, over time, more profound changes. After Two Sticks's hanging, newspaper editors did not write nor did public officials say to cheering crowds that "a good Indian is a dead Indian." Such blatant racism was no longer tolerated. The previously nearly constant diatribe in local newspapers bemoaning the "the sloth and sterility of Indian worthlessness"[27] and other derisive sentiments were curtailed. Blatant racism was no longer tolerated. Instead, after 1894 newspapers often acknowledged the difficulties faced by the Sioux and criticized the government for forcing the Oglala to become farmers on land unfit for cultivation, saddling them with an intractable economic system that resulted in generational poverty.[28]

There is a final reason to conclude that Two Sticks was a good Indian, and it is heart wrenching. In his autobiography, written in 1948, Philip Wells shared his recollection of the 1893 murders of the four cowboys and also the trial, part of which he attended. Wells believed it was the testimony of Fat Woman that convinced jurors that Two Sticks was at the murder scene and was therefore guilty of murder.[29]

"Snow had covered the ground the night before the murder," Wells related years later. "Four tracks, which led to the shack [the dugout] and back to the lodges of the murderers, were visible in the snow. I am sure that Two Sticks was not present at the murder. I carefully inspected him afterwards. I found that his right leg, which was crippled, was drawn up and that he had a stiff ankle, making it possible for him to step only on the tip of his toe. Had he been at the murder, I would have known it by his tracks in the snow, which were absent."[30]

Wells's conclusion was substantiated by Jake Herman of Kyle. Years later Herman sought out elders who knew Two Sticks. He related that Phyllis Garnette remembered Two Sticks and described him as "a nice man but easily aroused." She said he often visited their home on White Clay Creek. Jake Red Eagle, a former Indian scout, told Herman, "I knew Two Sticks well. He was a small man with hooded eyes, cunning and treacherous, who was continually agitating trouble." But Red Eagle was adamant that Two Sticks did not take part in the murders.[31]

As Two Sticks said minutes before his execution, "The white men will find out [in] time that I am innocent, and then they will be sorry they killed me."[32]

NOTES

PROLOGUE

1. Beck, *First Sioux War*.
2. Viegas, *Fort Laramie Treaty*.
3. Ostler, *Lakota and the Black Hills*.
4. Executive Documents of the Senate of the United States. First Session of the 51st Congress, *Congressional Edition*, vol. 2682, p. 353.
5. Annual Report of the Commissioner of Indian Affairs, 1890, 49.
6. Eli Ricker interview with Jack Whalen, Tablet 12, Nebraska State Historical Society.
7. Southerton, *James R. Walker's Campaign*, 107–26.
8. Utley, *Last Days of the Sioux Nation*, 57.
9. Utley, 261.

CHAPTER 1. STARING AT THE HANGMAN'S NOOSE

1. *Black Hills Daily Times* (Deadwood), December 29, 1894.
2. Florentine Digmann, History of the St. Francis Mission and Diary: 1886–1922, unpublished manuscript, Marquette University Archives.
3. *Black Hills Daily Times*, December 29, 1894.

CHAPTER 2. THE POLITICAL ROAD TO WOUNDED KNEE

1. Greene, *American Carnage*, 288.
2. Schuler, *South Dakota Capitol in Pierre*, 3.
3. Kingsbury, *History of Dakota Territory*, 137.
4. Lamar, *Dakota Territory*, 196.

5. Richard F. Pettigrew, Notes and Comments on Men and Events, Pettigrew Museum Archives.
6. Pettigrew, Notes and Comments.
7. *Dakota Republican* (Vermillion, S. Dak.), June 1, 1893.
8. *Argus Leader* (Sioux Falls), January 2, 1890.
9. *Great Bend* (Kans.) *Weekly Tribune*, November 23, 1883.
10. *St. Paul Globe*, November 3, 1888.
11. *Argus Leader*, November 12, 1888.
12. Pettigrew letter to Palmer, April 12, 1890, Pettigrew Museum Archives.
13. Annual Report of the Commissioner of Indian Affairs, 1890, 46.
14. Pettigrew letter to Shoenfelt, May 23, 1890, Pettigrew Museum Archives.
15. Pettigrew letter to Palmer, July 3, 1890, Pettigrew Museum Archives.
16. Pettigrew letter to Palmer, September 10, 1890, Pettigrew Museum Archives.
17. Pettigrew letter to Morgan, October 1, 1890, Pettigrew Museum Archives.
18. Pettigrew letter to Palmer, October 1, 1890. Pettigrew Museum Archives.
19. *Fort Worth Gazette*, November 12, 1891; *Bismarck Tribune*, November 12, 1891.
20. *Bismarck Weekly Tribune*, December 11, 1891.
21. *Daily Plainsman* (Huron, S. Dak.), January 25, 1891.
22. *Omaha Daily Bee*, July 11, 1889.
23. Pettigrew letter to Potter, March 18, 1890, Pettigrew Museum Archives.
24. Pettigrew letter to Wright, June 20, 1890, Pettigrew Museum Archives.
25. Pettigrew letter to Wright, July 2, 1890, Pettigrew Museum Archives.
26. Pettigrew letter to Wright, July 3, 1890, Pettigrew Museum Archives.
27. Pettigrew letter to Gifford, July 3, 1890, Pettigrew Museum Archives.
28. Pettigrew letter to Dixon, July 28, 1890, Pettigrew Museum Archives.
29. Pettigrew letter to Dixon, July 28, 1890. Pettigrew Museum Archives.
30. Pettigrew letter to Potter, March 18, 1890, Pettigrew Museum Archives.
31. Youngkin, Prelude to Wounded Knee, 333–51.
32. Pettigrew letter to Royer, March 17, 1890, Pettigrew Museum Archives.
33. Pettigrew letter to Royer, July 11, 1890, Pettigrew Museum Archives.
34. Pettigrew letter to Royer, August 4, 1890, Pettigrew Museum Archives.
35. Eli Ricker interview with R. O. Pugh, 1906, Tablet 12, Nebraska State Historical Society.
36. *Daily Plainsman*, August 29, 1889.
37. Eli Ricker interview with R. O. Pugh, 1906, Tablet 12, Nebraska State Historical Society.
38. *Sun* (New York), February 8, 1891.
39. Morgan, Reminiscences, 21–62.
40. Morgan.
41. Graber, *Sister to the Sioux*, 137.
42. Eli Ricker interview with Philip Wells, Tablet 4, Nebraska State Historical Society.

CHAPTER 3. THE INDIAN UNREST THAT BROUGHT CAN NOPA UHAH TO THE GALLOWS

1. *Daily Deadwood Pioneer-Times*, December 23, 1890.
2. Utley, *Last Days of the Sioux Nation*, 108.
3. Eastman, *From the Deep Woods to Civilization*, 94.
4. Eli Ricker interview with R. O. Pugh, 1906, Tablet 12, Nebraska State Historical Society.
5. Interview with R. O. Pugh.
6. Interview with R. O. Pugh.
7. Bureau of Indian Affairs, Miscellaneous Letters, Pine Ridge Agency, October 1890–June 1891, Royer telegram to Morgan, November 15, 1890, Microfilm 4476, South Dakota Historical Society Archives.
8. Mooney, *Ghost-Dance Religion*, 31; Smith, *Moon of Popping Trees*, 71.
9. Miller, *Ghost Dance*, 79.
10. Utley, *Last Days of the Sioux Nation*, 93.
11. Bureau of Indian Affairs, Miscellaneous Letters, Pine Ridge Agency, October 1890–June 1891, Royer telegram to Brooke, November 16, 1890, Microfilm 4483, South Dakota Historical Society Archives.
12. Eli Ricker interview with R. O. Pugh, 1906, Tablet 12, Nebraska State Historical Society Archives.
13. Utley, *Last Days of the Sioux Nation*, 111.
14. Utley, 118.
15. Coleman, *Voices of Wounded Knee*, 95.
16. Richardson, *Wounded Knee*, 210.
17. *Rapid City Journal*, November 23, 1890.
18. Spindler, *Tragedy Strikes at Wounded Knee*, 16–17.
19. *Pierre Weekly Free Press*, November 23, 1890.
20. Arthur Calvin Mellette Papers, Box 52, South Dakota Historical Society Archives.
21. *Pierre Weekly Free Press*, December 1, 1890.
22. Arthur Calvin Mellette Papers, Box 52, South Dakota Historical Society Archives; Hyde, *Sioux Chronicle*, 272.
23. Hagan, *Indian Rights Association*, 118.
24. Pettigrew letter to Royer, December 24, 1890, Pettigrew Museum Archives; Hendrickson, Public Career of Richard F. Pettigrew, 146–311.
25. Utley *Last Days of the Sioux Nation*, 120.
26. Miller, *Ghost Dance*, 157.
27. *Rapid City Journal*, December 2, 1890.
28. *Buffalo Gap* (S. Dak.) *Republican*, December 5, 1890.
29. *Buffalo Gap Republican*, December 5, 1890.
30. National Guard Papers, Box 3659A:3672, South Dakota Historical Society Archives.
31. Arthur Calvin Mellette Papers, Box 52, South Dakota Historical Society Archives.

32. National Guard Papers, Box 3659A:3672, South Dakota Historical Society Archives.
33. *Rapid City Journal*, December 7, 1890.
34. Lamar, *Dakota Territory*, 260.
35. *Rapid City Journal*, December 7, 1890.
36. Arthur Calvin Mellette Papers, Box 52, South Dakota Historical Society Archives.
37. J. B. McCloud unpublished manuscript, Box 3564A, South Dakota State Historical Archives.
38. J. B. McCloud manuscript; *Buffalo Gap Republican,* December 13, 1890.
39. Arthur Calvin Mellette Papers, Box 52, South Dakota Historical Society Archives.
40. Arthur Calvin Mellette Papers, Box 52, South Dakota Historical Society Archives.
41. Utley, *Lance and the Shield*, 296–301.
42. National Guard Papers, Box 3659A:3672, South Dakota Historical Society Archives.
43. *Rapid City Journal*, December 17, 1890.
44. *Rapid City Journal*, December 17, 1890.
45. *Battle River Pilot* (Hermosa, S. Dak.), December 17, 1890.
46. Pete Lemley oral history, Ben Reifel Visitor Center, Badlands National Park.
47. *Rapid City Journal*, December 19, 1890; Philip Hall interview with Hallie Young, June 15, 1976.
48. J. B. McCloud, unpublished manuscript, South Dakota Historical Society Archives.
49. Pete Lemley oral history, Ben Reifel Visitor Center, Badlands National Park.
50. J. B. McCloud, unpublished manuscript, South Dakota Historical Society Archives.
51. *Rapid City Journal*, December 20, 1890.
52. *Black Hills Daily Times*, December 23, 1890.
53. Coleman, *Voices of Wounded Knee*, 248.
54. Coleman, 252; Smith, *Moon of Popping Trees*, 174–75.
55. Philip Hall interview with Hallie Young, June 15, 1976.
56. Smith, *Moon of Popping Trees*, 175.
57. Yost, *Boss Cowman*, 151; *Belle Fourche* (S. Dak.) *Bee*, December 30, 1938.
58. Remington, *Pony Tracks*, 18–19.
59. Miller, *Ghost Dance*, 157.
60. Coleman, *Voices of Wounded Knee*, 258.
61. Utley, *Last Days of the Sioux Nation*, 191.
62. Remington, *Pony Tracks*, 20.
63. Remington, 24.
64. Remington, 26.
65. Hughes, *Pioneer Years in the Black Hills*, 249.
66. Pete Lemley oral history, Ben Reifel Visitors Center, Badlands National Park.
67. Remington, *Pony Tracks*, 26–28.
68. *Rapid City Journal*, January 4, 1891.
69. Remington, *Pony Tracks*, 28.
70. Miller, *Ghost Dance*, 214.
71. Remington, *Pony Tracks*, 30.
72. Miller, *Ghost Dance*, 176.

73. Miller, 214.
74. Utley, *Last Days of the Sioux Nation*, 233.
75. Remington, *Pony Tracks*, 30.
76. *Rapid City Journal*, January 3, 1891.
77. Utley, *Last Days of the Sioux Nation*, 233.
78. *Black Hills Daily Times*, March 12, 1891.

CHAPTER 4. THE KILLING OF IKE MILLER

1. *Los Angeles Herald*, December 31, 1890; *Salt Lake Herald*, December 30, 1890; *Omaha Daily Bee*, December 30, 1890; *Evening Star* (Washington, D.C.), December 30, 1890; *Mitchell* (S. Dak.) *Capital*, January 2, 1891.
2. *Columbus* (Neb.) *Journal*, December 31, 1890.
3. *Rapid City Journal*, December 31, 1890.
4. *Daily Deadwood Pioneer-Times*, January 3, 1891.
5. *Mitchell Capital*, January 2, 1891.
6. *Buffalo Gap Republican*, January 1, 1891.
7. *Buffalo Gap Republican*, January 8, 1891.
8. *Battle River Pilot*, January 8, 1891.
9. *Rapid City Journal*, January 11, 1891.
10. *Rapid City Journal*, January 3, 1891.
11. Thomas M. Littleton letter to Mellette, January 6, 1891, Arthur Calvin Mellette Correspondence, Box 3526B, South Dakota Historical Society Archives.
12. Philip letter to Mellette, Arthur Calvin Mellette Correspondence, January 12, 1891, Box 3526B, South Dakota Historical Society Archives.
13. National Guard Papers, Box 3659A:3672, South Dakota Historical Society Archives.
14. *Argus Leader*, January 7, 1891.
15. *Sturgis* (S. Dak.) *Weekly Record*, December 26, 1890.
16. *Macon* (Mo.) *Republican*, January 15, 1891.
17. *St. Paul Globe*, January 1, 1891.
18. *Pittsburg Dispatch*, January 1, 1891.
19. *Omaha Daily Bee*, January 8, 1891; *Chicago Tribune*, January 3, 1891.
20. *Inter Ocean* (Chicago), January 4, 1891.
21. *Los Angeles Herald*, January 6, 1891.
22. *Dalles* (Ore.) *Daily Chronicle*, January 3, 1891.
23. *Los Angeles Herald*, January 6, 1891.
24. *Buffalo Gap Republican*, January 9, 1891.
25. Bureau of Indian Affairs, Miscellaneous Letters, Pine Ridge Agency, October 1890–June 1891, F. E. Pierce letter to Miles, January 17, 1891, Microfilm 4476, South Dakota Historical Society Archives.
26. *Buffalo Gap Republican*, January 9, 1891.
27. Bureau of Indian Affairs, Miscellaneous Letters, Pine Ridge Agency, October 1890–June 1891, F. E. Pierce letter to Miles, January 17, 1891, Microfilm 4476, South Dakota Historical Society Archives.

28. Dakota Territory Census, 1885.
29. Bureau of Indian Affairs, Miscellaneous Letters, Pine Ridge Agency, October 1890–June 1891, F. E. Pierce letter to Miles, January 17, 1891, Microfilm 4476, South Dakota Historical Society Archives.
30. Yost, *Boss Cowman*, 154.
31. *Chicago Herald*, January 8, 1891; *Nebraska State Journal* (Lincoln), January 9, 1891.
32. *Buffalo Gap Republican*, January 9, 1891.
33. *Buffalo Gap Republican*, January 16, 1891.
34. Bureau of Indian Affairs, Miscellaneous Letters, Pine Ridge Agency, October 1890–June 1891, F. E. Pierce to Miles, January 17, 1891, Microfilm 4476, South Dakota Historical Society Archives.
35. *Black Hills Daily Times*, February 20, 1891.
36. *Helena* (Mont.) *Independent*, March 13, 1891; *St. Paul Globe*, March 13, 1891.
37. *Pantagraph* (Bloomington, Ill.), March 24, 1891.
38. U.S. Register of Civil, Military, and Naval Service 1863–1959, vol. 1, pp. 530, 577.
39. *Black Hills Daily Times*, April 22, 1891.

CHAPTER 5. THE PEACEMAKER

1. Agonito, *Young Man Afraid of His Horses*, 116–32.
2. Jensen, *Settler and Soldier*, 116–32.
3. Agonito, *Young Man Afraid of His Horses*, 79, 116–32.
4. Olson, *Red Cloud*, 301.
5. Olson.
6. Agonito, *Young Man Afraid of His Horses*, 79, 116–32.
7. *Black Hills Daily Times*, November 21, 1890.
8. *Black Hills Daily Times*, November 24, 1890.
9. *Sturgis Weekly Record*, November 28, 1890.
10. Waggoner, *Hunkpapa Historian*, 455.
11. *Abilene Weekly Reflector*, January 9, 1891; Utley, *Last Days of the Sioux Nation*, 258.
12. Eli Ricker interview with Peter McFarland, Tablet 31, Nebraska State Historical Society.
13. *Anaconda* (Mont.) *Standard*, April 14, 1891; Microfilm 983, pp. 1, 175, U.S. National Archives.
14. Eli Ricker interview with Peter McFarland, Tablet 31, Nebraska State Historical Society.
15. Remington, *Pony Tracks*, 18.
16. *Helena Independent Record*, January 9, 1891.
17. *Wahpeton* (N. Dak.) *Times*, January 15, 1891.
18. *Rapid City Journal*, January 20, 1891; Utley, *Last Days of the Sioux Nation*, 259–60.
19. *Rapid City Journal*, January 16, 1891.

CHAPTER 6. A GOOD INDIAN IS MURDERED

1. *Chicago Herald*, January 7, 1891; *Harrisburg* (Pa.) *Telegraph*, January 6, 1891.
2. *Rapid City Journal*, January 13, 1891.

3. *Rapid City Journal*, January 15, 1891.
4. *Sturgis Weekly Record*, January 16, 1891.
5. *Chicago Herald*, January 15, 1891.
6. Utley, *Last Days of the Sioux Nation*, 262.
7. *Rapid City Journal*, January 13, 1891.
8. Utley, *Last Days of the Sioux Nation*, 263.
9. *Sturgis Weekly Record*, January 9, 1891.
10. *Chicago Herald*, January 20, 1891; *Chicago Tribune*, January 20, 1891; *Sturgis Weekly Record*, February 20, 1891.
11. *Sun*, January 21, 1891; *Chicago Tribune*, January 20, 1891.
12. *Sturgis Weekly Record*, February 20, 1891.
13. Utley, Last Days of the Sioux Nation,, 263.
14. Brown and Willard, *Black Hills Trails*, 126.
15. Utley, *Last Days of the Sioux Nation*, 263–64.
16. *Sun*, January 20, 1891.
17. *Rock Island* (Ill.) *Daily Argus*, January 20, 1891.
18. *Sun*, January 21, 1891.
19. *Sturgis Weekly Record*, January 23, 1891.
20. *Sturgis Weekly Record*, January 28, 1891.
21. *Daily Deadwood Pioneer-Times*, March 11, 1891.
22. *Mitchell Capital*, January 23, 1891.
23. *Argus Leader*, May 16, 1891.
24. *Pierre Weekly Free Press*, June 18, 1891.
25. *Sun*, January 20, 1891.
26. *Detroit Free Press*, April 11, 1891.

CHAPTER 7. THE INDIAN WHO KILLED LIEUTENANT CASEY

1. Manhart, *A Dictionary*, 714, 728.
2. *McCook* (Neb.) *Tribune*, April 24, 1891.
3. Carlisle Indian School Digital Resource Center, Dickinson College, carlisleindian.dickinson.edu, accessed January 10, 2015.
4. *Sturgis Weekly Record*, February 20, 1891; *Bismarck Weekly Tribune*, January 30, 1891.
5. U.S. Register of Civil, Military, and Naval Service, 1863–1959.
6. Microfilm 982, 163–68, U.S. National Archives.
7. *Rapid City Journal*, February 20, 1891.
8. *St. Louis Post-Dispatch,* March 12, 1891; McGillycuddy, *McGillycuddy*, 272; *Black Hills Daily Times*, March 12, 1891.
9. Burns letter to Welsh, March 18, 1891, Indian Rights Association Archives, Reel 7, History Society of Philadelphia.
10. *Black Hills Daily Times*, April 11, 1891.
11. *Sturgis Weekly Record*, March 13, 1891.
12. *Black Hills Daily Times*, March 19, 1891.
13. *Omaha Daily Bee,* March 19, 1891.
14. *Daily Deadwood Pioneer-Times*, March 29, 1891.

15. *Omaha Daily Bee*, April 10, 1891; *Anaconda Standard*, April 14, 1891.
16. *Evening World* (New York), March 25, 1891.
17. *Argus Leader*, April 28, 1891.
18. *St. Paul Daily Globe*, April 14, 1891.
19. File 7097684, vol. 1, pp. 471–79, U.S. National Archives.
20. *Pierre Weekly Free Press*, April 23, 1891.
21. Lee, *Fort Meade*, 132; *Evening World*, April 29, 1891.
22. File 7097684, vol. 1, pp. 482–85, U.S. National Archives.
23. *Argus Leader*, April 24, 1891.
24. File 6037537, 106, U.S. National Archives.
25. *Argus Leader*, April 25, 1891; *St. Paul Daily Globe*, April 25, 1891.
26. *St. Paul Daily Globe*, April 30, 1891.
27. *Chicago Tribune*, April 26, 1891.
28. *St. Paul Daily Globe*, April 26, 1891.
29. *St. Paul Daily Globe*, April 26, 1891.
30. *Pittsburg Post-Dispatch,* April 27, 1891.
31. *Argus Leader*, April 27, 1891; *Pittsburg Post-Dispatch,* April 27, 1891.
32. U.S. Register of Civil, Military, and Naval Service: 1863–1959.
33. File 7097684, vol. 1, p. 487, U.S. National Archives.
34. *Argus Leader*, April 27, 1891.
35. *Argus Leader*, April 28, 1891.
36. *Argus Leader*, April 28, 1891.
37. *Evening World*, April 29, 1891.
38. *Evening World*, April 29, 1891.
39. *Evening World*, April 29, 1891.
40. Dickinson, Reconstructing the Indian Village, 2–14.
41. *Evening World*, April 29, 1891.
42. *Evening World*, April 29, 1891.
43. File 7097684, vol. 1, p. 488, U.S. National Archives.
44. *Argus Leader*, April 28, 1891.
45. *Evening World*, April 29, 1891.
46. *St. Paul Globe*, April 30, 1891.
47. *Chicago Herald*, April 30, 1891.
48. *Argus Leader*, April 30, 1891.
49. *Argus Leader*, April 30, 1891.
50. *Argus Leader*, April 30, 1891.

CHAPTER 8. PLENTY HORSES'S SECOND TRIAL

1. *Chicago Herald*, May 26,1891.
2. *Chicago Herald*, May 27, 1891.
3. *Sturgis Weekly Record*, May 29, 1891.
4. *Argus Leader*, May 25, 1891.
5. *Pierre Weekly Free Press*, May 28, 1891.

6. *Argus Leader*, May 25, 1891.
7. *Sturgis Weekly Record*, May 29, 1891.
8. *Argus Leader*, May 25, 1891.
9. *Argus Leader*, May 25, 1891.
10. *Argus Leader*, May 25, 1891.
11. *Argus Leader*, May 25, 1891.
12. *Chicago Herald*, May 27, 1891.
13. *Chicago Herald*, May 27, 1891.
14. *Argus Leader*, May 26, 1891.
15. *Argus Leader*, May 26, 1891.
16. *Argus Leader*, May 26, 1891.
17. *Argus Leader*, May 26, 1891.
18. *Argus Leader*, May 26, 1891.
19. *Argus Leader*, May 26, 1891.
20. *Argus Leader*, May 26, 1891; *Chicago Herald*, May 29, 1891.
21. *Argus Leader*, May 26, 1891.
22. *Argus Leader*, May 27, 1891.
23. *Sturgis Weekly Record*, June 5, 1891.
24. *Chicago Herald*, May 28, 1891.
25. *Sturgis Weekly Record*, June 5, 1891.
26. *Argus Leader*, May 27, 1891.
27. *Argus Leader*, May 27, 1891; *Chicago Herald*, May 28, 1891.
28. *Argus Leader*, May 27, 1891.
29. *Argus Leader*, May 27, 1891.
30. *Argus Leader*, May 27, 1891.
31. *Chicago Herald*, May 28, 1891.
32. *Chicago Herald*, May 28, 1891.
33. *Chicago Herald*, May 28, 1891.
34. *Argus Leader*, May 28, 1891.
35. *Sun*, May 29, 1891; *Omaha Daily Bee*, May 29, 1891.
36. *Omaha Daily Bee*, May 29, 1891.
37. *Argus Leader*, May 28, 1891.
38. *Argus Leader*, May 28, 1891.
39. *Chicago Herald*, May 29, 1891; *Argus Leader*, May 28, 1891.
40. *Argus Leader*, May 28, 1891.
41. *McCook Tribune*, June 5, 1891.
42. Pete Lemley oral history, Ben Reifel Visitor Center, Badlands National Park; J. B. McCloud, unpublished manuscript, South Dakota Historical Society Archives.
43. *Argus Leader*, May 29, 1891.
44. Bureau of Indian Affairs, Miscellaneous Letters, Pine Ridge Agency, October 1890–June 1891, Penney letter to Nock, June 6, 1891, Microfilm 4477, South Dakota State Historical Archives.

45. Carlisle Indian School Digital Resource Center, Dickinson College, carlisleindian.dickinson.edu, accessed July 5, 2017.

CHAPTER 9. FRONTIER JUSTICE

1. Meing, *Shaping of America*, 56.
2. Shell, *History of South Dakota*, 89.
3. Hall, *Roundup Years*, 602–3.
4. Welsh, *Civilization among the Sioux Indians*, 10.
5. *Rock Island Daily Argus*, January 26, 1891; Lee (1991), 131.
6. *Evening World News*, May 13, 1891.
7. Hagan, *Indian Rights Association*, 124.
8. Grand jury indictment, May 14, 1891, Eighth Circuit Court, courthouse records, 1891, Meade County, South Dakota.
9. *Mitchell Capital*, May 22, 1891.
10. *Sturgis Weekly Record*, May 22, 1891.
11. Lee, *Fort Meade*, 134.
12. *Sturgis Weekly Record*, June 19, 1891.
13. *Pierre Weekly Free Press*, June 18, 1891.
14. *Omaha Daily Bee*, June 24, 1891.
15. Courthouse records, 1891, Meade County, South Dakota.
16. *Omaha Daily Bee*, June 24, 1891.
17. Courthouse records, 1891, Meade County, South Dakota.
18. Lee, *Fort Meade*, 138.
19. *St. Paul Globe*, June 26, 1891.
20. *Rapid City Journal*, June 26, 1891.
21. *St. Paul Globe*, June 26, 1891.
22. *Chicago Herald*, June 26, 1891.
23. *St. Paul Globe*, June 27, 1891; *Chicago Herald*, June 27, 1891; *Queen City Mail* (Spearfish, S. Dak.), July 1, 1891.
24. *Queen City Mail*, July 1, 1891.
25. *Daily Deadwood Pioneer-Times*, July 2, 1891.
26. *Black Hills Daily Times* (Deadwood), July 2, 1891.
27. *Black Hills Daily Times*, July 2, 1891.
28. *Omaha Daily Bee*, June 30, 1891; *Black Hills Daily Times*, July 2, 1891.
29. *Freeborn County Standard* (Albert Lea, Minn.), September 14, 1882.
30. *Chicago Herald*, June 30, 1891.
31. *Chicago Herald*, June 30, 1891.
32. Courthouse records, 1891, Meade County, South Dakota.
33. *Omaha Daily Bee*, July 1, 1891.
34. *Omaha Daily Bee*, July 1, 1891; courthouse records, 1891, Meade County, South Dakota.
35. *Omaha Daily Bee*, June 30, 1891.
36. *Rapid City Journal*, July 1, 1891.
37. *Omaha Daily Bee*, July 2, 1891.

38. Courthouse records 1891, Meade County, South Dakota; *Bismarck Weekly Tribune*, July 3, 1891; *Omaha Daily Bee*, July 2, 1891.
39. *Daily Deadwood Pioneer-Times*, July 2, 1891; *Rapid City Journal*, July 2, 1891.
40. *Chicago Herald*, July 2, 1891.
41. Courthouse records 1891, Meade County, South Dakota; *Sturgis Weekly Record*, July 3, 1891.
42. Courthouse records 1891, Meade County, South Dakota.
43. *Rapid City Journal*, July 4, 1891.
44. *Sturgis Weekly Record*, July 3, 1891.

CHAPTER 10. FOR WHAT, SIMPLY KILLING AN INDIAN?

1. *Dakota Farmers' Leader* (Canton, S. Dak.), March 18, 1892; *Pierre Weekly Free Press*, March 31, 1892.
2. Hall, *Roundup Years*, 201.
3. Strain, Old Man on the Range, 12–13.
4. Strain, 12–13.
5. *Daily Deadwood Pioneer-Times*, March 13, 1892.
6. *Daily Deadwood Pioneer-Times*, March 13, 1892.
7. Bureau of Indian Affairs, Miscellaneous Correspondence Received, Rosebud, August 1891–July 1893, Whipple letter to Wright, December 31, 1891, Microfilm 5249, South Dakota Historical Society Archives.
8. *Dakota Farmers' Leader*, April 15, 1892.
9. Bureau of Indian Affairs. Miscellaneous Correspondence Received, Rosebud, August 1891–July 1893, Morris letter to Wright, March 22, 1892, Microfilm 5249, South Dakota Historical Society Archives.
10. Welsh, *Civilization*, 39.
11. Bureau of Indian Affairs. Miscellaneous Correspondence Received, Rosebud, August 1891–July 1893, deposition in the Indian agent's records, February 15, 1892, Microfilm 5249, South Dakota Historical Society Archives.
12. Bureau of Indian Affairs. Miscellaneous Correspondence Received, Rosebud, August 1891–July 1893, Sterling letter to Wright, March 26, 1892, Microfilm 5249, South Dakota Historical Society Archives.
13. *Daily Deadwood Pioneer-Times*, March 12, 1892.
14. *Daily Deadwood Pioneer-Times*, March 12, 1892.
15. *Daily Deadwood Pioneer-Times*, March 12, 1892.
16. *Daily Deadwood Pioneer-Times*, March 12, 1892.
17. Bureau of Indian Affairs. Miscellaneous Correspondence Received, Rosebud, August 1891–July 1893, Fry telegram to Wright, March 23, 1892, Microfilm 5249, South Dakota Historical Society Archives.
18. *Pierre Weekly Free Press*, March 31, 1892.
19. *Black Hills Daily Times*, January 26, 1892.
20. *Black Hills Union* (Rapid City), April 1, 1892.
21. *Pierre Weekly Free Press*, March 31, 1892.

22. *Black Hills Union*, April 1, 1892.
23. *St. Paul Globe*, March 29, 1892; *Turner County* (S. Dak.) *Herald*, April 7, 1892; *Sun*, March 27, 1892.
24. *Dakota Farmers' Leader*, April 15, 1892; *Hot Springs* (S. Dak.) *Star*, April 15, 1892.
25. *Rapid City Journal*, April 10, 1892.
26. *Argus Leader*, March 30, 1892.
27. *Bismarck Weekly Tribune*, April 1, 1892; *Pittsburg Post-Dispatch*, March 29, 1892.
28. Welsh, *Civilization*, 9.
29. *Argus Leader*, May 16, 1892.
30. *Pierre Weekly Free Press*, March 31, 1892.
31. *Black Hills Union*, April 1, 1892.
32. *Pierre Weekly Free Press*, April 21, 1892.
33. Bureau of Indian Affairs, Correspondence Received, Rosebud, August 1891–July 1893, Nock letter to Wright, May 13, 1892, Microfilm 5249, South Dakota State Historical Society Archives.
34. *Pierre Weekly Free Press*, May 19, 1892.
35. *Pierre Weekly Free Press*, May 19, 1892.
36. *Argus Leader*, May 20, 1892.

CHAPTER 11. PINE RIDGE 1891: A TIME OF GLOOM

1. Hyde, *Sioux Chronicle*, 229–40; *Evening Star*, December 6, 1889.
2. Reports and correspondence relating to army investigation of the battle at Wounded Knee and to the Sioux campaign of 1890–91, Microfilm 2, U.S. National Archives.
3. C. P. Jordan Papers, Box 3615B, South Dakota Historical Society Archives.
4. *St. Louis Dispatch-Post*, February 7, 1891.
5. Executive Documents of the Senate of the United States. First Session of the 51st Congress, *Congressional Edition,* vol. 2682, p. 359.
6. Annual Report of the Commissioner of Indian Affairs, 1890, 49.
7. Annual Report of the Commissioner of Indian Affairs, 1890, 49.
8. Annual Report of the Commissioner of Indian Affairs, 1891, 409.
9. Graber, *Sister to the Sioux*, 137.
10. W. K. Moorehead, Ghost Dances in the West, *Illustrated American*, January 24, 1891, 392.
11. Executive Documents of the Senate of the United States. First Session of the 51st Congress, *Congressional Edition*, vol. 2682, p. 368.
12. Executive Documents of the Senate of the United States. First Session of the 51st Congress, Congressional Edition, vol. 2682, p. 380.
13. Roosevelt, *Report of Hon. Theodore Roosevelt*, 12.
14. Smith, *Moon of Polling Trees*, xv.
15. *Daily Tobacco Leaf Chronicle* (Clarksville, Tenn.), January 14, 1891.
16. Lee and Williams, *Last Grass Frontier*, 185.
17. Simpson, *West River 1850–1900*, 72.
18. Annual Report of the Commissioner of Indian Affairs, 1891, 410.

19. Executive Documents of the Senate of the United States. First Session of the 51st Congress, *Congressional Edition*, vol. 2682, p. 359.
20. Roosevelt, *Report of Hon. Theodore Roosevelt*, 6.
21. *Argus Leader*, April 28, 1891.
22. *St. Paul Globe*, August 12, 1891; *Bismarck Weekly Tribune*, August 14, 1891.
23. Annual Report of the Commissioner of Indian Affairs, 1890, 50.
24. Warren, *Buffalo Bill's America*, 481.
25. Moses, Wild West Shows, 193–221.
26. Utley, *Last Days of the Sioux Nation*, 275.
27. *Sunday Herald & Weekly National Intelligencer* (Washington, D.C.), February 8, 1891.
28. *New York Times*, February 8, 1891; *Sun*, February 8, 1891.
29. Prucha, *American Indian Policy in Crisis*, 294–95; Smith, Anti-Catholicism, 213–33.
30. Annual Report of the Commissioner of Indian Affairs, 1889, 83.
31. *Herald-Advance* (Milbank, S. Dak.), September 30, 1892.
32. Eli Ricker interview with R. O. Pugh, Tablet 12, Nebraska State Historical Society.
33. *Sun*, February 10–11, 1891.
34. Executive Documents of the Senate of the United States. First Session of the 51st Congress, *Congressional Edition*, vol. 2682, p. 359.
35. Executive Documents of the Senate of the United States, 353.
36. Executive Documents of the Senate of the United States, 431.
37. *Chicago Tribune*, February 19, 1891; *Queen City Mail*, February 24, 1891.
38. *Chicago Tribune*, February 19, 1891.
39. *Chicago Tribune*, February 19, 1891.
40. *Bismarck Weekly Tribune*, February 20, 1891; *Chicago Tribune*, February, 19, 1891.
41. *Wessington Springs* (S. Dak.) *Herald*, February 27, 1891.
42. *Wessington Springs Herald*, February 27, 1891.
43. *Rock Island* (Ill.) *Daily Argus*, April 18, 1891.
44. *Lebanon* (Penn.) *Daily News*, April 18, 1891.
45. *Brenham* (Tex.) *Weekly Banner*, April 30, 1891.
46. *Buffalo* (N.Y.) *Commercial*, March 31, 1891.
47. *St. Louis Post-Dispatch*, April 1, 1891.
48. Executive Documents of the Senate of the United States. First Session of the 51st Congress, *Congressional Edition*, vol. 2682, p. 353.
49. Bureau of Indian Affairs, Miscellaneous Letters, Pine Ridge Agency, October 1890–June 1891, Cooper letter to Brown, May 19, 1891, Microfilm 4476, South Dakota Historical Society Archives.
50. *Inter Ocean*, May 8, 1891.
51. *Pierre Daily Capitol*, April 2, 1891
52. Arthur Calvin Mellette Papers, Correspondence and Reports: 1889–1892, Box 3527A, South Dakota Historical Society Archives.
53. Arthur Calvin Mellette Papers, Correspondence and Reports: 1889–1892, Box 3527A, South Dakota Historical Society Archives; *Buffalo Gap Republican*, April 18, 1891.

54. Bureau of Indian Affairs, Miscellaneous Letters, Pine Ridge Agency, October 1890–June 1891, Penney letter to Morgan, April 7, 1891, Microfilm 4476, South Dakota Historical Society Archives.
55. Lee, *Fort Meade*, 155.
56. *Bismarck Weekly Tribune*, July 10, 1891.
57. *Omaha Daily Bee*, July 5, 1891.
58. Lee, *Fort Meade*, 155.
59. Annual Report of the Commissioner of Indian Affairs, 1891, 408–10.
60. Ellis, Reservation Akicitas, 185–210.
61. Annual Report of the Commissioner of Indian Affairs, 1889, 153.
62. Annual Report of the Commissioner of Indian Affairs, 1891, 408–10.
63. Annual Report of the Commissioner of Indian Affairs, 1892, 453.
64. Bureau of Indian Affairs, Miscellaneous Letters, Pine Ridge Agency, October 1890–June 1891, Penney letter to assistant adjutant general, April 2, 1891, Microfilm 4476, South Dakota Historical Society Archives.
65. Bureau of Indian Affairs, Miscellaneous Letters, Pine Ridge Agency, October 1890–June 1891, Penney letter to Morgan, April 7, 1891, Microfilm 4476, South Dakota Historical Society Archives.

CHAPTER 12: PINE RIDGE 1892: A YEAR OF RESISTANCE

1. *Nebraska State Journal*, December 17, 1891.
2. Annual Report of the Commission of Indian Affairs, 1892, 453.
3. Bureau of Indian Affairs, Miscellaneous Correspondence Received, Rosebud, August 1891–July 1893, Brown letter to Wright, March 28, 1893, Microfilm 5249, South Dakota Historical Society Archives.
4. Bureau of Indian Affairs, Miscellaneous Letters, Pine Ridge Agency, August–October 1892, Morgan telegram to Brown, August 2, 1892, Microfilm 4484, South Dakota Historical Society Archives.
5. *Black Hills Union*, November 20, 1891; *Pierre Weekly Free Press*, November 26, 1891.
6. *Pierre Weekly Free Press*, November 26, 1891.
7. *Nebraska State Journal*, November 17, 1891.
8. *Hot Springs Star*, September 30, 1892.
9. Bureau of Indian Affairs, Miscellaneous Letters, Pine Ridge Agency, August–October 1892, Finlay letter to managing editor of *New York World*, August 20, 1892, Microfilm 4484, South Dakota Historical Society Archives.
10. Bureau of Indian Affairs, Miscellaneous Letters, Pine Ridge Agency, August–October 1892, Finlay letter to managing editor of *New York World*, August 20, 1892, Microfilm 4484, South Dakota Historical Society Archives.
11. Bureau of Indian Affairs, Miscellaneous Letters, Pine Ridge Agency, August–October 1892, Finlay letter to managing editor of *New York World*, August 20, 1892, Microfilm 4484, South Dakota Historical Society Archives.
12. Bureau of Indian Affairs, Miscellaneous Letters, Pine Ridge Agency, August–October 1892, Finlay letter to managing editor of *New York World*, August 20, 1892, Microfilm 4484, South Dakota Historical Society Archives.

13. Bureau of Indian Affairs, Miscellaneous Letters, Pine Ridge Agency, August–October 1892, Finlay letter to managing editor of *New York World*, August 20, 1892, Microfilm 4484, South Dakota Historical Society Archives.
14. Wells, *Ninety-Six Years*, 308.
15. Bureau of Indian Affairs, Miscellaneous Letters, Pine Ridge Agency, August–October 1892, Finlay letter to managing editor of *New York World*, August 20, 1892, Microfilm 4484, South Dakota Historical Society Archives.
16. Bureau of Indian Affairs, Miscellaneous Letters, Pine Ridge Agency, August–October 1892, Brown letter to Morgan, August 15, 1892, Microfilm 4484, South Dakota Historical Society Archives.
17. Bureau of Indian Affairs, Miscellaneous Letters, Pine Ridge Agency, August–October 1892, Brown letter to Morgan, August 15, 1892, Microfilm 4484, South Dakota Historical Society Archives.
18. Welsh, *Civilization*.
19. Roosevelt, *Report of Hon. Theodore Roosevelt*, 12.
20. *Chicago Tribune*, January 27, 1891.
21. Utley, *Last Days of the Sioux Nation*, 271.
22. *Sun*, February 14, 1892.
23. *Sun*, March 19, 1892; *Chicago Tribune*, March 19, 1892.
24. *Chicago Tribune*, September 11, 1892.
25. *Chicago Tribune*, September 11, 1892; *New Ulm* (Minn.) *Review*, September 21, 1892.
26. *Chicago Tribune*, September 11, 1892.
27. *Rapid City Journal*, September 21, 1892.
28. Bureau of Indian Affairs, Miscellaneous Letters, Pine Ridge Agency, August–October 1892, Brown telegram to Morgan, September 27, 1892, Microfilm 4484, South Dakota Historical Society Archives.
29. Bureau of Indian Affairs, Miscellaneous Letters, Pine Ridge Agency, August–October 1892, Richards telegram to Brown, August 20, 1892, Microfilm 4484, South Dakota Historical Society Archives.
30. Bureau of Indian Affairs, Miscellaneous Letters, Pine Ridge Agency, August–October 1892, Brown telegram to Humphrey, October 28, 1892, Microfilm 4484, South Dakota Historical Society Archives.
31. Bureau of Indian Affairs, Miscellaneous Letters, Pine Ridge Agency, November 1892–January 1893, Brown telegram to Humphrey, November 7, 1892, Microfilm 4486, South Dakota Historical Society Archives.
32. Bureau of Indian Affairs, Miscellaneous Letters, Pine Ridge Agency, August–October 1892, Belt telegram to Brown, October 10, 1892, Microfilm 4484, South Dakota Historical Society Archives.
33. *Mitchell* (S. Dak.) *Daily Republic*, November 12, 1891; *Bismarck Tribune*, November 12, 1891.
34. Bureau of Indian Affairs, Miscellaneous Letters, Pine Ridge Agency, November 1892–January 1893, West telegram to Brown, November 14, 1892, Microfilm 4486, South Dakota Historical Society Archives.

35. Bureau of Indian Affairs, Miscellaneous Letters, Pine Ridge Agency, November 1892–January 1893, West telegram to Brown, November 20, 1892, Microfilm 4486, South Dakota Historical Society Archives.
36. Bureau of Indian Affairs, Miscellaneous Letters, Pine Ridge Agency, November 1892–January 1893, Brown telegram to Harris, November 20, 1892, Microfilm 4486, South Dakota Historical Society Archives.
37. Bureau of Indian Affairs, Miscellaneous Letters, Pine Ridge Agency, November 1892–January 1893, Harris telegram to Brown, November 21, 1892, Microfilm 4486, South Dakota Historical Society Archives.
38. Annual Report of the Commissioner of Indian Affairs, 1889, 153.
39. Annual Report of the Commissioner of Indian Affairs, 1889, 134.
40. Executive Documents of the Senate of the United States. First Session of the 51st Congress, Constitutional Edition, vol. 2682, p. 376.
41. *Black Hills Union*, September 17, 1892.
42. *Evening Herald* (Shenandoah, Pa.), September 20, 1892; *Lincoln* (Neb.) *Evening Call*, September 20, 1892; *Dakota Farmers' Leader*, September 20, 1892; *Waterbury* (Conn.) *Evening Democrat*, September 20, 1892; *Wilmington* (Del.) *Daily Republican*, September 20, 1892.
43. *New Ulm Review*, September 21, 1892; *Rapid City Journal*, September 21, 1892.
44. *Rapid City Journal*, September 22, 1892.
45. *Omaha Daily Bee*, October 10, 1892.
46. *Chicago Tribune*, October 10, 1892; *Inter Ocean*, October 10, 1892; *New York Times*, October 10, 1892; *Los Angeles Herald,* October 10, 1892; *St. Paul Globe,* October 10, 1892.
47. *Sioux City* (Iowa) *Herald*, October 21, 1892; *Black Hills Daily Times*, October 23, 1892.
48. *New York Tribune*, October 22, 1892; *Evening World*, October 21, 1892.
49. *Omaha Daily Bee*, October 23, 1892.

CHAPTER 13: NO WATER AND HIS CAMP OF MALCONTENTS

1. Wells, *Ninety-Six Years*, 308.
2. Sandoz, *Crazy Horse*, 132.
3. Sandoz, 138–247.
4. Sandoz, 132.
5. Hyde, *Sioux Chronicle*, 3.
6. Blackburn, Historical Sketch, 459.
7. Marshall, *Journey of Crazy Horse*, 260.
8. Sandoz, *Crazy Horse*, 401–8.
9. Allen, *Fort Laramie to Wounded Knee*, 54.
10. Executive Documents of the Senate of the United States. First Session of the 51st Congress. *Congressional Edition*, vol. 2682, 390.
11. Wells, *Ninety-Six Years*, 308.
12. Mooney, *Ghost-Dance Religion*, 92.
13. *Chicago Tribune*, February 28, 1891.

14. *Helena Independent*, March 4, 1892.
15. Florentine Digmann, History of the St. Francis Mission and Diary: 1886–1922, unpublished manuscript, Marquette University Archives.
16. Bureau of Indian Affairs, Miscellaneous Letters, Pine Ridge Agency, September/November 1886–January 1893, Lemmon letter to Indian agent, September 11, 1886, Microfilm 4474, South Dakota Historical Society Archives.

CHAPTER 14. THE BROWN-EASTMAN DISPUTE

1. *Argus Leader*, March 30, 1892.
2. Skogen, *Indian Depredation Claims*.
3. U.S. Congressional Serial Set 3062, letter from secretary of the interior, 2–14.
4. *Omaha Daily Bee*, April 8, 1892.
5. U.S. Congressional Serial Set 3062, letter from secretary of the interior, 2–14.
6. *Omaha Daily Bee*, January 8, 1893.
7. Bureau of Indian Affairs, Miscellaneous Letters, Pine Ridge Agency, August–October 1892, Brown letter to Morgan, August 9, 1892, Microfilm 4484, South Dakota Historical Society Archives.
8. *St. Paul Globe*, February 9, 1893.
9. *St. Paul Globe*, February 9, 1893.
10. *St. Paul Globe*, February 9, 1893; *Dakota Farmers' Leader*, January 20, 1893.
11. Eastman, *From the Deep Woods*, 128–30.
12. Bureau of Indian Affairs, Miscellaneous Letters, Pine Ridge Agency, April–June 1892, Eastman letter to Morgan, May 2, 1892, Microfilm 4481, South Dakota Historical Society Archives.
13. Eastman, *From the Deep Woods*, 129.
14. Bureau of Indian Affairs, Miscellaneous Letters, Pine Ridge Agency, April–June 1892, Miller report to Morgan, May 28, 1892, Microfilm 4481, South Dakota Historical Society Archives.
15. Bureau of Indian Affairs, Miscellaneous Letters, Pine Ridge Agency, April–June 1892, Miller report to Morgan, May 28, 1892, Microfilm 4481, South Dakota Historical Society Archives.
16. Bureau of Indian Affairs, Miscellaneous Letters, Pine Ridge Agency, August–October 1892, Miller telegram to Noble, August 6, 1892, Microfilm 4483, South Dakota Historical Society Archives.
17. Bureau of Indian Affairs, Miscellaneous Letters, Pine Ridge Agency, August–October 1892, Miller report to Morgan, September 18, 1892, Microfilm 4484, South Dakota Historical Society Archives.
18. Bureau of Indian Affairs, Miscellaneous Letters, Pine Ridge Agency, August–October 1892, Eastman letter to Brown, September 20, 1892, Microfilm 4484, South Dakota Historical Society Archives.
19. Bureau of Indian Affairs, Miscellaneous Letters, Pine Ridge Agency, August–October 1892, Brown letter to Morgan, September 20, 1892, Microfilm 4484, South Dakota Historical Society Archives.

20. Wilson, *Ohiyesa*, 75.
21. Bureau of Indian Affairs, Miscellaneous Letters, Pine Ridge Agency, August–October 1892, Brown letter to Morgan, September 22, 1892, Microfilm 4484, South Dakota Historical Society Archives.
22. Bureau of Indian Affairs, Miscellaneous Letters, Pine Ridge Agency, August–October 1892, Brown letter to Morgan, October 15, 1892, Microfilm 4484, South Dakota Historical Society Archives.
23. Bureau of Indian Affairs, Miscellaneous Letters, Pine Ridge Agency, August–October 1892, Brown letter to Eastman, October 25, 1892, Microfilm 4484, South Dakota Historical Society Archives.
24. *Bismarck Weekly Tribune*, December 25, 1891.
25. Eli Ricker interview with White Eyes, Tablet 10, Nebraska State Historical Society.
26. Bureau of Indian Affairs, Miscellaneous Letters, Pine Ridge Agency, November 1892–January 1893, Cisney telegram to Morgan, December 8, 1892, Microfilm 4486, South Dakota Historical Society Archives; *Winfield* (Kans.) *Courier*, January 5, 1893.
27. Bureau of Indian Affairs, Miscellaneous Letters, Pine Ridge Agency, November 1892–January 1893, Brown letter to Cisney, December 26, 1892, Microfilm 4486, South Dakota Historical Society Archives.
28. *New York Evening Post*, November 16, 1892.
29. *Omaha Daily Bee*, November 22, 1892; *Churchman* 67 (February 4, 1893): 142.
30. Bureau of Indian Affairs, Miscellaneous Letters, Pine Ridge Agency, November 1892–January 1893, Brown letter to Cisney, November 24, 1892, Microfilm 4486, South Dakota Historical Society Archives.
31. Eastman, *From the Deep Woods*, 133.
32. Wilson, *Ohiyesa*, 72.
33. Bureau of Indian Affairs, Miscellaneous Letters, Pine Ridge Agency, November 1892–January 1893, Morgan telegram to Eastman, November 23, 1892, Microfilm 4486, South Dakota Historical Society Archives.
34. Bureau of Indian Affairs, Miscellaneous Letters, Pine Ridge Agency, November 1892–January 1893, Eastman telegram to Morgan, November 28, 1892, Microfilm 4486, South Dakota Historical Society Archives.
35. Bureau of Indian Affairs, Miscellaneous Letters, Pine Ridge Agency, November 1892–January 1893, Eastman letter to Morgan, December 2, 1892, Microfilm 4486, South Dakota Historical Society Archives.
36. Bureau of Indian Affairs, Miscellaneous Letters, Pine Ridge Agency, November 1892–January 1893, Morgan telegram to Brown, December 10, 1892, Microfilm 4486, South Dakota Historical Society Archives.
37. Wilson, *Ohiyesa*, 74.
38. *St. Paul Globe*, December 25, 1892.
39. Bureau of Indian Affairs, Miscellaneous Letters, Pine Ridge Agency, November 1892–January 1893, Brown telegram to Morgan, December 18, 1892, Microfilm 4486, South Dakota Historical Society Archives.

40. Bureau of Indian Affairs, Miscellaneous Letters, Pine Ridge Agency, November 1892–January 1893, Brown letter to Cisney, December 20, 1892, Microfilm 4486, South Dakota Historical Society Archives.
41. Bureau of Indian Affairs, Miscellaneous Letters, Pine Ridge Agency, November 1892–January 1893, Morgan telegram to Eastman, December 19, 1892, Microfilm 4486, South Dakota Historical Society Archives.
42. Bureau of Indian Affairs, Miscellaneous Letters, Pine Ridge Agency, November 1892–January 1893, Brown telegram to Morgan, December 24, 1892, Microfilm 4486, South Dakota Historical Society Archives.
43. Bureau of Indian Affairs, Miscellaneous Letters, Pine Ridge Agency, November 1892–January 1893, Morgan telegram to Brown, December 24, 1892, Microfilm 4486, South Dakota Historical Society Archives.
44. Bureau of Indian Affairs, Miscellaneous Letters, Pine Ridge Agency, November 1892–January 1893, Brown telegram to Morgan, December 25, 1892, Microfilm 4486, South Dakota Historical Society Archives.
45. Bureau of Indian Affairs, Miscellaneous Letters, Pine Ridge Agency, November 1892–January 1893, Brown telegram to Morgan, December 26, 1892, Microfilm 4486, South Dakota Historical Society Archives.
46. Bureau of Indian Affairs, Miscellaneous Letters, Pine Ridge Agency, November 1892–January 1893, Brown letter to Cisney, December 25, 1892, Microfilm 4486, South Dakota Historical Society Archives.
47. Bureau of Indian Affairs, Miscellaneous Letters, Pine Ridge Agency, November 1892–January 1893, Noble telegram to Cisney, December 27, 1892, Microfilm 4486, South Dakota Historical Society Archives.
48. Bureau of Indian Affairs, Miscellaneous Letters, Pine Ridge Agency, November 1892–January 1893, Cisney telegram to Noble, December 28, 1892, Microfilm 4486, South Dakota Historical Society Archives.
49. Bureau of Indian Affairs, Miscellaneous Letters, Pine Ridge Agency, November 1892–January 1893, Cisney telegram to Noble, January 2, 1893, Microfilm 4486, South Dakota Historical Society Archives.
50. Bureau of Indian Affairs, Miscellaneous Letters, Pine Ridge Agency, November 1892–January 1893, Brown telegram to Morgan, January 3, 1893, Microfilm 4486, South Dakota Historical Society Archives.
51. Bureau of Indian Affairs, Miscellaneous Letters, Pine Ridge Agency, November 1892–January 1893, Brown telegram to Morgan, January 3, 1893, Microfilm 4486, South Dakota Historical Society Archives.
52. Bureau of Indian Affairs, Miscellaneous Letters, Pine Ridge Agency, November 1892–January 1893, Brown telegram to Morgan, January 3, 1893, Microfilm 4486, South Dakota Historical Society Archives.
53. Bureau of Indian Affairs, Miscellaneous Letters, Pine Ridge Agency, November 1892–January 1893, Brown telegram to Morgan, January 5, 1893, Microfilm 4486, South Dakota Historical Society Archives.

54. Bureau of Indian Affairs, Miscellaneous Letters, Pine Ridge Agency, November 1892–January 1893, Wood telegram to Fry, January 6, 1893, Microfilm 4486, South Dakota Historical Society Archives.
55. Bureau of Indian Affairs, Miscellaneous Letters, Pine Ridge Agency, November 1892–January 1893. Fry telegram to Wood, January 6, 1893, Microfilm 4486, South Dakota Historical Society Archives.
56. Bureau of Indian Affairs, Miscellaneous Letters, Pine Ridge Agency, November 1892–January 1893. Morgan telegram to Elaine Eastman, January 6, 1893, Microfilm 4486, South Dakota Historical Society Archives.
57. Bureau of Indian Affairs, Miscellaneous Letters, Pine Ridge Agency, November 1892–January 1893, Wood telegram to Eastman, January 6, 1893, Microfilm 4486, South Dakota Historical Society Archives.
58. Bureau of Indian Affairs, Miscellaneous Letters, Pine Ridge Agency, November 1892–January 1893, Elaine Eastman telegram to Charles Eastman, January 6. 1893, Microfilm 4486, South Dakota Historical Society Archives.
59. Bureau of Indian Affairs, Miscellaneous Letters, Pine Ridge Agency, November 1892–January 1893. Eastman telegram to Morgan, January 8, 1893, Microfilm 4486, South Dakota Historical Society Archives.
60. *Omaha Daily Bee*, January 8, 1893.
61. Bureau of Indian Affairs, Miscellaneous Letters, Pine Ridge Agency, November 1892–January 1893, Brown telegram to Morgan, January 8, 1893, Microfilm 4486, South Dakota Historical Society Archives.
62. Bureau of Indian Affairs, Miscellaneous Letters, Pine Ridge Agency, November 1892–January 1893. Jarvis Richards telegram to Brown, January 9, 1893, Microfilm 4486, South Dakota Historical Society Archives.
63. *Evening Star*, January 20, 1893.
64. *Argus Leader*, January 23, 1893.
65. Bureau of Indian Affairs, Miscellaneous Letters, Pine Ridge Agency, November 1892–January 1893, Brown telegram to Morgan, January 24, 1893, Microfilm 4486, South Dakota Historical Society Archives.
66. Bureau of Indian Affairs, Miscellaneous Letters, Pine Ridge Agency, November 1892–January 1893, Cisney telegram to Noble, January 24, 1893, Microfilm 4486, South Dakota Historical Society Archives.
67. Bureau of Indian Affairs, Miscellaneous Letters, Pine Ridge Agency, November 1892–January 1893, Noble telegram to Brown, January 25. 1893, Microfilm 4486, South Dakota Historical Society Archives.
68. Bureau of Indian Affairs, Miscellaneous Letters, Pine Ridge Agency, November 1892–January 1893, Morgan telegram to Eastman, January 26, 1893, Microfilm 4486, South Dakota Historical Society Archives.
69. Bureau of Indian Affairs, Miscellaneous Letters, Pine Ridge Agency, November 1892–January 1893, Eastman telegram to Morgan, January 26, 1893, Microfilm 4486, South Dakota Historical Society Archives.
70. Wilson (1999), 175.

CHAPTER 15. LOOKING AT THE BROWN–EASTMAN DISPUTE THROUGH A OTHERS' EYES

1. Eli Ricker interview with George Bartlett, Tablet 45, Nebraska State Historical Society.
2. *Courier Journal* (Louisville, Ky.), March 12, 1911.
3. Eli Ricker interview with George Bartlett, Tablet 45, Nebraska State Historical Society; *Star Tribune* (Minneapolis), March 22, 1912.
4. *Star Tribune*, March 22, 1912.
5. *Daily Deadwood Pioneer-Times*, September 7, 1890.
6. Eli Ricker interview with George Bartlett, Tablet 45, Nebraska State Historical Society.
7. *Daily Deadwood Pioneer-Times*, September 7, 1890.
8. Bureau of Indian Affairs, Miscellaneous Letters, Pine Ridge Agency, February 1892–April 1892, Brown letter to the secretary of the interior, February 23, 1892, Microfilm 4480, South Dakota Historical Society Archives.
9. Bureau of Indian Affairs, Miscellaneous Letters, Pine Ridge Agency, August–October 1892, Brown letter to Miller, August 6, 1892, Microfilm 4484, South Dakota Historical Society Archives.
10. *Omaha Daily Bee*, July 26, 1892.
11. *Black Hills Weekly Times* (Deadwood), August 6, 1892.
12. *Black Hills Weekly Times*, November 5, 1892.
13. *Black Hills Weekly Times*, November 5, 1892.
14. *Black Hills Weekly Times*, December 17, 1892.
15. *Dakota Farmers' Leader*, January 20, 1893; *Girard* (Kans.) *Press*, November 24, 1892; *Argus Leader*, November 26, 1892.
16. U.S. Register of Civil, Military, and Naval Service 1863–1959, vol. 1, p. 175.
17. Bureau of Indian Affairs, Miscellaneous Letters, Pine Ridge Agency, June–July 1892, Brown letter to Miller, July 24, 1892, Microfilm 4482, South Dakota Historical Society Archives.
18. Bureau of Indian Affairs, Miscellaneous Letters, Pine Ridge Agency, August–October 1892, Brown letter to Miller, August 10, 1892, Microfilm 4484, South Dakota Historical Society Archives.
19. Bureau of Indian Affairs, Miscellaneous Letters, Pine Ridge Agency, August–October 1892, Morgan telegram to Brown, August 12, 1892, Microfilm 4484, South Dakota Historical Society Archives.
20. Bureau of Indian Affairs, Miscellaneous Letters, Pine Ridge Agency, August–October 1892, Brown telegram to Morgan, August 22, 1892, Microfilm 4484, South Dakota Historical Society Archives.
21. *Lincoln* (Neb.) *Evening Call*, December 21, 1891.
22. Bureau of Indian Affairs, Miscellaneous Letters, Pine Ridge Agency, January–February 1893, Morgan telegram to Meteer, February 4, 1893, Microfilm 4487, South Dakota Historical Society Archives.
23. Bureau of Indian Affairs, Miscellaneous Letters, Pine Ridge Agency, January–February 1893, Meteer telegram to Morgan, February 18, 1893, Microfilm 4487, South Dakota Historical Society Archives.

24. Florentine Digmann, History of the St. Francis Mission and Diary: 1886–1922, unpublished manuscript, Marquette University Archives.
25. Digmann.
26. Digmann.
27. Digmann.
28. Annual Report of the Commissioner of Indian Affairs, 1892, 455.
29. Hall, *Roundup Years*, 175.
30. Wells, *Ninety-Six Years*, 92–103.
31. Wells, 170; Philip Hall interview with A. E. Johnson, June 10, 1974.
32. Wells, 194–95.
33. Utley, *Last Days of the Sioux Nation*, 214; Wells, 169–87.
34. Eli Ricker interview with Philip Wells, Tablet 4, Nebraska State Historical Society.
35. Eli Ricker interview with Philip Wells, Tablet 4, Nebraska State Historical Society.
36. Bureau of Indian Affairs, Miscellaneous Letters, Pine Ridge Agency, August–October 1892, Comer telegram to West, October 26, 1892, Microfilm 4484, South Dakota Historical Society Archives.
37. "Col George LeRoy Brown," Find a Grave, 2019, http://www.findagrave.com/memorial/57758495, accessed August 26, 2019; U.S. Register of Civil, Military and Naval Service 1863–1959, vol. 1, 246.
38. "Capt George Daniel Wallace," Find a Grave, 2019, https://www.findagrave.com/memorial/5816415, accessed August 26, 2019.
39. Anderson, History of the Cheyenne River Agency, 464–67.
40. Florentine Digmann, History of the St. Francis Mission and Diary: 1886–1922, unpublished manuscript, Marquette University Archives.
41. *Council Fire and Arbitrator*, July–August 1884.
42. *Black Hills Daily Times*, October 26, 1882; *Council Fire and Arbitrator*, October 1884.
43. *Council Fire and Arbitrator*, September 1884; *Black Hills Weekly Times*, October 21, 1882.
44. *Council Fire and Arbitrator*, October 1884.
45. *Council Fire and Arbitrator*, October 1884.
46. *Mitchell Daily Republic*, December 22, 1891; *Bismarck Tribune*, December 25, 1891.
47. *Nebraska State Journal*, November 17, 1891.
48. Eastman, *From the Deep Woods*, 3.
49. Eastman; *Inter Ocean*, October 9, 1890.
50. Eastman, 112–13.
51. Bureau of Indian Affairs, Miscellaneous Letters, Pine Ridge Agency, November 1892–January 1893, Brown letter to Cisney, December 26, 1892, Microfilm 4486, South Dakota Historical Society Archives.
52. Bureau of Indian Affairs, Miscellaneous Letters, Pine Ridge Agency, November 1892–January 1893, Brown letter to Cisney, November 24, 1892, Microfilm 4486, South Dakota Historical Society Archives.
53. Graber, *Sister to the Sioux*, 152–53.

CHAPTER 16. CAN NOPA UHAH'S CRIME

1. Kingsbury, *South Dakota Biographical*, 898.
2. Hall, *Roundup Years*, 498.
3. *Black Hills Union*, April 1, 1892.
4. Hall, *Roundup Years*, 132.
5. Bureau of Indian Affairs, Miscellaneous Letters, Pine Ridge Agency, June–July 1892, Brown telegram to Humphrey, June 25, 1892, Microfilm 4482, South Dakota Historical Society Archives.
6. Bureau of Indian Affairs, Miscellaneous Letters, Pine Ridge Agency, August–October 1892, Brown letter to Morgan, October 18, 1892, Microfilm 4484, South Dakota Historical Society Archives.
7. Hall, *Roundup Years*, 106.
8. Bureau of Indian Affairs, Miscellaneous Letters, Pine Ridge Agency, August–October 1892, Humphrey telegram to Brown, October 29, 1892, Microfilm 4484, South Dakota Historical Society Archives.
9. Bureau of Indian Affairs, Miscellaneous Letters, Pine Ridge Agency, November 1892–January 1893, Humphrey telegram to Stenger, November 25, 1892, Microfilm 4486, South Dakota Historical Society Archives.
10. Bureau of Indian Affairs, Miscellaneous Letters, Pine Ridge Agency, November 1892–January 1893, Humphrey telegram to Rapid City postmaster, November 25, 1892, Microfilm 4486, South Dakota Historical Society Archives.
11. *Rapid City Journal*, February 5, 1893.
12. Utley, *Last Days of the Sioux Nation*, 76–77.
13. *Black Hills Weekly Times* (Deadwood), April 8, 1893.
14. Eli Ricker interview with Philip Wells, Tablet 4, Nebraska State Historical Society.
15. *Custer* (S. Dak.) *Chronicle*, February 11, 1893.
16. Wells, *Ninety-Six Years*, 308–9.
17. Wells, 308–9.
18. Wells, 308–9.
19. *Daily Deadwood Pioneer Times*, October 31, 1894.
20. Bureau of Indian Affairs, Miscellaneous Letters, Pine Ridge Agency, January–February 1893, Brown telegram to Humphrey, February 3, 1893, Microfilm 4487, South Dakota Historical Society Archives.
21. *Hot Springs Star*, February 3, 1893.
22. Bureau of Indian Affairs, Miscellaneous Letters, Pine Ridge Agency, January–February 1893, Brown telegram to Morgan, February 3, 1893, Microfilm 4487, South Dakota Historical Society Archives.
23. Bureau of Indian Affairs, Miscellaneous Letters, Pine Ridge Agency, January–February 1893, Brown telegram to Carlton, February 3, 1893, Microfilm 4487, South Dakota Historical Society Archives.
24. Bureau of Indian Affairs, Miscellaneous Letters, Pine Ridge Agency, January–February 1893, Carlton telegram to Brown, February 4, 1893, Microfilm 4487, South Dakota Historical Society Archives.

25. Philip Hall interview with Charley Edgerton Jr., June 24, 1974; *Buffalo Gap Republican*, February 11, 1893.
26. *Argus Leader*, February 8, 1893.
27. *Black Hills Daily Times*, October 24, 1894.
28. Philip Hall interview with Charley Edgerton Jr., June 24, 1974; *Buffalo Gap Republican*, February 11, 1893; *Custer Chronicle*, February 11, 1893.
29. *Buffalo Gap Republican*, February 11, 1893.
30. *Omaha Daily Bee*, February 8, 1893.
31. *Buffalo Gap Republican*, February 18, 1893; *Star Tribune*, February 3, 1893.
32. *Argus Leader*, February 8, 1893.
33. Bureau of Indian Affairs, Miscellaneous Letters, Pine Ridge Agency, January–February 1893, Brown telegram to Carleton, February 4, 1893, Microfilm 4487, South Dakota Historical Society Archives.
34. Bureau of Indian Affairs, Miscellaneous Letters, Pine Ridge Agency, January–February 1893, Morgan telegram to Brown, February 5, 1893, Microfilm 4487, South Dakota Historical Society Archives.
35. Bureau of Indian Affairs, Miscellaneous Letters, Pine Ridge Agency, January–February 1893, Brown telegram to Morgan, February 5, 1893, Microfilm 4487, South Dakota Historical Society Archives.
36. Bureau of Indian Affairs, Miscellaneous Letters, Pine Ridge Agency, January–February 1893. Cisney telegram to Noble, February 6, 1893, Microfilm 4487, South Dakota Historical Society Archives.
37. *Custer Chronicle*, February 11, 1893.
38. *Little Falls* (Minn.) *Transcript*, February 10, 1893.
39. Bureau of Indian Affairs, Miscellaneous Letters, Pine Ridge Agency, January–February 1893, Sheridan telegram to Brown, February 4, 1893, Microfilm 4487, South Dakota Historical Society Archives; *Omaha Daily Bee*, February 5, 1893.
40. Bureau of Indian Affairs, Miscellaneous Letters, Pine Ridge Agency, January–February 1893, Brown telegram to Sheridan, February 4, 1893, Microfilm 4487, South Dakota Historical Society Archives.
41. *Record-Union* (Sacramento), February 6, 1893; *Salt Lake Herald*, February 6, 1893; *New York Tribune*, February 5, 1893; *Helena Independent*, February 6, 1893; *Indianapolis Journal*, February 7, 1893; *Washington* (D.C.) *Bee*, February 11, 1893; *National Tribune* (Washington, D.C.), February 9, 1893; *Alexandria* (Va.) *Gazette*, February, 10, 1893; *Fort Worth Gazette*, February 9, 1893.
42. *Salt Lake Herald*, February 5, 1893.
43. *Morning Call* (San Francisco), February 8, 1893.
44. *Minneapolis Tribune*, February 7, 1893; *St. Paul Globe*, February 7, 1893.
45. *St. Paul Globe*, February 5, 1893.
46. *Custer Chronicle*, February 11, 1893.
47. *Custer Chronicle*, February 11, 1893.
48. *Omaha Daily Bee*, February 21, 1893.
49. *Argus Leader*, February 8, 1893.

50. *Hermosa* (S. Dak.) *Pilot*, March 31, 1893.
51. Kingsbury, *South Dakota Biographical*, 1357.
52. *Battle River Pilot* (Hermosa, S. Dak.), June 9, 1893.
53. *Battle River Pilot*, June 9, 1893.
54. Standing Bear, *My People*, 237.

CHAPTER 17. CATCHING THE CULPRITS

1. *Omaha Daily Bee*, February 6, 1893; *Kimball* (S. Dak.) *Graphic*, February 9, 1893.
2. *Argus Leader*, February 10, 1893.
3. *Black Hills Daily Times*, February 11, 1893; *Argus Leader*, February 10, 1893.
4. *Argus Leader*, February 10, 1893.
5. *Black Hills Weekly Times*, February 17, 1893.
6. Bureau of Indian Affairs, Miscellaneous Letters, Pine Ridge Agency, January–February 1893, Brown telegram to Fry, February 8, 1893, Microfilm 4487, South Dakota Historical Society Archives.
7. Bureau of Indian Affairs, Miscellaneous Letters, Pine Ridge Agency, January–February 1893, Brown telegram to adjutant general, Department of the Platte, February 9, 1893, Microfilm 4487, South Dakota Historical Society Archives.
8. Bureau of Indian Affairs, Miscellaneous Letters, Pine Ridge Agency, January–February 1893. Adjutant general, Department of the Platte telegram to Brown, February 9, 1893, Microfilm 4487, South Dakota Historical Society Archives.
9. *Black Hills Daily Times*, February 11, 1893; *Daily Deadwood Pioneer-Times*, February 11, 1893.
10. *Black Hills Daily Times*, February 11, 1893.
11. *Omaha Daily Bee*, February 11, 1893.
12. *Minneapolis Tribune*, February 16, 1893.
13. Bureau of Indian Affairs, Miscellaneous Letters, Pine Ridge Agency, January–February 1893, Brown telegram to Fry, February 18, 1893, Microfilm 4487, South Dakota Historical Society Archives.
14. *Daily Deadwood Pioneer-Times*, March 24, 1893.
15. John H. Burns Collection: 1877–1897, manuscript 3624C, South Dakota Historical Society Archives.
16. *Rapid City Journal*, November 30, 1890.
17. *Black Hills Daily Times*, December 2, 1890.
18. *Hot Springs Star*, December 8, 1890.
19. *Buffalo Gap Republican*, December 13, 1890.
20. John H. Burns Collection: 1877–1897, manuscript 3624C, South Dakota Historical Society Archives.
21. *St. Paul Daily Globe*, March 29, 1893.
22. *St. Paul Daily Globe*, March 29, 1893.
23. *St. Paul Daily Globe*, March 29, 1893.
24. *Omaha Daily Bee*, March 3, 1893; *Nebraska State Journal*, April 1, 1893.
25. *Nebraska State Journal*, April 1, 1893.

26. *Black Hills Daily Times*, April 1, 1893.
27. Ellis, Reservation Akicitas, 185–210.
28. *Argus Leader*, April 5, 1893.
29. *Argus Leader*, April 10, 1893.
30. *Argus Leader*, April 12, 1893.
31. *Omaha Daily Bee*, April 17, 1893.
32. *Black Hills Daily Times*, April 1, 1893.
33. *Black Hills Daily Times*, April 8, 1893.
34. Annual Report of the Commissioner of Indian Affairs, 1893, 291.
35. *Black Hills Daily Times*, April 7, 1893; *Daily Deadwood Pioneer-Times*, April 7, 1893.
36. *Hermosa Pilot*, April 14, 1893.
37. *Omaha Daily Bee*, April 9, 1893.
38. *Black Hills Daily Times*, April 30, 1893.
39. *Black Hills Daily Times*, May 28, 1893.
40. *Black Hills Daily Times*, May 28, 1893.
41. *Argus Leader*, May 29, 1893.
42. *Dakota Republican* (Vermillion, S. Dak.), June 1, 1893.
43. *Black Hills Daily Times*, July 6, 1893.

CHAPTER 18. THE FRONTIER PEERS INTO THE TWENTIETH CENTURY

1. Holton, *Reading Railroad*, 323–25.
2. Steeples and Whitten, *Democracy in Desperation*, 42–65.
3. Harris et al., *Grand Illusions*, 32.
4. Krupp'sche Gussstahlfabrik Essen, *Exhibition Catalogue*.
5. *Chicago Tribune*, June 18, 1893.
6. *Chicago Tribune*, June 18, 1893.
7. Moses, Indians on the Midway, 205–29.
8. Deahl, Chadron–Chicago, 166–93.
9. *Daily Deadwood Pioneer-Times*, April 14, 1893.
10. *Daily Deadwood Pioneer-Times*, April 14, 1893.
11. *Chicago Herald*, June 14, 1893: *Omaha Daily Bee*, June 14, 1893.
12. Hutton, *Doc Middleton*, 180.
13. Deahl, Chadron–Chicago, 166–93.
14. *Black Hills Weekly Times*, June 24, 1893.
15. Hutton, *Doc Middleton*, 5–7.
16. Hutton, 48.
17. Hutton, 192.
18. *Chicago Herald*, June 14, 1893.
19. *Buffalo Gap Republican*, June 24, 1893; *Chicago Tribune*, June 28, 1893.
20. Deahl, Chadron–Chicago, 166–93.
21. Hutton, *Doc Middleton*, 188.

22. Deahl, Chadron-Chicago, 166-93.
23. Hufstetler and Bedeau, *South Dakota's Railroads*, 9-17.
24. *Chicago Herald*, March 5, 1891.
25. Arthur Calvin Mellette, Correspondence, Box 3526B, South Dakota Historical Society Archives.
26. Robinson, *History of South Dakota*, 337.
27. Zimmerman, Promoting the Prairie Cornucopia, 281-300.
28. Zimmerman.
29. Zimmerman.
30. *Rapid City Journal*, March 5, 1893.
31. *Argus Leader*, July 12, 1893.
32. *Chicago Tribune*, July 13, 1893.
33. *Chicago Tribune*, July 13, 1893.
34. *Turner County Herald*, June 8, 1893.
35. *Black Hills Daily Times*, May 28, 1893.
36. Zimmerman, Promoting the Prairie Cornucopia, 281-300.
37. Turner, *Frontier in American History*, 1-38.
38. Turner, 38.
39. Eli Ricker interview with R. O. Pugh, Tablet 12. Nebraska State Historical Society.
40. Bureau of Indian Affairs, Miscellaneous Letters, Pine Ridge Agency, June-August 1893, John Ost telegram to Penney, acting Indian agent, July 13, 1893, Microfilm 4490, South Dakota Historical Society Archives; Eli Ricker interview with R. O. Pugh, October 26, 1906, Tablet 12, Nebraska State Historical Society.
41. Bureau of Indian Affairs, Miscellaneous Letters, Pine Ridge Agency, June-August 1893, Penny telegram to Morgan, July 14, 1893, Microfilm 4490, South Dakota Historical Society Archives.
42. Agonito, Young Man Afraid of His Horses, 116-32.

CHAPTER 19. THE WHEELS OF JUSTICE TURN SLOWLY

1. Annual Report of the Commissioner of Indian Affairs, 1893, 287.
2. *Weekly Pioneer-Times* (Deadwood), February 22, 1894.
3. *Black Hills Daily Times*, April 1, 1893.
4. *Minneapolis Tribune*, February 2, 1893.
5. Bureau of Indian Affairs, Standing Rock Agency, Correspondence Received, 1893, Peemiller letter to McLaughlin, August 1, 1893, Microfilm 5554, South Dakota State Historical Society Archives.
6. Bureau of Indian Affairs, Standing Rock Agency, Correspondence, January 1-August 11, 1893, McLaughlin letter to Peemiller, August 4, 1893, Microfilm 5485, South Dakota State Historical Society Archives.
7. Bureau of Indian Affairs, Standing Rock Agency, Correspondence Received, 1893, Peemiller letter to McLaughlin, August 7, 1893, Microfilm 5554, South Dakota State Historical Society Archives.

8. *Daily Plainsman*, August 26, 1893.
9. Bureau of Indian Affairs, Standing Rock Agency, Correspondence, January 1–August 11, 1893, Fry letter to McLaughlin, August 31, 1893, Microfilm 5485, South Dakota State Historical Society Archives.
10. Bureau of Indian Affairs, Standing Rock Agency, Correspondence, August 1893–March 1894, McLaughlin letter to Fry, November 1, 1893, Microfilm 5486, South Dakota Historical Society Archives.
11. *Argus Leader*, February 14, 1894.
12. Bureau of Indian Affairs, Standing Rock Agency Correspondence, August 1893–March 1894, McLaughlin letter to Peemiller, November 1, 1893, Microfilm 5486, South Dakota State Historical Archives.
13. Bureau of Indian Affairs, Standing Rock Agency, Correspondence Received, 1893, Tschetter letter to McLaughlin, December 15, 1893, Microfilm 5554, South Dakota State Historical Archives.
14. Bureau of Indian Affairs, Standing Rock Agency, Correspondence, August 1893–March 1894, McLaughlin letter to Tschetter, December 29, 1893, Microfilm 5486, South Dakota Historical Archives.
15. Bureau of Indian Affairs, Standing Rock Agency, Correspondence, August 1893–March 1894, McLaughlin letter to Cogley, January 11, 1894, Microfilm 5486, South Dakota State Historical Archives.
16. *Argus Leader*, February 14, 1894; *St. Paul Globe*, May 27, 1894.
17. Bureau of Indian Affairs, Standing Rock Agency, Correspondence Received, 1894, Cogley letter to McLaughlin, February 22, 1894, Microfilm 5557, South Dakota State Historical Society.
18. *Argus Leader*, February 22, 1894.
19. *Weekly Pioneer-Times*, April 5, 1894.
20. *Mower County* (Tenn.) *Transcript*, April 4, 1894; *Dakota Farmers' Leader*, May 18, 1894.
21. *Pierre Weekly Free Press*, April 26, 1894.
22. *Pierre Weekly Free Press*, May 5, 1894.
23. Annual Report of the Commissioner of Indian Affairs, 1893, 287.
24. Florentine Digmann. History of St. Francis Mission and Diary: 1886–1933, unpublished manuscript, Marquette University Archives.
25. *Black Hills Daily Times*, October 15, 1893.
26. *Black Hills Daily Times*, October 22, 1893.
27. *Black Hills Daily Times*, October 22, 1893.
28. Parker, *Deadwood*, 191.
29. *Daily Deadwood Pioneer-Times*, October 24, 1893.
30. *Black Hills Daily Times*, October 25, 1893.
31. *Daily Deadwood Pioneer-Times*, October 24, 1893; *Black Hills Daily Times*, October 25, 1893.
32. *Weekly Pioneer-Times*, October 26, 1893.
33. *lack Hills Daily Times*, October 26, 1893.

34. *Black Hills Daily Times*, October 25, 1893.
35. Robinson, *History of South Dakota*, 1123–26.
36. Lamar, *Dakota Territory*, 196.
37. Wysk, Dakota Images, 196.
38. Bureau of Indian Affairs, Miscellaneous Letters, Pine Ridge Agency, January–February 1893, Burns letter to John Shangreau, February 12, 1893, Microfilm 4487, South Dakota Historical Society Archives.
39. Bureau of Indian Affairs, Miscellaneous Letters, Pine Ridge Agency, January–February 1893, Brown letter to Burns, February 17, 1893, Microfilm 4487, South Dakota Historical Society Archives.
40. *Daily Deadwood Pioneer-Times*, October 18, 1893.
41. *Black Hills Weekly Times*, October, 21, 1893.
42. *Rapid City Journal*, October 26, 1893.
43. *Daily Deadwood Pioneer-Times*, October 27, 1893.
44. *Black Hills Daily Times*, October 24, 1893; Lamar, *Dakota Territory*, 251.
45. *Black Hills Daily Times*, October 28, 1893
46. *Black Hills Daily Times*, May 8, 1894.
47. *Deadwood Daily Pioneer-Times*, May 9, 1894.
48. *Weekly Pioneer-Times*, May 10, 1894.
49. *Black Hills Daily Times*, May 11, 1890.
50. *Black Hills Daily Times*, May 11, 1890.
51. *Black Hills Daily Times*, May 11, 1890.
52. *Weekly Pioneer-Times*, May 17, 1894.
53. *Weekly Pioneer-Times*, May 17, 1894.
54. *Weekly Pioneer-Times*, May 17, 1894.
55. *Weekly Pioneer-Times*, May 17, 1894.
56. *Black Hills Daily Times*, October 9, 1894.
57. *Black Hills Daily Times*, October 9, 1894.
58. *Black Hills Daily Times*, October 9, 1894.
59. Wishart, *Unspeakable Sadness*, 132–45.
60. Lead (S. Dak.) *Daily Call*, October 9, 1894; *Black Hills Weekly Times* (Deadwood), October 13, 1894.
61. *Black Hills Weekly Times*, October 13, 1894.
62. *Black Hills Daily Times*, October 9, 1894.
63. *Weekly Pioneer Times*, October 25, 1894.
64. *Black Hills Daily Times*, October 10, 1894.
65. *Black Hills Daily Times*, October 11, 1894.
66. *Weekly Pioneer Times*, October 18, 1894.
67. *Daily Deadwood Pioneer-Times*, October 31, 1893.
68. *Hot Springs Weekly Star*, October 12, 1894; *Black Hills Weekly Times*, October 31, 1894.
69. *Lead Daily Call*, October 16, 1894.
70. *Hot Springs Weekly Star*, October 12, 1894.
71. *Daily Deadwood Pioneer-Times*, October 28, 1894.

72. *Weekly Pioneer Times*, October 25, 1894.
73. *Black Hills Daily Times*, October 16, 1894.
74. *Black Hills Daily Times*, October 17, 1894.
75. *Black Hills Daily Times*, October 17, 1894.
76. *Hot Springs Star*, November 9, 1894.
77. *Black Hills Daily Times*, October 24, 1894; *Hot Springs Star*, November 9, 1894.
78. Bureau of Indian Affairs, Standing Rock Agency, Correspondence Received, 1894, Benoist letter to McLaughlin, April 4, 1894, Microfilm 5557, South Dakota Historical Archives.
79. *Black Hills Daily Times*, October 18, 1894; *Lead Daily Call*, October 18, 1894.
80. *Black Hills Daily Times*, October 27, 1894.
81. Eli Ricker interview with Alfred Coe, Series 3, Folder 5, Nebraska State Historical Society.
82. *Black Hills Daily Times*, October 18, 1894.
83. *Lead Daily Call*, October 19, 1894.
84. *Daily Deadwood Pioneer Times,* October 31, 1894; *Weekly Pioneer Times*, November 1, 1894; *Hot Springs Star*, November 9, 1894.
85. *Weekly Pioneer-Times*, November 1, 1894.
86. *Daily Deadwood Pioneer-Times*, July 7, 1895; *Argus Leader*, May 27, 1896.
87. *Argus Leader*, May 27, 1896.

CHAPTER 20. TWO STICKS'S TRIAL

1. *Daily Deadwood Pioneer-Times*, July 29, 1911; *Inter Mountain Globe* (Hulett, Wyo.), August 3, 1911.
2. *Black Hills Weekly Pioneer Times*, October 25, 1894.
3. *Black Hills Daily Times*, October 10, 1894.
4. *Lead Daily Call*, August 19, 1895.
5. *Black Hills Weekly Pioneer-Times*, December 25, 1879.
6. *Black Hills Weekly Pioneer-Times*, March 8, 1894.
7. *Black Hills Weekly Pioneer-Times*, August 9, 1894.
8. *Black Hills Weekly Pioneer-Times*, September 6, 1894.
9. *Black Hills Daily Times*, July 22, 1894.
10. *Black Hills Weekly Pioneer-Times*, June 14, 1894.
11. *Black Hills Weekly Pioneer-Times*, September 18, 1894.
12. South Dakota State Census, 1905.
13. *Black Hills Weekly Pioneer-Times*, June 14, 1894.
14. *Black Hills Daily Times*, March 10, 1894.
15. *Black Hills Daily Times*, January 17, 1894.
16. *Black Hills Weekly Pioneer-Times*, January 25, 1894.
17. *Black Hills Weekly Pioneer-Times*, December 27, 1893.
18. *Black Hills Daily Times*, April 3, 1894.
19. *Black Hills Weekly Pioneer-Times*, April 19, 1894.
20. *Lead Daily Call*, October 18, 1894.

21. *Black Hills Daily Times*, January 4, 1894.
22. *Black Hills Daily Times*, August 30, 1894.
23. *Black Hills Daily Times*, March 8, 1894.
24. *Black Hills Daily Times*, March 6, 1894.
25. *Weekly Pioneer-Times*, October 18, 1894.
26. *Black Hills Daily Times*, February 11, 1894.
27. *Weekly Pioneer Times*, January 13, 1894.
28. *Weekly Pioneer-Times*, November 29, 1894.
29. *Weekly Pioneer-Times*, October 25, 1894.
30. Records from Two Sticks's trial, 1894, Case 66, U.S. National Archives.
31. *Black Hills Daily Times*, October 24, 1894.
32. *Black Hills Daily Times*, October 24, 1894.
33. *Black Hills Daily Times*, October 24, 1894.
34. *Black Hills Daily Times*, October 26, 1894.
35. *Black Hills Daily Times*, October 26, 1894.
36. *Daily Deadwood Pioneer-Times*, October 31, 1894.
37. *Daily Deadwood Pioneer-Times*, October 31, 1894.
38. *Black Hills Daily Times*, October 26, 1894.
39. *Weekly Pioneer Times*, October 25, 1894.
40. *Black Hills Daily Times*, October 26, 1894.
41. *Daily Deadwood Pioneer-Times*, October 26, 1894.
42. *Inter Ocean*, October 31, 1894.
43. *Black Hills Daily Times*, October 26, 1894.
44. *Daily Deadwood Pioneer-Times,* October 26, 1894.
45. *Daily Deadwood Pioneer-Times,* October 26, 1894.
46. *Black Hills Daily Times*, October 26, 1894.
47. *Daily Deadwood Pioneer-Times*, October 31, 1894.
48. *Black Hills Daily Times*, October 26, 1894.
49. *Black Hills Daily Times*, October 26, 1894.
50. *Black Hills Daily Times*, October 26, 1894.
51. *Black Hills Daily Times*, October 26, 1894.
52. *Black Hills Daily Times*, October 26, 1894.
53. *Daily Deadwood Pioneer-Times*, October 26, 1894.
54. *Black Hills Daily Times*, October 26, 1894.
55. *Black Hills Daily Times*, October 27, 1894.
56. Philip Hall interview with Charley Edgerton Jr., June 24, 1974.
57. Philip Hall interview with Charley Edgerton Jr., June 24, 1974.
58. *Weekly Pioneer-Times*, November 1, 1894; *Daily Deadwood Pioneer-Times*, October 28, 1894.
59. *Daily Deadwood Pioneer-Times*, October 27, 1894.
60. Florentine Digmann, History of the St. Francis Mission and Diary: 1886–1922, unpublished manuscript, Marquette University Archives.
61. *Black Hills Daily Times*, October 27, 1894.

62. *Daily Deadwood Pioneer-Times*, October 27, 1894.
63. *Black Hills Daily Times*, October 27, 1894.
64. *Daily Deadwood Pioneer-Times*, October 28, 1894.
65. *Weekly Pioneer-Times*, November 1, 1894.
66. *Weekly Pioneer-Times*, November 1, 1894.
67. *Weekly Pioneer-Times*, November 1, 1894.
68. Records from Two Sticks's trial, 1894, Case 66, U.S. National Archives.
69. *Black Hills Daily Times*, October 31, 1894.
70. *Black Hills Daily Times*, October 31, 1894.
71. *Weekly Pioneer-Times*, November 1, 1894.
72. *Weekly Pioneer-Times*, November 1, 1894.
73. *Weekly Pioneer-Times*, November 29, 1894.
74. *Black Hills Daily Times*, December 15, 1894.

CHAPTER 21. THE HANGING

1. Florentine Digmann, History of the St. Francis Mission and Diary: 1886–1922, unpublished manuscript, Marquette University Archives.
2. Digmann.
3. Digmann.
4. Digmann.
5. Digmann.
6. *Lead Daily Call*, December 19, 1894.
7. *Black Hills Daily Times*, December 23, 1894.
8. Florentine Digmann, History of the St. Francis Mission and Diary: 1886–1922, unpublished manuscript, Marquette University Archives.
9. Digmann.
10. Digmann.
11. *Deadwood Daily Pioneer-Times*, December 28, 1894; *Weekly Pioneer-Times*, January 3, 1895.
12. *Black Hills Daily Times*, December 29, 1894.
13. *Argus Leader*, January 5, 1895.
14. *Black Hills Daily Times*, December 29, 1894.
15. *Black Hills Daily Times*, December 29, 1894.
16. *Omaha Daily Bee*, December 27, 1894.
17. *Black Hills Daily Times*, December 28, 1894.
18. *Daily Deadwood Pioneer-Times*, December 28, 1894.
19. *Black Hills Daily Times*, December 29, 1894; Florentine Digmann, History of the St. Francis Mission and Diary: 1886–1922, unpublished manuscript, Marquette University Archives.
20. *Black Hills Daily Times*, December 29, 1894.
21. *Rapid City Journal*, December 29, 1894.
22. Brown, *Bury My Heart at Wounded Knee*, 172.

23. Florentine Digmann, History of the St. Francis Mission and Diary: 1886–1922, unpublished manuscript, Marquette University Archives.
24. Annual Report of the Commission of Indian Affairs, 1897, 272.
25. Hall, *Roundup Years*, 46.
26. Hall, *Roundup Years*, 46.
27. *Battle River Pilot*, March 16, 1889.
28. *Omaha Daily Bee*, January 11, 1895.
29. Wells, *Ninety-Six Years*, 309–10.
30. Wells, 309–10.
31. *Rapid City Journal*, October 7, 1944.
32. *Black Hills Daily Times*, December 29, 1894.

BIBLIOGRAPHY

UNPUBLISHED MANUSCRIPTS AND ARCHIVED MATERIAL

Carlisle Indian School Digital Resource Center, Dickinson College
 Carlisle Indian Industrial School digital records, carlisleindians.dickinson.edu.
History Society of Philadelphia
 Indian Rights Association Archives. Reel 7.
Marquette University Archives
 Digmann, Florentine. History of the St. Francis Mission and Diary: 1886–1922. Unpublished manuscript.
Pettigrew Museum Archives, Sioux Falls
 Richard F. Pettigrew: Notes and Comments on Men and Events.
 Richard F. Pettigrew letters.
South Dakota Historical Society Archives
 Arthur Calvin Mellette Correspondence. Box 3526B.
 Arthur Calvin Mellette Papers, Correspondence and Reports: 1889–1892. Box 3527A.
 Bureau of Indian Affairs, Correspondence Received, Standing Rock Agency, 1893. Microfilm 5554.
 Bureau of Indian Affairs, Correspondence Received, Standing Rock Agency, 1894. Microfilm 5557.
 Bureau of Indian Affairs, Correspondence, Standing Rock Agency, January 1–August 11, 1893. Microfilm 5485.
 Bureau of Indian Affairs, Correspondence, Standing Rock Agency, August 1893–March 1894. Microfilm 5486.

Bureau of Indian Affairs, Miscellaneous Correspondence Received, Rosebud Agency, September 1887–August 1891. Microfilm 5248.
Bureau of Indian Affairs, Miscellaneous Correspondence Received, Rosebud Agency, August 1891–July 1893, Microfilm 5249.
Bureau of Indian Affairs, Miscellaneous Letters, Pine Ridge Agency, September/November 1886–January 1893. Microfilm 4474.
Bureau of Indian Affairs, Miscellaneous Letters, Pine Ridge Agency, October 1890–June 1891. Microfilm 4476.
Bureau of Indian Affairs, Miscellaneous Letters, Pine Ridge Agency, July–October 1891. Microfilm 4477.
Bureau of Indian Affairs, Miscellaneous Letters, Pine Ridge Agency, February–April 1892. Microfilm 4480.
Bureau of Indian Affairs, Miscellaneous Letters, Pine Ridge Agency, May–June 1892. Microfilm 4481.
Bureau of Indian Affairs, Miscellaneous Letters, Pine Ridge Agency, July–August 1892. Microfilm 4482.
Bureau of Indian Affairs, Miscellaneous Letters, Pine Ridge Agency, September–October 1892. Microfilm 4483.
Bureau of Indian Affairs, Miscellaneous Letters, Pine Ridge Agency, November 1892–January 1893. Microfilm 4484.
Bureau of Indian Affairs, Miscellaneous Letters, Pine Ridge Agency, February–April 1893. Microfilm 4485.
Bureau of Indian Affairs, Miscellaneous Letters, Pine Ridge Agency, May–June 1893. Microfilm 4486.
Bureau of Indian Affairs, Miscellaneous Letters, Pine Ridge Agency, July–August 1893. Microfilm 4487.
Bureau of Indian Affairs, Miscellaneous Letters, Pine Ridge Agency, November 1893–January 1894. Microfilm 4490.
C. P. Jordan Papers. Box 3615B.
J. B. McCloud, unpublished manuscript. Box 3564A.
John H. Burns Collection: 1877–1897. Manuscript 3624C.
National Guard Papers. Box 3659A:3672.
National Guard Papers. Box 571.
Report of Colonel E. A. Carr and Monthly Returns of the Regiment, November 1890–January 1891. Microfilm 666.
U.S. National Archives and Records Administration, Kansas City
  Microfilm 982, 163–68.
  Microfilm 983, 1, 175.
  Records from Plenty Horses's trial (handwritten). File 6037537, 106.
  Records from Plenty Horses's trial (typewritten). File 7097684, vol. 1, p. 487.
  Records from Two Sticks's trial, 1894. Case 66.
  Reports and correspondence relating to army investigations of the battle at Wounded Knee and the Sioux campaign of 1890–1891. Microfilm 2.

GOVERNMENT DOCUMENTS

Annual Report of the Commissioner of Indian Affairs, 1889.
Annual Report of the Commissioner of Indian Affairs, 1890.
Annual Report of the Commissioner of Indian Affairs, 1891.
Annual Report of the Commissioner of Indian Affairs, 1892.
Annual Report of the Commissioner of Indian Affairs, 1893.
Annual Report of the Commissioner of Indian Affairs, 1897.
Courthouse records, 1891. Meade County, South Dakota.
Dakota Territory Census, 1885. Central Portion, Fall River County, South Dakota.
Executive Documents of the Senate of the United States. First Session of the 51st Congress, *Congressional Edition*, vol. 2682.
U.S. Congressional Serial Set 3062, 2–14.
U.S. Register of Civil, Military, and Naval Service: 1863–1959. Department of the Interior.

BOOKS AND ARTICLES

Agonito, J. (1998). Young Man Afraid of His Horses: The Reservation Years. *Nebraska History* 79: 116–32.
Allen, C. W. (1997). *Fort Laramie to Wounded Knee: In the West That Was*. Lincoln: University of Nebraska Press.
Anderson, H. (1956). A History of the Cheyenne River Agency and Its Military Post, Fort Bennett, 1868–1891. In *South Dakota Historical Collections*, vol. 28. Pierre: State Historical Society.
Beck, J. P. N. (2004). *The First Sioux War: The Grattan Fight and Blue Water Creek, 1854–1856*. Lanham, Md.: University Press of America.
Blackburn, W. M. (1902). Historical Sketch of North and South Dakota. In *South Dakota Historical Collections*, vol. 1. Pierre: State Historical Society.
Brown, D. (1970). *Bury My Heart at Wounded Knee: An Indian History of the American West*. New York: Henry Holt.
Brown, J., and A. M. Willard. (1924). *The Black Hills Trails: A History of the Struggles of the Pioneers in the Winning of the Black Hills*. Rapid City: Rapid City Journal.
Buecker, T. R., ed. (2004). Henry P. Smith's Diary during the Ghost Dance Movement, 1890–1891. *South Dakota History* 34(3): 197–236.
Coleman, W. S. (2000). *Voices of Wounded Knee*. Lincoln: University of Nebraska Press.
Deahl, W. E. (1972). The Chadron–Chicago 1,000 Mile Cowboy Race. *Nebraska History* 53: 166–93.
Dickinson, E. (2006). Reconstructing the Indian village on the Little Big Horn: The Cankahuan or Soreback. *Greasy Grass* 2(1): 2–14.
Eastman, C. A. ([1916] 1977). *From the Deep Woods to Civilization*. Lincoln: University of Nebraska Press.
Ellis, M. R. (1999). Reservation Akicitas: The Pine Ridge Indian Police, 1879–1885. *South Dakota History* 29(3): 185–210.
Graber, K., ed. (1978). *Sister to the Sioux: The Memoirs of Elaine Goodale Eastman*. Lincoln: University of Nebraska Press.

Greene, J. A. (2014). *American Carnage: Wounded Knee 1890*. Norman: University of Oklahoma Press.
Hagan, W. T. (1985). *The Indian Rights Association: The Herbert Welsh Years 1882–1904*. Tucson: University of Arizona Press.
Hall, B. L. (1956 [2000]). *Roundup Years: Old Muddy to the Black Hills*. Pierre: State Publishing.
Harris, N., William de Wit, J. Gilbert, and R. W. Rydell. (1993). *Grand Illusions: Chicago's World Fair of 1893*. Chicago: Chicago Historical Society.
Hauk, J. K. (1954). The Story of Gus and Jessie Craven. In *South Dakota Historical Collections*, vol. 27. Pierre: South Dakota State Historical Society.
Hendrickson, K. E. (1968). The Public Career of Richard F. Pettigrew of South Dakota: 1848–1926. In *South Dakota Historical Collections*, vol. 34. Pierre: State Historical Society.
Holton, J. L. (1989). *The Reading Railroad: History of the Coal Age Empire*. Vol. 1, *The Nineteenth Century*. Lewisburg, Pa.: Garrigues House.
Hufstetler, M., and M. Bedeau. (1998). *South Dakota's Railroads*. Pierre: South Dakota Historic Preservation Office.
Hughes, R. B. ([1895] 2002). *Pioneer Years in the Black Hills*. Rapid City: Dakota Alpha.
Hutton, H. (1974). *Doc Middleton: Life and Legends of the Notorious Plains Outlaw*. Chicago: Swallow Press.
Hyde, G. E. (1956). *A Sioux Chronicle*. Norman: University of Oklahoma Press.
Jefferson, G. (2014). *The Life and Times of John Baptiste Richard*. Glendo, Wy.: High Plains Press.
Jensen, R. E., ed. (2005). *The Settler and Soldier Interviews of Eli S. Ricker*. Lincoln: University of Nebraska Press.
Kingsbury, G. W. (1915) *History of Dakota Territory*, vol. 2. Chicago: S. J. Clarke.
———. (1915). *South Dakota Biographical*, vol. 4. Chicago: S. J. Clarke.
Krupp'sche Gussstahlfabrik Essen. ([1923] 2001). *Exhibition Catalogue of the Cast Steel Works of Fried: Krupp, Essen on the Ruhr (Rhenish Prussia) World's Fair Exposition, 1893*. Charleston, N.C.: Nabu Press.
Lamar, H. R. (1956). *Dakota Territory 1861–1889: A Study in Frontier Politics*. New Haven, Conn.: Yale University Press.
Lee, R. (1991). *Fort Meade and the Black Hills*. Lincoln: University of Nebraska Press.
Lee, R., and D. Williams. (1964). *The Last Grass Frontier*. Sturgis, S. Dak.: Black Hills Publishers.
Manhart, Paul, ed. (1983). *A Dictionary: OIE Wowapi Wan of Teton Sioux*. Vermillion: University of South Dakota Press.
Marshall, J. (2004). *The Journey of Crazy Horse*. New York: Penguin.
McGillycuddy, J. B. (1941). *McGillycuddy Agent*. New York: Oxford University Press.
Meing, D. W. (1993). *The Shaping of America: A Geographical Perspective of 500 Years of History*, vol. 2. New Haven, Conn.: Yale University Press.
Miller, D. H. (1959). *Ghost Dance*. Lincoln: University of Nebraska Press.
Mooney, J. (1965). *The Ghost-Dance Religion and the Sioux Outbreak of 1890*. Chicago: University of Chicago Press.

Morgan, T. (1958). "Reminiscences of My Days in the Land of the Ogalalla Sioux." In *South Dakota Historical Collections*, vol. 29. Pierre: State Historical Society.

Moses, L. G. (1984). Wild West Shows, Reformers, and the Image of the American Indian. *South Dakota History* 14(3): 193-221.

———. (1991). Indians on the Midway: Wild West Shows and the Indian Bureau at the World's Fairs: 1893-1904. *South Dakota History* 21(3): 205-29.

Olson, J. C. ([1965] 1975). *Red Cloud and the Sioux Problem*. Lincoln: University of Nebraska. Press.

Ostler, J. (2010). *The Lakota and the Black Hills: The Struggle for Sacred Ground*. New York: Penguin Library of American Indian History.

Parker, W. (1981). *Deadwood: The Golden Years*. Lincoln: University of Nebraska Press.

Prucha, F. P. (1976). *American Indian Policy in Crisis: 1855-1900*. Norman: University of Oklahoma Press.

Remington, F. ([1895] 1982). *Pony Tracks*. New York: American Legacy Press.

Richardson, H. C. (2010). *Wounded Knee: Party Politics and the Road to an American Massacre*. New York: Basic Books.

Robinson, D. (1904). *History of South Dakota*. Logansport, Ind.: B. F. Bowen.

———. (1930). *History of South Dakota*, vol. 1. Chicago: Chicago Historical Society.

Roosevelt, T. R. (1893). *Report of Hon. Theodore Roosevelt Made to the United States Civil Service Commission upon a Visit to Certain Indian Reservations and Indian Schools in South Dakota, Nebraska, and Kansas*. Philadelphia: Indian Rights Association.

Sandoz, M. ([1942] 1992). *Crazy Horse: The Strange Man of the Oglalas*. Lincoln: University of Nebraska Press.

Schuler, H. H. (1985). *The South Dakota Capitol in Pierre*. Pierre: State Publishing.

Shell, H. S. (1975). *History of South Dakota*. Lincoln: University Nebraska Press.

Simpson, J. (2000). *West River 1850-1900: Stories from the Great Sioux Reservation*. St. Francis, S. Dak.: Rattlesnake Butte Press.

Skogen, L. C. (1996). *Indian Depredation Claims: 1796-1920*. Norman: University of Oklahoma Press.

Smith, B. M. (1988) Anti-Catholicism, Indian Education and Thomas Jefferson Morgan, Commissioner of Indian Affairs. *Canadian Journal of History* 22: 213-33.

Smith, R. A. (1975). *Moon of Popping Trees*. New York: Reader's Digest Press.

Southerton, D. (2004). James R. Walker's Campaign against Tuberculosis on the Pine Ridge Reservation. *South Dakota History* 34(2): 107-26.

Spindler, W. H. ([1955] 1985). *Tragedy Strikes at Wounded Knee*. Vermillion: University of South Dakota Press.

Strain, D. (1978). Old Man on the Range, *Dakota West* 34(4): 12-13.

Standing Bear, L. (1928). *My People, the Sioux*. Lincoln: University of Nebraska Press.

Steeples, D., and D. O. Witten. (1998). *Democracy in Desperation: The Depression of 1893*. Westport, Conn.: Greenwood Press.

Turner, F. J. ([1920] 1947). *The Frontier in American History*. New York: Henry Holt.

Utley, R. M. (1963). *The Last Days of the Sioux Nation*. New Haven, Conn: Yale University Press.

———. (1993). *The Lance and the Shield: The Life and Times of Sitting Bull.* New York: Ballantine Books.

Viegas, J. (2006). *Fort Laramie Treaty, 1868: A Primary Source Examination of the Treaty That Established a Sioux Reservation in Black Hills of Dakota.* New York: Rosen Publishing.

Waggoner, H. A. (2013). *A Hunkpapa Historian's Strong-Heart Song of the Lakota.* Lincoln: University of Nebraska Press.

Warren, L. S. (2005). *Buffalo Bill's America: William Cody and the Wild West Show.* New York: Knopf.

Wells, P. F. (1948). Ninety-Six Years among the Indians of the Northwest. *North Dakota History* 15.

Welsh, H. (1893). *Civilization among the Sioux Indians: Report of a Visit to Some of the Sioux Reservations of South Dakota and Nebraska.* Philadelphia: Office of Indian Rights.

Wilson, R. (1999). *Ohiyesa: Charles Eastman, Santee Sioux.* Urbana: University of Illinois Press.

Wishart, D. J. (1995). *An Unspeakable Sadness.* Lincoln: University of Nebraska Press.

Wysk, G. M. (1997). Dakota Images: Granville G. Bennett. *South Dakota History* 27(3): 193–96.

Younkin, S. D. (1974). Prelude to Wounded Knee: The Military Point of View. *South Dakota History*, 4(3): 333–51.

Yost, N. S. (1969). *Boss Cowman: Recollections of Ed Lemmon: 1857–1946.* Lincoln: University of Nebraska Press.

Zimmerman, K. (1993). Promoting the Prairie Cornucopia: South Dakota at the 1893 World's Columbia Exposition. *South Dakota History* 23(4): 281–300.

INTERVIEWS

Bartlett, George. Interview by Eli Ricker. Tablet 45. Nebraska State Historical Society.
Coe, Alfred. Interview by Eli Ricker. Series 3, Folder 5. Nebraska State Historical Society.
Edgerton, Charley. Interview by Philip Hall, June 24, 1974.
Horn Cloud, Joseph. Interview by Eli Ricker. Tablet 12. Nebraska State Historical Society.
Johnson, A. E. Oral history archived at the Ben Reifel Visitors Center. Badlands National Park.
Johnson, A. E. Interview by Philip Hall, June 10, 1974.
Lemley, Pete. Oral history archived at the Ben Reifel Visitors Center, Badlands National Park.
McFarland, Peter. Interview by Eli Ricker. Tablet 31. Nebraska State Historical Society.
Pugh, R. O. Interview by Eli Ricker, 1906. Tablet 12. Nebraska State Historical Society.
Wells, Philip. Interview by Eli Ricker. Tablet 4. Nebraska State Historical Society.
Whalen, Jack. Interview by Eli Ricker. Tablet 12. Nebraska State Historical Society.
White Eyes. Interview by Eli Ricker. Tablet 10, Nebraska State Historical Society.
Young, Hallie. Interview by Philip Hall, June 15, 1976.

INDEX

References to illustrations appear in italic type.

Agreement of 1877, 2
akicitas, 119–20
Akin, Gene, 25–26, 30
Alkali Creek, 52–54
Allen, Charley, 25, 29
Allison Commission, 47
American Horse, 15, 18, 75, 109, *116,* 126; as Lakota delegate, 114–16; at Plenty Horses's trial, 75
Argus Leader, 57, 173
Ash, Ben, 205–6
Attack Him (Julio), 98, 100–101

Bacon, Clark, 169, 172, 214
Bacon, James, 166, 172, 214, 219, 222
Baldwin, Frank D., 126, 128–29; at Few Tails's trial, 92; at Plenty Horses's trial, 72–73, 76–77
Baldwin, George M., 92
Ballance, John G., 64, 70, *81*
Barber, Amos, 40
Bartlett, Arthur, 5

Bartlett, George, 31, 100–101, 130, 173; background of, 149–50; and Brown, 150–51; at Plenty Horses's trial, 71, 79
Battle Creek, 25–26, 34–35, 163, 173
Battle of the Little Bighorn, 1, 67, 135, 155, 157–58
Battle River Pilot, 29
Bear Eagle, 121–24, 131, 215, 227
Bear Louse, 175
Bear That Lays Down, 65, 68, 71, 73–74, *81*
Beaver, V. M., 55, 88–89, 93
Beaver Creek, 25
Beiglemeir, Frank, 5, 25, 226–27
Belt, Guy, 123
Belt, Robert, 19, 106, 122, 127, 170
Bennett, Emanuel, 166–67, 176, 217
Bennett, Granville G., 177, 201–2, 204, 208–9
Benoist, William "Billy Benway," 10, 208
Big Foot, 32, 36, 55, 67, 123
Big Mouth, 133
Big Road, 17, 31, 115, *116,* 133

INDEX

Black, Mr. (special agent Cooper's brother-in-law), 139
Black Buffalo Woman, 132–33
Black Heart, 113, 176
Black Hills Daily Times, 49, 62, 203
Black Hills Weekly Times, 175, 188
Black Shawl, 134
Blakely, Ed W., 5
Bland, T. A., 57
Board of Indian Commissioners, 157
"Boss Farmers." *See* Farmers
Boston Indian Citizens Committee, 160
Bozeman Trail, 46, 133, 159
Brennan, John, 23, 29, 31
Brewster, James, 198
Broken Arm, 65–66, 71, 73, 78, *81*
Broken Arrow band, 38, 165; and halfway camp murders, 216, 219; and Moccasin Top, 123; and No Water's village, 131, 169; and Wells, 135, 167
"Broncho Bill," 100, 104–5
Brooke, John R., 19–20, 23, 34, 170–71, 173
Brown, Charles, 102, 213
Brown, George LeRoy, 121, 125–28, 130, 161–62, 164–65, 196, 202; and adversaries, 149–59; and Eastman, 139–48; and Moccasin Top, 122–24; response to murders, 167–72, 175–76, 178–79
Brown, Thomas H., 193
Brown, William, 194
"Buffalo Bill." *See* Cody, William
Buffalo Bill's Wild West Show, 27, 113, 186–87
Buffalo Gap, S.Dak., 23, 29
Buffalo Gap Republican, 23, 178
Bureau of Indian Affairs, 8, 11, 16–17, 109, 114, 117, 126–27, 140, 229
Burns, John H., 101–2; attorney for murder suspects, 61–62, 177–79, 201–2, 204, 208
Bush, Joe, 176, 178, *182,* 202, 206; and No Water's village, 165, 169–70
Byron, Joseph, 32–34, 50, 60, 168

Camp Cheyenne, 55
Camp Leavenworth, 36–37, 41, 43, 50, 56, 72, 78
Can Nopa Uhah. *See* Two Sticks (Can Nopa Uhah; Red Elk)
Carlisle Indian Industrial School, 28, 59–60, 112, 141–42
Carlton, Caleb, 167–68, 170
Carr, Eugene A., 78
Casey, Edwin W., 34–36, 58; death of, 50–51; Plenty Horses's trials, 61–69, 71–81
Catholicism, 224–26, 228. *See also* Florentine Digmann, Francis Craft
Chadron, Neb., 27, 41, 144, 169, 187
Chadron-Chicago horse race, 187–91
Chadron Democrat, 144
Chamberlain, S.Dak., 24, 185, 191
Chamberlain-Rapid City freighting route, 56
Cheyenne River Reservation, 8, 9, 32, 123, 138, 157–58; and Eagle Bear, 121–22, 131; fraud and mismanagement, 10–11, 142, 159
Cheyenne scouts, 32–35, 50, 60, 65, 71
Chicago World's Fair, 82, 150, 185–86, 192–94
Cih Hu Ha Tum band, 48
Cisney, James H., 141–45, 147, 159, 170
Civil Service Commission, 124
Cleveland, Grover, 4
Clown, 54–56, 78; as witness at Few Tails's trial, 87, 90, 92–93
Cody, William F., 125, 186–87, 190–91, 193
Coe, Albert, 200, 204, 209–10, 214, 220
Cogley, Martin, 199, 205–6
Colby, Leonard, 41
Cole, M. D., 28–30
Coleman, Sydney A., 60, 80
Columbian Exposition. *See* Chicago World's Fair
Comer, George, 144, 150–51, 156, 176, 204–5

Comes Crawling, 21, 216
Conquering Bear, 1
consumption. *See* tuberculosis
Cook, Charles E., 115, *116*
Cooper, James, 117, 137–43, 160
Cosgrove, George, 25–27, 29
Court of Indian Offenses, 48, 119
Craft, Francis, 117, 129, 152
Craven, Gus, 56, 72, 78–79
Crazy Horse, 131–34, 180
Crook, George, 48, 108
Crook Commission of 1889, 128, 134
Crow Creek Reservation, 8, 11–12, 24
Crow Dog, 20
Crow Eagle, 22
Culbertson, Andrew, 52, 54–55, 87, 88–92
Culbertson, August "Pete," 52, 54–55, 87, 91–92
Culbertson, Nelson, 87, 91–92
Cuny Table, 23, 32, 35–36
Custer, George Armstrong, 134, 155, 157, 186
Custer, S.Dak., 23, 28
Custer Chronicle, 172

Dahlman, James, 41
Daily Deadwood Pioneer-Times, 57, 150, 205
Dakota Militia, 24–31, 35, 40–41
Dakota Territory legislature, 8
Dakota War of 1862, 160
Daly, Jack, 25, 27
Daly-Torkelson Ranch, 25–27, 74, 81
Daniel, Z. T., 180
Darr, John, 43
Davis, Clement, 93
Davis, James, 142
Dawson, A. R. Z., 203
Day, M. H., 24–25, 28, 39
Dead Arm, 30
Deadwood, S.Dak., 120, 176–78, 180, 192, 211–13; death of Cyrus Fry, 183–84; incarceration of Indian prisoners, 31, 38, 44, 101–2, 183, 200–201; site of March 1891 grand jury, 60, 62; site of U.S. district court proceedings, 200, 204–5, 207
Delaware College, 125, 158
Dennis, Neal, 26–27
Department of the Platte, 19, 170–71, 173, 176
Digmann, Florentine, 4, 136, 152, *153*, 154, 224–28
Dismounts (Hiyuiciya; Thomas Two Sticks), 21, 220
Division of the Missouri, 3, 20, 70, 81, 104, 125, 158
Dixon, Andrew, 111–12
Dollard, Robert, 88
Drake, Thomas, 208, 210, 213
Drexel Mission, 4, 36, 66–68, 77, 152
drought, 62, 108, 185, 192
Dundy, Elmer S., 180, 205–8, 210, 216–17, 220–23

Eagle Hawk, 44
Eagle Louse, 166–67, 208, *209*, 214–15, 226
Eastman, Charles A., *147*, 156, 160–62, 171, 197; and Brown, 139–48
Eastman, Elaine Goodale, 16, 108, 143–44, 146–48, *147*, 156, 161–62
Eastman, John, 146
East River, 57, 62, 71, 83–85, 87
Edgerton, Charley, 169, 219
Edgerton, Alonzo J., 60, 62–63; and Deadwood trials, 200–201, 203–5, 221; and Plenty Horses's trials, 68–69, 70–80; and Wets His Lips, 105
education, 15–16, 109, 111–12, 113, 114–15. *See also names of individual schools*
Evening World, 87, 130

farmers (boss farmers), 16, 154, 156. *See also* Craven, Gus; Smoot, W. C.; Wells, Philip
Farnham, Ellen, 29–30

INDEX

Farnham, John, 29, 30, 212
Fast Horse, 45
Fat Woman, 216–17, 220
Few Tails, 54–58, 60, 62–63, 87–88, 90–93
Fields, George. *See* White Face Horse
Fights With (Wasaglefis; Mark Red Elk), 5, 20, 25, 33, 35, *209*, 222; capture of, 175–76; death of, 210; and halfway camp murders, 169; incarceration of, 177, 181, 184, 200; trials of, 201–4, 211–14, 216–19
Files, C. H., 79
Finlay, James, 138–39, 170
First Eagle (Wanbli Tokaha), 5, 20, 25, 33, 35, 222; and halfway camp murders, 169, 181, 184, 214, 216–19
Fishing Skunk, 178
Flandreau, S.Dak., 8, 144–46, 160
Flood, Thomas, 74, *81*, 98, 101
Forsyth, James, 155
Fort Keogh, Mont., 50
Fort Laramie, 133–34
Fort Laramie Treaty, 1, 133
Fort Meade, 36, 40, 49, 92, 167, 170, 173, 175; and confinement of prisoners, 44, 60, 62–63
Fort Nendle, 21
Fort Pierre, 40, 211
Fort Pierre–Fort Laramie Trail, 32, 34, 36
Fort Robinson, 20, 134, 170, 188; surrender of Crazy Horse, 67, 134
Fort Sheridan, Ill., 70, 125–26, 135
Fort Sheridan, Nebr., 134
Fort Yates, N.Dak., 166, 198
Foster, Charles, 109, 112
Franklin, N. E., 212
Fry, Cyrus, 63, *81*, 101–2, 146, 150–51, *182*; arrests convicts, 176, 180; background of, 7–8; death of, 183–84
Fry, Frank, 184, 198, 200

Galigo, Frank, 168
Gallagher, Charley, 32, 212
Gallagher, Hugh, 14, 75, 113, 120, 127–28, 224
Gardner, John H., 176
Garnette, Phyllis, 229
Garnier, Baptiste, 50
General Order No. 28, 118–19
Gettysburg, S.Dak., 199–200
Ghost Dance, 71, 178, 195; description of, 19, 66–67; on Pine Ridge Reservation, 21, 22, 76, 135
Gifford, O. S., 11–12
Gleason, Bishop J., 14
Goodale, Elaine. *See* Eastman, Elaine Goodale
Good Boy, Herbert, 141
Gossage, Joseph, 29, 228
"Grandmother" (Lays on His Mother-in-Law), 97–105
Grant, Ulysses, 156–58
Grass, John, 114
Grass Creek, 23, 36, 56, 135, 227
Grattan, John L., 1
Great Dakota Boom, 84
Great Father. *See* Harrison, Benjamin
Great Sioux Reservation, 1–2, 30, 40, 48, 86, 133, 149

Haaser, Gus, 26, 32
halfway camp, *214*, *215*, 216–17, 219–21; description of, 136, 164; scene of murders, 166–69
Hampton Normal and Agricultural Institute, 112, 158, 161
Harney Hotel, 23, 34, 38, 111
Harney Springs, 34
Harrington, Henry M., 57
Harris, E. C., 127
Harrison, Benjamin, 9, 20, 22, 108–9, 112–14; and Lakota delegation, 115
Hart, Frank, 29–30
Harvey, Thomas, 88, 93
Haskell Indian School, 122
He Dog, 46, 67, 77, *81*, *116*, 133; and halfway camp murderers, 168, 170, 179

Hemia Yelo, 227
Henry, Guy V., 34
Herman, Jake, 229–30
Hermosa, S.Dak., 23, 34–35, 39–40, 51, 163, 168–69, 173, 175–77
High Forehead, 1
Holland, John, 22
Hollow Horn Bear, 96, 108
Hollow Wood, 165, 179–80, 201
Holy Rosary Mission. *See* Drexel Mission
home guards, 23–24, 39–41, 54. *See also* Dakota Militia
Homestake Mine, 202, 212
Hot Springs, S.Dak., 23, 28, 151, 167, 206–7
Hot Springs Star, 178, 207
Howard, Charles, 64, 69–70, 200, 203
Hughes, Richard, 35
Hughes, Will, 159
Hughes County Jail, 104, 200, 205
Humane Society of America, 188, 190
Humphrey, Isaac "Ike": as beef contractor, 122, 126, 163–64, 166–67; and halfway camp murders, 169, 214, 226
Hunts the Enemy. *See* Sword, George
Hurley, Barney, 212
Hutson, Thisba, 15–16
Hyde, James D., 139

Ickes, W. A., 212
Indian Affairs Committee, U.S. Senate, 8, 22
investigations, 140–44, 158–59. *See also* Cisney, James; Miller, Benjamin; Pollock, W. J.; Townsend, Eddy
Iowa National Guard, 41
Iwicakeze. *See* Fights With
Indian Depredations Act, 137
Indian Rights Association, 22, 61–62, 64, 87, 103, 113, 145

Jackson County, 102–3
Jarchow, Gus J., 176, 183
Jones, Abe "Squire," 53–54, 90, 92

Jones, George, 188, 191
Jordan, C. P., 107
Joslyn, Merrit L., 158
Juelfs, Julius "James," 87–89, 91–94
Julio (Attack Him), 98, 100–101

Kelly, James, 172
Kelly, Sally, 96
Kelly, William, 166, 219
Keyes, Frank, 104
Kicking Bear, 3, 19, 30, 33, 134, 158, 187; returns to Pine Ridge, 125–26
Kills the Two. *See* Two Two (Kills the Two)
Kirkpatrick, George, 168

Ladd, George W., 55, 93
Lake Mohonk Indian Conference, 106
Lakota delegation of 1891, 113–16, *116*
Lamont, Daniel, 173
Larvie, Thomas, 99–100
Lawrence County Jail, 31, 176–77, 181, 200, 204–5, 207–8, 221, 224
Lays on His Mother-In-Law (Grandmother), 97–105
Lea, A. T., 106–7
Leaves His Woman (Young Skunk), 44, 60
Lemley, Pete, 29–30
Lemmon, Ed, 111
Lewis, William, 213–14
Lip's camp, 20–21, 55, 135
Little, 17–18, 31, *37*, 38
Little Bighorn. *See* Battle of the Little Bighorn
Little Big Man, 47
Little Coral Draw, 29
Littleton, Thomas, 40
Little Wolf (Oglala), 123
Little Wound, 31, *116*
Living Bear, 62–64, 67, 69, 71, 79, *81*
Lob, 215, 220, 227
Lower Brule Reservation, 11, 138, 161

Maher, John G., 187
Man Who Carries the Sword. *See* Sword, George
Marshall, Francis (soldier), 55
Marshall, Frank, 87
Marshall, John B, 150
Marty, Martin, 225
Marvin, Alva, 53, 87–88, 91, 97
Matthiessen, Chris, *81*, 93, 176–79, *182*, 183; and Plenty Horses, 62–63; and Two Sticks, 200, 226
McCall, Alex, 55, 62, 87–88
McChesney, Charles, 9, 127–28
McClelland, Paul, 29, 169
McClelland, William, 40
McCloud, Joe, 26–27, 30
McDonough, John, 68
McFarland, Will, 29, 31
McGaa, William, 77, 109
McGillycuddy, V. T., 44–45, 48, 60, 119, 158–59, 179; and Indian unrest, 22–23, 29, 31, 104, 129–30, 137
McLaughlin, James, 28, 197–99
McLaughlin, William L., 4, 211, 214, 220–23, 226
Meade County, 57, 62, 95
Meade County Jail, 63, 88
Mellette, Arthur C., 55, 118, 178, 192–93; response to Indian uprising, 21–25, 28, 40, 92
Mellette, Charles E., 25, 200, 206
Menard, Louis, 204
Merriam, Henry C., 55
Messiah craze, 48–49, 54, 66, 75, 78–79, 122, 135; government response to, 19, 50, 125–26, 137–38; leaders of, 187. *See also* Ghost Dance
Meteer, James H., 144, 151–52
Middleton, Doc, 188–91
Miles, Nelson A., 3, 55, 104, 113; and Indian prisoners, 125, 135; Indian unrest, 20, 49–52, 56–58, 117; justice for Few Tails, 57–58, 60–63; response to Messiah craze, 22, 24, 34–35; Plenty Horses's trial, 70, 76–77, 79–80, 87; Wounded Knee Massacre, 38, 46, 49–52

Miller, Benjamin H., 140–41, 143, 150–51
Miller, Ezra, 200–201, 203–6, 210–11, 213, 216, 221, 226
Miller, Isaac "Ike," 26, 37, 42–45
Miller, Riley, 27, 29
Miniconjou, 30, 36, 38, 121, 123
Minneapolis Tribune, 171
Minnehaha County Jail, 63, 179, 180
Minnesela, S.Dak., 40, 48–49
Missouri Valley & Elkhorn Railroad, 38–39, 127, 156, 191, 194, 200, 206
Mitchell Capital, 57
Moccasin Top, 122–24, 128, 131, 133, 164
Moody, C. C., 57, 88, 95
Moody, Gideon, 6, 13
Moon That Ever Shines, 59
Morgan, Thomas J., 9, 121–22, 124, 150–52, 154, 162, 195; allocation of monies, 137–38; and Brown-Eastman dispute, 140–42, 144–47; and halfway camp murders, 167, 170; and Lakota delegation, 113–15; and Messiah craze, 19, 22
Morris, A. Judson, 98, 101

National Indian Defense Association, 57
Nebraska State Militia, 41
Netland, John, 92
Noble, John, 20, 22, 122, 159; allocation of monies, 137–38; and Brown-Eastman dispute, 141, 143–47, 170; and Lakota delegation, 106–7, 113–15
Nock, George, 63–64, 66, 68–70, 72, 81, *81*, 104–5
No Flesh, 165, 179–80, 201
No Neck, 113, 194
Nopa Nopa. *See* Two Two (Kills the Two)
Notley, Scott, 212
No Water, 124, 129, 135, 178–80; and Crazy Horse, 131–34; and halfway camp murders, 165–66, 169
No Water's camp (village), 56, 105, 126, 131–36, *132*; and Casey, 71, 73; and

malcontents, 36, 38, 46, 48, 50, 52, 60, 67–69, 121–24; and Miller, 42–43

Offley, Robert H., 34–35
Ohiyesa. *See* Eastman, Charles
Omaha Daily Bee, 88, 129, 172
One Feather, 54–55, 87, 90, 92–93
Oonagazhee. *See* Stronghold Table (Oonagazhee)
Otter Robe, 54, 87, 93

Palmer, C. S., 194
Palmer, Perain P., 8–11, 122, 127, 142, 159
Palmer, S. N., 71, 80
Parker, George, 212
Pawnee (Oglala man), 221
Pawnee (tribe), 59
Peemiller, Otto, 184, 197–200, 206–7; and Two Sticks, 5, 225–27
Penney, Charles, 81, 111, 118–22, 159, 163, 195–96
Pennington County, 102–3
Pennington, John, 201
Pettigrew, Richard F., 6–14, 7, 22, 111, 151, 184, 202
Philip, James "Scotty," 21–22, 40
Pierce, F. E., 57, 121
Pierre, S.Dak., 6, 199–200
Pierre Weekly Free Press, 57
Pine Ridge Indian agents, 121. *See also names of individual agents*
Pine Ridge Reservation, 107, 110; confinement of Oglalas, 110, 113, 142; factions, 46, 48; fraud, 111, 126, 139, 150–51, 156, 158–59; ghost dancing, 19, 126, 130, 131; jobs and unemployment, 108–9, 112–14, 118–19; patronage on, 112–16; trespassing of cattle, 110–11, 200, 207, 229. *See also* education; rations
Plenty Horses, 33, 60, *61*, *81*; and Carlisle Indian School, 28, 59, 61; first trial of, 61–89; second trial of, 70–81
Polk, Charles, 88, 91, 93
Pollock, W. J., 158

Porter, John, 90–91
Powell, John Wesley, 107
Powers, David E., 63–64, 66–67, 69, 70, 74–78, 80–82, *81*
Pratt Commission (1877), 2
Pratt, Richard H., 142
Price, Hiram, 159
Proctor, Redfield, 20, 24, 44, 63, 113
Ptay Ptessau Hacksilau. *See* White Face Horse
Pugh, Robert, 14, 18–20, 75–76, 114, 195
Pyramid Lake, Nev., 19, 135

Quinn, David, 87, 92
Quinn, Peter, 56
Quinn, Sheridan, 87
Quinn Draw, 35
Quinn's ranch, 54

Rankin, W. A., 212
Rapid City, S.Dak., 23, 28, 177, 192, 212
Rapid City Journal, 29, 35, 52–53, 103, 203, 228
rations, 2, 57, 73–75, 79, 106–8, 110, 113, 115, 165; rotten meat, 128–29
Rebsamen, Julius, 213
Red Cloud, 65, 73–74, 77, 129, 131, 133, 159
Red Cloud, Jack, *81*
Red Cloud Agency, 47, 134, 189
Red Eagle, Jake, 230
Red Elk. *See* Two Sticks (Can Nopa Uhah; Red Elk)
Red Elk, Mark. *See* Fights With (Wasaglefis; Mark Red Elk)
Red Owl, 54, 87, 93
Red Shirt, 78–79
Reilly, James M., 188–91
Remington, Frederic, 35, 37
Richard, Peter, 65–66, 73–74, *81*, 166, 172
Richards, Bartlett, 126
Rock Road, 50, 65, 71–72, 78, *81*
Roosevelt, Theodore, 112, 124–25, 142
Rosebud Reservation, 11, 38, 52, 96, 138
Rossiter, Bryan, 212–13

Roush, Francis, 27, 169
Rowland, William, 71, *81*
Royce, Rodney, 166–69, 176, 217, 219–20
Royer, Daniel F., 12–14, *13*, 16–20, 22, 75, 121
Rushville, Nebr., 27, 50, 183; and Indian unrest, 19, 39, 41; as railway transportation site, 22–23, 79, 93, 117, 167, 176–77; as supply point, 127, 139

Saint Paul Globe, 171–72
Santee Reservation, 8
Santee Training School, 160, 209
Schofield, John M., 118–19
Scholfield, Ike, 178
Schwing, Joseph, 213
Shangreau, John, 202
Shangreaux, Louis, *116*, 149–50
Sheldon, Charles H., 193
Sheridan, M. V., 171
Sheridan, Philip, 228
Sherman, William T., 157
Shiras, Oliver P., 64, 66, 69, 70, 76, 80
Shoenfeldt, George B., 10–11
Shoots the Enemy, 45
Short Bull, 125–26, 135–36, 175, 187; leader of Indian uprising, 19–22, 31, 36
Shoun, V. P., 54, 92
Sidney–Black Hills Trail, 189
Sioux Bill of 1889, 2, 11, 106–7, 109, 113, 117, 134
Sioux Bill commissioners, 11, 108–9, 111–12, 115
Sioux City, Iowa, 79, 81, 149, 155, 190, 192
Sioux City Herald, 130
Sioux Falls, S.Dak., 210; site of Plenty Horses's trials, 62–63, 70–71, 76, 79, 146, 176, 179–80, 191, 194
Sioux Indian Wars, 1, 17
Sits in Lodge. *See* Two Sticks, Mrs. (Sits in Lodge, Timahel Yanka)
Sitting Bear, 169, 176
Sitting Bull, 21

Slohan Ku (Comes Crawling), 21, 216
Smith, Frank, 54, 213
Smith, S. R., 228
Smoot, W. C., 154
South Dakota Republicans, 7–14, 184
South Dakota State Penitentiary, 210
South Dakota World's Fair Commission, 193
Sprague, Farley, 26, 30
Springfield Republican, 146
Spotted Tail's band, 133–34
Standing Bear, Luther, 173–74
Standing Bear (Indian policeman), 18
Standing Bear (Ponca chief), 205–6
Standing Rock Reservation, 138, 196–97, 199
Stenger, Ed, 163–64, 168, 226
Stephens, James, 11
Sterling, William B., *81*, 101, 105, 151, 194; prosecutes Few Tails's killers, 62–63, 87–93; prosecutes Plenty Horses, 64–69, 70–77
Stewart, Frank, 43–44
Stronghold Table (Oonagazhee), 23, 25, 27–37, 42, 50, 135
Struthers, L. H., 34
Sturgis Weekly Record, 53, 57, 88
Sumner, Edwin V., 32, 44, 62–63
Swartz, Charles, 168, 219
Sweeney, John M., 108
Sword, George, 46–48, 115, *116*, 133, 171, 179–80

Tarbox, George, 26, 30
Tasunka-Ota. *See* Plenty Horses
Teller, Henry, 159
Ten Eyck, B. L., 65, 72
Thomas, Charles, 88–89, 94
Thompson, Henry C., 66
Thompson, William "Americus," 31, 35, 37–38, 72, 78, *81*
Thornby, William J., 173
Three Stars, Clarence, 15

Thunder Bear (Lakota policeman), 17–18, 122, 176, 200, 206
Thunder Bull, 122–23
Thunder Hawk, 208
Timahel Yanka. *See* Two Sticks, Mrs. (Sits in Lodge, Timahel Yanka)
Tongue River Reservation, Wyo., 138
Touch the Clouds, 134, 158
Townsend, Eddy, 159
Traynor, Matthew, 226, 228
Tschetter, Jacob, 199
tuberculosis, 2, 81, 210
Tuplin, Noah "James," 208, 213, 225
Turner, Frederick Jackson, 194
Turner County Herald, 194
Turton, Alfred, 87, 90
Twiss, Henry, 173
Two Sticks (Can Nopa Uhah; Red Elk), 3, 20, 52, 69, 105, *182*, 203, 206–7; arrest of, 175, 177–79, 180–83; and halfway camp crime, 167, 169–73; hanging of, 4–5, 6, 224–30; indictment of 200–201; trial of, 211–23
Two Sticks, Mrs. (Sits in Lodge, Timahel Yanka), 20, 217, 220
Two Sticks, Thomas (Dismounts; Hiyuiciya), 21, 220
Two Strike, 20, 31, 77, *116*, 187
Two Two (Kills the Two), 200–201, *209*, 210, 211, 214, 216–20, 222; arrest of, 175–77, 181, 184, 200; and halfway camp murders, 5, 169; incarceration of, 181, 184; trials of, 203–5, 206–8

Underwood, D. M., 217, 227
U.S. District Court for the District of South Dakota, 184, 200, 204
U.S. Military Academy, 156–57

Von Wedelstaedt, H.A.L., 228

Wak-anhdi Ota, 160
Waldron, Charley, 21

Walters, J. P., 207, 225
Wanbli Tokaha. *See* First Eagle
Warner, Porter, 57, 202–3, 205
Warner, William, 108
Warren, T. M., 26, 37
Warren ranch, 26
Wasaglefis. *See* Fights With (Wasaglefis; Mark Red Elk)
Weekly Pioneer Times, 71–72
Wells, Almond, 32, 36
Wells, Orman, 165–66
Wells, Philip, 66–68, 71, *81*, 155, 165, 220, 224; as boss farmer, 135, 155–56; at Few Tails's trial, 87, 89; and halfway camp murders, 166–67, 172, 208, 229; at Plenty Horses's trial, 213–15, 221
Wells, William "Wallace," 155
Welsh, Herbert, 22, 61–62, 64, 87, 113, 142–43, 145
Werthheimer, Louis, 213
West, J. E., 127, 156
West River, 86, 107, 211–12; geology of, 83–85; inhabitants of, 85–86, 163–65; prejudice in, 49, 62, 87–88, 89, 95, 97, 102–3
Wets His Lips (Broncho Bill), 100, 104–5
Whipple, Devine A. "Jack," 96, 101–5, 121; and killing of Lays on His Mother-in-Law, 97–100
White, E. P., 78
White Clay Creek, 21, 23, 36, 135, 220
White Face Horse, 5, 175, 205, 211; alleged death of, 181, 184; capture of, 199–200; escape of, 196–99; and halfway camp murders, 169; trial of, 200, 202–3, 206, 208–10, 214, 216–22
White Face Horse, Mrs., 216, 220
White Horse, 27–28, 74, 81
White Moon, 50, 65, 71–73, 78–79, *81*
Whitfield, Robert, 21
Woman Dress, 78
Women's National Indian Rights Association, 161

Wood, Frank, 146, 160
World's Fair. *See* Chicago World's Fair
Wounded Knee Creek, 17, 38–39, 135, 150, 161
Wounded Knee Massacre, 2, 6, 118, 120, 135–36, 155, 157
Wovoka, 19, 135. *See also* Ghost Dance
Wright, James, 11
Wright, J. George, 11, 97–98, 101–2, 104–5, 121
Wyoming State Militia, 40

Yankton, S.Dak., 193

Yankton Reservation, 8, 149, 209
Yellow Thigh, 22
Young, Frank, 5
Young Man Afraid of His Horses, 47, *116*, 175–76, 179–80, 196–97; background of, 46–48, 133; death of, 195; as Lakota delegate, 115, 126; as peacemaker, 50–51, 56–58, 168–71; visits Wyoming friends, 48–49, 195
Young Skunk (Leaves His Woman), 44, 60

Z-Bell cowboys, 165, 168–69, 214, 217, 219
Z-Bell Ranch, 163–65

www.ingramcontent.com/pod-product-compliance
Lightning Source LLC
Chambersburg PA
CBHW031430160426
43195CB00010BB/684